D1563905

Liberal Economics and Democracy

Liberal Economics and Democracy

KEYNES, GALBRAITH, THUROW, AND REICH

Conrad P. Waligorski

University Press of Kansas

Published by the University Press of Kansas (Lawrence, Kansas 66049),
which was organized by the Kansas Board of Regents and is operated and
funded by Emporia State University, Fort Hays State University, Kansas
State University, Pittsburg State University, the University of Kansas, and
Wichita State University

Library of Congress Cataloging-in-Publication Data

Waligorski, Conrad.
    Liberal economics and democracy : Keynes, Galbraith, Thurow, and
Reich / Conrad P. Waligorski.
    Includes bibliographical references.
    ISBN 0-7006-0803-6
    1. Economics—United States—History—20th century.
    2. Liberalism—United States—History—20th century.   3. Democracy—
United States—History—20th century.   I. Title.
    HB119.A2W18   1996
    330.1—dc20   96-42442

British Library Cataloguing in Publication Data is available.

Printed in the United States of America

10   9   8   7   6   5   4   3   2   1

The paper used in this publication meets the minimum requirements of the
American National Standard for Permanence of Paper for Printed Library
Materials Z39.48-1984.

To my wife
Ann Waligorski

Contents

Preface

Politics, policy, ideology, and economics are inseparable. In recent years the United States has entered into momentous debate over the nature of American civil and political society, the obligations we owe to one another, and the character and role of government. Though argued in what seem to be economic terms of deficit spending, balanced budgets, limits to growth imposed by fear of inflation, government sponsored health care, taxes, welfare spending, corporate responsibility, job security, growing inequality, and public broadcasting, the real issues are much deeper, involving philosophical, ideological, and moral images of our most profound values and the kind of society in which they might reach fruition. Within this context, current efforts to effectively dismantle activist and welfare government are led by conservative intellectuals and members of Congress who embrace a market ideology opposed to and contested by the arguments in this book.

To reform liberals economic problems, issues, theories, and proposals dominate public debate over fundamental political values and relations: the meaning and scope of freedom, equality, equal opportunity, individualism, community, justice, and democracy; the role of government; the question of who will benefit most from and who will bear the costs of public policy; and the central issue of what kind of society we choose to have. Although it includes use of abstract models and mathematical analysis, public debate is irrevocably normative, necessarily involving goals, purposes, priorities, and moral assumptions. This book is about normative ideas and arguments in political-economic policy recommendations. It examines political-social-economic values, beliefs, and policy prescriptions *shared* among a group of seven theorists who epitomize reform liberal political economy. Three early twentieth-century noneconomists—Louis Brandeis, John Dewey, and L. T. Hobhouse—are briefly discussed in historical juxtaposition to the main figures, four more recent liberal economists—John Maynard Keynes, John Kenneth Galbraith, Robert Reich, and Lester C. Thurow—who reformulate many of the earlier themes into a contemporary context, placing all of them within the neoclassical political-economic model each criticizes. More than academic theorists, though six had or still have university careers, these writers are genuine "worldly philosophers"[1] engaged with the continuing interaction of values, political-economics, and public policy. Each has written extensively for the broad public and has attempted to influence public policy. All were political activists at some point in their careers. Brandeis, Keynes, Galbraith, Thurow, and Reich participated in campaigns for high office, advised candidates, and, except for Thurow, advised cabinet officials, prime ministers, and/or presidents. Dewey and Keynes, and to a lesser extent Galbraith, have been highly influential in changing the way we understand and interpret the world. Brandeis was a Supreme Court justice. Keynes and Galbraith had responsibility for administering important public programs and both represented their country abroad. Reich is secretary of a cabinet department.[2] These seven authors have been chosen because they are concerned with politics, address how politics and economics interact, and attempt to influence public opinion and policy. Together, they offer a coherent, century-long defense of an active government role in the economy.

All relevant theorists cannot be included. First, we emphasize liberals who are primarily economists—mirroring what many critics see as liberalism's fatal flaw, its emphasis on economics; therefore, writers such as Charles Lindblom and Robert Dahl who have contributed enormously to this area are not included. Second, we examine liberals who have written extensively and for the public about policy and politics as well as economics. Economists such as James Tobin, Robert Solow, Alvin Hansen, or Paul Samuelson are less politically oriented than the theorists in this book. Third, although there are other historical possibilities, such as the British theorist John Hobson (1864–1929), Brandeis, Dewey, and Hobhouse give a good flavor of earlier reform liberal concerns.

One begins a book on liberalism with some trepidation because liberalism is deeply reviled and under attack. Results of the 1994 election, as in elections since 1972, are widely seen as repudiating liberalism. Government seems caught in gridlock and people are deeply discontented and worried about the future. Calls for new political parties and for stripping government of resources and many social-economic responsibilities are multiplying, while anger against "special interests" intensifies[3] and liberals are blamed. Popular and sometimes academic discussion of liberalism often sinks to liberalbabble: the solemn and frequently pompous invocation of the dreaded "L-word," as in the 1988 presidential election; or assurance this is a "postliberal age" where one can distinguish a "preliberal" from a "postliberal" based on policy. Liberal candidates flee the liberal label, saying such "'old categories are defunct.'"[4] The theorists in this book, especially Keynes and Galbraith, are often seen as representing what the public rejects and politicians are afraid to discuss—active government, economic intervention, and paying taxes to support popular public services. Commentators claim liberals are unable to form coherent policy and liberalism is dead. Indeed some people call liberal anything they dislike. "Liberal" is used in character assassination, and as a bludgeon to silence opposition. Liberals are called baby murderers, patrons of promiscuity, criminal coddlers, big spenders, creators of divisive political correctness, campaigners "against middle-class values and convictions," irreligious, anti-God, taxers, alien to real Americans. Such passionate demonology overlooks the liberal content in many widely accepted fundamental values and institutions. Both liberals and their critics often focus on superficialities, ignoring principles, goals, and values, and offering no criteria by which a person or policy is called liberal or conservative.[5]

The theorists in this book dissent from such false assuredness in which complexity and reality are sacrificed to a simplicity that promises certainty and security. Their world is more complex: multiple causation, intricate interrelations, impermanent solutions and successes, ever-changing problems, admission that a solution for one issue may cause new problems, and constant policy adjustment to pursue fundamental values. Many liberals may have acquiesced in conservatives' definition of basic values, but reform liberals have not. Their dissent is no mere response to the moment. For several generations conservatives and liberals have clashed over the political-economic issues discussed in this book. Throughout, reform liberals have offered a conscience, a considered rejoinder to market ideology, and a warning about how much can be lost.

Two fundamental assumptions structure my examination of the common themes in reform liberalism's normative political economy. First, values, preferences, and judgments shape and color economic theories and policies, and second, politics and economics are closely related.

Each of us does not see the same world. Theories often tell us what are "facts" and how we ought to proceed. In political economy one cannot simply "test" which ideas "work" because values guide and even determine what is a valid test and result. Beliefs about motivation, freedom, legitimacy, or individualism are mental filters that color perception of problems and possible or acceptable solutions. These beliefs in action (ideology) underlie much political conflict. For example, in the continuing debate over budget policy or the role of government in health care, substantial disagreement results from philosophical differences about public versus private spheres, freedom, responsibility, obligation, motivation, and what must be accepted as part of the order of things and what can or should be changed. Economics and abstract economic theory are frequently secondary to politics as they are marshalled by various sides to support their respective positions. If education and health care are personal responsibilities with slight social-political impact, government must have a small role in these areas. If on the other hand, they expand freedom or have a wide impact, government may be active in their provision. Starting points do not determine policies, but they widen or narrow possible public action and predispose people toward one or another outcome. They produce "visions" that interpret and explain reality, determine who must justify policy, encourage one perspective and not another, and set limits to permissible policy. When confronted with different choices, we use values and judgments to help us select among them. The most serious problems arise when people deny having values, claiming such values are irrelevant to policy conclusions, or distort factual reality to fit assumptions and values.[6] More than most of their contemporaries, the theorists in this book acknowledge having values and the role of values in shaping policy.

The second fundamental assumption that structures this book is that politics and economics are closely related and interdependent. Unlike laissez-faire theorists, reform liberals insist policy must accommodate this interaction. Because this book emphasizes the interrelation of politics and economics, it does not cover all reform economic or social-political ideas, values, and arguments. It is neither biography, history, public policy comparison, economics, or economic theory. Throughout, it explores common values and shared ideas rather than disagreement. It examines political theory—the social-political values, principles, and reasoning that inform political-economic policy proposals—and the normative interrelation of politics and political-social relations with economics, not economics per se. Given the role of economists and quasi-economic arguments in politics and public policy, economic theory has become political. Politics and economics cannot be understood separately from each other. Economic theories and proposals are a form of political theory when they employ political values such as freedom, equality, and democracy, prescribe public goals, or propose changes in government.[7] The proper relation of politics and economics, the economic component of issues such as environmental protection and gender relations, and the proper role of government in the economy are contentious political matters crucial to future social viability and stability. The book illustrates that liberalism is not just a philosophical concept[8] but a political-economic theory and ideology, concerned with context, concrete societies, and infusing basic values into public policy.

I am in broad sympathy with these authors, believing their values and general policy preferences best fit the contemporary world. Because so many others have claimed to explain liberalism, my primary goal is to let these theorists speak for themselves on the relation of politics and economics, and to explicate their arguments and purposes, but not to criticize them. My criticisms are immanent. I share many assumptions with these authors, but sometimes critique their depth of understanding, conclusions, or the likelihood of reaching stated goals. References to conservative arguments are to the form of individualistic liberalism now properly called conservatism, which I examined in an earlier book.[9]

The first chapter discusses reform liberalism and, briefly, the role of economics in liberalism. Chapters 2 through 6 examine individual arguments and chapter 7 attempts to illustrate common arguments within the context of problems for and criticisms of liberalism and how these theorists respond.

Acknowledgments

Many people have contributed to this book and I thank them for their support and criticism. Kenneth M. Dolbeare and Charles E. Lindblom read this book in manuscript and I owe them a special debt. Authors miss what diligent readers see is important and their suggestions have strengthened this book. Kenneth M. Dolbeare and Kenneth R. Hoover read the original proposal and greatly aided my thinking. Three people graciously shared their time and ideas with me in interviews: John Kenneth Galbraith, the late Lord Kahn, and Donald Moggridge. Several friends and colleagues commented on conference papers that explored some aspects of this book. Edward J. Harpham, Denny Pilant, David Lorenzo, Arthur Di Quattro, Richard Fralin, and Jaan Whitehead prove that discussants take their task seriously. I also thank JAI Press for allowing me to use part of an article, "Keynes and Democracy," *The Social Science Journal,* 31 (1994) and the anonymous reviewers at *The Social Science Journal.* The University of Arkansas has been generous in its support. The university provided an off-campus duty assignment, 1992–93, that allowed me to complete much of my research. The final writing was greatly aided by a research leave, Fall 1994, from the Fulbright College of Arts and Sciences. My graduate assistants, especially Ronda King and Kyle Hawley, checked references, ran searches, and read parts of the manuscript. Interlibrary Loan personnel at Mullins University Library always found what I needed. The staff at the John Fitzgerald Kennedy Library, at Kings College Library, Cambridge, and at the Public Records Office, London, provided superb support. The editors at the University Press of Kansas, especially Michael Briggs and Susan Schott, always give their support and I appreciate them very much. Two friends continuously aid my interest in normative political economy: David Gay and Thomas Hone. Finally, I thank my wife, Ann Waligorski. She knew how important this book has been to me and somehow managed to tolerate the perpetual disorder in my study.

1

Themes

If a term has many diverging definitions, it is better to begin by assuming that it is full of meanings. For none of the main ideas of our civilization has a single meaning.
—Walter Lippmann, *Essays in the Public Philosophy*

Did y'ever think, Ken, that making a speech on ee-conomics is a lot like pissing down your leg? It seems hot to you, but it never does to anyone else.
—Lyndon Johnson to John Kenneth Galbraith, John Kenneth Galbraith, *A Life in Our Times*

WITH THE APPARENT DEMISE of Soviet communism and the Marxist version of socialism, many claim that liberal-democracy, and perhaps capitalism, won the Cold War.[1] But the crucial question is, about which liberalism, which democracy, and which capitalism is this claim made? Liberalism encompasses distinct, even incompatible images of basic liberal values, political-economics, and democracy. This book examines reform liberalism and its political economy. Reform liberals reject any simple picture of liberalism or democracy and do not equate either with any of the many varieties of capitalism, some of which are more successful than others. They offer a complex vision of enhanced possibilities that differs significantly from a laissez-faire philosophy. For them, economic success, social welfare, inclusive freedom, democracy, and political-social stability require that active, democratic government regulate, maintain, and on occasion restrain some economic activities. Many writers, however, insist that there is only one liberalism.[2] Frequently they identify liberalism with specific policies or present it as continuous from its seventeenth-century origins and inextricably linked to a nineteenth-century laissez-faire, individual utility maximizing economics. This book argues that liberalism is multifaceted,[3] continually changes policies, and cannot be forced into a single continuum, even though liberalism has a core of common values.

Liberalism does not rest on a single value or dimension of human expe-

rience, although freedom from perceived oppressive forces is fundamental.
It has rarely concentrated on one thing, even property rights, to the exclusion of others. Insistence that everything is subordinate to one value may be
dogmatically comforting or philosophically exhilarating but offends reality
by ignoring that goods cannot be subsumed under a single head and often
clash. Leading liberals attempted to balance inevitably conflicting claims:
freedom and equality, participation and protection of nonpolitical rights,
freedom of association and tolerance, individualism and community, free
expression and being left alone. Of course liberals fail to achieve a final balance because there is no single, ultimate, or everlasting answer. Circumstances change, requiring minor and major policy alterations. The success
of one generation of liberals in realizing some of its goals provides a base
from which subsequent generations may further refine values, goals, and
policies; it does not supply a resting place. A number of complexly interacting themes recur in this book: the interconnection of politics and economics, particularly economics' impact on politics; criticism of laissez-faire
political economy; desire to expand freedom, equality, democracy, and individuality; and promotion of common interest, accountable power, a wider
sphere for the public, an active role for government, and the legitimacy of
public intervention to ameliorate economic dislocation.[4] Liberalism need
not include laissez-faire, complete property freedom, unchecked markets,
or purely negative freedom. Agreeing on the names of basic values, however, means little until one understands how these concepts are employed,
what they include or exclude, perceived obstacles to their realization, and
what policies follow from or may implement them.

Liberalism and Economics

Liberalism's long association with economics has historically colored liberalism's perception of values and political possibility. Although liberalism
cannot easily be separated from economic relations, it is not primarily an
economic theory. Its link with economics, however, has been and continues
to be controversial. Liberals and critics of liberalism cannot agree on the
nature of liberal economics or the interrelation between economics and politics in liberalism.[5] This difficulty is compounded by political and economic
writers who employ similar language—freedom, individualism, equality,
public versus private—to mean very different things. Particularly among
laissez-faire theorists the distinction between public and private spheres is,
erroneously according to the theorists in this book, equated with that

between economy and polity. The following subsections identify several themes in the development of liberal political-economy, briefly exploring classical and laissez-faire liberalism as an introduction to reform liberalism and its major concerns.

CLASSICAL LIBERALISM

Classical liberalism developed first in England during the Civil War of the 1640s. Whether one looks at John Locke, Thomas Jefferson, Thomas Paine, Voltaire, or some aspects of John Stuart Mill, they primarily emphasized negative freedom and political rights, and only incidentally touched on economics. Classical liberalism emphasized religious freedom—an important source for tolerance that defends a sphere of autonomous thought and behavior, the right to dissent, and social-individual concerns as distinguished from public and government ones—as well as freedom of thought, expression, and press; constitutional guarantees; contract; some individualism, though not individuality; limited government; and tolerance. The most important assumption for our purposes is that people are naturally social while government is artificial, or at least secondary. John Locke distinguished between society, which is natural, and government, which is created by consent and is limited to protecting preexisting individual rights brought into civil society from the state of nature. A century later, Thomas Paine in *Common Sense* popularly expressed that concept: "Society is produced by our wants, and government by our wickedness; the former promotes our happiness *positively* by uniting our affections, the latter *negatively* by restraining our vices."[6] By postulating a clear distinction between private and public, classical liberals laid the groundwork for later claims that the economy is separate from and superior to the political system.

Classical liberals saw government as the major danger to freedom, including economic freedom. These theorists did not share any single view of the relation between politics and economics, in part because economics had not yet fully developed as a separate theory—the earliest wrote during the ascendance of mercantilism—and in part because early liberals were not united. Dewey and Galbraith correctly observe that Jefferson does not today defend a laissez-faire, limited government, because urbanization and industrialization destroyed the economic system that made such a model possible.[7] Nevertheless these early theorists and politicians were not afraid to discuss how politics and economics are related—especially in terms of class conflict. Locke may have found the origin of property in labor, but the tacit, consent-based invention of money ensured that laborers had few claims on property held by the wealthy. Property may have included personal property and individual rights,[8] but rights involving real property often had priority among rights. If government was the major danger to freedom and if social relations were natural, voluntary, and consensual the latter could scarcely be dangers to freedom.

INDIVIDUALISTIC OR LAISSEZ-FAIRE[9] LIBERALISM

Two major approaches contend for the economic soul of modern liberalism: individualistic or laissez-faire liberalism and reform liberalism. Both claim the title of liberalism, and both have roots in classical liberalism.

Laissez-faire liberalism is unabashedly and primarily economic in orientation and is dominated by the assumption that self-interested individuals compete in markets and market-like situations, the results of which are just, even democratic. Laissez-faire liberalism includes, for our purposes, much of classical and neoclassical economics,[10] social Darwinism, and such contemporary forms as monetarism and libertarianism—the last three seeing the market as the primary arena of and model for human activity. These theories, while not identical, share politically relevant assumptions and characteristics. Laissez-faire descends directly from and modifies classical liberalism. The two theories share assumptions about natural social order, voluntary behavior in the absence of coercion, mistrust of and a small role for government, defense of property rights, a tendency to subordinate political participation to property rights, insistence that careers be open to talent, separation of private from public concerns, and appeals to natural lawlike processes and behavior. These, together with a seeming incorporation of fundamental values such as individualism and freedom lent laissez-faire popular appeal.[11] The claim that power dissolves in the market is an example. It incorporates Lockean theory into political-economics, equating the presumably peaceful and noncoercive market with Lockean natural social relations and societal structure, thereby rendering markets the functional equivalent of classic liberal society.

Laissez-faire liberalism was first identified with Adam Smith, for whom the economy determined the role of government. Its fuller political content and implications have been developed by theorists as diverse as David Ricardo, Thomas Robert Malthus, Herbert Spencer, Milton Friedman, George Gilder, F. A. Hayek, and recent conservative critics in Congress. Despite their deep differences, all laissez-faire theorists claim that a free economy resolves social problems. Politics and social relations are secondary to the economic system and must be adjusted to fit what is perceived as economic necessity. Laissez-faire liberalism emphasizes limited government and negative freedom defined as allowing people to seek their own interest and use their resources as they choose in markets and marketlike situations. Such self-interested, self-determined behavior generates order, equilibrium, and justice. Although Smith viewed government as having a role in creating supporting conditions for the economy and believed its role should change with the economy, government's primary duty has become keeping out of the economy. Smith's argument for noninvolvement arose partly in reaction to corrupt government and mercantilism, although he also assumed that commerce could soften manners, improve government, and give people an acceptable outlet for their energies[12]—a point John Maynard Keynes later elaborated. But this theme in Smith's writings has been elevated by his successors to the status of a first principle. The market, individualized motivation, and self-seeking behavior set impenetrable limits to political possibility, prohibiting active government, extensive regulation of the economy, widespread welfare provisions, and public attempts to promote equality. Intervention undermines the economic order and, for some writers, fosters immorality; therefore, government lacks any legitimate role in economic and social relations beyond protecting the right to compete.

According to laissez-faire theorists, the market is a natural, noncoercive and self-regulating sphere of voluntary behavior that rewards people according to their contribution to the welfare of others. As a result it produces the maximum possible levels of freedom, equality, and welfare. People are self-contained, have mostly contractual links or responsibilities, and are largely uninfluenced by others. Each person seeks her or his own advantage and is equally able to enter markets and bargain. Pursuit of individual want satisfaction and self-interest leads to spontaneous order or natural harmony, social advantage, the common good, and benefit to others. Companies produce what the consumer—collectively—wants, in the quantities and qualities wanted, and at prices they will pay. In a market free of government intervention, no one person, group, seller, buyer, or manufacturer determines what is produced or what prices are paid. Large and small participants are equally subject to the market. As no one controls production, prices, or what is offered, no identifiable individual has power over any other identifiable individual, each of whom voluntarily participates or not at the prices and quantities offered, thereby protecting freedom. Competition regulates behavior, preventing self-interest from harming others. Competition thus becomes the key moral imperative—one lacking in government—and means to organize society. If free, markets take over and depoliticize many of the distributive and regulatory functions others assign to government. Noninterventionist public policy, limited government, and leaving people to their own devices follows.[13] Such laissez-faire arguments provide the context and primary contrast for reform liberalism.

Reform Liberalism

Reform liberalism[14] epitomizes the contemporary concept of political-economic liberalism. For a century it has helped shape modern understanding and practice of the interrelations among politics, government, and economics. The seven theorists examined in this book form a tradition of argument that developed much of the perspective, language, and ideas currently employed by people who defend the legitimacy of active government involvement in the political-economy. These theorists reinterpret the soul of liberalism against libertarian claims and communitarian critics, attempting to fit liberalism to the continually changing environment of industrial and postindustrial society. Reform liberals attack the philosophical-economic base on which the current conservative reaction's political-economic policies depend. Their systematic, ongoing moral-political-economic engagement with and criticism of the leave things alone philosophy and its political-social implications is the only viable democratic alternative to an increasingly assertive conservative theory of public policy.

Louis Brandeis, John Dewey, and L. T. Hobhouse represent a definitive and (in the cases of Dewey and Hobhouse) conscious break from older-style liberalism. Although not economists, they criticized social Darwinism and confronted the impact of economic change and large organization on individuality, politics, and society. Dewey explicitly links Progressivism,[15] which emphasized consequences and focused on public control of the perceived adverse effects of industrialization, and liberalism. America's most famous philosopher, he insisted that industrialization had transformed the conditions that once supported freedom and individualism. Arguing that real individual liberation could not occur without deep changes in ideas and the social-economy, he attempted to adapt liberalism to a society in which the majority had little control over large parts of their lives. Louis Brandeis illustrates the progressive effort to address industrial concentration, power, and large organization. A prominent member of the U.S. Supreme Court, he was for forty years one of America's leading defenders of both civil rights and an active role for government in solving social-economic problems. Hobhouse's book *Liberalism* (1911) contains many twentieth-century liberal concerns. Accepting the basic values of classical liberalism, he argued that people are social creatures, that individuals develop their full human capacities only in society, and that individuals and society are interdependent.

No twentieth-century philosopher, economist, or political theorist has had more impact on policy than John Maynard Keynes. Before Keynes, economic "law" and economic "necessity" could be invoked against any reform. Keynes changed the way people understand the role of government in the economy, opening the possibility of a large-scale interventionist, welfare government. Whereas earlier reform liberals employed moral and social criticism to attack laissez-faire, Keynes developed sophisticated and plausible economic arguments for intervention and against economic inequality—arguments that reform liberalism hitherto had lacked. His analysis challenged the foundation of laissez-faire thinking, especially its basis in natural law and the assumption that the market naturally tends toward equilibrium. In the process he provided the technical justification for government intervention that remains at the intellectual core of reform liberalism and much of social democratic theory.

John Kenneth Galbraith participated in Democratic administrations from Franklin Roosevelt to Lyndon Johnson and campaigned for seven Democratic presidential hopefuls, from Adlai Stevenson in 1952 to Edward Kennedy in 1980. His readiness to confront the gaps between theoretical orthodoxy and practical reality made him the leading reform liberal in the third quarter of the twentieth century. Galbraith's greatest influence on American society came from helping formulate agricultural and anti-poverty policy under Kennedy and Johnson. Through his arguments about the maladies and imbalances of what he called the "affluent society," and his attack on market ideology, he helped people to recognize poverty amidst wealth. With less success, he tried to reintroduce the issue of power—the most ignored factor in conservative political economy—into economic argument. Galbraith insists that power is an essential factor in modern economic conditions. His arguments about organization parallel those of Brandeis and Dewey.

Lester Thurow and Robert Reich[16] signal a shift in reform liberal focus. While continuing to adhere to basic reform values and assumptions, the context within which they write—renewed conservatism and a radically altered United States and world economy—has changed. Government intervention in the market has been assailed by theorists such as Frank Knight, Milton Friedman, George Gilder, F. A. Hayek, James Buchanan, George Stigler, and Robert Nozick and by politicians such as Margaret Thatcher, Ronald Reagan, George Bush, Newt Gingrich, and Jack Kemp. Rather than experiencing expected or realized economic success, Thurow and Reich face relative economic decline, low productivity, intensifying inequality, and heightened international economic challenges that none of the others, except Keynes in the 1920s and 1940s, had experienced. This situation defies currently accepted answers and reintroduces the possibility of severe social and political conflict over economic inequality and social position. Thurow addresses these issues in economists' terms. Reich brings reform language into the policy argument among New Democrats.[17] Thurow and Reich agree that capitalism is not stable and that leaving things alone is not a viable option. They criticize the assumptions and the social-political-economic results of the pure market model. They worry that capitalism is not working well enough to support economic well-being, equality, democracy, and community. But while they ask many questions similar to those Keynes raised, many answers are different. For Keynes, the central problem in the 1930s was how to put people back to work, and the immediacy of this task permitted him to focus on the short run. For Thurow and Reich—as for Keynes after World War II—the focus is on the long run of five to fifty years and on long-term competitiveness. They are less involved in immediate, detailed social-political policies than was Galbraith, but they share with both Keynes and Galbraith a worry over long-term social-political viability that is missing from contemporary conservative argument. Thurow and Reich rephrase the classic liberal question, first stated by Adam Smith: What social-political policies, relations, and role for government are necessary to promote growth and prosperity in a highly competitive world? Given resurgent neoclassical political economy, powerful international competition, concern over social dislocation, and the need for social-political-economic reconstruction, their answers are very different from those of Smith, Ricardo, or their neoclassical descendants.

Despite theoretical and policy differences among themselves, reform liberals reject core laissez-faire claims and conclusions. Even though they share many values and principles of classical and laissez-faire liberalism, they interpret these more broadly and insist on distinguishing between fundamental principles and the policies that might implement them. In contrast, proponents of laissez-faire maintain a theory and policies no longer applicable to existing conditions, thereby endangering the principles they ostensibly defend. By reinterpreting values, rethinking obstacles, applying the spirit of fundamental principles to new issues, and considering unconventional policies, reform liberals seek to modify and adapt traditional liberal principles to altered circumstances. This adaptive and reforming impulse is what makes them *reform* liberals. Their unifying theme is that traditional liberal concepts and policies must be redesigned to fit drastically altered twentieth-century circumstances.[18] Adjustment is necessary because habitual applications, means, and policies no longer protect or attain classic liberal ends and values. Changed conditions include new links between politics and economics, a failure of markets to attain acceptable levels of equilibrium, democracy, powerful economic actors, deeply felt inequality, reappraisal of the state's potential, and recognition of horrendous social-political consequences of leaving the market alone. In short, the hands-off approach of earlier liberalism ignored evils generated by unrestrained markets, private power, and deep-seated inequality. New policies and organizations are necessary to realize historic liberal principles. Dewey, for example, argued that the "significance" and private nature of property had "changed," and so must policy. Liberalism could attain its ends "*only* by" abandoning the laissez-faire policies "to which early liberalism was committed." For Hobhouse, changes from older noninterventionist concepts of freedom and equality, such as were implicit in factory legislation, "are in reality departures by which the principles of liberty and equality are developed and extended." Reform liberalism thus extends classical concerns into previously ignored areas of social and economic relations. Reform liberals do not hesitate to employ government to achieve desired economic and social goals, expand opportunities, and reduce the harmful impact of economic dislocation on democracy.[19] They also assert that their theories produce superior economic, social, moral, and political results.

Although it has a large economic component, reform liberalism is not just economic.[20] Rather, it argues that policy makers must address economic matters in conjunction with social-political issues. Reform liberalism began to develop in the late nineteenth-century in response to the emergence of large concentrations of wealth and economic power—which threatened the social and political order, social justice,[21] and democracy—as well as social Darwinism and the patterns of late nineteenth- and early twentieth-century industrialization. Reform liberalism moved away from the prevailing mechanical systems and quasi-determinism of classical political economy toward willingness to experiment and modify received policies. Evolving first in Britain, it was associated initially[22] with theorists such as T. H. Green, J. A. Hobson, and L. T. Hobhouse, and became identified as liberalism by 1900. In the United States, reform liberalism is related to Progressivism; it may be identified first with Louis Brandeis, Jane Addams, and John Dewey, and only acquired the name liberalism in the 1930s.[23] What most people today call liberalism refers to what this book calls reform liberalism, in contrast to classical and laissez-faire versions.[24]

Although the relation between turn-of-the-century "new" liberalism and liberalism since 1930 is controversial, this book assumes that a strong element of continuity exists, despite the frequently idealist nature of new liberalism. Robert Skidelsky claims that "Keynes had no connection with" new liberal idealism, emphasis on democracy, or positive freedom. Whether or not this is accurate it slights the assumptions and policy goals that new and later liberals share, including criticism of laissez-faire and insistence that freedom and equality can be expanded.[25] Philippa Strum confirms the continuity between nineteenth- and twentieth-century liberals when she argues that Brandeis made proposals comparable to "nineteenth-century English reform liberals. . . . faced with similar problems, he came to many similar solutions."[26] To the extent that new liberals "insisted on retaining the emphasis on wealth and production as the essential financial source of a social reform policy," on concern for social justice, and on desire "to replace laissez-faire economics,"[27] all of the theorists discussed in this book concur.

American reform liberalism reached maturity during the Great Depression. Although unrestrained capitalism received intensive criticism from roughly 1890 to 1920, a dominant and unifying theme did not emerge until the 1930s. The Depression is a defining and justifying moment for modern liberalism because it led to widespread agreement that the market is not inherently stable and that the role of government in the social economy can be significant. John Maynard Keynes provided the intellectual justification for intervention by creating a widely accepted political-economic alternative that reform liberalism had hitherto lacked. He saw Franklin Roosevelt as crucial to saving liberal democracy. Roosevelt, who never understood Keynes, presided over policies that for fifty years—except in the area of civil rights—reflected the reform liberal approach. Roosevelt believed that "'in many instances the victory of the central Government was a haven of refuge to the individual'" from a "'new industrial dictatorship.'"[28] Keynes and Roosevelt may have dreamed radical thoughts, but they never broke with fundamental political-economic institutions. At bottom their goals were deeply conservative: to maintain continuity with central progressive and liberal values, to preserve capitalism (and as a result much of the power of business), to head off more radical alternatives, to maintain established institutions, and to achieve limited common ends. In addition to continuing an American tradition of active government involvement in the economy, the New Deal partly extended "it so as to protect the weak as well as the strong." It also solidified for almost half a century a shift from belief in self-equilibrating markets and weak government to acceptance of a positive government role in "social and economic progress" and in expanding economic freedom[29]—policies and principles under profound attack today.[30]

Common Values in Reform Liberalism

Reform liberals share much more than an insistence on distinguishing principle from policy. Their continuity of concerns helps set reform liberals apart from earlier liberals. A number of themes common to reform liberalism recur throughout this book: criticism and rejection of pure laissez-faire theory and policy; expansion of the meaning and scope of traditional liberal values such as freedom, equality, democracy, and individualism; concern with power in the economy; rejection of a rigid separation between the public and private spheres; and justification of a positive government role in economic relations. Although each theme does not receive equal weight in each chapter, and some, such as democracy or how government will perform its role, are not fully explored, they are defining elements in reform liberalism. To simply note recurrent themes is to outline alternatives to century-old and recent social Darwinism. The themes are examined again in the last chapter in connection with critics and problems of liberalism. As Hobhouse wrote, "No one element of the social life stands separate from the rest. . . . public policy must be conceived in its bearing on the life of society as a whole."[31]

REFORM LIBERAL POLITICAL ECONOMY

The response to laissez-faire is the key common substantive element in reform arguments. One line of argument runs through each chapter: in current conditions the economy and the polity do not operate as laissez-faire claims; politics and economics are closely related; laissez-faire makes for bad economic and public policy, because it produces undesirable social, political, and economic results; and better alternatives are available. Reform liberals attempt to shape an economy compatible with liberal and democratic values in the world as people confront it in their lives.

Let us settle one point of abuse immediately. Reform liberals do not spurn the free market. They like it so much that they want to see it work better. This is one of the values that makes them liberals. But their market is different from the laissez-faire market. They are more optimistic than laissez-faire theorists about how much control people can successfully exert over social-economic forces. Markets cannot justify themselves. Unrestrained markets do not ensure efficiency, equilibrium, a high degree of prosperity, or fairness, but can produce disorder, inequality, and injustice. There are no necessary trade-offs between efficiency and equity, markets cannot replace government for important matters, and they require public intervention to attain more of the social and economic good they can achieve. Moreover, economic order and public life are not dichotomous and political-social effects are relevant in judging markets.[32] The authors presented in this book attempt to move beyond traditional political economy[33] to judge markets by other criteria. The economy cannot be considered in isolation from the social relations of which it is a part. While an efficient economy is important, it is instrumental, not an end in itself.[34] Far from being secondary to economics, social-political ends, values, and relations have at least equal significance in public policy. Claims that economic efficiency justifies reducing government are wrong, because, reform liberals insist, narrow efficiency criteria are important but do not define justice, the good life, or the appropriate limits of democracy. In fact, efficiency must be defined in terms of these ends. Concurrently, each theorist is sensitive to the political content of economics—Brandeis and Galbraith in particular.

These arguments are the basis for many policies associated with liberalism, including full employment, support for education and economic regulation. Despite some shortcomings, such policies change the rules and beneficiaries of a market economy. They legitimate political-social considerations in economics, reduce economic power, and serve to some extent to empower workers and consumers.

FREEDOM

Although it is the central liberal value, freedom cannot be understood merely by reference to a one-dimensional definition; rather we must ask what it means, where it applies, what obstacles restrain it, and what may government do to enhance it. Answers to these questions distinguish one type of liberalism from another. The theorists in this book do not have identical concepts of freedom, but as a group they have a more expansive concept of freedom than that propounded in classical and laissez-faire theory. This is especially true with regard to perceived obstacles to freedom. Classical and economic liberals insisted that government interference with individual rights is the major impediment to being free. Dewey exemplifies the reform liberal argument that freedom is historically contingent and its meaning and required institutional framework change over time: "the conception of liberty is always relative to forces that at a given time and place are felt to be oppressive."[35] Obstacles to freedom include laissez-faire policy, concentrated economic power, discrimination, poverty, ignorance, and economic conditions beyond individual control such as market failure and economic instability. Freedom in social and economic relations means more than allowing people to compete. Reform liberalism embraces limited positive freedom understood as aid in achieving formal freedom.

EQUALITY

Equality is a protean concept.[36] Though important for liberals, equality is often secondary and instrumental to freedom. This makes contemporary efforts to define liberalism in terms of equality[37] problematic because liberalism has always been ambiguous about equality except for the same right to freedom. Economic theory has traditionally justified economic and in some cases social and political inequality. The theorists in this book conceive of equality as comprehending more than historic liberal concepts such as the opening of careers to talent and the identical treatment of each person by the law. Each rejects such traditional justifications of inequality as claims by neoclassical writers and contemporary conservatives that extensive inequality fosters economic growth, rewards initiative, and encourages contributions to the welfare of others. They accept Keynes' argument that great inequality retards growth. While some inequality is justifiable, the existing degree of inequality is not equitable, causes social discontent, and undermines general economic welfare. Although this view does not make reform liberals thoroughgoing egalitarians, it does mean that if great or greater inequality—as proposed by supply-side theory in the 1980s—is unnecessary for economic growth or for benefitting the poorest, inequality must be defended on other grounds. These theorists focus on increasing equality, not on making everyone the same. In most problems facing the social-economy, enhanced equality need not interfere with freedom although the two may conflict at the margin. More equality of power, educational opportunity, economic rewards, or real as opposed to formal equal opportunity, enhances freedom understood in terms of political and economic autonomy. Under pressure from conditions ignored by classical and laissez-faire theory it is legitimate to encourage more equality through active public policy. Meaningful or expanded equality of opportunity requires some equality of results and limited redistribution. Reform liberals further assert that gross inequality is unjust, frustrates economic efficiency, and undermines social-political stability. Brandeis, Dewey, Reich, and Thurow add that concern with economic equalization is necessary to political equality.

DEMOCRACY

An acute tension exists between much economic theory and democracy. Many economists, from Thomas Robert Malthus to contemporary theorists such as F. A. Hayek or Milton Friedman, have been indifferent to political democracy and actively opposed to anything resembling economic democracy. This indifference and aversion have come to be associated with liberalism in general; yet reform liberals demonstrate that liberalism need not have a weak connection to democracy.[38] Although none of the seven theorists examined here are participatory democrats—Brandeis and Reich come closest—all are concerned with the impact of economics on democracy. Given economic inequality and an imbalance of economic power, markets are not the sphere of real democracy. Historically, reform liberals have sought to foster the conditions within which democracy can operate. They have consistently attempted to protect democracy—initially from monied interests and large organizations (Dewey and Brandeis), and more recently from the threat of economic disequilibrium (Keynes, Thurow, Reich, and to a limited extent Galbraith). Economics and economists must accommodate democracy, not tailor democracy to fit economic theory, and government must be free to respond to popular needs and demands about the economy. Keynes, for example, assumed that public opinion was ahead of elite opinion on addressing economic crises. Dewey, Brandeis, and Reich discuss the more positive benefits of democracy and participation the most,[39] although other reform liberals accept increased popular participation.

INDIVIDUALISM

Individualism is central to all varieties of liberalism but, as with freedom, liberals sharply disagree about the meaning, content, impediments to, and supportive public policies for individualism. They also disagree about the nature of community. Reform liberals argue that the traditional liberal concept of individualism as self-interested utility maximization, which is satisfied by allowing competition in markets—Reich's "opportunistic individualism"[40]—is inadequate for three reasons: it fails to value individuality, individuals, and individual ends; it ignores the social context in which decisions are shaped and made; and it slights situations where "what is to the advantage of each of us regarded as a solitary individual is to the disadvantage of each of us regarded as members of a community."[41] Among reform liberals, Keynes' concept of community is the weakest, and Dewey's and Hobhouse's the strongest, but all agree that individuals are not isolated from the community. Supporting structures which contour perceptions and definition of self-interest are essential for individual development which in turn alters the society in which individuals define their self and social interests. For example, Brandeis and Thurow identify the work environment as pivotal to individual satisfaction and development of a sense of community.

POWER

Concepts of power are closely related to notions of freedom, equality, individuality, and the role of government. Except for theorists such as John Stuart Mill and Alexis de Tocqueville, classical and laissez-faire liberals disregarded nongovernmental power. Classical liberalism was satisfied that power was not a problem so long as individual rights were protected from government. Laissez-faire theory argues that since power can be exercised only through coercion, power disappears in a free market because each action is voluntary and self-interested. Power cannot be exercised because, in pursuing his or her self-interest, each person does only what he or she determines is beneficial. Both classical and laissez-faire liberalism assume that only government has power harmful to freedom. Neither conceives that holders of private power, which in theory cannot exist, might endanger the freedom of other individuals and groups. Reform liberals reject the image of the market as being free of economic power. They assert that unequal power to affect social and economic outcomes is a problem for society. "Voluntary" acts may not be free when people lack reasonable alternatives. Consequently, social and economic relations may be as oppressive as those created "by force and violence."[42] Galbraith analyzes power in greatest detail, but several others also consider its role. Brandeis, Dewey, Hobhouse, Galbraith, and Thurow agree that many "economic" decisions can restrain individual freedom as severely as government decisions.[43] Dewey, Brandeis, and Galbraith worry about the ability of large-scale organizations to bend people to the will of the controlling elite. Inequality of power causes social injustice and prevents the economy from performing well. If political economy is to address reality, these theorists agree, it must acknowledge the full range of power holders in society.

PUBLIC-PRIVATE SPHERES

Traditional liberal theory claims there is a clear distinction between the arena of the private and the public. Early liberalism associated the private realm with moral or religious conscience, which helped justify religious freedom and tolerance. Adam Smith's discovery of natural liberty in market relations, John Stuart Mill's effort to secure a realm of individuality and noninterference, and contemporary concern with privacy illustrate continuing engagement with the nexus of public and private. Although not the same as the contrast between state and society, this distinction is related to it and to individualism and has been a frequent liberal defense for individual rights. Except for limited externalities, laissez-faire theory has assimilated virtually all market relations into the private sphere. To the extent that a public realm exists at all, it results from summing the private interests and wants of separate individuals and has no existence apart from the coincidence of individually held preferences.

Reform liberals challenge any simple separation between "private" and "public" and emphatically reject the notion that the economy constitutes a realm of private behavior equivalent to classical liberal society. That the economy exhibits significant elements often ascribed to the state, such as power and authority, weakens a simple public-private distinction. People are not isolated but are embedded in an environment that shapes and affects them and is in turn shaped by people pursuing self-interest. Individuals therefore have overlapping public and private selves. This is not to claim that reform liberals favor the public over the private. Rather, they assert that economic behavior is neither protected by natural law nor isolated from community. The market does not consist of simple one-to-one personal transactions with generally beneficial or at least innocuous impact on others. Collective consequences exist. Economic behavior is itself often political, as those at the top of the machine bargain, manipulate, and exercise authority and power over the livelihood, status, and essential amenities of the large majority. Some conservatives may claim that, except for labor unions, workers voluntarily place themselves in authoritative and hierarchical enterprises, and that corporate leaders therefore do not possess power over them, so the economy remains the realm of private behavior, but the theorists in this book consider that explanation to be unrealistic in ignoring constrained choice and how individuals actually feel.

POSITIVE ROLE OF GOVERNMENT

Most people locate the biggest change between earlier liberalism and reform liberalism in the increased role envisioned for government. Popular and journalistic accounts allege that liberalism is dedicated to big government. This erroneous assertion illustrates that liberals have come to be associated with expansion of government into *new*—for this century—areas of activity. Conservative dogma insists active government must fail because only market competition can effectively control self-interest. Government cannot successfully intervene in economic relations broadly understood.[44] Government action inevitably reduces freedom and worsens the situation. Conservative policy follows with rigid necessity: (1) The market solves problems such as discrimination, regulation of financial institutions, unsafe work conditions, and poor education. (2) Welfare breeds dependence, crime, riots, and promiscuity, while destroying freedom. (3) Public policy to promote specific parts of the economy should be abandoned. (4) Institutions such as the Corporation for Public Broadcasting, Environmental Protection Agency, Commerce Department, or the Council of Economic Advisors should be eliminated. Reform liberalism, which developed in response to market philosophy, claims that conservatives ignore the reasons for allowing government a larger role. Real governments have for generations intervened significantly in the economy, particularly to aid large enterprises. The form of capitalism that has triumphed over communism was aided, protected, and reformed by government. Examples include tariffs, public works, in the United States free land and protection of corporations under the Fourteenth Amendment, public research, nineteenth- and early twentieth-century suppression of worker organizations, laws of incorporation, and interpretation of laws so as to benefit concentrations of property.[45] The authors discussed in this book do not love government. Some find it distasteful. They are not apologists for everything governments have done in the last sixty-five years. None denies that government actions can fail. All are caught in the liberal dilemma of simultaneously needing and mistrusting government. Nevertheless, they believe that government must be responsive to "the mild but continuous repressiveness of everyday social life."[46] Each agrees that economic and environmental changes and a legitimate concern for what happens to the majority have compelled governments to take on a larger role. Given modern economies, any other course would be disastrous.

The Reform Enterprise

Reform liberalism is more than the sum of these parts. As with all important ideological perspectives, it changes the world while interpreting it. We examine these arguments not simply because they are interesting and offer an alternative to currently dominant political-economic practice, but, more importantly, because they have become a lens through which many liberals, and conservatives, view and understand reality. Both economists and noneconomists made similar arguments. This makes it possible to examine continuity and development in assumptions and goals, though not policies, over one hundred years of debate, from reactions to social Darwinism and early twentieth-century industrialization, through the Great Depression, to the War on Poverty, welfare reform, industrial policy, and international economic challenge.

Emphasizing continuity does not mean that reform liberals are indistinguishable.[47] Each theorist responded to distinct historical circumstances. Brandeis, Dewey, and Hobhouse wrote during a period of rapid expansion and deeply felt social injustice; Keynes and Dewey (in his period of active involvement with political-economy) during what was feared to be the collapse of capitalism and western democracy; Galbraith, when United States' economic and political dominance was at its peak and could be taken for granted; Reich and Thurow, during a time of increasing external economic challenge and growing internal inequality. Keynes and Galbraith never let the Depression experience disappear from their writing or advice. Perceived problems and themes therefore shift and change. For example, Thurow sees a less open international economy than does Reich. In his major published work, Galbraith virtually ignores international economics; Keynes, Thurow, and Reich are attentive to its impact on the domestic system (this book focuses on domestic matters). Galbraith is deeply concerned with power; Keynes with restoring capitalism and preserving conditions for parliamentary democracy; Reich with participatory democracy, international competition, and rebuilding America so it can better compete; Thurow with the sources and nature of domestic and international conflict. But these are differences within an ideological family sharing numerous values, approaches, and assumptions. These authors are exemplars of a broad thesis, but they are not identical in focus, problems addressed, or degree of explicit political consciousness. It is these essentially secondary differences that cause misunderstanding of liberalism. Differences highlight the values, problems, responses, and opponents these theorists share. The interrelation of politics and economics never disappears.

Recent conservative victories and efforts to dismantle the interventionist state in the name of returning to the free market have demoralized many liberals, but the theorists in this book also faced powerful conservative policies and arguments. Spanning a century, these seven liberals provide a persistent, reasonably coherent alternative model to widely accepted social Darwinian, laissez-faire, supply-side, libertarian, and monetarist political-economic practice and philosophy, including much that was called liberal. Their liberalism is oriented to policy and improvement. These theorists attempt to create a workable political-economic public philosophy that acknowledges social-political responsibility between individuals and government, and reflects the impossibility of completely separating politics and economics. They insist on looking at what happens to individuals—at the limits on their lives, and at the economic obstacles to democracy and freedom. Asserting that politics and social relations are important, they reject economic determinism, claiming that economic practices can be made to conform to social, moral, and political values. Despite embracing values similar to those of traditional liberals, reform theorists offer new social and political goals and organization. They illuminate the diversity of meanings and policies for freedom, equality, and democracy, and demonstrate that these are not delimited by market "efficiency." Government is not their enemy: they insist that individualism and freedom can be enhanced by positive government, while social and economic relations can be oppressive. They offer a framework within which a revamped liberalism may once again form public policy.

2

Beginnings

Every economic and social question is an ethical question about ultimate and intermediate ends and about the moral appropriateness of ends.
—Walter A. Weisskopf, "Normative and Ideological Elements in Social and Economic Thought," *Journal of Economic Issues*

But Liberalism is not a creed that, in fulfilling itself, extinguishes itself. It is a spirit, an attitude of mind, a principle of action of infinite application to the changing conditions of society.
—A. G. G., "The Spirit of Liberalism," *The Nation and the Athenaeum*

JOHN DEWEY (1859–1952), Louis Brandeis (1856–1941), and L. T. Hobhouse (1864–1929) epitomize the moral and critical element in reform liberal political-economy, without the sophisticated economic theory that was developed later to support their challenge to existing political-economic relations. Neither economists nor economic writers, they criticized social Darwinism, inactive government, and the social-political consequences of unconstrained economic power, and their criticism is reflected in later reform economists. Economic concerns such as the interrelation of politics and economics, vulnerability to social and economic forces, and the impact of economic power and inequality on social-political life permeate their work, especially that of Dewey and Brandeis. This chapter focuses on "the practical effects of thought," including what Galbraith refers to as "conflict between ideology and the dynamics of change,"[1] not on philosophy or other aspects of their work.[2] Rather than considering differences, it emphasizes six shared normative themes and conclusions that characterize reform liberal political-economy: liberalism, individualism, freedom, democracy, economic practice and theory, and the role of government. Focusing on the link between politics and economics, this chapter accentuates Dewey's writing in the 1930s when he was most actively engaged with social-economic and political-economic issues, Brandeis, especially before Woodrow Wilson appointed him to the Supreme Court in 1916, and Hobhouse before World War I.

Liberalism

Brandeis, Dewey, and Hobhouse criticized liberalism from within liberalism, condemning the way liberalism was practiced, especially its dominant economic expression. As with Keynes, Galbraith, and Reich, they agreed principles must be distinguished from policies that might implement them. Economic-social transformations are at the center of this chapter. Fundamental industrial and economic changes transformed the real, as opposed to imagined, social-economy. Ideas, ideologies, and movements initially arise in forms that fit their time and conditions. As circumstances change, they may cease to speak to people's experience and instead be enlisted to support reaction: "[O]nce harmless" practices "may, owing to changed conditions, seriously threaten the public welfare." Resisting the widespread desire to cling to "older creeds" like "magic formula" liberalism must change its orientation, perceived obstacles to values, and policies in order to remain faithful to basic liberal values.[3] But liberalism did not change fast enough and this failure was destructive. "*[L]aissez-faire* liberalism" still dominated public policy, leading to deeper class division, injustice, and defense of anti-liberal ends. Sharing the theme with subsequent reform liberals, Dewey argued for a "renascent liberalism" that spells out its ends "in terms of means that are relevant to the contemporary situation." "The idea that liberalism cannot maintain its ends and at the same time reverse its conception of means by which they are to be attained is folly. The ends can now be achieved only by reversal of the means to which early liberalism was committed." If liberalism takes "cultural liberation and growth of individuals" seriously, it must replace laissez-faire policy and favoring wealth with social direction of industry. This approach does not abandon "liberty . . . development of the inherent capacities of individuals . . . free intelligence in inquiry, discussion and expression" or individuality, but recognizes new obstacles to their attainment and, for their support, new policies adapted to a technological age of large organizations.[4]

As did Galbraith later, Hobhouse argued that many problems of liberalism were due to its success. "The great middle class has become contented with its lot" and opposed to further changes to bring justice to the rest of society.[5] Hobhouse wanted liberals to "'restate the fundamental principles of Liberalism in the form which modern circumstances require.'"[6] Faced with a changing economic and social environment, liberalism must revivify principles such as liberty by redefining their meaning and identifying new obstacles to their achievement. To maintain existing policy is to risk revolution. Thus legislation protecting workers or supporting labor unions may look socialistic to conservatives but has become "a necessary means to" fulfilling the promise of freedom and equality. The core values of liberalism remain, especially commitment to safeguarding individuals.[7] For Brandeis, older liberal interpretations no longer applied to urban-industrial America where social-economic change made it impossible to pursue traditional values in old ways. "'Rights . . . [and] liberty of the individual must be remolded from time to time'" to meet society's changing needs, especially under pressure of large concentrations of wealth and capital.[8]

Individualism

Adherence to a narrow definition of individualism as the right to pursue one's economic self-interest illustrates liberalism's failure to adapt. Individuality is context dependent. Environment shapes the possibility of and expression of individuality. Yet despite drastic alterations in their world, special interests and even people hurt by changes cling to older meanings and policies. New forms of industry, large-scale organization, concentrated economic power, interdependence, the key role played by "dominant corporatedness" in defining opportunity and choices, and "precarious conditions" for the "vast multitude" have shattered the setting and basis of classic and laissez-faire individualism, which prove inadequate to the new situation. These new circumstances leave most people with no control over the events that shape their lives and no margin for experiment. Brandeis believed they provide training in oppression and undermine opportunities to develop personality. These changes caused a centralization of private power that is camouflaged by traditional thinking.[9]

Dewey, Brandeis, and Hobhouse criticized atomistic individualism. They agreed people are not self-contained. Individual or specific group interests can clash with "the interest of all considered collectively and permanently."[10] Early, especially economic, liberalism ignored restraints on the liberty of individuals in the nongovernment environment where people imagined possibilities, found or created opportunities, and formed plans. Although early liberalism emancipated individuals from many restrictions, Dewey argued that it failed to see and therefore was ineffective in addressing "problems of social organization and integration." Early liberal individualism, according to Hobhouse, cannot solve the problems created by large-scale industry. Dewey observed that early liberalism saw individuals as alone and separate, and "individuality as something ready-made, already processed, and needing only the removal of certain legal restrictions to come into full play." It could not consider how dependent people were on "social conditions" or imagine how changed circumstances ravaged previous methods for protecting individualism and freedom. Instead it provided an apologia "for the existing economic regime."[11]

Rather than being systematically individualistic, older liberal individualism focused on a narrow range of behavior—pursuing economic self-interest. Despite its professed commitment to individualism, earlier liberalism was unconcerned with what happened to individuals. Individualism's "whole significance" had "shrunk to a pecuniary scale and measure." Otherwise, it suppressed "individuality in thought and speech" to maintain an economic system that allowed "opportunity of personal expression" to only a small minority. But economic self-interest should not be the primary meaning of individualism. "Concentration" of power and "corporate organization" isolate individuals who are "lost" and virtually helpless. They cannot control the economic machine, bear no responsibility for its success or failure, and if unorganized must accept economic conditions as they find them—a situation often still celebrated by laissez-faire theory. Dewey and Hobhouse, in an argument congenial to Brandeis, Galbraith, Reich, Keynes, and Thurow, say that individuality is constrained by older ideas that fail to acknowledge the significance of new developments. This results in submerging "the individual" into corporate growth and power.[12]

The purpose of reform is not to abandon individualism but to complete the evolution of individualism by creating a "new individualism" that recognizes existent reality: "the collective age," "mental collectivism," and "standardization" imposed by new productive methods, economic needs, encouragement of consumption, and the concentration of power. In response to these new conditions, Brandeis urged developing "manhood," a concept that included growth of talents and development of the capacity to act. By ignoring situations people actually face, market philosophy missed the controlling impact of social-economic conditions and the large element of cooperation in all activities. A lack of concern for association and community was a primary failing of older liberalism. For Dewey, if liberalism stresses "the importance of individuality with sincerity," it "must be deeply concerned about the structure of human association." Association and community "negatively and positively" shape the "development of individuals." Support for full individuality requires "elimination of the older economic and political individualism," "economic revision," and a more complete concept of community to "liberate imagination and endeavor."[13] Nevertheless the new individualism is less clearly developed than is criticism of the old concept.

In varying forms but with the same result, these theorists argue community and individual are interdependent. They agree with Brandeis that individual development "is attained in the processes of living" and people are fundamentally social. According to Hobhouse, a person is embedded in a "social milieu which . . . turns his individuality into a creation of the time and place" so that, Dewey asserts, "it develops" and takes form "only through interaction with actual conditions." The rise of business civilization represents a change in "social constitution" that has transformed interaction and individualism.[14] Thus these theorists accept and attempt to expand the role of community, thereby rectifying a primary failing of earlier liberalism, which perpetuated the myth of atomistic individualism. Dewey argues liberty "and development of individuality as ends" do not "exclude the use of organized social effort as means."[15] Although Hobhouse used organic language about society, none of these theorists consolidate individuals into a collectivity that speaks their real will. For Hobhouse, organic refers to interdependence and mutual aid, not a mystical "physical organism." It "means that, while the life of society is nothing but the life of individuals as they act one upon another, the life of the individual in turn would be something utterly different if he could be separated from society. A great deal of him would not exist at all." Society and community are means to achieve expansive individuality and individual freedom. Either extreme—atomistic laissez-faire individualism or absolute incorporation into the whole—would cause disaster.[16]

Freedom

The conditions for freedom and the meaning of freedom are affected by the same economic-social transformations that impacted individualism. Real individuality requires effective freedom. Hobhouse illustrated this. Freedom means removal of constraint, yet freedom requires some restraints to ensure no one prevents others from exercising freedom. In *Liberalism* he virtually identified freedom with liberalism. Civil liberty—rule of law, elimination of and protection from arbitrary public action—is the necessary first step on which to build other freedoms; without it they cannot be secure. But freedom from arbitrary government is not the end of freedom. Freedom includes fiscal liberty, social liberty, economic liberty, domestic liberty, and so on. Each is a necessary not sufficient component of freedom. At each step in the development of freedom, different constraints and obstacles arise. Frequently, government may be the main impediment. Once government's worst oppressive behavior is tamed, it starts to become responsive to more citizens, and once functional democracy develops, government can better protect freedom. When government no longer poses the primary danger to

freedom, "other enemies of liberty besides the State" such as private power
and unequal bargaining positions become relevant. Then, government intervention may eliminate or obstruct the force of these obstacles, or, as Hobhouse argued, help ensure the conditions that make a moral life and
independence possible.[17]

Dewey also addressed constraints. The meaning and content of freedom
have changed over time as new relations have been defined as oppressive—
Hobhouse's notion of expanding concepts of unacceptable injury. People
and freedom are not such "that . . . abolition of oppressions exercised by
church and state . . . produce and maintain free institutions." Freedom and
perceived obstacles to freedom evolve and cannot be addressed by a single
policy. Freedom is "always relative to forces that at a given time and place
are increasingly felt to be oppressive. Liberty in the concrete signifies release
from the impact of *particular* oppressive forces; emancipation from something once taken as a normal part of human life but now experienced as
bondage." The reality of freedom "is a function of the social conditions existing at any time."[18]

That people "voluntarily" enter into employment or other economic relations does not eliminate coercive, nonfree elements in these relations that
limit and harm individuals and society. Dewey accused older liberalism of
holding a time-bound concept of liberty that is too limited to the individualistic economic sphere. Once revolutionary ideas are now used to defend
the status quo. Early liberals failed to distinguish "formal freedom or legal
liberty" from "effective liberty" or "to grasp the historic position of" their
"interpretation of liberty," leading to policies that have become "a chief
obstacle to attainment of the ends they professed." Laissez-faire freedom is
a "fallacy," and merely "liberty of the entrepreneur," but genuine liberty
requires "a degree of security" and equality for everyone. "[P]rivate control
of the new forces of production" came to "operate in the same way as private unchecked control of political power" destroying the chance for freedom and individualism of those lacking power. Thus contemporary freedom
must confront vulnerability to forces outside individual control, and seek
"liberation from material insecurity . . . coercions and repressions."[19]

Hobhouse too distinguished "nominal freedom . . . the absence of legal
restraint" from "real freedom" that prevents "the stronger party" from coerc-
ing "the weaker." Form is insufficient to ensure freedom. Circumstances can
deprive people of influence over the terms of a contract. Nominal consent
to a contract does not ensure freedom, given the constraint and unequal
influence in choosing or rejecting terms among the contracting parties, and
given that a contract does not have the same importance to all parties. There

is often a fundamental "inequality which results in unfreedom"—or inability to reject terms because of very painful results. It "is erroneous" to assume "that a labor contract cannot be of a servile character" on grounds that a person enters it "freely, and with his eyes open." In the past people could sell themselves into slavery. Guaranteeing that people are not subject to excessive influence has been the motivation for "a very large part of the modern development of social control as motivated by the desire for a more effective liberty."[20]

Brandeis argued economic relations pose the greatest contemporary challenge to freedom. Suitable economic conditions are necessary for freedom and democracy because people trained to subservience at work cannot be independent citizens. Brandeis insisted that large-scale industry and capital aggregation produce "necessary conflict" between American "political democracy and . . . industrial absolutism." "[B]usiness methods and practices" can be as effective and disastrous in oppressing people as "force and violence." Work relations may be "benevolent absolutism" or "benevolent despotism"; both are harmful to workers and managers. Industrial absolutism produces great inequality between corporations and employees who are wholly dependent on their employer for livelihood and direction at work. When managers make all relevant decisions, employees have no control or opportunity to exercise intelligence, which undermines their individuality, actual freedom, and capacity to exercise industrial or political freedom.[21] In such a situation, despite any material benefits, people are not fully free but face "'an insidious menace to the liberty of citizens.'" Brandeis long advocated profit sharing, but in the years before World War I concluded profit sharing, or "satisfaction merely of material needs, however high these needs are raised," was morally and politically insufficient to develop initiative, freedom, and individuality. Though material abundance is necessary, even with it we may still "have a nation of slaves." Government policies, such as unemployment compensation and other social insurance can help people obtain "real freedom of contract" as opposed to fancied freedom.[22]

These arguments point toward a working concept of positive freedom. Government or the state has the duty to limit private power and help people acquire the resources for achieving freedom conceived of as the ability to act and expanded individual control over significant parts of one's life. Freedom is thus related to the power to act or to prevent others from acting. This more positive freedom is associated with a broader conception of the constraints on freedom than that found among conservative theorists, and it is linked to the claim that collective effort is compatible with individual freedom, responsibility, dignity, and democracy.[23]

Democracy

As their counterparts do today, conservative contemporaries of Dewey, Brandeis, and Hobhouse argued that democracy is a limited political procedure for electing governments and protecting individual rights. It has nothing to do with economics, and it does not require active participation. Brandeis, Dewey, and Hobhouse strongly disagreed. Democracy is endangered by inequality and by concentration of power generated by economic, industrial, and organizational changes. It is enhanced through education and by reshaping the political-economy and power relations. Though their images of democracy diverged, Brandeis, Dewey, and Hobhouse have a richer understanding of democracy than that found in either the practice and theories they criticized or in those ascribed to liberalism by many contemporary critics of liberalism. They insisted there are multiple spheres of democracy. Democracy is not just a set of procedures for deciding who makes political—and economic—decisions; rather democracy has goals that include social justice, development of individuality, and solving public problems. All three authors called for expanding democracy, and Brandeis and Dewey made proposals, which Hobhouse could accept, that are compatible with direct and industrial democracy. Once again, we focus on economic content.

Brandeis argued that democracy—as individual involvement in decisionmaking—is not just political, "and we cannot successfully grapple with the problem of democracy if we confine ourselves to political democracy." If work situations as presently constituted are a training ground for servitude, only a shell of representative democracy is possible. Brandeis agreed with Jefferson that democracy requires economic independence to cultivate alert, self-governing citizens who have the ability and confidence to participate in public affairs. Spending most of one's day taking orders in a large, powerful hierarchical organization whose means and purposes appear alien, and being fearful of losing one's livelihood, is corrupting. Such a situation damages the social-economic basis for political democracy and democratic relations with others. Dewey agreed. Most workers "have no share" in directing enterprises vital to them, execute others' plans, and have limited opportunities, which leads them to become crippled, passive individuals. But if work can train people for tyranny, it can also educate them in the skills of democracy: decisionmaking for the common good, taking responsibility, and thinking in cause and effect terms, all of which Brandeis claims are essential to democracy. Liberty requires participation in enterprise. Workers share in the problems of a business, therefore, they should participate in its decisions, direction, and responsibilities. Implying workers can have rights in a job, Brandeis concluded that something like "industrial democracy" is necessary: "rule by the people" requires "industrial as well as political democracy" to make work more efficient and supportive of individuality, freedom, and political democracy.[24]

Demanding worker participation, Brandeis made a number of undeveloped recommendations to curb employers' "autocratic power." Collective bargaining was a first step, but if it maintained relations of control and subordination it was inadequate. More was necessary: expanding labor unions; electing members of the board of directors, which alone is insufficient to have industrial democracy; "a share of the responsibilities and management, and a utilization of" workers' "latent powers"; making more decisions at the shop level; and sharing in the advances and failures of an enterprise. This level of worker participation requires "practically an industrial government" in which issues and problems are considered between workers and employer on a continuing basis: "something akin to a government of the trade before you reach a real approach to democratization." This government included developing "cooperative enterprises" in which workers would eventually assume "responsibility for the conduct of business."[25]

Democracy is possible only "if side by side with political democracy comes industrial democracy." Industrial democracy furthers the evolution or deepening of democracy in America and is the next logical step in the continuing removal of obstacles to a democratic society. Of the many different possible forms of industrial democracy, Brandeis favored workers electing accountable representatives for industrial decision making, much more than direct worker involvement in making decisions. Though there would be some direct participation at the shop level, Brandeis argued that his proposals would end industrial despotism, thereby improving economic efficiency and educating workers. Brandeis believed "social justice" is part of democracy, "not only . . . in the sense of avoiding things which bring suffering and harm, like unjust distribution of wealth." Rather, social justice is "an incident of our democracy. . . . the result of democracy—perhaps its finest expression."[26]

Power is never given up voluntarily. "[I]ndustrial democracy will not come as a gift." Government must act to compensate for unequal power. When workers and their unions cannot achieve industrial democracy "the State must in some way come to the aid of the workingmen if democratization is to be secured." The state will not play a continuing, centralized, or dominant role, but must help to create the conditions within which people can take responsibility for themselves.[27] Brandeis, however, did not develop his ideas in detail and left few clues about how to achieve industrial democracy. Nor did he amplify proposals for expanding political democracy as such, though he wanted more citizen participation[28] and believed that decentralizing government would expand popular activity. Industrial democracy therefore applies enriched representation—workers and their representatives have close ties—from politics to large industrial organizations, thereby supplementing political democracy. To the extent it involves direct democracy it seems confined to industry, not expanded to the broad public for whom representation remains the most important expression of democracy at the national level.

As with Brandeis, Dewey argued that "political democracy is not the whole of democracy." Universal suffrage and representative government were insufficient to define or achieve democracy, and "hardly more than externally touched" the problems of democracy extended into "all the areas and ways of living." Democracy and unrestrained, individualistic capitalism are not necessarily harmonious. "[D]emocracy is not in reality what its name implies until it is industrial, as well as civil and political." Despite the "form" of democratic institutions the system tended "to favor in substance a privileged plutocracy." Though this is a problem *of* government—especially given "interconnections and interdependence of industry and government"—it is not only a problem *with* government. Changes in scale, new industrial and economic institutions, and shifts in power significantly diminish the rough equality, individuality, and face-to-face relations necessary to democracy. Although modern industry and commerce may have helped develop democracy and aspirations for social justice, they are also obstacles. They have produced the growing inequality, class divisions, and "extreme divisions of work" that subvert democracy while reducing the labor of "great masses of men" to a "mechanical and servile" level. Democracy remains "an ideal of the future" until the problems of modern industry are dealt with. Moreover, during the Depression, both the possessing class and those with little become willing "to surrender democratic forms" for security. Political democracy is possible only when supported with social democracy and the will to make "the spirit of democracy permeate industry." Then, people might benefit from the "intellectual and moral effects" and the "enormous liberation of mind" that result from reducing managerial control and allow workers to exercise their abilities. Until then democracy is threatened and incomplete.[29]

Dewey shares a problem with many critics of democracy; he fails to specify how alternatives will be instituted and operate. His arguments are both more critical of existing practice and less precise about alternatives than those of Brandeis. Dewey wrote more about democracy, especially its relation to education, than anyone else in this book, but outside the area of education his argument is curiously incomplete. Although his critique of existing democratic practice is thorough and fairly radical, and self-government was very important, Dewey rarely discussed democracy "in its narrow, strictly political sense."[30] And although he was temporarily active in politics in the 1930s, Dewey did not elaborate organizational means for achieving or relevant institutions for maintaining democracy. Even the face-to-face associations he frequently[31] called for remain abstract.

For Hobhouse, democracy is necessary to liberalism, just as democracy requires the liberal values of liberty, equality, and community. More than a procedure for selecting governors, democracy can be realized only when "the generality of men and women are not only passive recipients but practical contributors." Citizenship is the crucial modern way of uniting people and has evolved as the type of authority appropriate to "higher civilization." As Brandeis and Dewey argued, participating in "popular government" educates and trains the citizen, allowing people to share a common life and understanding. Democracy requires applying "ethical principles to political relations," community self-government, and well-informed active citizens. But citizenship and the "civic bond" are torn by "modern economic conditions" that "engender" large-scale capital, economic inequality, and "industrial organization which constantly reduce political and civic equality to a meaningless form of words." For Hobhouse "[p]eople are not fully free in their political capacity when they are subject industrially to conditions which take the life and heart out of them."[32]

Political-Economy

A number of political-economic themes run through the work of Brandeis, Dewey, and Hobhouse, though Hobhouse deals least with the economy. These include claims that industrialization, growth in organization, capital accumulation, and "potential plenty"[33] have transformed economic relations, associated politics, and social interaction. In a central reform liberal argument, each agrees economics is not autonomous but can impair fundamental political and social values, relations, and institutions. People are not remunerated according to effort or justice, in part because dominant individuals and large organizations have power. We sample several of these continuing reform arguments.

That economic relations have changed society and can harm freedom, individualism, or democracy has already been discussed. Rejecting strict economic determinism, Brandeis, Dewey, and Hobhouse agreed that the inevitable and close interactions between economics, politics, and society require challenging laissez-faire's incorrect and dangerous subordination of politics to narrow economic ends. Dewey insisted that politics and economics are closely related. Economic conditions and popular desire for protection from seemingly impersonal forces deeply affect political demands, combination, thinking, personality, the possibility of a moral life, and indi-viduality—points with which Brandeis and Hobhouse agreed. "[T]he rela-tion of the economic structure to political operations" has elemental importance and "economic factors are an intrinsic" and shaping "part of the culture." Fundamental problems have developed from creation of a corpo-rate civilization that thwarts individualism, concentrates power, and pro-duces insecurity that is inherent in the existing system. Though incomplete, Dewey's political-economic analysis is more radical in demanding basic changes than that of his contemporary, Keynes, but like Keynes he consid-ered "established material security" a prerequisite for achieving liberal ends.[34]

Industrial, financial, and commercial problems "necessarily became politi-cal questions." Brandeis considered unemployment the most important "social or industrial problem," one that obstructs "industrial efficiency and . . . social justice." He believed that imposing strict divisions between politics and economics disguised the actual situation. To ignore that eco-nomic organization shapes social and political institutions is to court disaster. As with the other theorists, Brandeis neither attacked capitalism itself, nor was he anti-business. He and Galbraith favor public aid for smaller en-terprises. The problem is not capitalism or the growth of capitalism, but current practices and public policy that favor concentration of capital and power at the expense of workers, smaller businesses, and the common good.[35]

Hobhouse agreed political questions cannot readily be disconnected from the social-economy. Market philosophy is weak, and its separation of economics from the rest of society ignores their interdependence. Laissez-faire's faulty picture of motivation crippled its political and social vision. "[T]o suppose that men are governed entirely by a sense of their interests is a many-sided fallacy. Men are neither so intelligent nor so selfish." Its the-ory of the role of government was especially confused, failing to explain the criteria by which it chooses some state functions and rejects others. "Why should the state ensure protection of person and property?" That protection can be bought like anything else. The claim that economic intervention pau-perizes people and robs them of independence—an argument Dewey said came from people who "would leave intact the conditions" that lead to demand for welfare—applies to protection from theft as much as to pro-tection from unsafe working conditions. Preserving a rich person from rob-bery deprives him or her of self-reliance as much as saving workers from dangerous machines or protecting welfare recipients from destitution deprive them of self-reliance. Hobhouse could find no reasonable grounds "to spec-ify certain injuries which the State may prohibit and to mark off others which it must leave untouched."[36]

Early laissez-faire theory and social Darwinism were supported by appeals to natural law and scientific reasoning that, given its moral and political content and conclusions, was the functional equivalent of older natural law theory. As with similar arguments today, these appeals lent their theories a strength absent from "pure" moral, political, or economic analysis, by wrapping normative conclusions within ostensibly objective reasoning. This natural law argument subordinated "political to economic activity" by identifying "natural laws with the laws of production and exchange" that supposedly guaranteed harmony between "personal profit and social benefit." By arguing that economics and economic relations were protected by natural law and natural rights or followed from evolution, or that the pursuit of self-interest in economic relations is natural, these theorists set absolute limits to political possibility. Twisting Lockean themes, natural law became "much more concrete," with "a more directly practical meaning" that they applied to production, exchange, and justification of market inequality. Political action was turned into "an invasion of individual liberty . . . [and] a conspiracy against the causes that bring about social progress." This argument "still provide[s] the intellectual system of apologetics for the existing economic regime."[37]

Brandeis, Dewey, and Hobhouse emphatically denied that economic relations, rights, and inequalities follow from natural law; are fundamentally moral and/or correct; are ultimately unchangeable for the better by human intervention; or work out for the best and require leaving people to their own devices. That laissez-faire vision was not scientific nor is it morally, socially, or politically acceptable. Dewey and Hobhouse argued that economic relations are not the result of natural law–like or evolutionary processes, natural law had been misapplied to economics, and natural right did not exist. Therefore, putative necessity did not dictate tolerating undesirable conditions.[38] All three criticized social Darwinian theory and its failure to distinguish moral law from empirical hypotheses. Analyzing assumptions and results, Hobhouse saw social Darwinism as providing a "philosophy for . . . reaction" much as Malthus's theories had done in the early nineteenth century.[39] Ineluctably normative, tautological, structurally confused, and scientifically contradictory, social Darwinism justifies power and position, ignoring what happens to losers in the economic struggle.[40] It assumes that blind, mindless change and conflict produce progress that necessarily benefits survivors (who are the only ones who matter). But evolution or change with no assured direction differ from progress. Progress is measured against a standard or goal and usually requires human direction. For Hobhouse, progress includes mutual aid, happiness, and "mental development." "Natural" evolution ensures none of these.[41]

Economic relations are not self-justifying but are subject to exogenous moral analysis and demands. Dewey argued, and Hobhouse and Brandeis agreed, that the economic system can be made to conform to ideas of justice and morality, not that justice and morality come from or should be defined and limited by economic relations. Economics should be instrumental to achieving larger values and ends than monetary goals or increased wealth for the owners of the system. Keynes and Galbraith would agree. The measure of economic good should be what kind of people and relations are formed through economic interaction, not what degree of success is achieved in competition, production, or material goods. "[E]conomic activities" should be converted "into servants of the development of the higher capacities of individuals." For Dewey "private gain does not satisfy the full human nature even of those who profit by it."[42] Social responsibility for business was crucial to Brandeis, who saw competition serving social ideals as well as profit making.[43] Both emphasized moral development through individual and social growth, and community good as the source of values.

Brandeis, Dewey, and Hobhouse rejected claims that power does not exist in markets and that people are compensated according to their contribution to the self-defined welfare of others. In fact coercion helps maintain the political-economic system, but coercion is not the only way to exercise power. For Brandeis, power includes great influence, especially when people have few or no alternatives. Brandeis and Hobhouse saw successful opposition to labor unions as an exercise of power. Power therefore entails ability to frustrate the will and purposes of others, as well as to achieve one's own ends and purposes, making power both an obstacle to and a means to achieve individuality. Power also refers to shaping attitudes and behavior, including manipulation, advertising, and creation of opinion—what Galbraith later called "conditioned power." Brandeis, who opposed big government and big business, and Dewey contended that large economic organizations had become a state within a state that often dominated the political state and the lives and property of workers and investors. For Dewey "[i]t is foolish" to argue that only governments have power. Indeed, their power pales "in contrast with that exercised by concentrated and organized property interests." Early liberals' image of liberty had become a cover for "power possessed by the few." Democracy, Brandeis insisted, requires that all power be limited and made accountable to people affected by that power, but concentrations of economic power are almost uncontrollable. A large corporation or trust was sometimes "so powerful that the ordinary social and industrial forces existing are insufficient to cope with it."[44]

When those with wealth and power use their position to justify inequality, power causes inequality, and unequal opportunity mirrors and is perpetuated by unequal power. Brandeis argued that development of a "privi-leged class" and "great inequality in power . . . necessarily" destroys liberty. Hobhouse and Dewey agreed. Free bargains became impossible. Desperate need and few resources constrained action of the less powerful when deal-ing with those who could choose from among thousands of unorganized workers or consumers. Brandeis and Hobhouse accepted that "combination was necessary to place the workman on something approaching equal terms with the employer."[45]

To meet such challenges these theorists called for major though not foundational changes in economic power, political-economic relations and social conditions. Keynes' economic theory was not available,[46] and it is doubtful that Brandeis and Dewey would have approved post–World War II Keynesian emphasis on aggregate demand stimulation as the alternative to political-economic reform, though they shared many values with Keynes. In his preference for smaller business and less centralized government, Bran-deis would have liked to disagree with Dewey's and Hobhouse's wary accep-tance of large-scale organization and more expansive government. Based on his legal work, Brandeis became convinced that mere size did not ensure efficiency. His argument for industrial democracy and modification of inter-nal corporate relations, however, accepts the existence of large businesses. Large enterprises that did not dominate their market should be the result of efficiency and skill, not an aggregation of miscellaneous parts, too large for one person to understand, created as an expression of power, and alien to workers and stockholders. Brandeis was not a primitivist seeking return to a golden age of small business, but, like the others, was concerned with the political and moral implications of control by private organizations over mil-lions of people. It is no criticism that Brandeis' willingness to weaken what Galbraith later called the technostructure, and to introduce limited indus-trial democracy, might reduce production and available goods. These were not his primary end: people are not just economic utility maximizers—indi-viduality and democracy matter more. Moreover, public as well as private needs were legitimate. Brandeis did not perceive the choice as either no lim-its or poverty, but saw much poverty as the result of unregulated power and inequality. Brandeis doubted that limiting size and power would impover-ish society. If large organizations were often inefficient, and smaller firms more efficient, there was much room for both social justice and increased production, not decline.[47]

Like many people, Dewey and Hobhouse tended to call any alternative to laissez-faire capitalism socialism, but they were not frightened by the word.[48] Non-Marxist socialism was possible. A reaction to concentrated eco-nomic power and the "mental collectivism by massed methods" that business created might generate "some kind of socialism, call it by whatever name we please." Hobhouse asserted that, when individualism looks at the real, exist- ing situation, in order to protect itself, it "is driven no small distance along Socialist lines." Dewey claimed that society must go beyond social legisla- tion and the welfare state to "socialize the forces of production" as the only means to "free individual development." As with Keynes' "liberal socialism"— Hobhouse used the same term—this is not socialism in any conventional sense. Dewey, for example, did not call for public ownership of the means of production, spurned state and militant socialism, rejected the dictatorship of the proletariat and elimination of the bourgeoisie through violence, denied that there is just one interest in society, and believed social-political values could direct economic relations. For Dewey, the choice was "blind, chaotic . . . unplanned" change or "socially planned and ordered develop- ment"—that is, "between a socialism that is public and one that is capitalis- tic." Along with many 1930s reformers, Dewey talked vaguely about planning. He did not advocate centralized direction of the economy but sug- gested something analogous to what Reich later called industrial policy, with a more elaborate social policy. As with Keynes' discussions of limited plan- ning, he intended to make the system work, including protecting democracy and capitalism. His idea was to coordinate and gain control of economic forces, apply collective intelligence to social-economic issues, and prevent the few from monopolizing inventions and processes that are the result of col- lective intelligence. Although Dewey and Hobhouse denied that property rights trump all other considerations, they claimed that by holding to free- dom and individuality their systems remained liberal. For Hobhouse, social- ism must be democratic and develop from and take into account the needs of individual people, thereby accommodating liberalism and socialism.[49]

Government

An active government is a necessary tool for addressing contemporary prob- lems, though it is not desirable in itself. According to Hobhouse, trusting government more than old liberals did not mean that new liberals valued "liberty less." For each of these theorists, as for later reform liberals, growth of government and bureaucracy is at least partly in response to growth in private organization, bureaucracy, and power. Government cannot be neu- tral in contemporary struggles over individuality, freedom, power, and dis- tribution. For Hobhouse, forbidding all restraint ignores "that all social liberty rests upon restraint" as a condition for freedom in other respects.

Dewey insisted there is always an alternative to doing nothing. "To foresee consequences of existing conditions is to surrender neutrality and drift; it is to take sides in behalf of the consequences that are preferred." Brandeis insisted that, in complex societies, dealing with reality necessitated recognizing (according to Felix Frankfurter) "variations in . . . needs, opportunities, and coercive power."[50]

What is government to do about problems generated by economic change and social dislocation? If there are no a priori natural laws, natural rights, or evolutionary rules determining the role of government, government has the potential to be very active. These theorists offer both vague and well developed proposals of what government should do, but not how (other than through education) people can be organized to change public policy, how government will be made to carry out these proposals, or how government will be administered.[51] Hobhouse argues that the role of government depends on circumstances and the types of compulsion people face. There are no general rules which apply everywhere at all times. But there are common purposes. Hobhouse concurs with Brandeis and Dewey in his argument that "The function of the state is to override individual coercion." This is the first step in creating conditions for individual morality and securing such circumstances, as with Keynes later, "that the normal man"—Dewey's "normal individuals"—can have a decent wage and livelihood. For many people this may require either assurances of employment or "as an alternative, of public assistance." But these policies require change in how people understand values such as individualism or freedom, and how they view government.[52]

New conditions required a different role for government. Jefferson's "principles of self-government," freedom, popular authority, and public welfare cannot, Dewey claimed, be used to defend policies that subvert those principles. Jefferson was no apologist for twentieth-century big business and would have supported policies today that curb private power. Strum associates Brandeis with this perspective. The link with Jefferson is most apparent in Dewey's proposals regarding education, protecting people from abuse of power, and expanding popular participation. Although Brandeis saw the possibility of more decentralization than did Dewey, opposed centralized planning, and contested some New Deal legislation, he favored much higher taxation of the very rich and more massive public works projects than did New Deal advocates.[53]

None of these theorists was a revolutionary attacking the political, social, or economic system. They sought to reform what they saw as abuses and shortcomings, to make things better, and to expand or create conditions that would support fundamental values. Always, policy was to be implemented with appreciation of the impact circumstances have on individual lives, and for the liberation of individuals, not in service to venerable abstractions or august practices that do not respect what happens to people in concrete situations. Anything else risked losing liberal and democratic values and institutions. In this they addressed similar dilemmas to and pointed the way to a reform liberalism that would be fortified with an economic theory that justified expanding government to protect reinvigorated liberal values and institutions. That later reform liberalism is less social and political does not abrogate continuity of values and goals between earlier and contemporary reform liberalism. All searched for answers to continually recurring problems generated by an evolving economy and conservative arguments against public action.

3

John Maynard Keynes: What Future for Capitalism and Liberal Democracy?

I confess I am not charmed with the ideal of life held out by those who think that the normal state of human beings is that of struggling to get on; that the trampling, crushing, elbowing, and treading on each other's heels, which form the existing type of social life, are the most desirable lot of human kind, or anything but the disagreeable symptoms of one of the phases of industrial progress.
— John Stuart Mill, *Principles of Political Economy*

Great objects . . . are evidently not necessary in order to occasion the greatest exertions. Rivalship and emulation render excellency . . . an object of ambition, and frequently occasion the very greatest exertions.
— Adam Smith, *The Wealth of Nations*

THE ENGLISH ECONOMIST JOHN MAYNARD KEYNES (1883–1946) is the critical transitional figure in reform liberalism.[1] His economic critique of classical and neoclassical theory, claim that the accepted model of capitalism worked badly, denial that economic prosperity requires significant economic inequality, and justification of public intervention into economic relations made Keynes the most influential liberal of this century. He supplied the economic theory that justified concern for social justice, equality, democracy, and community, turning reform liberalism into a powerful force for political-economic reconstruction. His arguments transformed the liberal approach to public policy, set the agenda for economic debate for at least a generation, and provided a target for sixty years of conservative criticism.

Keynes remains controversial half a century after his death, his economics subject to revision, exegesis, and condemnation, the political-social content of his work often misunderstood or reviled. The meaning, impact, and nature of Keynes' economics,[2] his political-social values, and how they blend are fiercely debated. He has been called both savior and wrecker of capitalism and democracy. On the "right" he is called the destroyer of traditional morality, violator of freedom, liberator of selfish impulses, and creator of an economic system that unleashes democracy's intrinsic disorder.[3] On the "left" he is frequently criticized for promoting technocratic government, being hostile to genuine democracy, favoring the wealthy, weakening demands for fundamental political change, and propping up the capitalist system.[4] Others focus on the literary and artistic dimension of his life and analysis. That he was an elitist is accepted throughout the political spectrum though for different reasons. His political orientation is disputed. Keynes is seen as a conservative, a liberal, and a radical; the inherent ambiguity and exact meaning of these terms often remains unspecified and unexplored. As an "enlightened" conservative he opposed socialism and demonstrated its invalidity, favored supply-side economics, and sought to preserve the essentials of capitalism.[5] He was also a radical, emphasizing the frailty of capitalism and arguing for more equality.[6] Joan Robinson said he swung from right to left and back to right.[7] Each perspective—some more accurately than others—identifies a part of his complexity, but this chapter looks at Keynes as a liberal within the framework of liberalism.[8] Keynes considered himself a liberal, defended the fundamental principles of liberalism, and argued that public policy must change to preserve liberal principles.

Politics and Economics

Orthodox economic theory separated politics and economics. Keynes did not. He was very much the *political* economist,[9] serious about political-social issues though not a deep political thinker, concerned with public policy and social-political stability. His political importance lies not in his writing about politics but in his attention to the interrelation between politics and economics and in the political possibilities opened by his economics. For Keynes political, social, and economic issues were mutually related and interdependent. Although economics can provide a base for political reform, it can also undermine the political system. Thus, *Economic Consequences of the Peace,* 1919, and popular pamphlets such as "The Economic Consequences of Mr. Churchill," 1925, or "How to Pay for the War," 1940, are deeply social and political. In his service in the Treasury during two world wars and in major books such as *The General Theory,* he was attuned to political implications and political limits. Economics was neither autonomous nor an extension of natural law, absolutely specifying values such as freedom or individualism, setting stern limits to public activity, neutrally distributing goods and services, and imposing its imperatives upon other relations. Economic and political needs and problems overlapped. Economics was vital but ultimately instrumental, secondary, and supportive of the more important aspects of life. Unemployment, deflation, inflation, exchange instability, or severe foreign competition threatened freedom and democratic government, produced class conflict, and caused political-social turmoil, necessitating public intervention to avoid or reduce such social-political repercussions. Thus, "in the future, more than ever, questions about the economic framework of society will be far and away the most important of political issues." "[T]he largest of all political questions . . . the economic questions."[10]

Like religion, successful ideologies offer answers to current pains and problems and project a better future. Keynes' work is no exception. From 1919 until his death Keynes was concerned with current problems and possible futures for capitalism and their relation to democratic society. Although his focus and policy proposals changed repeatedly, he persistently criticized laissez-faire capitalism and its social-politics. Claiming it was inefficient, immoral, and unstable, he proposed to replace individualistic capitalism—rejecting socialism as another obsolete answer to problems of the past—with an alternate version, one better conforming to social, political, and moral values, and better fitted to contemporary conditions, while attaining our economic ends.[11] Developing this alternate capitalism involved Keynes in an economic, social, political, moral, and aesthetic critique of the existing political economy, and in crafting broad proposals for its reformation. This chapter focuses on the political-social elements in Keynes' image of capitalism, what it might become, and democracy.

Past and Present

Since capitalism had evolved and would continue to evolve, outlining future possibilities required analyzing and understanding earlier developments and determining whether existing conditions would lead to the continuation of past and present relations or to their transformation. Given the interaction between economics and politics, the future of capitalism was both economic and political-social. The past was not an appropriate guide to the future. There was no golden age, no utopia in an age of innocence, but poverty, inevitable inequality, and the possibility of improvement if entrepreneurs increased investment. Earlier class and economic conditions allowed for and necessitated a different form of capitalism than was needed after World War I.[12] Keynes considered laissez-faire theory in its inception to have been substantially correct, but the conditions that allowed for significant individually generated accumulation, investment, and growth no longer existed. European capitalism from midcentury until World War I was an "extraordinary episode in the economic progress of man," despite many elements of instability and inequality. Politically it depended "on a double bluff or deception": whether "from ignorance or powerlessness" workers had acquiesced in possessing little of what they produced, while "the capitalist classes were allowed to call the best part of the cake theirs . . . on the tacit underlying condition that they consumed very little of it in practice." It was "the duty and the delight of a large class" to save. Continued investment justified inequality because it promised that consequent growth would produce enough for all. This situation no longer exists. It "depended on unstable psychological conditions, which it may be impossible to re-create." War, demands for more comfort, loss of confidence in the future, a growing gap between ownership and management, displacement of family firms, monetary instability, less need for inequality to generate investable funds, consumption-driven demand and employment, and reduced opportunities for investment created new conditions, in turn causing the lost possibilities Keynes criticized from 1919 until his death in 1946.[13]

Failure of Laissez-faire Theory and Policy

These changes and a pervasive refusal to acknowledge that transformed circumstances required a reinterpretation of basic values and new policies to implement them, generated what Keynes saw as fundamental economic, social, political, and moral problems. Then current application of laissez-faire was rooted in erroneous assumptions and as a policy led to disastrous and avoidable political-social consequences. "The decadent international but individualistic capitalism, in the hands of which we found ourselves after the war, is not a success. It is not intelligent, it is not beautiful, it is not just, it is not virtuous—and it doesn't deliver the goods."[14] Keynes neither completely rejected classical or laissez-faire ideas nor elevated them to fundamental principles. Given existing circumstances he saw them as limited cases, inapplicable under actual experience, but valid if public intervention were to assure sufficient demand to maintain something approximating full employment.[15] Laissez-faire and its attendant political-social apparatus produced policies that should be changed when they interfered with achieving basic principles—freedom, individualism, democracy, social justice, Keynes' version of the good life and material plenty—and employed when useful. Just as politics and economics are closely related, economics has significant moral components, and capitalism depends on specific social, psychological, class, and political conditions and relations. Keynes' criticism of laissez-faire is multifaceted and interdependent—social, political, logical, moral, and economic[16]—but it is his economic theory that gave force to his other criticisms. This section samples his criticisms.

Keynes focused on laissez-faire's operational assumptions and policy results. Believing presuppositions shaped how people see and respond to the world, Keynes rejected many laissez-faire philosophical and political assumptions as "unreal" in presuming characteristics which "happen not to be those of the economic society in which we actually live, with the result that its teaching is misleading and disastrous if we attempt to apply it to the facts of experience."[17] Belief in a natural, harmony producing system was particularly disturbing. This supposition had no support in experience and led people to ignore economic reality and the impact of laissez-faire policy on economic efficiency, justice, and social-political stability. There was "too much dependence upon the operation of what one might call natural forces." Even so-called natural methods, such as the use of interest rates to indirectly change behavior, are artificial. Keynes counted himself among "those who fear that there is no design but our own, and that the invisible hand is merely our own bleeding feet moving through pain and loss to an uncertain and unprofitable destination." Belief in "some law of nature" ensuring optimal results and precluding intervention was "nonsense."[18]

More important, the economic system did not automatically achieve equilibrium at an acceptable level of output and employment. This is a constant theme. Along with effective demand, equilibrium is one of Keynes' most politically charged concepts because if the market is not self-equilibrating at an acceptable level this can justify public intervention to achieve economic, social, and political goals. "The system is not self-adjusting. . . . [E]conomists, in their devotion to a theory of self-adjusting equilibrium, have been, on the whole, wrong in their practical advice." Such belief is "doctrinaire delusion." Many different conditions of equilibrium were possible, at various levels of unemployment, maladjustment, and pain. All could last indefinitely, with differing impact on diverse groups and classes. There was no assurance that the equilibrium society fell into combined best use of resources, high employment, and social justice. The economy could enter "pseudo-equilibrium" and was "capable of remaining in a condition of sub-normal activity" for extended periods, without either recovery or collapse. Letting things work themselves out may achieve a desired result but often at very high cost and contrary to one's purposes.[19]

Keynes deliberately refuted classical theory's equilibrium/full employment connection.[20] His rejection of the tendency to equilibrium and full employment was a fundamental break from classical theory[21] and the social-political relations that it supported. Classical theory saw unemployment as either frictional or voluntary, neither of which can be helped by government action. If it is frictional, it will cure itself. If it is voluntary, only willingness by workers as a group to accept lower wages can provide employment. In either case public action is not needed. Economic instability, large-scale unemployment, waste of people and resources, and the political extremism he feared they were generating led Keynes to address unemployment as society's foremost concern. Keynes argued that significant involuntary unemployment exists during a depression or recession because of insufficient demand to maintain production and employment. Wages and prices adjust slowly and unequally. Reducing wages might help some firms if "the same advantages are not extended to *all* entrepreneurs." Flexible wages are incapable "of maintaining a state of continuous employment." Moreover, even if wage reductions could work, they were unjust, bad public policy, psychologically damaging, and pitted class against class.[22]

Attempts to lower wages are naturally resisted. Effective credit restriction and deflation create unemployment and are policies "for the benefit of other classes" at the expense of unemployed workers caught in "the economic juggernaut." Lacking any mechanism for simultaneously reducing wages and prices for everyone, "each separate group" is attacked "in turn," leading to almost "certain . . . violent social struggle," where "it must be war, until those who are economically weakest are beaten to the ground." Those most likely to "suffer losses are people who are anyhow rather near the edge." Simultaneously, the burden of debt increases and rentiers receive a substantial and unwarranted bonus. Under conditions of unemployment, rentiers' greater tendency to save withdraws purchasing power from the economy, reducing production and demand. One result is a cut in investment, savings, and profits along with employment, leading to less investment and prolonging disequilibrium in the future. This destroys the community's wealth along with livelihoods, confidence, and people's sense of self-worth, while encouraging fear and wild experiments.[23]

Wage reduction decreased aggregate or total economic demand, further depressing the economy. Keynes' concern with aggregate demand is a major innovation with deep political and policy implications. Classical theory denied the possibility of a general glut or general failure of purchasing power, thereby supporting laissez-faire policy. For Keynes, depression was due primarily to a failure of aggregate demand and the "subsequent cessation of" investment. Lack of "effective demand" helped explain "the paradox of poverty in the midst of plenty" and could "bring the increase of employment to a standstill *before* a level of full employment has been reached." Given weaker marginal propensity to consume and fewer attractive investment opportunities, richer communities needed more stimulus to invest than poorer ones. Demand consisted of "[p]ersonal consumption," "[g]overnment expenditure," and net investment. Each of these, representing different policy approaches for subsequent Keynesians, could be stimulated by government to increase levels of demand and employment at acceptable equilibrium.[24]

Uncertainty challenges people's confidence that the economic system is at or near equilibrium and things always work for the best.[25] Keynes merged the argument that psychology, opinion, and confidence help determine economic behavior with the assumption that the economy does not function automatically. Error, chance, surprises, and mistakes are normal. Although his analysis had static elements, there was no overall certainty in Keynes' political economy. Accepting uncertainty did not imply that everything is unknown and unknowable or that there are no rules, necessary correlates, or valuable tautologies. Uncertainty means significant imponderables and "discontinuity" reduce determinism, precision, and the ability to predict. Results cannot be deduced from a few simple assumptions, and future events are fundamentally and irremediably unknowable. Risks cannot be calculated with precision and no one can be sure of the outcome of a major problem or action. In this sense Keynes reintroduced problem solving into political economy. "[K]nowledge of the future is fluctuating, vague, and uncertain." Political economy has many areas where "there is no scientific basis on which to form any calculable probability whatever."[26]

If natural order and equilibrium do not exist, individual pursuit of self-interest need not produce social good and there is no assurance things work out for the best. Leaving the economy alone does not ensure optimal use of resources but permits disaster when something goes seriously wrong. Although Keynes was deeply affected by human, material, and psychological loss in World War I, his persistent insistence on the fragility of capitalist society is striking, perhaps obsessive. From his first book, *Indian Currency and Finance* (1913), to speeches in the House of Lords defending the Bretton Woods Agreements and the United States postwar loan,[27] he was absorbed in how order can decay and the contribution of economics to that decay. Equilibrium was transitory,[28] change and flux normal. To Keynes the existing social-economic system was very recent, and in 1919 few realized its "intensely unusual, unstable, complicated, unreliable, temporary nature." In 1938 he wrote: civilization is "a thin and precarious crust" much more easily disturbed than even he had earlier believed. He castigated nineteenth-century capitalism, and some of his contemporaries, for believing monetary and social arrangements were permanent. If the monetary and other sub-systems were impermanent and unstable, they could not ensure current or future success. Chaos is possible. Economic disorder is not neutral in its impact. Despite many regularities order is created not discovered. Advantages enjoyed by Europeans were neither immutable nor part of the order of nature. Nothing guaranteed their continuance. To let things drift was to run terrible risks. In 1922, Keynes marveled "at the lethargy and apparent impotence of what may be called . . . the forces of capitalism. They are running the most enormous risks. . . . Nothing but peace and moderation can serve their cause." Deep and "profound modifications . . . will not be the work of the doctrines of Marx, nor of the disciplined force of international labour, but of the timid and short-sighted ways and stupid heads of its own conservative leaders."[29]

As with other reform liberals, Keynes was concerned with the social-political impact of economic policies. He saw orthodox public economic policy as unjust and biased in its effects. Both inflation and policies of deflation menaced social-political stability. Economic instability generated disorder that was incompatible with the continued existence of either democratic government or capitalism.[30] The gravest threat from unrestricted laissez-faire was its "general regardlessness of social detail" and reliance "on the eventual working out of blind forces." In an argument that Galbraith echoes, he observed that economists and bankers have ignored "the character of the causal process through which" money supply manipulation lowers prices or reduces inflation, causing them to be too light-hearted in contemplating and consequently surprised at ensuing unemployment, business loss, and public discontent. Alternating "boom and slump . . . undermine the foundations of society." The capitalist order and "the social stability of every country" were at stake during the Depression. Economic failure lent plausibility to Marxist, Fascist, and Nazi—the new barbarians with the potential to destroy civilization—willingness to sacrifice political liberty "to change the existing economic order." Yet, "achievement of economic reform would make the defence of political liberty much easier."[31]

Classical and laissez-faire theory and policy are ostensibly individualistic, but Keynes, like Dewey, found accepted notions of individualism inadequate and laissez-faire's image of competition antagonistic to individualism. People were not autonomous, purely self-seeking and self-motivating, operating in a law-like, self-stabilizing economic system. Laissez-faire competitive individualism had become invalid under new circumstances. Rigid insistence on it endangered both capitalism and democracy. Political and economic order required that economic individualism be reformed with intelligent, collective intervention. It had to be "purged of its defects and its abuses," including excessive inequality, while protecting the essential values of individualism: "efficiency . . . decentralisation . . . the play of self-interest. . . . personal liberty . . . personal choice. . . . the variety of life."[32]

The traditional image of individualism was also defective in asserting that individual pursuit of self-interest alone conduces to the common good. Under modern conditions individual pursuit of self-interest is insufficient to achieve either individual or community good, and "private advantage and the public good" are not necessarily harmonious. Pursuing self-interest could be harmful when "what is to the advantage of each of us regarded as a solitary individual is to the disadvantage of each of us regarded as members of a community." For example, individual saving did not ensure investment or increase the community's saving. Individual action, such as wage cuts, could generate conflict that makes such action incapable of protecting individuals or solving society wide problems. Often "the cure lies outside the operation of individuals; it may even be in the interest of individuals to aggravate the disease."[33]

Concern with the fate of individuals runs through Keynes' major work, from *The Economic Consequences of the Peace* through *The General Theory* to discussions of taxes in 1944–1945, and is reinforced by his life-long interest in philosophy, art, and literature. *How* changes are effected, *who* paid for corrections in the economy, and *how* people respond in a democracy were significant considerations. Concern for "social detail" included impact on individual people. Reducing unemployment and stimulating aggregate demand and investment expand individual choice. In language reminiscent of Locke, he charged that the Treaty of Versailles violated morality: "nations are not authorised . . . to visit on the children of their enemies the misdoings of the parents or the rulers." One generation could be bound, but not the individuals who comprised the next. Government policy during World War II should attempt to secure "the maximum freedom of choice to each individual" in income use.[34]

The major dangers to individualism were economic disaster, needless inequality, and adherence to obsolete and dangerous policies, not government. As John Stuart Mill argued earlier, individuality included a right to be different and singular, and according to Keynes embraced individual welfare and an enhanced opportunity to succeed. Individuality and government are not incompatible. Increased intervention could protect individual autonomy and pursuit of individual interests. Without it the blind workings of an unstable economic system would overwhelm individual and community welfare. Unthinking insistence that government can do no more than a private person "render[s] impossible the continuance of an individualist society." He expressed a core reform liberal assumption: "extension of the traditional functions of government" by modifying "the environment within which the individual freely operates" would allow "a wide field for the exercise of private initiative and responsibility."[35] Free governments could take such collective action. "[D]irective intelligence," a "coordinated act of intelligent judgement," and "collective action" were necessary supplements to prevent destruction of the economic, social, and political orders.[36]

Keynes did not reject what he saw as the basis of capitalism—private ownership, money making, individualism—but saw himself as implementing Adam Smith: "capitalism, wisely managed, can possibly be made more efficient for attaining economic ends than any alternative system yet in sight," despite its many "objectionable" features.[37] There is an intimate link between past and current problems and future requirements, possibilities, and desiderata. Contemporary problems illustrated what needed to be changed, and the process of correcting them revealed what the future of capitalism could be with the right public policy. With public planning, capitalism's inherent disequilibria could be eliminated or reduced, and capitalism evolve to achieve its potential. His image of a possible future is as much social—and to a much smaller extent political—as economic.

Future Possibilities

Keynes represents reform or what he called "New Liberalism," preferring "reform by the methods of political liberalism."[38] The future we choose— it was always a matter of choice whether one drifted or actively intervened— would be one in which laissez-faire no longer dominated public policy; planning and energetic government had a large role; and a revamped economy would support different and better social and moral relations. This section examines the social economics of the future, social justice, equality, moral behavior, democracy, and the role of government.

SOCIAL ECONOMICS OF THE FUTURE[39]

Keynes believed that capitalism and related institutions were still evolving but his image of their evolution is different from that of his contemporaries F. A. Hayek or Joseph Schumpeter, both of whom painted an essentially pessimistic picture in which reinterpreting basic values or altering traditional policies would necessarily destroy capitalism. For Keynes, laissez-faire was not the essential part of capitalism, and capitalism was not limited to one possibility. Indeed, "The Conservative Party ought to be concerning itself with evolving a version of individualistic capitalism adapted to the progressive change of circumstances."[40] Psychological, organizational, and moral defects not material obstacles or inevitable class struggle impeded the progressive evolution of capitalism. Physical means were available to address the Depression and remake the future, but the will and belief to use them were lacking, crushed under a "hag-ridden" theory that claimed nothing can be done, it is better to do nothing rather than risk doing something, if something is done the future will be made worse. Keynes was convinced that "the economic problem . . . the problem of want and poverty and the economic struggle between classes and nations, is nothing but a frightful muddle, a transitory and an *unnecessary* muddle." In a frequently used simile, the political-economic situation was like two drivers meeting in the middle of a road. They did not need new cars or new engineering to allow them to pass each other, but rather a new "rule of the road," an act of mind and will to let each proceed.[41]

It is easy to solve the economic problem of want, poverty and class and national struggle because it was due to error and faulty thinking.[42] In the long run, that was not even the really important problem facing society. Unlike some of our contemporaries who foresee a better future with reduced consumption, Keynes saw expanding national income and limited redistribution as the means to enlarge individual and social possibility frontiers, thus reducing conflict over shares. He envisaged a future with less need to save for investment, less need to perform physical work, less competition, less private control over all aspects of the political-economy, and less inequality. Instead there would be more material goods and leisure, with the accompanying possibility of individual development and expression for an increasing proportion of the population. Keynes recognized the role of work in occupying, defining, and giving people a sense of membership in society. A mistrust of play, useful in a society desperately trying to accumulate capital, ran deep. Ignoring stimulation of new wants, he worried about having sufficient work to keep people occupied until they developed and accepted the arts of leisure. "For many ages to come . . . everybody will need to do *some* work if he is to be contented." How people learn to use leisure is a serious problem and he dreaded "readjustment of the habits and instincts of the ordinary man." The wealthy were not a model. They failed to constructively use leisure and their boredom and lack of purpose were depressing.[43] Although the age of plenty had not yet arrived,[44] society must begin addressing its possibility. Thus, in 1943, Keynes wrote that society must prepare to live in "an era of abundance not . . . poverty" when, if international challenges can be met, the issue will be "profound moral and social problems of how to organise material abundance to yield up the fruits of a good life." In 1945: "we are entering into the age of abundance," but, as he wrote fifteen years earlier in "Economic Possibilities for Our Grandchildren," society was not yet there.[45]

The age of abundance will not come immediately. Because poverty was due to transitory muddle does not mean the transition from poverty has occurred or that accumulation of capital can safely end. To expand the material base for a better life, undesirable, immoral, or aesthetically unpleasing relations must continue for some time longer. Corrupt though it might be, the old economic morality was useful for capital accumulation. Quoting the witches in *Macbeth* (Act I, sc 1)—in a comment on the morality of capitalism—Keynes cautioned, "The time for all this is not yet. . . . we must pretend to ourselves and to everyone that fair is foul and foul is fair; for foul is useful and fair is not. Avarice and usury and precaution must be our gods for a little longer still. For only they can lead us out of the tunnel of economic necessity into the daylight."[46]

Given compound interest, technical development, and continued accumulation, however, eventually the old gods could be put to rest. Between 1928 and 1936, Keynes shortened the required time period. In "Economic Possibilities for Our Grandchildren," it must be "at least another hundred years," "the *economic problem* may be solved, or be at least within sight of solution, within a hundred years." In 1931, "the day is not far off when the economic problem will take the back seat. . . ." "A very few more quinquennia of equal activity might" be sufficient to fairly begin the process. In 1936, it might take only a single generation to reduce "the marginal efficiency of capital" to zero.[47] But change required civil peace, stability, planning, and "no important wars and no important increase in population." World War II retarded the process for Britain. In 1942 "We can do almost anything we like, *given time*. We must not force the pace." In 1945, "the euthanasia of the rentier should not take place just yet." And, in 1946, in his last article, he cautioned "No one can be certain of anything in this age of flux and change," but inexorable uncertainty must not paralyze society. The change, already begun, will be gradual. More and more people will move into comfort, itself only means for a more significant readjustment of "habits and instincts." The future will finally arrive when there is a moral change to accompany the material one, satisfactory conditions becoming "so general that the nature of one's duty to one's neighbour is changed."[48]

Keynes disputed the claim that liberalism assumes wants are unlimited. The economic problem could be solved because human beings are not endlessly acquisitive. Human needs "may seem to be insatiable" but must be separated by object. "[T]hey fall into two classes. . . ." Needs 1 "are absolute in the sense that we feel them whatever the situation of our fellow human beings may be." Needs 2 are morally more significant. They "are relative in the sense that we feel them only if their satisfaction lifts us above, makes us feel superior to, our fellows." Such needs "which satisfy the desire for superiority, may indeed be insatiable. . . . But this is not true of the absolute needs—a point may soon be reached . . . when these needs are satisfied in the sense that we prefer to devote our further energies to non-economic purposes."[49]

Keynes was not specific about the content of these two sets of needs— a third set, friendship and community, which are elsewhere very important, is not included—and in his policy advice he neglected the second set, yet clues are available. Keynes did not assume fixed wants or that in the future people will be content with less. Rather, with an average 2 percent per year increase in capital equipment, leading in a century to a seven-and-a-half fold expansion in capital goods, concomitant increases in production and services, more even distribution of the resulting product, and a standard of living four to eight times higher than when he was writing, material scarcity could virtually disappear.[50] Meeting Needs 1 required more than simple food, shelter, and clothing. Plentiful basic necessities, leisure, meaningful activity, and agreeable physical surroundings are essential. Satisfying basic needs could reduce zero sum conflict and open the possibility of focusing on "our real problems . . . life . . . human relations . . . creation and behaviour and religion." But Keynes was not interested in "transmuting" passions, only "managing" them, or arranging things so "as to appeal to the money-motive as little as possible." Presumably, desire for power over others will have less of an object and be less rational when scarcity and physical insecurity end, reducing the stakes of conflict. Greater economic equalization, euthanasia of the rentier, macro-economic manipulation to reduce destructive aspects of competition, and proposals for implementing social justice indicate a partial approach to addressing Needs 2.[51]

If the economic problem, as opposed, perhaps, to the moral problem of desire for superiority could be solved, how could it be done? Keynes proposed shifting from dependence on mythical natural forces to enlarging the public economic role. Part of the dilemma was that a wealthy community had a weaker propensity to consume, therefore "the opportunities for further investment are less attractive." How then was capital to become so abundant as to allow "euthanasia of the rentier, and, consequently, the euthanasia of the cumulative oppressive power of the capitalist to exploit the scarcity-value of capital?"[52] Some of the answer lay in normal growth and the nearly magical properties of compound interest and capital goods accumulation across generations. By themselves, however, they were insufficient. Assuring expanded growth required political stability, social justice, coordination through planning and "directive intelligence" to rapidly increase the supply of capital.[53] Keynes thought "that the demand for capital is strictly limited," and it would "be comparatively easy to make capital-goods so abundant that the marginal efficiency of capital is zero," or very low, thereby "gradually getting rid of many of the objectionable features of capitalism." This required lower interest rates, significant expansion of public investment, and public direction of investment. In a double criticism of laissez-faire, because individual self-interest can be harmful in and to the aggregate, "the duty of ordering the current volume of investment cannot be left safely in private hands."[54]

As capitalism had failed the task of capital accumulation, an essential means to expand capital is "communal saving through the agency of the State to be maintained at a level which will allow the growth of capital up to the point where it ceases to be scarce." State direction of investment did not require complete government control, manipulation of all investment, ownership, "State Socialism," or nationalization. The latter two were irrelevant to real twentieth-century problems. Rather, government would promote capital accumulation, influence direction of investment, and expand public investment—"a somewhat comprehensive socialisation of investment"—to move Britain out of the nineteenth century into the next stage of capitalist development, that of "liberal socialism." "The true socialism of the future" "may be found in co-operation between private initiative and the public Exchequer."[55] In 1943 he estimated that to eliminate "serious fluctuations," "the bulk of investment" might have to be "under public or semi-public control"[56] perhaps "something like two-thirds or three-quarters of total investment." This might occasion "the evolution of a form of social economy which lies between the rival and equally old-fashioned doctrines of our great allies to the East and to the West."[57]

SOCIAL JUSTICE

The economic component of the future was not an end in itself but the means to a better more just society than was possible in the past. Economic stability and expansion were necessary, though far from sufficient to the qualitative aspects of life Keynes cherished. If economic insecurity engenders political and social instability, distasteful morality, and injustice, then material change through rapid growth and more equality can occasion, or at least permit, purposeful social and moral improvement. A reformed and expanded economy opened for Keynes a portrait of a cultured yet bourgeois society in which mass life followed paths blazed by the literary and artistic avant-garde. But the good society required social justice, especially for the classes who paid the highest costs for laissez-faire policy while not fully sharing in its promise.

Justice was specified in part by the new mechanisms of distribution. Although Keynes did not describe the process in detail, a redefinition of justice and morality away from emphasis on acquisition and keeping acquisitions in market relations became possible with changes in material conditions of the social-economy. Lessening waste, anxiety, and uncertainty generated by individualistic competition could reduce insecurity, which in turn could help manage people's needs for power and superiority. Businesses would still fail and people lose jobs, but not from laissez-faire policies and macro-economic conditions completely outside their control. People of ordinary talent would have a chance at success in relatively stable and expanding conditions, and a smaller premium would be placed on luck—the art of being in the right place at the right time—permitting more humane possibilities.

Keynes frequently referred to social justice.[58] As with economic improvement, reaching a better world that encompassed social justice required conscious decisions as to who will benefit from policy, planning, and intervention. In the past some "social injustice" allowed capital to accumulate for "social progress," but now—as Dewey, Brandeis, Galbraith, and Reich also argued—social justice was compatible with and necessary to efficiency. It is possible "to promote social and economic justice, whilst respecting and protecting the individual—his freedom of choice, his faith, his mind and its expression, his enterprise, and his property."[59] Belief in an automatic system, which justified laissez-faire policies that disregarded social-political consequences, was one of the prime obstacles to social justice. Keynes never specified the meaning or content of social justice but defined it negatively. Examples of social injustice included unnecessary inequality; deliberate harm to a class of people, such as causing unemployment to further another policy; deflation as benefiting "receivers of interest at the expense of the rest of the community"; wage cuts forced on public employees such as teachers; the likelihood that wage cuts will be larger than price cuts; and poor housing and inadequate public services in a wealthy community. A slightly more even distribution of earning power, more economic equality, expansion of public services, support for the arts, social-communal direction of important common enterprises including determination of aggregate demand and investment, and assurance that the poor gained a proportionally greater share from policy than the wealthy, figured in his image of a more just society.[60]

Keynes' primary policies for attaining social justice—full employment and equalization through planning and investment—represented partial means to achieve the society portrayed in "Economic Possibilities for Our Grandchildren." Full employment was both an economic *and* social-political goal. It represented a middle way which would encourage "liberty . . . initiative and . . . idiosyncrasy of the individual in a framework serving the public good and seeking equality of contentment." Although some involuntary unemployment[61] would remain, public determination of aggregate demand would promote fuller employment and with it more class peace, social justice, and equality.

Issues of social justice arise over conflicts of interest, implying the market ensures neither justice nor harmony of interest.[62] Testimony to the central role of economics in social justice is provided by conservative criticisms that it is a subversive, dangerous mirage.[63] Despite that claim, laissez-faire economics is a model and theory of distributive justice vindicating how wealth and privilege are apportioned. Keynes said social justice was important only in a free society—other societies could impose sacrifices on the non-elite—and was necessary to political stability.[64] Ignoring substantive social justice undermined a society's claims to be free or democratic. Keynes expressed social justice in terms of jobs and expanding minimum standards. There can be no real movement to social justice until its economic grounds are established. Today, descendants of the theories Keynes criticized are the major obstacles to social justice and income redistribution. But Keynes' arguments are deeper than theirs. If the economic system and its results are not due to natural law, painful economic situations can be improved, and if society can be reorganized according to collective moral preferences, social justice legitimately belongs on the agenda of public debate.

EQUALITY

There is broad agreement Keynes was not an egalitarian.[65] His importance for the reform liberal concept of equality lies less in his own treatment of equality than the implications of his arguments. Keynes did not directly challenge the economic or social institutions upon which inequality was based, but he attacked their economic rationale. Unlike the classical and laissez-faire traditions, his economics provided little justification for inequality. Although Keynes did not support extensive economic inequality, neither Keynes nor most Keynesians explored the radical implications of his economic argument for equality. Indeed, it is necessary to reject Keynes' economics to defend inequality.

Neither an avowed egalitarian nor a principled critic of equality, Keynes criticized economic inequality, called for more equalization, and argued that unemployment and the "arbitrary and inequitable distribution of wealth and incomes" are the greatest problems facing society. Keynes saw consumption rather than saving as the key to economic growth in conditions of unemployed resources. He said that movement toward economic equalization promoted social justice, social peace, and economic efficiency through increas-

ing demand. The traditional economic justification for inequality as necessary to accumulate savings for capital investment, and its accompanying
defense of "much social injustice and apparent cruelty as an inevitable incident in the scheme of progress" were wrong. Inequality was unnecessary,
unjust, and inhuman under contemporary conditions. He believed *The General Theory* proved that social injustice in the name of private saving for economic growth—as supply-side theorists again argued under Ronald Reagan—was neither justified during depression nor required in the age into
which capitalism was moving. Only gross capital accumulation needed
greater economic inequality. New conditions necessitated more equalization. Without demand there was little incentive to invest, and since inequality depressed demand, savings would be wasted. In order to avoid depression and its associated problems, consumption-driven economies required
more equality of purchasing power, by "direct taxation" and "redistribution
of incomes or otherwise" and less saving by the rich, so as to increase "the
propensity to consume" and thus employment. This argument removed
"One of the chief social justifications of great inequality of wealth" though
"social and psychological justification for significant" but smaller than existing "inequalities of incomes and wealth" remained, for example to defuse
potentially destructive drives and passions.[66]

Within this context, raising working class wages, which as Brandeis also
argued, could never rise high enough to secure a basis for social justice, was
less important than welfare, limited redistribution,[67] and collective consumption as "ways of assigning to them [the working class] a larger proportion of the total national income." Keynes offered several methods for
achieving greater equality including "social insurance," "pensions," state
expenditure on "health, recreation, and education," family allowances, and
improved housing, all of which put the burden of social improvement on
the entire nation where it belonged.[68] Future abundance could also encourage improved morality.

MORALITY

For Keynes existing economic theory specified one's duty and relation to
others but had little concern for moral values. It overvalued "economic criterion," and as embodied in "the Benthamite tradition, . . . [is] the worm
which has been gnawing at the insides of modern civilisation and is responsible for its present moral decay." Excessively narrow economic conceptual-
izations of freedom and individualism prevented their attainment. "[A]ppeal
to the money motive in nine-tenths of the activities of life, with the universal striving after individual economic security as the prime object of

endeavour, with the social approbation of money as the measure of constructive success, and with the social appeal of the hording instinct," and their denial of human relations and obligation to others, was the "moral problem of our age."[69]

While monetary motivation may have been appropriate for a period requiring rapid capital accumulation, solving the material problem would eliminate the need and justification for such behavior and could support a more satisfactory moral and aesthetic life by altering, as with Needs 2, how people behave and interact. For Keynes, economics did not determine morals but could support many possibilities, and its policy proposals should be subject to external moral shaping and criticism. Moreover, economics was also a "moral science" in that "it deals with introspection and with values. . . . motives, expectations, psychological uncertainties," as well as ethical concerns, especially in policy recommendations.[70] To call economics a moral science implies not only the necessity of making choices but the legitimacy of doing so. Economics was not an end in itself or the most important aspect of life but secondary and instrumental to what really mattered: traditional moral-economic relations and the qualitative arts of living—moral judgment, friendship, aesthetic enjoyment, leisure, justice, and individual supporting relations. It is in this context that leisure becomes a problem. An improved society will come to esteem things other than pursuit of private economic ends. This will allow

> great changes in the code of morals. We shall be able to rid ourselves of many of the pseudo-moral principles which have hag-ridden us for two hundred years, by which we have exalted some of the most distasteful of human qualities into the position of the highest virtues. . . . the money-motive. . . . will be recognised for what it is, a somewhat disgusting morbidity. . . . social customs and economic practices, affecting the distribution of wealth and of economic rewards and penalties . . . because they are tremendously useful in promoting the accumulation of capital, we shall then be free, at last, to discard.[71]

THE LONG RUN

This "gradual evolution of a reformed society which shall be acceptable, just, and efficient in the changed conditions of the age"[72] is relevant to a controversial question, the short versus the long run. In its defense of inactive government, belief the economic system is self-correcting, and assurance things work out as well as they possibly can, laissez-faire claims to focus on the long run. Keynes did not believe that when serious problems arise we must or can wait. Perhaps Keynes' most famous and misunderstood remark is, "*In the long run* we are all dead."[73] This does *not* justify selfishness but rejects the laissez-faire contention that if left alone the future will take care of itself. Although much of Keynes' policy advice[74] focused on the short run—increased spending and reduced savings during depression were short run solutions, which must not be allowed to retard accumulation for the future excessively[75]—most is consistent with his concern for and frequent reference to the future. Neither democracy nor any form of capitalism would survive unless their current crises were resolved. A better future was contingent upon the present. It would not result from the inevitable march of history or the operation of natural relations, nor—rejecting both Marxism and laissez-faire[76]—should we invariably sacrifice the present for the sake of the future. Lost opportunities and squandered resources may be gone forever. Long lasting trends might take too long or seriously harm the weak. With large unemployment, poverty, and the growing appeal of fascism and communism, ignoring current pain might destroy what is valuable and permanently cut off the possibility of a better future. "A 'short period' . . . thinks nothing of living longer than a man. A 'short period' is quite long enough to include (and, perhaps to contrive) the rise and the fall of the greatness of a nation." The present was more than the threshold of tomorrow and society could not "afford always to take long views."[77] The sometimes rival demands of present and future could be balanced. Approximating his image of society one hundred years from now would drastically reduce conflicting claims between justice and consumption versus accumulation for and expansion in the future. Solving some of the economic problem reduces pressure on democracy and the existing political system.

Democracy

Keynes did not systematically argue for or analyze democratic theory or practice but rejected the economic basis of conservative criticism of democracy[78] and provided the first widely accepted economic justification capable of supporting expanded participation and/or public intervention into the economy. Keynes did not propose more participation but asserted that preservation and expansion of liberal democracy necessitated economic intervention. His analysis removes most economic rationale for limitations on democracy and democratic government, including justification of inequality and hostility to popular participation for fear democracy will subvert economic relations. Because his analysis potentially justifies social democracy, intervention, and democratizing the economy, it has contributed to the current debate about democracy.[79] Explicating the relation between Keynes' economics and democracy helps illuminate his political economy and hints at an alternative image of democracy. Keynes did not explore that alternative,[80] but his arguments can support a more social and egalitarian democracy than that found in the work of conservative economists. Keynes has been called ambivalent about democracy and even anti-democratic,[81] but focusing on the word "democracy" is too limiting. A theorist's conception of democracy includes conditions for democracy—supports for and obstacles to democracy—and concern for the components of democracy.

Keynes believed intervention would protect democratic government and liberal values because, as noted above, (1) the economic system is not self-stabilizing and (2) instability undermines political-social order, including democracy. Keynes' concern with democracy was largely defensive. He believed the basic struggle for democracy—suffrage and parliamentary government—had been won, and "partly [as] a result of the victory of democracy" liberalism was shifting to economic issues and concerns.[82] Unemployment, instability, and unresolved economic problems undermined and destroyed popular belief in and support for capitalism and democracy, weakening democratic governments' ability to respond to emergencies. This proved "a dangerous enterprise in a society which is both capitalist and democratic" and "might easily mean the downfall of our present system of democratic government."[83]

Things cannot be left to chance and the arbitrary exercise of power. Enhanced economic stability and popular welfare promote democracy and free government. The "task . . . of government within a democracy" is to find a way to foster stable economic order to avert "a social catastrophe."[84] But, is this task compatible with democracy? "It is perhaps *the* problem of problems" but he believed it is compatible. Unrestrained capitalism contained the seeds of its own and democracy's destruction. Reforming capitalism could save both. Intervention and public planning could protect democracy from internal despair and totalitarianism, enhance capitalism, and would not require fascism, socialism, or state ownership. This argument also made his theory "moderately conservative in its implications." "The idea that we cannot do what seems necessary without endangering our personal liberties and democratic institutions is a bogy." Danger lay with theorists and politicians who labored "finding plausible reasons for not doing things which public opinion almost overwhelmingly demands." As "facts" and conditions "shift" policy must keep pace while preserving basic political and economic values.[85]

To understand how Keynes envisaged democracy one must look at the common constitutive elements and values which make up every theory of democracy. Four major components are present: freedom, equality, consent, and the type of democracy.[86] An expansive concept of one element, such as equality, supports wider application of the others, whereas a narrow concept of one element constricts the range and meaning of the others. Public opinion and social justice provide further clues to Keynes' image of democracy.

Keynes did not discuss freedom or equality in political terms but his economic argument can support participatory claims. As for most liberals his primary value was freedom. There can be no democracy without freedom, but the issue is what kind of freedom and how much. Keynes criticized laissez-faire in part because policies such as wage flexibility were possible only in "a highly authoritarian society." He rejected laissez-faire freedom, in which markets are the primary area of freedom, in favor of what he called "deeper freedoms" of thought, expression, employment, achievement of some self-chosen ends, and artistic expression. Government was not the sole obstacle to freedom, but, through planning and intervention—he used rules of the road as an example—could promote conditions that would expand choices and help to actualize formal freedom. The conditions under which people exercise freedom are important. Although rarely discussing political freedom or linking freedom to democracy as such, Keynes wanted to expand the arena of freedom. Preservation of civil and political freedom was of "extraordinary importance"; violations of freedom of opinion, security of person, and property "destroy civilisation whatever they may preserve." On the other hand, achieving "economic reform would make the defence of political liberty much easier." "A great deal is at stake . . . we have to show that a free system can be made to work." This required new policies to fulfill traditional principles. Favoring "planning and management does not mean a falling away from the moral principles of liberty, which could be formerly embodied in a simpler system."[87]

The conditions for freedom had changed. Attempts to link Keynes to Locke[88] fall short because Keynes recognized individual and community can clash, and argued active government preserves and enhances freedom. Freedom had a limited positive meaning: augmenting the potential for agency through public action that strengthens economic security and develops resources, conditions, and opportunities to take advantage of and enrich formal freedom. Social justice is one element in positive freedom. Jobs, smaller economic gaps between classes, curbing the economic freedom of a few to benefit the many, limits on private power, even art and beautification of public places expand awareness and autonomy. Keynes saw the women's suffrage movement as a partial start and symptom "of deeper and more important issues below the surface" involving autonomy, expanded choice, self-control, and relief from restrictive customs and laws.[89]

A previous section discussed economic equalization which can be instrumental to political equality. Keynes, however, is almost silent on political equality.[90] He neither distrusted, as did Burke, Schumpeter, and Hayek, universal suffrage—which is a limited form of political equality—nor called for more popular input. His defense of public intervention, however, is compatible with expanded political equality while sanctioning more responsive government. By denying the justification for large economic inequalities Keynes' economics potentially empowers people and promotes democracy by removing some of the basis for class differences, economic policies that benefit people with high incomes or generate unemployment to fight inflation, and arguments that political equality undermines a free economy.

Although occasionally employing the term, Keynes rarely addressed consent. Democratic systems had two advantages over autocratic ones: they could utilize voluntarily a wider range of "disinterested talent" and they have, and must secure, "consciousness of consent" to legitimate their behavior.[91] Beyond such limited references, Keynes often spoke about public opinion, which he equated with consent. Public opinion is not democracy but under some circumstances may be part of democracy.

Keynes distinguished inside from outside opinion. This did not correspond to true and false opinion, but opinion expressed by or for the public and that by opinion leaders: "upstairs and back-stairs, expressed in limited circles."[92] Outside (and inside) opinion might be mistaken, and the gap between inside and outside opinion was a problem for democracy, but freedom and democracy required that outside opinion be respected, especially on major issues such as war, peace, and economic intervention. Although his primary theoretical concern was to convince other economists, that was a first step toward emancipating opinion not an alternative to informing mass opinion. Great changes required "an instructed and educated public opinion."[93]

Public opinion should limit government but respecting outside opinion did not require blindly following it, when wrong, but encouraging, shaping, and educating it.[94] Keynes believed great public opinion is created not spontaneous. In contrast to some contemporaries,[95] he asserted public opinion can and must be courted, that the public can learn to understand, want, and support better policies—Keynes broadcast and wrote extensively for the popular press—indicating that he believed people are capable of understanding and legitimately influencing policy. In examining a hypothetical defense of Lloyd George's conduct at Versailles, the common charge that public opinion forces democratic politicians into destructive policies, Keynes agreed this is sometimes valid but refused to accept it as the norm. He called Versailles a failure of leadership in its lack of vision and understanding of what he considered realities of international economics. Democracy like any system needs effective leadership, especially leaders who do not lie to or manipulate the public. Elites opposed or obfuscated needed changes more than the public, and secrecy and claims of superior knowledge obstructed "informed outside criticism." Educating outside opinion[96] is illustrated by his *Economic Consequences of the Peace* which appealed to public opinion—whistle-blowing—to revise the Treaty of Versailles. Experience changes "the living, indefinite belief of the individual." The public, thereby democracy, could learn from clear presentation of facts and possibilities: "it is not self-interest that makes the democracy difficult to persuade" but the dilemma of knowing what is correct.[97]

Keynes has frequently been called an elitist, and has sometimes been said to have opposed democracy.[98] Part of the elitism charge against Keynes, that his system—like that of Fabians, Labour, and Conservatives—required experts, is correct but not necessarily anti-democratic. There was no widely accepted model of participatory democracy readily available to Keynes if he had wanted one. Even the Labour Party did not expand popular decision making and rejected worker control of industry, claiming parliamentary government was sufficient for democracy.[99] Public involvement in the economy required changes in government, especially in values and administration, but not in politics or political sovereignty. Planning, necessary to achieve popular aspirations and ensure democracy's survival, needed advice, discretion, and "utmost decentralisation" of expert control. Keynes saw experts working within the framework of public opinion and Parliamentary supremacy as necessary to, not incompatible with democracy. Their role was to meet popular demand for stability and employment. As Woodrow Wilson also believed, democratic government would not supervise day to day activities, but would lay down "principles," general policy, and be "judges, not of first, but of final instance." Keynes distinguished determination of ends—the realm of public opinion and Parliament—from technical ability to achieve those ends—the realm of bureaucracy and experts. This distinction applied to reviving the Liberal Party, where "With strong leadership the technique, *as distinguished from the main principle,* could still be dictated above" [emphasis added]. Distinguishing ends and means is difficult. Power to determine means almost always leads to determining ends. Keynes did not address problems of bureaucratic control. He insisted, however, that bankers, administrators, economists, and decentralized semi-public corporations must not determine public policy goals, only the means to achieve goals—"can never, and should not, have the last word or the power, but must be a necessary ingredient in the decisions of those who have been entrusted by the country with the last word and with the power."[100]

Keynes emphasized intelligence and governance by the best, and frequently expressed contempt for ignorance and lack of imagination. What, then, is at issue? What is elitism? Except for conservative claims that market intervention is anti-democratic and elitist—the market, not politics, being the true arena of democracy—the elitism charge lacks specificity. Does elitism mean government by the best, a kind of Jeffersonian natural aristocracy; or belief in an identifiable group or class that has a prescriptive right to rule; or claims that the ruling class can or should ignore demands from the ignorant masses and rule in their name? Keynes never limited democracy to choosing between rival elites and might have accepted Jefferson's concept, but, given his faith in human reason and his emphasis on the importance of public opinion, he clearly rejected the last two alternatives. Moreover, frequent reference to "madmen in authority"[101] indicates contempt for powerful people who through ignorance or malice abuse their trust. Keynes, as did Dewey, Hobhouse, Galbraith, Thurow, and Reich, saw two alternatives: reliance on mythical automatic forces to produce the best possible results, or attempts to make the system operate according to moral and political ideals. As he considered the first impossible, intervention became necessary, and successful intervention required intelligence.

What type of democracy was this? It is more than procedural, much less than participatory, but he did not despair of democracy. As with most of his Conservative and Labour Party contemporaries Keynes defended parliamentary democracy, accepted the existing constitutional system, and never envisaged direct popular decision making. This approach weakened reform in later years. Keynes recognized the changes in capitalism in the previous century much more than those in democracy. If he had been more of the "political animal" he referred to in 1925 he might have realized the need to give the mass public a central role in his politics, as he did in his emphasis on aggregate demand, thus developing support and public acceptance to carry out his proposals. Instead, he emphasized parliamentary sovereignty, responsive bureaucracies, party reform, popular elections, and concern with public opinion to control the economic dislocations he saw destroying democracy in the 1930s.[102]

The image of indirect, quasi-popular influence over economics—not economic determination of the limits of government—applies to political democracy not economic democracy. If economic democracy refers to increasing direct participation in economic decisionmaking, Keynes was not an economic democrat. If it includes economic equalizing, his work is compatible with economic democracy. Keynes advocated limited social democracy—intervention, regulation, and welfare within a parliamentary setting. This would promote "social and economic justice" which only democracy required.[103] Unlike many conservatives, he felt social justice was compatible with, provided substantive content for, and helped define both democracy and the good society.

For many in the 1930s, democracy lacked vitality, had failed, or needed replacement, but Keynes agreed with those who insisted it could work. He saw his economics as promoting that end. Without realizing the potential in his argument, Keynes expanded political-economic possibility by insisting that economic intervention and equalization are compatible with and frequently necessary to democracy, legitimating a substantive social and potentially participatory democracy. Other economic theories can support further democratization, and Keynes is not necessarily a model for today, but, in the current political climate a hands-off economics is usually hostile to enlarging the scope and depth of democracy. Keynes never considered markets as the essence of democracy because he rejected the laissez-faire theory on which that claim is based. He insisted democracy suffered from doing nothing and democratic systems could successfully develop the public intervention necessary to their survival. Thus Keynes gave economists a modest task, finding ways to accommodate popular feelings and needs, in his metaphor the role of dentists;[104] and gave democracy a greater one, designing intelligent intervention so that it might survive and grow.

Role of Government

Keynes had high level experience in government, but, like Galbraith later, resisted proposals that he run for public office. After graduating from King's College, Cambridge, he entered the India Office, leaving after two years. Keynes joined the Treasury Department in 1915 where he dealt with foreign exchange, was the chief representative of the Treasury at the 1919 peace conference ending World War I, and broke with the government over the Treaty of Versailles. In World War II he had a more informal and influential relation with the Treasury, working tirelessly on financial relations with the United States, on trade, and on exchange issues. His proposals influenced the development of the World Bank and the International Monetary Fund. His justification of active government made his economics essential to reformers and a sixty-year target for conservatives. Although subsequent reform liberals modified Keynes' work, his defense of public intervention remains at the center of reform arguments.

Keynes accepted the basic structure of British government and assumed that constitutional integrity and traditional methods of parliamentary and bureaucratic government could be maintained. Like Dewey or Galbraith, he proposed changing the philosophy and role of government, not its structure. If error, bad thinking, and lack of moral clarity were obstacles to reform, these could change and institutions could take on new roles. That would be sufficient. Keynes' justification of active government is more important than and can be separated from specific policy recommendations and images of government. Economic theory did not annihilate or determine politics. Keynes repudiated the laissez-faire model of government in favor of public action to promote the good life. A successful future for capitalism was possible only with a new, permanent government role in the economy. He assumed that intervention can be successful, that it is certainly not doomed to failure. "Experience does *not* show that individuals, when they make up a social unit, are always less clear-sighted than when they act separately."[105]

Keynes proposed a wide variety of government activities in the social economy, including socialization and control of some or much investment, stimulation of the propensity to consume, partial redistribution of wealth, welfare, monetary policy, fiscal policy such as low interest rates and progressive taxes, creation of public works, and participation in international organizations for monetary and trade stability. In contrast, most of his discussion of government and administrative structure is incomplete. Except for his Clearing Union proposal, Keynes did not work out structural and operational details, or explain how government could deal with political pressures. Planning, which today might be called industrial policy, especially through stimulation and control of investment, was the clearest though not necessarily permanent domestic government duty. Here too, he discussed goals—fuller employment, more equality, social justice, more efficient use of resources, cheaper capital, political-social stability and achievement of a better future—more than institutional arrangements. State planning would grow from already existing examples. It would supplement individual initiative because conditions for the exercise of individualism had changed. Individuals had not failed but had achieved so much that the system could no longer function without some "central deliberation." Government would focus on "*general* organization of resources as distinct from the *particular* problems of production and distribution which are the province of the individual business technician and engineer." Competition, pursuit of self-interest, and democratic government would remain as planning was designed to "modify and condition the environment within which the individual freely operates with and against other individuals." Otherwise, individuals will be crushed.[106]

The right environment for domestic experimentation was crucial. Keynes directed his extensive work on international economics toward the long-range goal of creating a new system compatible with and supportive of domestic reform. He asserted that the existing international order subjected the domestic political economy to destabilizing influences, thereby precluding an expansive social-economic policy. Unlimited free trade and an unregulated gold-based international economy could not be part of the future because they transferred international disequilibria to the domestic system, forcing it to conform to often disruptive pressures from international monetary and trade flows. Keynes proposed new institutions and methods that would insulate the domestic system from adverse international impact: a Clearing Union which evolved into the International Monetary Fund and the International Bank for Reconstruction and Development; commodity agreements to stabilize prices and supplies; and policies to regulate and restrict currency flows between nations. To succeed, "[t]here should be the least possible interference with internal national policies and the plan should not wander from the international terrain." To encourage expansion and prevent unemployment, a Clearing Union must guard that "the pressure of [balance of payments] adjustment should not fall, as it has in the past, almost wholly on the weaker country, the debtor."[107]

Conclusions

Keynes' economics changed twentieth-century liberalism *and* government responsibilities. Although he may not have been comfortable with recent theoretical developments in the areas of freedom, equality, and participation, his rejection of natural economic harmony and equilibrium transformed liberal political-economy and laid the economic foundation for current theory and policy. He was unconcerned with formal liberal theory, even if well aware of changing meanings of liberalism, but aimed instead at reforming policy. Keynes recognized liberalism was multidimensional and employed various phrases to describe his own liberalism—"progressive Liberal," "real Liberals," "New Liberalism"—and distinguished "old Liberals" who "are blind" to the economic problem from Liberals willing to go beyond the policies and issues of a previous generation.[108]

Keynes regularly argued that as conditions change policies must be adjusted to protect basic principles. As the economic, social, and political circumstances that gave birth to capitalism evolve it must adapt to new conditions. Laissez-faire and its related political-social theory produced once sensible policies that now interfered with realizing freedom, individualism, democracy, social justice, and material plenty. Capitalism and democracy had a future only if society modified its laissez-faire orientation, redefined individualism, embraced social justice, acknowledged that pursuit of self-interest is as likely to be chaotic and zero-sum as to be order producing, and accepted that capitalism will not achieve its wealth maximizing potential without intervention, guidance, and general direction of the macro-economy. The future will retain what Keynes considered the essence of capitalism and historic liberalism—private ownership[109] of most of the means of production, money making, freedom, and individuality; but will go beyond historically contingent elements—laissez-faire policy, great inequality, and narrow individualism. Even if he had approved of the existing economic system, a die-hard attitude meant the good in it would be destroyed along with the bad.[110] Keynes saw his theory as sustaining individual pursuit of self-interest and money making at lower stakes, with classical theory remaining relevant to the analysis of what is produced and to whom it is distributed.

Are we the future that Keynes envisioned? No. Despite widespread acceptance of "Keynesianism" until the 1970s, the full, radical, and equalizing elements in Keynes' image of the future were never achieved. In our current period of population growth, continued war, high arms spending, radical conservative dismantling of Keynesian and social policy, relative economic decline, and growing inequality, with all their potential for racial, gender, regional, class, and international conflict, we are moving away from his ideal. That his social-economic theory needs updating and refinement attenuates neither its positive support for embattled democracies in the 1930s and 1940s nor its reminder that sometimes new economic policies, which are workable in a system where the mass public is not excluded from power, must be created to protect basic political-social principles.

Keynes' political-economy is sometimes incomplete. Keynes identified two categories of needs: one satisfied by material goods and the other through a sense of power over others. Although he believed material abundance encourages changes in morality and presumably reduces or redirects drives for power, he hardly discussed the second category of needs or considered how advertising plays upon and creates desire for superiority over others. Occasionally referring to economic power as control, he did not analyze how it operates in modern society; he assumed that conquest of the economic problem would require and bring about more equality, and that tyrannizing over one's bankbook is sometimes an alternative to tyrannizing over people.[111] Full employment empowers people and reduces the potential for exercising the kind of control on the job that Brandeis discussed, but, as Galbraith argues, it does not eliminate power relations. Yet, Keynes made almost offhand remarks that hint at greater awareness of the problem of power. He notes that Ricardo's theory "commended it[self] to authority" in part because it justified inequality. Given the centrality of expectations, "economic prosperity is excessively dependent on a political and social atmosphere which is congenial to the average business man." He noted elsewhere that workers are often presented with a "choice between starvation and submission."[112] But he did not develop these observations into a consistent part of his theory. Keynes saw ignorance as the fundamental obstacle to reform, not wickedness, class conflict, power, or vested interests. Reform was a matter of convincing opponents, not defeating them.[113] Thus both class and distribution conflict remain unexplored, and, along with them the question Reich asks, are elites willing to weaken their positions at the top of the economic machine to allow a better future for all? Moreover, Keynes offers little discussion of how a value system can be developed and accepted that allows his future, and no strong sense of the inevitability of ideological conflict over these issues despite his emphasis on ideas, assumptions, and reason.

Finally, one must ask whether government is strong enough to accomplish Keynes' ends. Leaving aside the fashionable conservative claim that pursuit of self-interest causes the inevitable failure of intervention, and the recent assault not only on active government but government authority, this question is vital and perhaps unanswerable. One thing is certain. Current pluralist systems are not modeling policies or dominant liberal and democratic theories on the public roles or seizing the opportunities opened up by Keynes' economics. In the last twenty-five years these systems have become less inclined to pursue expansive, equalizing experiments. Confronted with massive mistrust of experts and government, treating citizens as consumers, as Keynes tended to do, aggravates these trends. Whether Keynes' specific arguments are appropriate in our situation of growing inequality, the principles he attempted to establish—refutation of the claim that the economic system is autonomous and self-equilibrating in a desirable manner, attention to social-political consequences of economics, defense of an active government role in the social-economy, reinvigoration of traditional and liberal values through new policies to implement them, and concern for social justice—remain the heart of modern liberalism's alternative to the philosophy of leaving things alone.

4

John Kenneth Galbraith: Power and the Political-Cultural Context of Economics

People of the same trade seldom meet together, even for merriment and diversion, but the conversation ends in a conspiracy against the public, or in some contrivance to raise prices.
—Adam Smith, *The Wealth of Nations*

CONSERVATIVE THEORIST Irving Kristol's critical review of *The New Industrial State* captures John Kenneth Galbraith's (b. 1908) intended approach to political-economy: "it ingeniously combines the tradition of moral-social criticism with a professional and plausible economic analysis."[1] While slighting the long practice of liberal discourse and criticism, as partly seen in this book, Kristol illuminates Galbraith's effort to go beyond conventional economics to view economics in its political and cultural context. Galbraith blends the social and political concerns of Dewey, Brandeis, and Hobhouse with Keynes' emphasis on the instability of capitalism, but his work is more social and political than Keynes. Galbraith, who was born in Canada and has been associated with Harvard University most of his adult life, is the least conventional and least growth-oriented of the four economists. His books have sold millions of copies,[2] and they deeply influenced popular thinking in the 1950s and 1960s. In addition, Galbraith served as deputy director of the Office of Price Administration, or head of price control, from 1941 to 1943, where Richard Nixon briefly worked; was a co-director of the United States Strategic Bombing Survey at the end of World War II; was a co-founder and eventually chairperson of Americans for Democratic Action; became president of the American Economic Association; advised John F. Kennedy and, until he broke with him over Vietnam, Lyndon Johnson on agriculture and poverty; wrote speeches for and/or advised and campaigned for six Democratic presidential hopefuls; and was ambassador to India from 1961 to 1963. This chapter examines Galbraith's political-social-economic ideas, values, and policy prescriptions, and with that the interrelation between politics and economics. It surveys his interpretation of the current situation, the social-political nature of market failure, power, and justification for expanding government's role in the social-economy; and it offers a sampling of Galbraith's conclusions. We will not discuss Galbraith's opposition to the Vietnam war, his foreign policy proposals, his novels, or his interest in the developing nations.

Galbraith has always been a liberal,[3] despite conservative claims that he is a socialist and despite his own occasional calls for planning and/or some form of socialism. Liberalism has a vital function in modern society: "Conservatives accumulate the unsolved problems. The task of liberals is to keep pace with the solutions." Liberalism "is . . . the only practical [political-economic] faith."[4] Although Galbraith's liberalism has been called "the first major reevaluation and reinterpretation of American liberalism since the Progressive era," it does not represent a radical break with liberal tradition. Galbraith accepts a large role for the market, some inequality, and the inevitability of large organization; moreover he rejects class conflict[5] and values individuality and freedom. But Galbraith is not precise as to the meaning of liberalism; and while he is critical of others, he reads no one out of liberalism.[6] From Ricardo to John Stuart Mill, liberalism "centered on the liberal market society—that in which economic life was regulated by the market and not by the state."[7] Once liberating and appropriate, this is no longer suitable. Problems, opportunities, and understanding change, and liberal ideas and policies must evolve to meet altered circumstances and new challenges. Social, political, and economic needs and problems—and liberalism itself— have progressed beyond laissez-faire and/or narrow Keynesian political-economy and Galbraith criticizes liberals and so-called liberal policies that fail to do so. Liberalism "is ceasing to be" what it once was, "a determined faith." Liberals are growing comfortable, conventional, safe, and contented. They reflect too much, emphasize speech over action, ignore inequality, overemphasize production for solving social-economic problems, make liberalism "a cover for convenient belief," and endorse irrelevant policies such as antitrust, in the process thinking they are doing something significant.[8]

What does this mean for Keynesian liberalism? Galbraith considers his own work, like that of all modern economics, to follow from Keynes; but like Thurow he does not accept everything "Keynesian," especially emphasis on production as the highest goal. Many ostensibly Keynesian policies defend an increasingly intolerable status quo. Keynes' revolution was "extraordinarily conservative": it did not alter the dominance of markets; it had only "limited effects on larger economic policy"; and it left "the power and independence of the business enterprise untouched."[9] For Galbraith, liberalism is living and evolving, and it needs to focus on power, equality, distribution, and the adaptation of basic values to altered circumstances. If it does not, society ossifies.

Galbraith rejects the mainstream or "central tradition" claim that economics is autonomous from and superior to politics and political considerations. He insists that economics is inseparable from and interrelated with the political-social environment. The boundary between economics and politics is often arbitrary, and it "must truly be an imaginary one." Issues cannot be studied in isolation. Policy must consider its impact on all political, social, and economic relations. As with Keynes, Dewey, and Brandeis, Galbraith considers the economy a volatile source of social-political discontent and conflict. "[E]conomics does not usefully exist apart from politics." "In government there are no exclusively economic, political, not even purely medical judgments."[10] Separation leads to error, misjudgment, and sterility in economics; irrelevance and frequent harm in public policy. Professional economists who ignore the social and political context in offering necessarily political policy recommendations discredit economics and foster bad public policy. Failure to respect political needs and interests is as much an "error" as focusing solely on the wants and interests of affected groups.[11] Moreover, separating politics and economics ignores that political stability, popular security, and participation provide the foundation for economic development—"the intimate association between responsible, honest democratic government and economic progress."[12]

The Existing Relation Between Economy and Polity

Politics and economics are closely related in contemporary society. Galbraith sees analysis and practice commanded by ideology, lack of consumer sovereignty, planning system dominance, and the all-pervading presence of power which, according to the "central tradition," does not exist.

Galbraith insists that political-economic thinking is dominated by *ideology*, which he sees as unquestioned acceptance of traditional, convenient belief regardless of conditions or impact. "Ideas are inherently conservative." Liberals, conservatives, and socialists are captives of their ideas. Galbraith is closer to Keynes than are contemporary Keynesians in asserting that unquestioned assumptions are pivotal in shaping understanding of the world, perceptions of reality, and policy advice. As with Dewey, Galbraith criticizes theorists who place theory and ideological purity over experience, and he ridicules inflexibility in face of change. Trouble frequently lies "not with the world but with the ideas by which it was interpreted." Technology more than thinking shapes our world, but arguments and theories explain, justify, defend, and modify the results. They are also obstacles to needed improvements. *Affluent Society* and *Culture of Contentment,* written thirty-four years apart, argue that conventional ideas of social order, accepted ways of doing things, and dominant understandings of power are insufficient for the problems we face. Leading political-cultural practice, supplemented by economic ideology, is at odds with common, collective needs and problems, and it is incompatible with the ultimate satisfaction and well being of the majority.[13]

Subordinating experience and reality to market ideology lies at the heart of economics. In a paper given at the American Economic Association—indicating the importance he attaches to this argument—Galbraith claimed: "Economics has been not a science but a conservatively useful system of belief defending that belief as a science." People embrace ideology as "a substitute for the painful process of thought." Much economics "does not describe the world as it is." Too often "economic theory combines interpretation with justification. . . . [and] explicit defense." An ideology of the benign self-adjusting market ignores power and the impact of conventionally acceptable policy on those with little power, and supports the egregious belief that things work out for the best if left alone. Socially injurious corporate performance and other communally harmful behavior follow from adherence "to outdated and irrelevant ideology." Much "socially inconvenient analysis" is ignored. Private power, corporate bureaucracy, and inequality are neglected or explained away. Thus economics "serves the controlling economic interest. It cultivates the beliefs and therewith the behavior that such interest requires."[14] Market abstractions such as competition take on mythic stature, serving more as political images of the good life than as economic concepts.[15] The role of ideology in economics reappears in Galbraith's discussions of power, consumer sovereignty, imbalance, and inequality, as well as in his recommendations.

Galbraith's claim about ideology is fundamentally political, and has important policy implications. Two major consequences follow: the market cannot function as a regulator of and model for social relations or government; and conventional theory is incapable of analyzing or intelligently prescribing for contemporary conditions. This argument complements the reform liberal claim that policy is not neutral. Economics thus becomes "not . . . a search for, and expression of truth" but an adjustment to an "insistent process of change."[16]

Galbraith's ideology argument is associated with his repeated insistence—in books from *American Capitalism* through *The New Industrial State*

to *The Culture of Contentment*—that policy must change to fit new circumstances if it is to protect basic values, and with his examination of economic
history.[17] Once-valid policies no longer apply when conditions change: "the
same action or event occurring at different times can lead to very different
results." For this reason Galbraith is sometimes called a technological deter-
minist. Thus, the neoclassical system "is not implausible as a description of
a society that once existed. Nor is it entirely unsatisfactory as a picture of
that part of the economy . . . called the market system." Nineteenth-century
liberal emphasis on increasing production by almost any means was relevant
under remnants of "feudal and mercantilist society," low productivity, and
absolute shortages of goods and services necessary for a decent life. Laissez-faire policies made sense before major economic actors acquired power
over markets and consumers. But in the contemporary situation, "[w]hat
was sound economic behavior before cannot be sound economic behavior
now." Economic tasks, and related political-social possibilities, concerns,
and government responsibilities are very different in an advanced society.
Adherence to the policies of the past, even if attractive to powerful interests, induces great error and perhaps disaster.[18]

Galbraith believes that reform liberal solutions risk becoming another
obsolescent orthodoxy if they do not change to meet new circumstances;
but he does not specify where answers are to be found if received models of
political-economy are questionable and often irrelevant. Galbraith does not
believe that everything is ideology, but he fails to explain fully how we are
to avoid ideological thinking. He can see a relation between himself and
Dewey in terms of pragmatism, and his approach to economics and policy is
essentially pragmatic, but he says there is no direct link.[19] Galbraith fits a
pragmatic perspective: he emphasizes everyday results of theory and policy;
searches for workable solutions; mistrusts received opinion; claims that the
validity of policy depends on changing circumstances and context; asserts
that understanding develops from experience and observation of the interaction between environment, people, and policy; and attributes many problems to vestiges of traditional thinking. Like Dewey, Galbraith claims that
adaptation, acceptance of change, experimentation, and examination of the
impact of policy on specific persons—as opposed to accepting a set of ideas
as guiding in all circumstances—provide the only means to workable
answers, even though new answers are needed as soon as problems are
solved and circumstances change. Galbraith implies that this approach is
more likely to avoid ideological limitations. Presumably we are to decide
what to do by looking at problems and results; but lacking Dewey's emphasis on experience per se, Galbraith gives little specific guidance for determining what is a result and how it should be measured. Although pragma-

tism is no longer a major philosophical movement, Galbraith misses the opportunity to justify his theory through fuller appeal to this American philosophy, and to ground his work in at least a quasi-philosophical argument, as early liberal political economists did with appeals to natural law, and as some contemporary conservatives do by referring to "spontaneous order." By missing this opportunity and by not providing a more explicit explanation of his essentially evolutionary approach to political economy, Galbraith discourages wider support for his argument.

As with Dewey, Galbraith believes that modern life is dominated by "something new": large-scale organization, with real power and its own purposes and goals, which supersede and supplant individual and public ones. Such organization commands the most important parts of the economy, dominating consumers and the state. Size and market concentration produce power that is unacknowledged in classical, neoclassical, and laissez-faire theory—the "central tradition"—allowing economic power virtual free reign. Ours is an "age of organization," and "[t]he real world is one of great interacting organizations." Organization is "[t]he transforming force, the engine of historical change"; and its common purpose "is to take power away from the market and lodge it," as much as possible, with producers.[20]

Root and branch, Galbraith rejects the argument that consumer sovereignty controls the market, ensuring market freedom while limiting power in economic relations. Consumers and citizens are not sovereign. Manipulation and organization have reduced individualism and consumer and citizen sovereignty to little more than myths. Galbraith considers "The surrender of the sovereignty of the individual to the producer or producing organization is the theme, explicit or implicit, of two books, *The Affluent Society* . . . and *The New Industrial State*"—to which one can add *Anatomy of Power*. Economics must abandon the assumptions of consumer sovereignty and citizen sovereignty because these assumptions hide bureaucratic and producer power and manipulation, making economics "a shield for the exercise of producer sovereignty." "[E]conomic and associated political theory," by maintaining the illusion of "consumer and citizen sovereignty," fails "to interpret reality," turning popular sovereignty into "the servant . . . of a conservatively useful myth that conceals the reality. . . . adding to frustration and conflict." Simultaneously, the myth "raises barriers against a wide range of social action" and helps "sanction income inequality." Consumers—and presumably citizens—could not be dissatisfied if they really were in control.[21]

This argument challenges "the very foundations of classical economics"—and of the contemporary congressional resurrection of social Darwinism—by calling into question the doctrine of individualism that has become a "cloak for organization."[22] Galbraith finds the ultimate moral sanction for the neoclassical model in the supposed subordination of the market to individuals operating through the market. This adds powerful ideological support for retaining the concept against evidence of producer and bureaucratic control. Even if "management of the consumer" is incomplete and hardly operates at all in the most competitive part of the economy—control is a matter of more or less, not either/or—its existence undermines the philosophical defense for non-intervention and inequality.[23] Who is sovereign? Large organizations.

Galbraith distinguishes between the planning system and the market system. The planning system, the epitome of organization, is characterized by extensive planning and is composed of about a thousand large firms and associated labor unions, which he says produce more than half of the output in the United States. These large, well-organized firms enjoy significant independence from market forces. They do not passively accept market prices, but, well into the 1970s, and to a lesser extent today, mitigate market forces by exercising significant control over suppliers, customers, government, and the market system. With a fair amount of success, they "seek to control the social environment," and are able to "impose their values on the society and the state." Their planning is made necessary by the imperatives of modern technology and the high costs of capital and production.[24] These firms are controlled by the technostructure—"all who bring specialized knowledge, talent or experience to group decisionmaking"—not their stockholders. "This, not the narrow management group, is the guiding intelligence—the brain—of the enterprise," effectively wielding power and determining goals. Top members of the technostructure often own little stock, are concerned less with price or profit maximization than with their own security, perquisites, and power, and often share a group orientation.[25]

The market system is composed of millions of smaller firms producing the remaining output. Unlike the planning system, but in conformity with neoclassical theory, it is inherently stable and tends toward equality. Individuals in the market system have little power. They are unable to "influence" customer, supplier, or government behavior significantly or to control prices directly. Moreover, since the planning system can manipulate its political-economic environment, while the market system cannot, there is built-in inequality between them. Top corporate officials have "a prescriptive right, on visiting Washington, to see the President of the United States." Individual farmers or retailers have "no similar access to the Secretary of Agriculture [or] . . . Secretary of Commerce. It would be of little value if they did." Bureaucracy influences bureaucracy.[26]

The specific details of the planning-market system distinction and its possible applicability to the 1990s and beyond are less important than the fundamental assumptions on which it is based and the conclusions about power that it supports. The central tradition's competitive markets and the attendant political-social requirements for and limits on government and politics are not accurate or applicable for the leading sectors of the economy. Consequently, the central tradition is a poor policy guide. There are no beneficent automatic market forces, and there is no moral, political, or economic requirement to accept all market results. Circumstances change in a dynamic system, so Galbraith would not expect his specific planning–market system formulation to remain unaltered. The inherent "sclerosis" of the technostructure—and all organization—aside, the technostructure remains an oligarchy, but international competition has begun to weaken its power.[27] Galbraith's crucial claim is that the planning system, due to its size, organization, and resources, has meaningful power, whereas the market system does not.

Power

Traditional theory limits government involvement in the economy partly on the basis of claims that no one has power over any one else in the market.[28] Galbraith disagrees. Power is related to his analysis of ideology, the problems of conventional political-economic analysis, and democracy. Galbraith's is the most complete and elaborate discussion of power in this book, and one of his most important political arguments. As with Keynes' different justification of intervention, Galbraith's concept of power undermines the politically limiting market claim and opens the way for extensive public involvement in the economy. According to Galbraith, analysis of power reveals not the invisible hand of free markets but the visible hand of corporate planning, manipulation, and control.[29]

In 1953, Galbraith claimed that "regulation of economic power" was "the oldest of economic problems," manageable only by functioning markets or government. In 1985, he reiterated that power was the "most troublesome, even intractable, problem. . . . the great black hole of economics." Possession and use of power are disguised by market theory, which removes "most of the justification for exercise of government authority over the economy" and frees large enterprises from meaningful external control. The traditional model of dissolved power retains validity for the competitive part of the economy, but it is irrelevant to prevailing planning system conditions, where wages and executive compensation are set by "human agency" rather than by impersonal markets.[30] Ideology vindicates power. Conventional economics has "slipped imperceptibly into its role as the cloak over corporate power."

Its concealment of power makes economics into a powerful instrument for conditioning people to the needs of the planning system. "This power would be much more remarked and resisted were it not for" denying and disguising it behind a "theology" in which the market, as if by a "miracle," forces private ambition to serve others.[31]

Power includes imposition of adverse consequences broadly understood, influence, control, and shaping options. It is exercised less through force than through belief formation, manipulation, and compensation. Successful use of power is demonstrated by the "ability of an individual or a group to impose its purposes on others," to induce a person "to abandon the goals he would normally pursue and accept those of another person or organization," or to "command the efforts of individuals and the state." Power is successfully exercised "when the individual submits to the purposes of others not only willingly but with a sense of attendant virtue."[32] Galbraith, however, compounds the means of exercising power with types of power, identifying three types: "condign, compensatory, and conditioned power." Condign power includes threatened or actual physical coercion, painful emotional situations, and, as in Mill's *On Liberty*, "conspicuous condemnation" and "personal or public rebuke." Condign power has become less important in socio-economic relations, chiefly because the planning system has other, more effective means to bend people to its needs.[33]

Belief and behavior exist in a social, cultural, and political environment. Conditioned power—"cultivation of belief"—changes belief through education, persuasion, manipulation of perceptions, individual identification with group goals, unquestioning acceptance of existing rules and opinions, corporate use of revered symbols, and advertising.[34] Conditioned power is most closely associated with organization. It leads people to submit to the planning system without recognizing that their behavior is being manipulated. Conditioned power is the central means for winning public and government support for planning system needs and wishes. Eliminating the possibility and desirability of alternatives encourages individuals to believe that they are acting voluntarily or are motivated by their "own moral or social sense." Affecting belief becomes "[t]he major exercise of power over the legislator or public official."[35]

Compensation—offering positive rewards—is pervasive but little resembles the purely voluntary behavior portrayed in much economic literature. Circumstances determine the extent to which it is an exercise of power. Galbraith claims many exchanges are only formally free. People frequently have little or no choice but to accept an offer. Compensatory power—"the bending of the will of one person to another by straightforward purchase"—along with organization, is crucial to planning system control, and wins compliance by "the offer of an affirmative reward." It is power because it enables some to command others, and this ability is unequally distributed, depending on wealth and property.[36]

Organization is the most important means of acquiring and employing power. In arguments reminiscent of Charles Lindblom,[37] Galbraith emphasizes business influence and control over government, whereas conventional theory claims that such power does not or should not exist. The acquisition of power by the planning system, with its accompanying conditioning of belief, gives large private organizations "power over the state." In a politically charged argument he prosecutes more by example rather than systematically proves, Galbraith asserts that their purposes become public purposes, their interests public interests and policy. How is this power exercised? The planning system can command the resources of the state through continuing, regular, and direct access to decisionmakers and the bureaucracy; whereas small business and unorganized labor act primarily through the less effective and more public electoral system. The planning system can manipulate, influence, and control beliefs about the proper role of government, the nature of socioeconomic relations, and the identification of corporate needs with public needs. And, finally, it has the means to buy support. Elections give power to money because money is necessary to finance campaigns, ensuring the wealthy direct access to decision makers and electoral influence.[38]

Galbraith sees a "deep and enduring contradiction in modern industrial society. The public and the corporate purposes diverge." Government is not autonomous of the planning system. Conditioned power transforms essentially private wants into public ends through corporate cultivation of "belief in" its "needs or purposes." In many areas, especially but not limited to defense contractors and the military, private bureaucracy has entered into a "symbiotic relationship with the public bureaucracy" and dominates public opinion and the legislature, ensuring primacy for planning system interests.[39] Concurrently, the planning system depends heavily on government. In Keynesian terms, intervention, especially "regulation of aggregate demand," is required by the planning system, which otherwise "is prone to depression or inflation." Public purchases, provision of educated workers, development of advanced and often "socialized technology," and scientific innovation are also essential. The political and economic systems become linked, and the line between them becomes "a traditional fiction." "In notable respects, the mature corporation is an arm of the state. And the state, in important matters, is an instrument of the planning system." This new industrial state epitomizes private-public symbiosis. Most liberal and conservative theorists ignore that "the line between public and private

authority in the planning system is indistinct and in large measure imaginary"; yet this "abhorrent" relation "is normal." Reasoning backward from
results to cause, Galbraith claims that "distribution of public resources
reflects the power of the planning system over the state." This is not, however, complete control or "absolute power."[40] Still, its influence forcefully
shapes opinion, macro-economic policy, and military and defense policy to
its benefit. Other less powerful groups compete to appropriate some of the
power of government to their purposes, and some real democracy persists.
Nevertheless, the planning system is powerful, remains unexplained and
unexamined in traditional theory, and exercises more influence than any
other actor.[41] Galbraith admits that this implies a "theory of the state. . . .
[that] comes close to being the executive committee of the large producing
organization—of the technostructure."[42] This relation is radically different
from that with the market portion of the economy.

    If Galbraith's assessment of power is valid, both traditional theory and
the market as an institution have suffered a massive failure to curb private
power and ensure real competition, especially in the planning system. The
competitive market model describes not the existing situation, but one producing "ideal results."[43] In real life, competition may neither promote the
general good nor curb or eliminate private power. Claiming that competition describes reality, rather than admitting it is an idealized prescription,
justifies existing relations.[44] Galbraith's argument reverses laissez-faire theory by identifying power and coerciveness where it sees peaceful relations
and/or passive servants of the market. Given such power, the market is not
competitive over its full range of activities, does not always protect freedom,
and cannot substitute for government. Moreover, the market cannot be
Pareto optimal. What can protect people? Often for Galbraith, the only
answer is government.

Justifying Active Government: Market Failure

Laissez-faire theorists locate government limitations in the market's spon-
taneity and success; Galbraith locates government responsibilities in the
market's failures, omissions, and inabilities. Galbraith sees two types of
related market failure: (1) the market does not function as traditional economic theory claims; and (2) economic failure harms social and political
goals and relations, regardless of narrow economic efficiency.[45] These failures distinguish categories that apologists sometimes collapse or, especially
with the second, deny.

The first type of market failure refers to Keynesian economic instability, inefficiency, and unemployment, as well as to such externalities as pollution and industrial disease. Galbraith agrees with Keynes that the economic system is not self-stabilizing or self-correcting at desirable levels of output and employment and that it may need stimulus to achieve satisfactory performance and prevent "stasis" in recession or depression. In the original Keynesian formulation, solutions emphasized stimulating employment and aggregate demand to lift the economy out of depression. Today, according to orthodox theory, government, whether faced with depression or inflation, should stimulate or restrict demand, thereby restoring presumably natural market forces to normal operation. The heavy burden this assigns to government is consistent with a conservative image of capitalism because it leaves intact internal corporate decision making, consumer decisions, and the social structure of the economy. Intervention is absolutely necessary, given "the deeply inherent and self-destructive tendencies of the economic system."[46] But it is not enough. The market fails in more than not providing adequate employment.

The second type of market failure has broad political implications and is closer to Brandeis, Dewey, and Hobhouse than to modern Keynesians. A picture of market failure that includes the social-political impact of market relations and the inability of markets to meet public goals such as freedom, social justice, and reduced class tension, justifies deeper public intervention than limited pictures that deny market failure is a problem. It goes beyond classical liberalism and conventional Keynesianism to include the social and political results, costs, and impacts of both economic relations and orthodox policies such as monetarism. In contemporary conditions, Galbraith, like Keynes, says fiscal and monetary policies formulated to address market problems often harm those with little power. He believes that the failure to produce socially optimal results is intrinsic to the market, as seen with power and inequality.

The market can neither curb private power in the planning system nor ensure real competition; and its direct results are often undesirable, even destructive. Consequently, the market fails to perform economic, social, and political tasks—such as promoting equality, ensuring freedom, and acting as the real realm of democracy—ascribed to it by conservative economists or to society in classic liberal theory. Social-political costs of disorder can be very high, even terminal. Agreeing with Keynes, Galbraith argues that, "left to themselves, economic forces do not work out for the best except perhaps for the powerful."[47] But he also adds something new. Social-political failure includes an overemphasis on and unceasing propaganda in favor of private consumption, to the virtual exclusion of and harm to public purposes. Constant advertisement for private consumption undermines a sense of being part of the public, separates people, and makes defense of public goods and efforts to meet common needs difficult. Within this environment Keynesian fiscal policy cannot solve economic and social problems. "[I]ncreased production is not the final test of social achievement, the solvent of all social ills," because it cannot eliminate shared, communal problems such as deteriorated public services and facilities, pollution, and poverty among those unable to participate fully in a competitive economy, and it cannot address inequality of market power: "in starving our public services and in placing so much of our faith in the general curative powers of increased production, we were inviting grave social ills." Even the subordinate position of women in 1970s America served planning system needs.[48]

Classical, neoclassical, supply-side, and other contemporary conservative theories of political economy justify and accelerate significant economic, and in some cases social and political, inequality.[49] Again and again Galbraith returns to the central tradition's repeated celebration of inequality, which he sees as linked to ideological reasoning. The two-hundred-year-old task of defending inequality has "commanded some of the greatest, or in any case some of the most ingenious, talent of the economics profession." Supply-side economics is simply the most recent example. Galbraith identifies many defenses of inequality: encouragement of work, investment, capital formation, and savings; assurance of the survival of the fittest and belief that hardship culls out the weak; God's blessing on the wealthy; "natural law and equity"; the notion that equality promotes uniformity; criticism that equality is "spiritually suspect" and "unworkable"; assertions that too much equality exists; the iron law of wages; the view that good fortune is earned and that people deserve their fate; the absolution of the affluent from any moral responsibility for others; consumer sovereignty; and (the oldest and most influential justification) preservation of freedom. Although some of these arguments may have had partial validity in a poorer society, Galbraith rejects each justification, though not all inequality.[50]

Galbraith is impressed by the power of forces defending inequality, appalled at the end of equality as a major social-political issue, and convinced that he was wrong when he said in *Affluent Society* that inequality was being solved.[51] Equality has many possible meanings, though Galbraith rarely explores these. Critics of equality frequently charge that it requires identical results or treatment for all, a concept Galbraith rejects. Once again, his focus is on correcting failures in existing theory, policy, and the economic system. Unnecessary inequality is one of the gravest intrinsic ills in planning system dominance: "income inequality [is] inherent in capitalism" fostering other forms of inequality, including a seemingly permanent underclass, division of society, a "laager mentality," and the probability of "increasingly oppressive authority in areas of urban desolation." Such effects of inequality confront us with "the most serious social problem of the time," and "the greatest threat to long-run peace and civility." The neoclassical expectation that markets and economic growth lead to more equality—a claim that undermines "the moral energy of belief" in reform—is proved wrong by growing inequality.[52]

The power of the planning system is a major obstacle to equalization, and establishing identical policies for everyone perpetuates inequality. Economic growth is important but does not in itself reduce inequality. Market forces cannot and will not end inequality. Deliberate public efforts are required: "in the absence of energetic reform, the tendency of the economy is to one comparatively affluent, one comparatively impoverished working force." Current wage differentials are "egregious and indefensible" and are not based on the rarity of executive talent. If we want to promote equality, "a reasonably equal distribution of income is superior to an unequal distribution which is then remedied by taxation." Still, "progressive taxation is indispensable in the civilizing effort to attain a greater measure of equality in the planning system."[53] Galbraith sees inequality as such a serious problem between the planning and market parts of the economy that he proposes public intervention to make the market system more competitive with and more nearly equal to the planning system.[54]

How far equal opportunity extends and what happens to those unable to compete successfully are important measures of an author's seriousness about equality. Galbraith favors a hard equality of opportunity, beyond identical treatment by the law and the opening of careers on the basis of talent. Active efforts to ensure that people can compete are necessary; and for those who cannot, Galbraith defends an extensive safety net, including "*provision of a guaranteed or alternative income as a matter of right to those who cannot find employment*," though like the others in this book he is less interested in establishing welfare systems than in changing the political economy to promote individuality and human welfare. He has argued for major financial and human investment in education, focusing first on the poorest parts of the United States. In the 1970s, he defended affirmative action for women and racial minorities because the planning system was not and is not today adequately subject to the market, and then as now the market—contrary to conservative claims—neither punished nor removed discrimination. "When the effects of past discrimination have been erased . . . selection can become blind. But only then."[55] This link between equality and market failure contains an unarticulated theory of social justice.[56] For Galbraith, as for Reich, "[t]he reasonable goal of an economic system is one that allows all individuals to pursue socially benign personal goals regardless of sex" or race.

Inequality based on accidents of power, birth, or place must be reduced. Because Galbraith is willing to make interpersonal utility comparisons, he argues that equalization promotes individual and social welfare, improves economic performance and stability, and reduces the threat of recession or depression. "Income inequality . . . distorts the use of resources," shifting them from the needs of the many to the discretion of the few. Genuine risk, intelligence, and hard work—not positions of power—are legitimate sources of income differences.[57]

Given unequal power, public policy is not neutral. Its impact is unequal, depending on one's power position, reinforcing Galbraith's claim that society must choose who benefits and who does not. The lack of balance he discusses in *Affluent Society* reflects unequal power. Policy serves first the needs of the planning system and those with influence. Thus, public policy has been "relatively comprehensive" where the interest of the "contented" is concerned, but "relatively limited" for the poor. It frequently addresses problems caused by or important to the planning system and ignores the resulting impact on the rest of society. For example, monetary policy has high social costs such as unemployment and unequal impact between the planning and market systems. It reduces investment especially in the market part of the economy, creates unemployment, discriminates "against the small businessman," and most sharply affects "those least able to bear it." It favors "those with money. . . . [and] is also a very crude, imperfect and unscientific way of guiding an economy." Monetary policy is acceptable to those with power, because, Galbraith claims, it hardly affects them, or does so only after having a much deeper impact on others, and it is permissible to conventional political-economic theorists because it seemingly requires little government involvement.[58]

Justifying Active Government: Positive Social Ends

A narrow concept of market failure provides little justification for public intervention into the economy, beyond perhaps macro-economic regulation. As a result, government necessarily has a restricted role, regardless of social-political conditions. Defending public action in terms of market failure broadly understood allows a wider but still restricted range of legitimate government activities. Galbraith's discussion of the social-political impact of markets forms a continuum with his argument for positive good from public activity. Galbraith contends that private consumption is not the only desirable end. There is a public sector where we must act if we are to live well;[59] a realm where people share and can achieve common interests beyond putatively private consumption, buying, selling, and seeking fulfillment in these activities. Public action to achieve public goods beyond the sum of private goods is legitimate. Public interest is more than a temporary coincidence of private interests, and a collective public exists distinct from the separate individuals of whom it is composed. Moreover what is advantageous to private interests may not be so to the public. Public and private, individual and community interest can clash. Need for government grows as society and organization become more complex, so that organization and government expand together. Because some ends can be pursued only through public action, the classic liberal-libertarian limits on government's role (based on reaction against rapacious kings enriching themselves at public expense) must be abandoned in favor of meeting urgent needs resulting from new wealth.[60] Galbraith's discussion of conservation has wider application. Individuals need do little planning beyond their own, or their family's lifetime. "No one can deplore as prodigal an action that will reduce an individual's income a hundred years hence; no one can condone action which will impoverish the community a hundred years from now." Who is to protect public interest? Not the market. "It is on the state that the public must rely for the assertion of the public interest."[61]

Galbraith's argument confronts us with "fundamental value choices."[62] How will we, as a "good society," employ resources that are socially produced? What is needed for the good life? Once basic necessities are met people "begin to desire other things. . . . services which must be rendered collectively, although they enter the general scheme of wants after the immediate physical necessities, increase in urgency more than proportionally with increasing wealth." For Galbraith, as for Reich, this means increasing public investment and provision of goods and services. Galbraith argues for a better balance than now exists between private production and public investment and goods. A proper balance is even more important than increasing equality through the tax system or tax reduction. "A well rounded or balanced life consists of both" private goods and "[c]ommunity goods and services." Maintaining this balance is crucial. Society is directly and indirectly harmed by lack of balance between private and public production. Many "social disorders . . . are the counterpart of the present imbalance." Failure "to expand public production" causes missed "opportunities for enjoyment which otherwise we might have had."[63]

Again ideology, power, and the economic structure obstruct socially desirable action. Liberals, conservatives, and economists of all persuasions are overwhelmingly preoccupied with production for the sake of output and jobs. This was necessary up through the 1930s; but given our relative wealth, private production as the highest social goal should be replaced by attention to a better life, real individuality, and more social balance. This is not a prescription for zero growth but a serious assessment of how wealth is and should be employed. The presumptions that private production responds to autonomous consumer wants, that it is paramount—"a moral sanction"—and that (except when directed toward defense) public investment and public goods are suspect, wasteful, and need special apology, invite "grave social ills."[64]

Equality, democracy, "quality of life," security, social stability, reduced social tension,[65] and freedom illustrate nonmaterial positive social goods. Galbraith rejects the view that the market is the primary arena for and bulwark of freedom—conceived of as allowing people to use their property as they wish in pursuit of self-interest—and that government is the principal impediment to freedom. To the contrary, economic relations can undermine freedom as much as oppressive government. Planning system power and inequality severely compromise the market as an agent of freedom. A strong element of ability— "an exercise-concept"[66]—informs Galbraith's image of freedom. Actual freedom is contingent on removal of legal obstacles *and* on a reasonable opportunity to succeed. Freedom must include the conditions under which people exercise freedom, people's capacity to act, a reasonable chance of success, and enjoyment of a wider sphere of activity than only protection from physical coercion. Having an income is one of the first and most important freedoms because it confers status, allows participation in market and society, provides some independence, and promotes self-development. Poverty circumscribes freedom. The conservative fear that "the state might reach out and destroy the vigorous, money-making entrepreneur" misunderstands the real problem. Danger lies in uniting business interests with the state and in subordinating individuals to organization. Freedom requires "emancipation of belief. . . . to win freedom from the doctrines that, if accepted, put people in the service not of themselves but of the planning system."[67]

Freedom for Galbraith is both negative—allowing wide scope for independent action and autonomy—and positive—in ensuring the basic resources and social structure necessary to protect negative freedom and promote individual and common ends. Galbraith hopes that people will make better use of their opportunities, but he will not and cannot impose his preferences, even while declaring that consumerism "is a false ideal . . . that leisure, free time and intellectual achievement are the real thing."[68] Providing the resources needed to reach some self-chosen ends recognizes—even while deploring consumerism and imbalance—that imposing a pattern of life destroys the other conditions of freedom. Freedom does not contain any notion of transcendent ends or of forcing people to be free.

As with other reform liberals, Galbraith considers freedom context-dependent and multidimensional. Depending on circumstances, government and private power, market and polity can be obstacles. Expanding available choices enhances freedom, permitting people to develop more autonomy by resisting control. In this process, government can play an important role. Autonomy and choice may be seen as negative forms of freedom, but their attainment requires reorientation of active public policy, and they are directed toward the private sphere. In this context, any form of social equality, such as women's rights, is freedom-enhancing. Galbraith does not directly address conservative claims that welfare reduces taxpayers' freedom, and he would dismiss as nonsense the proposition that it obstructs recipients' freedom. If having an income is crucial to being free, welfare programs—like affluence, generally—are freedom-enhancing because they expand choice and remove the compulsion of taking work at any wage under any conditions, thus allowing "escape from the compensatory power once associated in compelling form with property." Policies countering depressions, creating minimum-wage laws, requiring more flexible hours, establishing social insurance, and supporting the market system or slum renewal enlarge choice and reduce costs of resisting control by others. Intervention is not contrary to economic freedom but may promote freedom in other ways. Even farm price support programs can expand freedom. "Freedom is served in different ways. . . . Farmers who" kept "their farms" with government aid in the 1930s "preserved a degree of freedom and economic independence that would hardly have been theirs if the government had not intervened."[69]

In the absence of a classical free market, economic freedom must encompass more than allowing the market free reign, so that market freedom does not trump other aspects of freedom. For instance, individual small entrepreneurs often face severely limited options because others exercise power over them. Economic freedom is an active concept that requires extensive public participation and the curbing of corporate power over workers and consumers if it is to be realized. It "is a two-dimensional concept." First it consists of "a free choice in economic matters"—a point with which conservative economists agree. But Galbraith departs from economic orthodoxy by insisting that free choice means "The individual must be able to resist the control by others of these [livelihood, use of income, and so on] decisions," to which his later work adds grinding poverty and pressure to consume. Second, there must be "an [effective] opportunity to choose." Although his 1954 examples are innocuous, his later work incorporates "avenues for self-expression" and resistance against planning system control. Economic freedom is a pragmatic concept where restraint on some may increase freedom of others. Often, cumulative individual and social choice determines which restraints are allowed. Labor unions, farm organizations, or small business associations, by resisting pressure to conform to power, may enhance the freedom of their members.[70]

Resistance to manipulation also strengthens individuality. Like all liberals, Galbraith honors individuality, linking it to freedom. Unfortunately, laissez-faire individualism too frequently limits itself to attacking government, ignoring real opportunities and positions, and opening those without power to abuse and restraint in an economic system that requires suppression of individuality for its operation. Galbraith and Dewey agree that organization power is the main danger to individuality, but Galbraith adds two other obstacles: conformity to conventional wisdom, and ideological obsolescence. Individualism is an inclusive, result-oriented concept that active government can promote. This image is distinct from individualism in classical and neoclassical economic theory, where it stands for the right to compete with whatever resources one can command. Galbraith believes that economic power is a prime obstacle to the development of personality, but he holds that the principal purpose of organization should be to champion individuals—their interaction, happiness, and safety. Individualism should mean that individuals are ends in themselves, not instruments of private or public bureaucracy. This requires release from constraint, even to the point of changing the structure of work options, adding leisure so that people can cultivate interests other than work, "development of personality," and "opportunity for the individual to fashion his own existence." It includes growth and self-discipline. In an argument similar to Dewey's and Hobhouse's, and to a lesser extent Reich's and Thurow's, Galbraith asserts that improving individuals improves society. Planning and government intervention—denounced by conservatives as collectivist—help individuals escape subordination if accompanied by understanding, skepticism, and "political pluralism."[71]

Capitalism has been successful, but less so than conservatives claim, especially in its social, political, and cultural effects. Failures in such areas as substandard housing, inadequate health care, unemployment, poverty, neglect of public goods, and subordination of individuals to organization need correction. However, the market remains a necessary social and political instrument. As noted above, Galbraith wants to make the market work better and recommends employing public policy to strengthen the market part of the economy against the highly organized part. This has been a theme of his since the 1930s and includes his major arguments, from countervailing power to the new industrial state. For providing mass consumer goods, nothing can substitute for the market and its coordinating, decentralizing role. But this role is neither the controlling coordination claimed by F. A. Hayek and Milton Friedman nor the conscious power elite of C. Wright Mills. Under the best of circumstances, the market needs public guidance.[72]

The inseparability of politics from economics means that the conservative argument that government intervention always fails is simplistic and overstated. Galbraith acknowledges government fails. But the cause is not mass-based groups pressuring government to loot the wealthy minority; it is bureaucratic symbiosis and the frequent actions of large business against the public interest. The planning system's capture of government and government's responsiveness to the powerful, rather than to those in need, are persistent themes. But there is hope. People need not tolerate bad conditions, do nothing, or pretend that the market produces optimal results. "The role of government, when one contemplates reform, is a dual one. The government is a major part of the problem; it is also central to the remedy." Today, market failure is a more serious problem. "The . . . modern capitalist, or more precisely the modern mixed economy all but exclusively involves the role of government." To think otherwise is to take "a highly selective view of the role of the state," in which benefits to the powerful and contented are normal while all other programs require a rigorous burden of proof. Much of the inadequacy of public policies lies in the attitude that government must fail, and many failed programs have been administered by their opponents. Moreover, economic criteria alone are insufficient bases for judging welfare, regulation, and intervention.[73]

That government has done much good—saving capitalism during the Depression to expanding educational opportunities—and is capable of still more is central to Galbraith's argument. Again he claims that needs and therefore relevant policies have changed. Echoing Dewey, "'Where,' someone will ask, 'is the Jeffersonian principle that the government governs best which governs least?' The answer is that urbanization destroyed the society where that rule was possible. And that it would do so was well recognized by Jefferson himself."[74] Without denying that public policies fail, saying that government must fail, as opposed to saying that it may fail, is heavily freighted with ideological presuppositions: competitive self-interest, narrow negative freedom, and strong preference for "private" action. For Galbraith, government does not replace the market, even when it extensively supplements it; and economy should not replace government. Economy and polity are not either-or phenomenon but parts of a continuum of possibilities. The crucial question is who will exercise power: large organizational interests for themselves, or the public through government. The latter will sometimes achieve public interest; the former, expressed only through private interest and consumption, almost never will.

Role of Government

Government's proper role depends on the problems and public capabilities one envisions. Galbraith embodies twentieth-century reform liberal expansion of government. "It would be better had we accorded the modern state the position in principle that it must have in practice. Then we would not have to be defensive about its role." "Good government is a good thing. Government services are not a threat to our liberties. Not dangerous forms of collectivism." The market cannot solve our problems. "All that remains is the state."[75] The power structure and economic system generate major social-political problems that can be addressed only through public—that is, government—action. "The line between public and private activity" shifts and changes. "[T]radition, ideological preference, social urgency and political convenience" help define the public and private spheres. More importantly "functions accrue to the state because, as a purely technical matter, there is no alternative to public management."[76] This applies to redressing the imbalance between private consumption and public services, thereby achieving more equality, and expanding opportunities, as well as to such mundane matters as building roads for increasing numbers of private automobiles and sanitation facilities for the disposal of private consumption detritus.

Galbraith recognizes few hard-and-fast rules as to when government should intervene. His guide is a simple, unanalyzed pragmatism that slights both the laissez-faire ideological challenge and the conflict over ends. Government action is not inherently good or bad. "The test of public action is a practical one. If needful good can be achieved only by government, or if it can be better achieved by government, the responsibility should be theirs." Each act of government can "be judged on its merits" if such acts "are viewed comprehensively." But this leaves unspoken the underlying assumptions about "needful good" and "merits." Nevertheless, one cannot determine in advance the most important problem, such as inflation or recession. "Policy must always be against whichever one has." There are no perfect solutions. Any answer generates other problems. Neither point should prevent reform, however, if policy provides some improvement over existing conditions.[77]

Galbraith has recommended a wide range of policies. Many of his proposals aim at restoring what he calls social balance and promoting individuality. Galbraith has argued for farm price supports; until 1985, wage and price controls in the planning part of the economy, as a more equitable way than monetary and fiscal policy to deal with inflation and inequality; various types of public planning; expanded welfare programs, which influenced anti-poverty policy in the 1960s; reduction in the size and scope of the American military; numerous development proposals; more extensive regulation of pollution; massive aid to education; urban reform; redressing inequality of private power; aid and support for the arts; promotion and regulation of aggregate demand and macro-economic performance; a more progressive tax system; more and "scrupulous regulation"; and enlarged regulation of economic speculation.[78] Interested in yet critical of socialism, and skeptical of public ownership, he has been willing to countenance limited public ownership where public-private symbiosis has gone far.[79] His reasons for tending to oppose tax reductions illustrate the positive role he envisions for government.

Galbraith opposed the 1964 tax cut, as well as those of the early 1980s, because of his broad picture of the public sphere and of shared responsibilities. Galbraith believes that, if fiscal stimulus is necessary, it is better to increase public spending for public needs than to reduce taxes. Tax cuts take resources from public services, increasing the imbalance between satisfying public and private needs, while doing little to address economic and social inequality. Public spending tends to benefit those with less, promoting equalization and, Galbraith believes, social tranquility. Tax cuts emphasize private consumption of private goods, rather than public spending on shared needs, which further separates people and requires expanded public services to support private consumption. Frequently, tax reduction is an "excuse for holding back on the needed tasks of government." Finally, increasing the demand for planning system goods enhances the power and prestige of those at the top of the planning system, allowing them still more penetration of the political system. For Galbraith, a substantial public sector is essential if government is to provide the countercyclical intervention demanded by large businesses.[80]

Galbraith favors an evolutionary, not a revolutionary approach to change: "my instinct is for action within the political framework." "For better or for worse I am a reformer and not a revolutionist." His desire to work within the system—even when opposing the war in Vietnam or supporting public control over the planning system—limits the scope of possible reform. Reform is a slow process, requires compromise and distinguishing "between what might be perfect and what is achievable," and "is not served by jumping rapidly from one issue to another." Though once active in politics, Galbraith does not have a theory of government, and he uses state and government virtually interchangeably. Lacking a clear theory of the nature of government, Galbraith provides stronger arguments for public action than proposed means to accomplish his ends. His policy prescriptions are often modest compared to the boldness of his criticism and analysis. In *Economics and the Public Purpose*, he offers "A General Theory of Reform"; but this overly ambitious phrase, echoing Keynes' *General Theory*, does not fulfill its promise. What

follows is more a discussion and listing of problems, goals, and needed policies, together with general statements of the basis and structure of reform,
than a theory or detailed strategy of reform. Political specifics are missing.
Unlike conservative economists, Galbraith does not recommend structural
political changes. Pursuing reform does, however, require emancipating the
state. By this he means freeing government from the overwhelming influence of the planning system and its interests, creating instead a "public state"
that is responsive to the needs of the broad public and of the market system.
Unfortunately, he does not develop the political-social details of this public
state, except to argue that reform must begin with the legislature.[81]

Government has the capacity to be independent of corporate bureaucracy because government is also organized and bureaucratic. Indeed public organization and bureaucracy, developed in response to private power
and bureaucracy, make "the state extensively the instrument of its own purposes." The vagueness of this statement is disturbing. Despite his inten-
tion—that government can be independent of corporate power—the
statement seems to imply the state is independent of popular control but,
like corporations, is subject to bureaucracy. Such control weakens reformers' ability to employ government for their ends unless they capture the
bureaucracy—which happened during Galbraith's tenure in government—
or to make it in the interest of the bureaucracy to foster reform. For incom-
pletely specified reasons, Galbraith, who is more worried than Keynes about
dangers of public and private bureaucracy, believes "the autonomous
processes of government. . . . [need not be] socially inimical. On the contrary, it serves the highest civilized purposes—protection of the people from
hardship, exploitation, and abuse . . . regulation of the exercise of condign
power . . . advancement of knowledge . . . arts." Galbraith claims he does
"not pass judgment on" the "social merits" or "legitimacy" of such
processes.[82] Government is not simply the extension of society nor the neutral balancer of group conflict, as in simple pictures of pluralism. It can have
an active, partly independent role, and it can serve the public interest, not
just the interest of the powerful.

How is emancipation—making the public and the government autonomous of the planning system—to be accomplished? Here again Galbraith
offers an outline. Ideas are crucial. "Reform begins. . . . with belief," not
"with laws and the government." And belief is altered by circumstance.
Echoing centuries of liberal argument, Galbraith asserts that reason and
education can effectuate reform. People must emancipate themselves from
identifying planning system purposes with public good. This requires
"knowledge of the forces by which one is constrained . . . [as] the first step
toward freedom" and "some political force for accomplishing what the plan-

ning system ignores and, indeed, holds to be unimportant." Who or what is this? Assuming that education is more autonomous of corporate influence and conventional wisdom than it is, Galbraith concludes, "It is to the educational and scientific estate . . . that we must turn for the requisite political initiative." Education and science are in touch with reality. They have the best chance of seeing through the cloud of corporate influence and identifying the public interest. Through "social invention" they can "emancipate belief," on which all reform depends. Galbraith says large corporations and concentrations of power cannot be dismantled or eliminated, but they can be neutralized through an understanding of their behavior and power, which is the key to advancing public control over the planning system. This means resisting bureaucratic and executive pronouncements until these are demonstrated in the public interest, rejecting belief that "economic goals are the only goals of the society," and (as with Voltaire or Veblen) attacking the bases for beliefs that support present attitudes.[83]

Emancipating belief is a necessary though not sufficient step, but Galbraith does not fully address how it is to be accomplished and what is to be done next; though thinking, education, reform, and pluralism are essential components. Nor will education or analysis, on his own evidence of power-serving scholarship and ideology, necessarily lead to emancipation. Given his limited institutional mechanisms for reform, Galbraith depends on a combination of circumstance and alternative proposals to convince people to demand change. Once this is accomplished, however, he offers few specifics on what to do next. He is not alone. Other liberals offer a program not a platform. Conservative political-economics also fails to provide a convincing answer. Marx depended on a virtual miracle. But Galbraith hopes for reform.[84] In leaving us with well-defined goals but an incomplete map to pursue them, he leaves us to face the same problem as did Enlightenment theorists such as Voltaire and Diderot: what do we put in place of the errors that are removed through enlightenment? Galbraith seems to believe people might discover in themselves and in interaction with others the richness and potential of personality and real individuality, but he does not develop this possibility.

Emancipation requires a stronger, more participatory democracy, but Galbraith has not incorporated expansive democratic procedures into his proposals. Only recently has he argued for making democracy more "inclusive" and that creation of a good society requires "a more nearly perfect expression of democratic will." This requires at least two things: development of and commitment to the values for which he has argued throughout his career, and organization, especially among the poor and those committed to improvement, to ensure that all citizens vote. But Galbraith does not fully link his concern for economic power with democracy or political equality, although he occasionally discusses the impact of money on politics. He believes that the state is not entirely dominated by corporate interests—even when large organizations, necessary for other purposes, escape democratic control—but instead can have an independent and public role that a strict reading of his own analysis would seem to deny. The franchise is a potentially independent "claim on the powers of the government."[85]

At the heart of Galbraith's democracy are open, effective elections and the right to criticize government, supplemented by freedom, equality, and personal development. Criticism of government becomes the equivalent of consent, since an informed and frequently protesting public is the primary limit on government power. Thus democracy is both a procedure for selecting those who govern and is goal-oriented. Given his stress on circumstances, Galbraith believes that democracy will emerge in nondemocratic systems as those societies become more open, as contributions are needed from more people, and as the process of development creates classes of people who demand a greater voice in how they and others are governed.[86]

But all is not well. Democratic government is necessary for economic progress, but the problems Galbraith discusses compromise its possibilities. Our problem is not democracy "but that democracy is imperfect." The United States does not embrace "the interests and votes of all the citizens." It has become "a democracy of the contented and the comfortable." They "monopolize or largely monopolize the political franchise," while "the uncomfortable and the distressed do not have candidates who represent their needs and so they do not vote." Alienated, their interests are ignored. Military power remains uncontrolled, and "the greater power of democratic process and constraint has yet to be proved." Monetary policy—which Galbraith generally opposes—and bank regulation are "partially outside the democratic process" yet he finds no satisfactory way to incorporate them into democracy. Inflation undermines the public services that hold a democracy together.[87]

Planning system power is a huge dilemma for democracy, with profound and threatening implications for popular control. Unlike Brandeis, Galbraith hardly analyzes the relation between private power and democracy, and has not connected power to his hope for democratic development in Eastern Europe. For Galbraith, disappearance of classical competition and development of planning system power mean that the market cannot be democratic. Corporate managers are usually "responsible only to themselves," a fact often concealed by "democratic liturgy," which becomes subversive of democratic processes. In union with government bureaucracies, corporate elites make decisions affecting the entire nation. The classic democratic model does not hold. Citizens are not fully sovereign. Lack of consumer sovereignty parallels and reinforces lack of citizen sovereignty, but Galbraith does not develop this as part of his picture of democracy. Although organizations compete for voters, confining myths and conditioned power obscure the reality of private power.[88] This undermines his hope for emancipation. If demand and public opinion are developed, shaped by, and ultimately subservient to corporate interests—even when not directly political, as with emphasis on private consumption—public opinion is not autonomous and cannot independently shape policy. Even the hope for effective pluralism is weakened by unequal power, unequal access to decision makers, and manipulation of opinion and demand.

Other theorists surveying similar circumstances find the solution in participatory and/or economic democracy. Participatory democracy has no single meaning, but it frequently includes worker involvement in corporate decision making, as for Brandeis. Galbraith advocates expanded electoral democracy, not participatory democracy, and doubts that narrow pictures of economic democracy would be effective; yet stronger democracy could aid emancipation. His analysis of power precludes one of the most common suggestions: placing worker and citizen representatives on boards of directors. This conveys no popular control, Galbraith argues, because there is no real power at this level. Rather power resides in the technostructure, which is immune in most day-to-day decisions from such outside intervention. Moreover, unless they formed a majority, these representatives would be isolated and subject to co-option.[89] This argument also undermines hope for popular control over government bureaucracy. There, too, a few citizen representatives are unlikely to exercise real power. Galbraith's criticism of how democracy operates in the United States gives few clues about how these problems might be addressed and little vindication for more expansive democracy. Thus, the basic institutions of democracy remain. Galbraith would eliminate none of them, but he offers little hope for the mass public to gain control. Realizing that one's power is lost despite the pretense that one has power is potentially liberating. The problem is how to realize that potential.

Conclusions

Galbraith presents a fundamental criticism of conservative political economy and of Republican Party ideology at the end of the twentieth century—not a call for revolution, nationalization, or immediate redistribution of power. With Keynes, Galbraith expands the economic limits to political possibility, justifying more active government. Intervention is legitimate because narrowly framed economic goals do not trump all other considerations. Because producers not consumers are sovereign, one cannot claim that intervention to address social-political problems abrogates consumer sovereignty and is thus inherently undemocratic or elitist. Freedom is not protected by laissez-faire policy; to the contrary, it is left undefended before private power.

Galbraith epitomizes reform liberalism even while criticizing many aspects of liberalism. In its failure to grow and offer better alternatives, liberalism is part of the problem. "In the Western-style economies the belief required by the planning system is achieved in the name of liberalism." But Galbraith does not abandon liberalism. Some observers see his unwillingness to embrace a more radical perspective, such as socialism or even European-style social democracy as a failure, at least of nerve.[90] But Galbraith like the others believes the core values of liberalism are the only means by which problems can be addressed. "[B]ecause liberalism is a cover for convenient belief, liberalism is not wrong. The remedy is not illiberal suppression of the techniques for compelling belief but a truly liberal resistance to such belief."[91] We must learn to cope with large size, organization, and the consequences of power, because a return to the innocence of an ideally competitive system is impossible. In classic liberal fashion, Galbraith believes that liberation comes through education, emancipation of perception and opinion, and faithful adherence to representative democracy. Contrary to Lockean and laissez-faire models, equality, freedom, opportunity, and choice require government involvement in economics. In place of a market model of the relation between politics and economics, Galbraith argues for active government that is more democratic than that found in classical, neoclassical and laissez-faire liberalism or their political-economies. He is also more attuned to the social-political costs of economic relations. This frequently necessitates employing government to achieve desired economic and social goals, expand opportunities, and reduce the harmful impact of economic dislocation. The political mechanism for accomplishing this, however, remains unclear especially in face of the need to convince business people to go along if Galbraith's goals are to be realized.

5

Lester Thurow:
Drift, Gridlock, and Equity

... when one is unemployed one loses one's standing in America.
—Judith N. Shklar, *American Citizenship*

PLACING HIM at the end of a list of "a younger generation of economists" who question and amend the neoclassical model, Galbraith calls Lester Thurow (b. 1938) "marginally more orthodox."[1] Despite, or perhaps because of, being "more orthodox" Thurow acknowledges and reinterprets liberal tradition into what he sees as radically altered conditions that require new ideas and responses to achieve growth and an equitable society. His orthodoxy lies in accepting a larger role for the market (than some of the other theorists considered here) and not calling for major political or social restructuring. Thurow is not as overtly political as Galbraith or Reich, presenting his economic argument in economic more than in social-political terms. His later work addresses justice less than his earlier work, but he is cognizant of the political content and implications of his and others' economic proposals, and has regularly advised Democrats. Thurow is on Galbraith's list because Thurow rejects classical, neoclassical, supply-side, and monetarist belief that the market is autonomous and self-stabilizing at a politically viable level. Along with Robert Reich he represents contemporary liberal, political-economic response and alternatives to resurgent conservatism, relative economic decline, and growing inequality. Thurow achieved prominence with publication of *The Zero-Sum Society* [1980] in which he argued that the inability to fairly allocate costs and benefits is a major reason the United States economy is not performing well. He holds an M.A. from Oxford and a Ph.D. from Harvard. Thurow was on the staff of President Johnson's Council of Economic Advisors and also advised Paul Tsongas. He teaches at the Massachusetts Institute of Technology and was dean of the Sloan School of Management at Massachusetts Institute of Technology from 1987 to 1993. Thurow calls for significant though not fundamental changes in American business and the economy. He recognizes that political legitimacy and economic policy are interrelated, fears that the social and political results of market relations can be disastrous, and advocates actively employing government to stabilize and reform capitalism, create more equity, and increase social justice.

The post–World War II, liberal international regime, and in a strong sense the domestic regime also, has ended. America has a critical problem: "America is now a First World economy with a large, growing Third World economy in its midst."[2] The situation Galbraith implicitly assumed in the 1950s and 1960s is gone. With the collapse of European communism, the international economy is the primary competitive arena, and the United States is not well positioned to compete. Rapid American growth and relatively easy economic and political dominance for the twenty-five years after World War II cannot be revived. American mastery of world markets is disappearing, competition increasing, technological supremacy in civilian goods vanishing, and the infrastructure decaying. American workers are no longer the best educated, and labor-management relations in America are more adversarial than those in most major economic rivals. Balance of payments problems and budget deficits reflect political and economic unwillingness and inability to cope with new conditions. As with Reich, Thurow argues that two fundamental changes have occurred. The first is international. The United States, irrevocably enmeshed in the world economy, is losing control over its domestic economic and social welfare policy. The second related problem is domestic. The United States is increasingly dividing along economic lines, with the top 20 percent gaining income and wealth and the bottom 60 percent losing real income over the last twenty years. As inequality grows and willingness to help others decreases, those at the bottom face an increasingly hopeless situation. "History is far from over. A new competitive phase is even now under way." Conflict and national decline are real possibilities.[3]

Americans can compete. The choice is how. The current course forces wages down for more and more people, creating worse conditions of homelessness, poverty, family breakup, falling income, inequality, low growth, and despair. The laissez-faire capitalist market alone cannot solve these problems, and our situation is generating zero-sum conflict that has important domestic and international political implications. Zero-sum conflict occurs when important changes produce different groups of winners and losers, and losers, who are not compensated for their losses, oppose change. Past success and present conditions require changing older ideas and policies: "new realities force the creation of new virtues—new procedures, new rules, and new institutions." Leaving the economy alone accepts "a standard of living that gradually falls relative to the world's industrial leaders," causing loss of economic, political, and eventually military leadership.[4] In this environment, achieving social justice, more equality, and the common good—much less maintaining democracy and past economic gains—becomes difficult and less probable.

Failures of Dominant Economic Theory

To criticize claims that market behavior spontaneously produces order or to argue that leaving things alone is inadequate to address current and developing problems, is not to reject a coordinating role for markets. As did Keynes, Thurow believes, "One cannot fight the market, but one can channel it." The market is, however, deeply flawed as a social instrument, and widely accepted market theory is deficient in its fundamental assumptions, its understanding of behavior, and its policy applications. As with the others in this book, Thurow presents a multidimensional criticism of laissez-faire theory. He explicitly rejects the dominant market or price-auction image in contemporary political economy, arguing it has produced political, social, and economic failure, placing economic theory and public policy in fundamental disarray.[5]

For Thurow, it is legitimate to consider political and social factors in evaluating economic theories, problems, and policies. The market does not automatically solve problems or settle controversies in nonpolitical or socially and politically acceptable ways. Ignoring linkages between economics and politics fosters bad public policy and ultimately undermines economic success. "[R]elative economic decline has both economic and political impacts." Americans are accustomed neither to foreign living standards rising faster than their own nor to growing domestic inequality. Expanding income gaps and falling standards may be politically contained in a dictatorship but strain democracy, generating a search for scapegoats. As belief in neutral markets that fairly distribute rewards declines, government is attacked and often expected to intervene, further straining a political system that has never had to allocate gains *and* losses. Yet such equity issues are the essence of contemporary decision making.[6]

The dominant model "assumes that economic events never have social consequences," only individual, and ignores that "slow productivity growth is apt to produce unacceptable social and political results." Families are "destroyed . . . by a modern economic system that is not congruent with 'family values.'" Governments can lose office. People demand more security. "Renewed class warfare" is possible. Radical alternatives may appear attractive. Violence may result. Democracy is threatened. Political reaction is inevitable and economists must recognize it is more than just a market imperfection. "[S]ocial and political concerns," "constraints," and intervention are always part of economics because stable economies "are needed to serve social and political purposes and because economic outcomes have an impact, sometimes a heavy one, on social and political events." Once unrest actually develops, "it will be very difficult to solve." Prevention always costs less politically than remediation, but, given dominant economic ideas and current political stalemate, Thurow fears we will not face our problems. He asks us to imagine people—such as many "in South Central Los Angeles in 1992"—with few skills, less opportunity, incomplete work experience, and "no economic future in America." What will happen to them? They will not just go away. How will they react? We? Deficiencies in collective organization, not individual moral failure cause their economic problems. Fighting inflation with recession also risks social unrest. As Galbraith and Keynes observe on deflation, "we draft inflation fighters in a very uneven pattern." Each group does not pay the same costs. Anti-inflation policies weigh most on the unskilled, young, and minorities, producing deep-felt grievances against the system.[7]

Thurow claims the accepted model disguises reality. Facts and changed circumstances "are very difficult to deal with when they conflict with both theory and previous experience." Accommodating reality is painful because one must give up comfortable ideas. Because people wish to retain beliefs that once accorded with conditions, they "spend long periods of time pretending that the facts that conflict with their theories don't exist, hoping that such facts will somehow magically go away, or denying that the facts conflict with their theoretical views of the world in any important way."[8] Laissez-faire is such an image of reality. As in Dewey and Keynes, it was once reasonably congruent with economic need and social-political reality but is increasingly divorced from successful foreign practice, modern political conditions including democracy, and current domestic problems. "The equilibrium price-auction view of the world. . . . is . . . also a political philosophy, often becoming something approaching a religion." It "has become an ideology rather than a set of working hypotheses."[9]

Starting assumptions are crucial because they shape how one sees and understands the world, determine where one puts the burden of proof, and structure allowable public policies. Common price-auction assumptions, some of which "are absurd," illustrate what Thurow sees as ideological thinking and an inability to address "mushy reality." Too many of its fundamental concepts cannot be proven wrong. Ideas such as utility and psychic income are "nonobservable" and allow any activity to be counted as maximizing individual utility. Individual decisions cannot be questioned because whatever a person does maximizes his or her self-determined self-interest. Many assumptions apply only in limited circumstances that do not reflect the entire political-economy. Actual behavioral theories are missing. "Too much of real individual behavior . . . is unexplained or explained away." "[D]eviant observations" are dismissed, often with inconsistent theories. Realities such as labor unions, which have persisted for generations, are considered market imperfections making it unnecessary to incorporate them into the dominant model. While internally consistent, "unobservable" concepts rob the model of "empirical content," yet its adherents try to adjust reality to theory, not theory to reality. Assumptions that the market achieves equilibrium ignore how long it takes, "what happens during the period of adjustment (disequilibrium) and how that period affects the future course of the economy." There are real costs that losers oppose, and recurrent shocks may prevent the economy from ever reaching acceptable equilibrium. "If Newton and his contemporaries . . . had had access to the modern computer" and behaved as contemporary economists do, "it is likely that the law of gravity would never have been discovered" because "deviant celestial" observations could be explained by adding "another epicycle to the system. Given enough epicycles, all patterns were theoretically explainable."[10]

Thurow agrees with Dewey and Galbraith that "economists can't find hard empirical constants. . . . When the world changes, the observed behavior of the economic actors follows it." Economics is not a hard science. It makes no sense to talk about politically conservative or liberal physics, but it makes great sense to discuss liberal and conservative theory and policy. Value judgments are inevitable. "Prescription dominates description." Definitive experiments are impossible. Even efficiency statements depend on "underlying . . . value judgments."[11] The continual debate over the minimum wage illustrates the role of values in analysis and prescription. Conservatives insist a minimum wage hurts the market and reduces employment. Liberals contend that employment effects are small compared to impetus to consumer demand, reduced welfare, and added social benefits from a higher minimum wage. Here, as elsewhere, it is not basic economic facts but their significance and the legitimate role of government and markets that are in dispute. Many controversies are less technical than ethical and political—"who ought to be hurt and who ought to be helped." Supply-side claims to increase savings by shifting resources to those at the top illustrate how value preferences color policy choice. Advocating *any* policy requires judgment. All recommendations therefore involve "two major elements"—hard data about what may happen, and "the ethical value judgment" as to what should happen. Pretending that only the first is relevant violates reality.[12]

Capitalism thinks in short run terms and lacks any norms to compensate for individuals focusing on the immediate. An emphasis on individual utility maximization presumes that pursuit of self-interest in competitive markets produces social good and stability. Thurow says relying on individual utility maximization is not wrong but insufficient because it takes no account of society, social context, or common interest. Group or common good may clash with that of individuals taken separately. Given uncertainty and risk, "what is rational behavior for the individual . . . may be irrational for the society as a whole." Inflation fighting is an example where individual rationality "is socially irrational." Cost of living provisions change the shape and nature of the economy and remove potentially effective tools against inflation. "What is privately profitable . . . need not be socially productive." Labor practices that make money in the short run—such as replacing permanent with temporary employees—may undermine the cooperation and training necessary to long term growth. The system produces "[s]hort time horizons" where "the sum total of those individual rational choices is social stupidity." The zero-sum society and its accompanying turmoil, gridlock, and division are the necessary consequence of pursuing individual and group interest regardless of circumstances.[13]

Domestic and international zero-sum conflict is an important outcome of the dominant theory and its policy proposals. Self-interested competition and hostility to collective solutions obstruct needed changes and make it impossible to compensate losers. The costs of unemployment, rebuilding the education system, changing labor-management relations, or abandoning obsolete concepts do not result from forces of nature, are not fairly mediated by a neutral market, and uncomfortable changes are "caused by identifiable human actions that can be controlled" whether or not they should be. No matter how much majorities benefit from needed changes, individuals who lose income naturally resist, obstructing change, leading to conflict between winners and losers. That winners and losers are often different individuals, groups, or nation-states is usually ignored in conventional theory and policy proposals. Thurow would enforce Pareto efficiency by compensating losers, but dominant economic theory abandons its individualism by retreating "to the weak form of Pareto efficiency," which is satisfied if winners *could* compensate losers but need not do so.[14]

Zero-sum conflict says much about Thurow's image of motivation. People are both self-interested *and* capable of teamwork and community. Rules encouraging cooperative behavior reduce conflict if people are assured they will not be made suckers. "Humans were and are the same, but their cultures lead them to express themselves in very different ways." They are not just utility maximizers in an operationally meaningful way. "Narrow individual economic self-interest" is "powerful . . . but not the only human motive." Yet, the price-auction model clings to utility maximization and ignores psychological and sociological evidence. People "are learning animals who change over time." They are also "tool-using," and it is in work that one "determines who one is." Preferences are not isolated but are interdependent and may even be "determined" by a social-political environment that shapes wants and allowable ways to pursue wants. To account for interdependent preferences, "words such as 'motivation' and 'voluntary cooperation' have to re-enter the vocabulary" and, as a result, mutual aid becomes possible.[15]

Alternatives

These criticisms of the dominant model structure Thurow's proposals for assuring the future of capitalism and the future of the United States. The nation must address challenges the market alone cannot solve. American capitalism has deep problems: inequality; "unfettered" it tends toward "instability or monopoly," requiring government to intervene during crises to "rescue" the system; it has no internal mechanism to address "'unfair'" and politically divisive property distributions; and, for very good reasons, we are reluctant to allow people to fail too badly, weakening one motive force of capitalism.[16]

As Keynes also observed, there is not just one form of capitalism, one set of possible rules, or one successful pattern of rewards. Society has choice. It does not simply discover rules but must "pick which fair game we wish to play . . . which distribution of prizes we want."[17] United States capitalism is only one variant of capitalism, not necessarily the one most successful in contemporary conditions. Insistence on following once effective policies regardless of a changed environment will devastate the American future. Given their "different histories and present circumstances," Japan and the emerging European Community operate capitalism with different domestic and international rules than those in the United States, forcing "[s]harp changes" on the United States. The "individualistic . . . British-American form of" managerial capitalism, emphasizing solitary, lone ranger values and behavior, weakly confronts the more "communitarian German and Japanese variants of capitalism" with their alternative attitudes and forms of organization. These variants of capitalism are not innocent of individual pursuit of self-interest, but values, rules, and structures channel self-interest into more community-minded behavior. Despite serious problems in Japan and Europe, communitarian capitalism includes focus on long term growth and investment, teams, investment in worker skills, aid to industry, admitting the validity and necessity of business-government cooperation, and accepting "social responsibility for success."[18]

Thurow discounts claims that markets and public policy can be neutral between individuals, groups, and classes. Every policy has unequal impact. Distribution decisions are inevitable, whether they are conscious or not, just or not. Society and policy makers must choose between claimants and groups, to determine who will pay and who will benefit from necessary changes. Any economic rule or regulation benefits some at the expense of others, and whether the result is good or bad depends on one's theory of justice. Claims that the market gives fair treatment to everyone attempt to de-politicize a highly charged process of determining shares by hiding behind supposedly neutral mechanisms. The market is not simply a natural process. Normative choices are inevitable because the market gain-loss allocation mechanism does not treat everyone alike. People bring drastically different resources, including inheritance, to the market game. One's assets, ability, and situation determine how one is treated. Thurow says that from the 1960s through early 1990s it became harder to distribute losses to the politically weak, such as unorganized workers or the lower middle class, and this compounded the problem of making a market system operate without public intervention. Political and economic realities do not allow the pretense that distributive and equity decisions are made by impersonal market forces. Though we lack explicit, politically accepted mechanisms for making these decisions, they are and will be made.[19]

Neutrality and equity are closely related. Equity refers to a popular sense of justice and fair treatment, including a feeling of economic justice. Echoing Keynes on equilibrium, Thurow's argument returns moral questions to political economics. We have no choice but to choose, and conscious and unconscious equity decisions guide our choices. "[I]t is not possible to pick a value-free, fair economic game." Deciding on the goodness or badness of a policy such as a tax, expenditure, or welfare policy requires a prior decision as to what constitutes fair distribution. "The Issue Cannot Be Avoided." It is "inescapable." As Keynes and Galbraith claimed, leaving things alone is as much an equity decision as direct intervention. Equity decisions cannot be put aside as non-scientific. Accepting the inherited distribution is an equity decision that affirms "the arbitrary initial income distribution given to us by history." Difficult as it is to define equity, "[t]o have no government program for redistributing income is simply to certify that the existing market distribution of resources is equitable. One way or the other, we are forced to reveal our collective preferences about what constitutes a just distribution of economic resources."[20]

As other liberal economists have argued, equity and efficiency are related. Both are determined on the basis of value judgments and decisions about distribution and relative standing. Defining efficiency requires that one define "equity or justice." Concepts of efficiency, equity, and justice precede policy decisions. "Once the value judgments have been accepted, it is possible to think economically." The supposed tradeoff between equity and efficiency is "[n]onexistent." One theme that recurs from *Generating Inequality* to *The Future of Capitalism* is that efficiency does not conflict with equity. Equity and higher productivity complement one another. "[T]o obtain the efficiency the United States needs, it is going to have to promote equity." This is related to motivation and community. People cannot be driven to cooperate freely, but they will cooperate if satisfied, and satisfaction increases efficiency. Efficiency "requires motivation, cooperation, and teamwork"— "'soft' productivity"—all of which develop only when people feel that costs and benefits are fairly allocated. In a democracy, perceived "equity is the key" to generating popular support for policies that require changes or sacrifices. Unlike many conservative economists, Thurow does not find the necessary value system in the market. Education, leadership, and a "sense of crisis" are required to create it.[21]

Equality

Although Thurow sometimes uses equity and equality interchangeably, as in the early 1980s arguing for reducing income inequalities among full time workers, he insists they are different. Equalization, or movement toward greater equality, may be an element in equity. Equity or a feeling of justice may or may not require more equality. Equality may or may not be just, depending on underlying value judgments.[22] Throughout his writings, Thurow focuses on economic and social equality with, until recently, rare references to political equality.

What is the problem? Laissez-faire theorists claim that the market produces all the equality that is possible. Thurow, like Galbraith, asserts capitalism generates inequality, even while producing more goods and services.[23] Economic changes over the last generation are causing "[a] significant and disturbing shift," a "surge toward inequality" of income and wealth. The United States has experienced a sharper "shift in the distribution of earnings" than any country not affected by "revolution or a military defeat." As Reich too has argued, the share of income going to the top 20 percent is at "the highest level recorded since data were first collected in 1947." The portion for the bottom 60 percent was "the lowest ever recorded." Only income transfers prevented the bottom quintile's share of national income from falling still further. Wealth is even "more unequally distributed" than income, which will lead to greater future income inequality. Moreover, from roughly 1970 into the 1990s, real income for labor fell across all age groups, especially among those with fewest skills. This decline is what Thurow means by a "growing Third World economy" in the United States. Compared to Japan and Germany we have more and increasing inequality. Thurow believes these distribution differences are ethically and politically significant. Whereas price-auction theory claims that only absolute not relative income matters, Thurow says relative income, feelings of relative deprivation, and a sense of fairness are crucial in maintaining productivity and social cohesion. Rising inequality, however, makes redistribution proposals "even more divisive" than previously.[24]

What causes inequality? In a theme found throughout this book, great inequality is not economically necessary. It has little to do with "natural" differences. Welfare and transfer payments are not at fault. Though power, discrimination, and attacks on welfare are factors, they are less important for Thurow than they were for Galbraith. The primary reason for inequality lies in "an economy that did not perform well" and the refusal of government and business to make the changes necessary to improve performance. International competitive pressure and trade difficulties reduce income for middle class males, although increased participation by women who receive lower pay accounts for some of the decrease. "[F]actor price equalization struck with a vengeance," especially among the less skilled, and forced the United States into competition with developing states. In the absence of significant public efforts to improve education and skills, and to organize for competition at all levels, these tendencies toward greater inequality will continue.[25]

Internal processes in American capitalism accentuate such trends. Skills, education, and intelligence do not explain the earnings distribution. The original or starting distribution deeply affects what people receive subsequently. Impersonal market forces do not reward effort or distribute income as traditional theory claims. Thurow insists that most inequality cannot be traced to skill differences. Much of the growth in inequality has occurred among people "with identical skills." He can find "no known distribution of talents that is as unequal as the distribution of earnings." Access to opportunities for jobs is more important than any inherent differences among people. The random walk—luck—ensures "a highly skewed distribution of wealth regardless of the normal distribution of personal abilities." "Stochastic processes," chance, and "economic lotteries rather than . . . individual characteristics," gradual reinvestment, or accumulation produce most large fortunes. Once such inequality is created it tends to persist and "be magnified" because "[t]here is no feedback principle . . . to equalize the distribution of wealth once it has become unequal." Individuals are not paid according to their marginal productivity, and equals often have different incomes.[26]

Thurow emphatically rejects the traditional economic justification of inequality and associated claims that protecting the economy may require restricting political equality.[27] Assuming people are essentially equal leads to a different set of policies from, and places the burden of proof on, those who argue for inequality. People do not "have to be driven to work with harsh punishments and large rewards."[28] In the same way there is no trade-off between equity and efficiency, there is none between equality and efficiency. Thurow finds no correlation in "real-world economies" between high levels of inequality and increased investment and productivity. The United States has more income inequality and larger income differentials between top management and average workers than most of its major economic rivals. Japan has the least. The fact that "our competitors" have not "unleashed work effort and savings by increasing income differentials" indicates that supply-side policies to shift resources to those at the top are not functionally necessary. The need to stimulate growth cannot justify even "current inequalities in the distribution of income." The economic prizes we choose to promote growth are political and "ethical" choices. They are not dictated by economic necessity, when, as in 1981, the top-bottom gap for full-time employed minorities was five times greater than among white males.[29] Trickle-down economics has not worked, and claims that taxes as high as 50 percent reduce work effort are not proven.[30]

What to do is problematic. International economic competition and capitalism's inherent tendency toward inequality complicate any proposed answers. Achieving equality in one area may increase inequality in another, again forcing equity decisions. Full employment is necessary to promote equalization but is not equality per se. Income differentials can and should be reduced, but this will require more extensive policies than simple welfare.[31] Active support for equal opportunity is highly desirable, but that is the start not the conclusion of debate. Defining equal opportunity confronts the equity question of what is a fair game and how ought economic prizes be structured. The market does not assure equal opportunity. In his early work Thurow asserted common arguments for equal opportunity evaded serious consideration of equality. Despite widespread "verbal attachment to the idea of equal opportunity" there was not much "attachment . . . to reducing relative income differentials." Rhetoric and cheap, unsuccessful policies are attractive. Effective policy is rejected as too costly or threatening. Judgments about whether equal opportunity exists can be made only by looking at groups, but market individualism calls this illegitimate.[32]

Conventional economic theory is innocent of groups and is unable to explain adequately why discrimination endures. On purely economic grounds, conservative economists should not oppose egalitarian race and gender policies, but they do. As discrimination cannot be a problem in a free market, affirmative action is not a solution. Thurow insists groups exist—witness zero-sum conflict—are legitimate, and appreciation of groups is essential to understanding political-economic processes. While discrimination affects individuals, "systematic discrimination" can be identified only at the group level. Discrimination against minorities and women exaggerates patterns of distribution, making them more unequal. Thurow's early work introduced "statistical discrimination" which is grounded on group identity to explain some continuing discrimination. "[S]tatistical discrimination" results from decision makers judging if an individual should be admitted to school or receive a job based on the real or imagined possibility of success of the group as a whole, not of the individual. If members of a group have historically lower graduation rates, or less success, even by a percentage point, and if the primary goal—efficiency?—is to have the largest number of people graduate and so forth, it can seem reasonable to ignore justice and putative individualism and exclude members of that group, especially when there are inadequate predictors of individual success.[33]

Acknowledging groups and "statistical discrimination" justifies positive public intervention such as affirmative action. Affirmative action is more a political than an economic issue. Like Galbraith, Thurow accepts it as a general policy to ensure real individual equal opportunity, that is guarantee a future where individuals are not judged adversely by race, ethnicity, or gender, or suffer from the aftereffects of past discrimination against members of their group. It is necessary for equal opportunity, not an alternative to it. Again Thurow returns to starting points and equity. The market has failed to solve income disparities between blacks and whites, and nothing less than an "unlikely" massive national political and economic mobilization that targets African-Americans but benefits everyone below the top has any hope of success. Society has violated its own individualistic ethic through discrimination and now allows individualism to defend the results of past discrimination. Those who have inherited socially desired genes start with an advantage they would retain even if discrimination were to end and real individualism were to be adopted. Ending discrimination does "not create 'equal opportunity.' " "The need to practice discrimination (positive or negative) to eliminate the effects of past discrimination is one of the unfortunate costs of past discrimination." Positive action is necessary, yet economic problems and lack of community feeling lead to paradigmatic zero-sum conflict.[34] Although in 1980 Thurow doubted growth could solve this problem, he has since embraced growth as prerequisite to any solutions.

"[A] good society simply does not tolerate poverty." Thurow's early work argued for increased redistribution, but political and economic conditions have changed. Welfare policies are as important to equity and equalization as ever, but expanding international economic competition has had the impact Keynes feared. It restricts domestic policy. Along with domestic zero-sum conflict, the politically limiting impact of "a breakdown in the social consensus" that previously supported limited redistribution makes effective welfare policy so contentious and costly that Thurow is not hopeful for a successful anti-poverty program. He therefore proposes more modest goals. Concern for equity and equalization remain, but he now focuses on increasing American output and expanding educational opportunities to make people better able to compete. Thurow proposes more investment and new government policies, so that welfare—a second best solution—is less needed and less divisive. This more traditional emphasis on growth as the key to providing jobs, increasing well-being, and reducing conflict is roughly what Keynes meant in "Economic Possibilities for Our Grandchildren." This does not mean leaving things alone or abolishing public welfare to generate savings for investment. Growth alone will not eliminate poverty or significantly reduce inequality. Society needs a "more egalitarian distribution of earnings." Given that the purely welfare component of the federal budget is small, as opposed to self-financed programs such as Social Security, eliminating welfare could never provide sufficient funds to generate savings for investment. More effective alternatives are available, if we can muster political leadership to develop them. The real limits to welfare are political. Reducing welfare "is an ethical decision and not one forced upon us by harsh economic imperatives." The welfare debate and discussions are dominated, however, more by "myth . . . than reality." People believe what they wish, "cannot see successful social welfare programs," and listen eagerly to seductive voices that reinforce myths about individual responsibility for poverty, eliminating guilt "about hurting people when" welfare programs are reduced.[35]

Equity aside, public welfare is necessary to capitalism, and its development has proven wrong theorists as diverse as Malthus, who claimed welfare would encourage revolution, and Marx, who claimed welfare could not prevent revolution. Along with Galbraith, Thurow claims Franklin Roosevelt's version of the welfare system saved capitalism in the 1930s; however, traditional liberal welfare has now reached a logical conclusion and needs reform and replacement. Rejecting the new social Darwinism, Thurow says that "[t]he welfare state is an essential ingredient in capitalism" and allows its continued survival and development. It "is hardly a foreign virus in the body of capitalism" but is capitalism's "immune system" preventing "it from becoming infected with . . . too much inequality." Because they remain Americans, people who do not thrive in the market will need far-reaching welfare provisions. Thurow proposes, as did Keynes in *How to Pay for the War,* to use an external crisis—here international economic challenges—for improving the domestic social economy and thereby providing "more jobs and a more egalitarian distribution of earnings." But the present political climate and simplistic slogans, such as government inefficiency or belief individual responsibility can replace welfare, prevent recognition of this reality and frustrate agreement over how far welfare should extend and how to ensure more and better employment.[36]

Democracy

Thurow is more concerned with protecting democracy from economic instability and from zero-sum conflict than with developing a theory of democracy or expanding the scope of democracy. He accepts existing practice, sees contemporary democracy as a process without vision or goals, and assumes institutions and forms of participation will remain essentially as they are. Thurow expresses two contrasting points: democracy is part of the problem, and economic theory and policy must accommodate democratic demands. It is part of the problem because people have acquired limited political means to protect themselves from economic dislocation, and governments must respond to their demands. In that sense the zero-sum society is a critique of pluralism. Groups can veto or exact excessive costs for the policies they see as detrimental to themselves, even if they are unable to impose their preferences on others. Drift, gridlock, and inability to address crises follow. They are the political costs of pursuing individual and group self-interest in the absence of common goals, purposes, or a framework that moderates grossly disproportionate gains and loses. Zero-sum conflict with its identifiable winners and losers, and growing inequality, are lethal to democracy, creating strains that democracies have always found "most difficult to solve." Thurow does not believe this situation requires limiting democracy, but in 1980 asserted democracy needed "a substantial majority of concerned but disinterested citizens" to prevent policy "being shaped by those with direct economic self-interests." Presumably, such citizens would as in Aristotle act as a balance between factions, but Thurow does not discuss where they come from or how they might operate politically. With everyone involved there is no one who is disinterested between outcomes.[37]

Thurow argues that the principles of capitalism and of democracy are in conflict. Contradictions between democratic egalitarianism and the inherent inequality of power and wealth in capitalism will become more obvious in a period of reduced public spending, falling wages, and growing inequality. In a democracy, however, what is politically necessary, such as a popular sense of fairness, must be accommodated by economics and economic policy. Traditional political-economy has refused to admit this need, preferring to define and limit democracy according to its economic theory. Thurow is adamant that economic failure not democracy causes our problems, and that it is completely unnecessary to weaken democracy to protect economic relations. Political democracies have "other considerations" than narrow market efficiency. The United States today is the first example of a democracy in which inequality has increased over a substantial period. The historic record offers little hope that democracies can survive "extreme" or growing "disparities in income and wealth." "Limits on economic inequality may be necessary to preserve political equality." No democracy can allow the market alone to determine distribution. "For a democratic government does what its citizens want—even if they happen to want something that interferes with the market." Yet growing inability to "deliver to a majority of voters what these voters want . . . and are used to having" undermines the legitimacy of democracy at the same time that people are increasingly critical of the performance of American capitalism. Democracy requires a "vision," including a sense of fairness "that transcends narrow sectarian self-interest," to create "common bonds," and to allow markets to operate. Only this can generate the "sense of economic justice" necessary for change. Without that feeling both democracies and markets fail because majorities and large minorities can cripple the operation of both.[38]

Although Thurow argues that lack of "worker participation" may be one cause of "our poor performance," he does not take advantage of the possibility that a more participatory democracy[39] could create the feelings of equity and community that are necessary to generate support for and legitimate policies that require changes and sacrifices. Instead, Thurow searches for another way to address our problems. Thurow's goal is to find a workable economic solution consistent with democracy, and not to dismantle democracy. Each potential answer to United States problems requires committed leadership, especially by the president in setting the agenda for debate and leading popular opinion. But leaders are deeply divided. A disinterested majority could provide an alternative to drift, but Thurow's zero-sum analysis undermines that hope. In an argument he does not fully develop, Thurow claims that America needs a dedicated, political establishment such as existed at the founding of the republic and again after World War II. Instead it has an oligarchy. Oligarchs are self-interested power holders who mold the system and its values to their own ends. Whether through merger mania, junk bonds, or tax systems rigged to shift resources to those with higher incomes, oligarchies destroy the popular sense of trust and fairness, thereby exacerbating conflict. The establishment-oligarchy distinction acknowledges that politics and economics are closely related, that leadership is drawn from both areas, and that democracy requires effective leadership. Our major choice is between leaders who have a popular mandate to govern in the common interest and who attempt to educate the public, or leaders who govern in their own interest. Thurow believes that in democracies, establishments attempt to ensure the system works well, including subordinating their narrow utility maximization to common needs, and are "disinterested" between self-interested groups. At the minimum, they have a broad concept of self-interest that encompasses the common good. Unlike oligarchies, they avoid even the appearance of placing their own interests first. Such an establishment does not, however, consist of "the wise Civil Servants" whom "Adam Smith" claims that Thurow "admires"—a notion that assumes markets are more democratic than elections—but leaders of a democracy who are willing to put common needs near the top of our national concerns.[40] Thurow does not suggest how to re-create such an establishment or how it might operate in contemporary conditions.

Power

Thurow disagrees with the orthodox assumption that power dissolves in markets as participants voluntarily pursue self-interest. Power includes influence and control. Those who can veto proposals harmful to their interest have power, even if they cannot impose their will on others. "In the past, political and economic power was distributed in such a way that substantial economic losses could be imposed on parts of the population if" power holders "decided that" was necessary. "Economic losses were allocated to particular powerless groups." Fewer groups are now powerless. Moreover, large companies and labor unions have substantial "power to stop their prices or wages from falling." Along with doubt "that market incomes are determined by impersonal forces outside of human control" this compels us to confront distribution issues.[41] Without an accepted mechanism to impose or allocate costs and benefits, ability to decide how costs and benefits are to be allocated, or ideological willingness to compensate those who lose from a change that is valuable to the majority, people will continue to resist change.

Disguising or ignoring power and the desire for power benefits the already powerful, whether business or labor, distorts analysis and understanding of political-economic relations, and makes reform difficult. Thurow worries that conventional economics does not examine economic power: "Yet in the world most of us live in, we see many people working to get economic power" as an end in itself or as a means to political influence. With world competition shifting from the political arena to the economy, modern corporations provide the "best opportunity for empire building." That corporate officials "can hand out real punishments and rewards" gives them power.[42] Thurow agrees with Galbraith that inequality generates power. Wealth and large size give access to government that is denied smaller enterprises and unorganized groups. Denying a major tenet of conventional theory, Thurow argues that significant power comes "out of the end of a dollar bill." Thurow emphasizes how people actually behave rather than how a market system might operate under minimal government. "Economic clout also gives . . . access to the political and cultural affairs of a society" and can sometimes "be used to buy political power." Arguing that "the American political system has lost sight of the economic well-being of the bottom 60 percent," Thurow does not directly link this to unequal power as do Brandeis, Dewey, and Galbraith.[43] Nevertheless, Thurow's proposals such as the active development of equal opportunity, job training, or aid to industry to better compete, would provide more power to those who out of fear or absolute necessity now have little choice but to accept what they are offered.

The Role of Government

Thurow provides neither a theory of government operation nor extensive analysis of government, but he does offer criteria for when government should become involved in the social economy. Even if not well organized for dealing with contemporary problems, government establishes the structure and rules within which every economy operates and is essential for addressing problems in the social economy.[44] "Market principles should be used in the necessary restructuring, but markets by themselves are not going to solve American problems . . . any more than they solved British problems at the turn of the century." If neither the market nor policy are fully neutral, if people experience real nongovernmental constraints that "affect economic behavior," and if there are no automatic forces ensuring equilibrium and efficiency, it cannot be claimed intervention upsets natural distribution processes. The key justification for government involvement is to mitigate undesirable conditions neither caused nor correctable by individual action, in order to avoid serious, harmful consequences. Talking about farming, Thurow says that problems "caused by individual stupidity" do not require social action, but those "caused by circumstances that no individual farmer could reasonably have foreseen" may be addressed by public action. If, as Thurow claims, capitalism is "inherently unstable," a third-world economy is developing for many citizens, and America is a community, "[o]nly government" has a sufficiently long "time horizon" to organize "necessary investments." As Reich also stated, "man-made comparative advantage" is the primary form of comparative advantage, justifying "government investment in skills, infrastructure, R&D, and plant and equipment."[45]

Like Keynes, Galbraith, and Reich, Thurow rejects the claim that government intervention into self-regulating markets must fail. Markets are not self-stabilizing and capitalism suffers from "myopia" about future needs. Government is not the enemy, certainly not the only problem; and conservative claims systematically ignore successful government intervention. Failure is always possible but is not so extensive as to preclude intervention. "THERE IS NO SIMPLE CORRELATION BETWEEN THE DEGREE OF ECONOMIC SUCCESS AND THE DEGREE OF ECONOMIC REGULATION." Nor are "social expenditures or government intervention and economic success" in conflict. Democracy and welfare have transformed the state, making it more than "an instrument of oppression." The argument that public officials waste taxpayers' money and not their own is disingenuous. Both public and corporate officials employ someone else's money, and neither bears the full cost of mistakes.[46] Historically the United States economy has worked best when government was directly involved. Foreign experience confirms this observation. The issue "is not rules versus no rules, but finding the right rules." As Galbraith also asserts, due in part to government sponsored research and demonstration projects, growth in agricultural productivity is an outstanding "success story." Accompanied by policies such as conservation and rural electrification, this public-private partnership furnishes, with improvements, a model for other forms of government involvement.[47]

Bad economic theory and advice occasion many public policy failures. Too often empirical evidence is soft and supplemented by myth, ideology, and assertion. "If the policy makers want to believe something, they will always find an economist who will confirm their beliefs." Increasing investment by expanding domestic inequality through shifting tax burdens has never worked. Monetarism is a failure. Fighting inflation with recession stops growth much faster than it stops inflation, and it undermines "efficiency and competitiveness." Wage and price controls—once a favorite Galbraith proposal—do not work well in a democracy and generate zero-sum

conflict. Thurow and Galbraith agree that anti-trust policy—Brandeis' preference—"has been a failure." Seemingly permanent budget deficits must be
ended, partly to free investable funds, partly to reduce inflation, partly to
allow "countercyclical fiscal policies when recessions break out." Defense
spending is too high and, more importantly, consumes too many scarce
resources, especially human talent. "America's investment, trade and education deficits all fall into this 'festering disaster' category."[48]

Despite this catalog of failure, Thurow does not despair of successful
intervention. Many policies have worked. Government has repeatedly res-
cued finance capitalism from failure, and it will continue to have a "central"
role in promoting "man-made brain power industries" under the new international conditions. Though Thurow no longer actively supports industrial
policy in its classical sense, policies resembling industrial policy will not disappear. Industrial policy, or "national strategies," can succeed. From *Zero-
Sum Society* to *Head to Head* he argued for some form of industrial policy,
though he uses the specific term less in his later work and hardly at all in
The Future of Capitalism. Thurow emphasized industrial policy because the
United States is in deep social-economic difficulty; industrial successes have
changed the environment and now we require new policies. Neither the
market nor the rejected policies above respond effectively to the new environment. Industrial policy was the primary public policy for internal reform
and expanding American competitiveness. In a society with a successful
competitive policy, cooperation and community are not only possible but
necessary. Government is not oppressively incompetent. Industrial policy
can also provide an answer to zero-sum clashes. It can reduce conflict by
ensuring that people who are hurt by necessary change will be protected or
compensated. It can be a vehicle for economic advance, equalization, guaranteeing jobs, and reducing discrimination.[49] Leaving equity aside, if reducing conflict requires bribing people not to oppose needed changes that hurt
them, so be it. The obstacles to successful market intervention are ideological not technical. "Much of the controversy is theological"[50] but despite
claiming we need a vision, Thurow does not propose a counter-ideology.

Industrial policy and all other successful policies require extensive public-private cooperation. Policy does not replace the market but is "a form of
cooperative coordination . . . to speed up the workings of the market and
remove some of the economic pain and suffering that" result from exclusive
reliance on the market. Government need not pick winners and losers.
Much initiative must come from industry, which bears a large part of the
cost, but the key is to adopt a "growth strategy": enhancing and developing
skills, improving education, increasing "savings and investment," making the
public sector a net saver, changing taxes, including adding some new taxes,

increasing federal civilian research, creating business groups that can cooperate and perform joint development, and improving infrastructure. Because the consequences of investment are not just a private matter, government must be more involved in "the economy's major investment decisions," formulating a national strategy directed at enhancing competitive and potentially competitive industries, not protecting from competition those industries that are failing. Such support does not produce a net drain on the economy. The European air industry is an example. Government aid has made Europe's plane manufacturing competitive with that of the United States while developing a reservoir of skills and technology applicable in other advanced areas. Reich and Thurow agree the United States has clandestine industrial policies. Thurow believes that some of these policies are valuable, but he agrees with Reich that they always benefit the powerful, who can demand them, and often protect the inefficient. Whereas conservative economists use the failings of protectionism to condemn all intervention, Thurow argues these failings are good reason for bringing policy making into the open and consciously engaging in industrial and other policy geared toward successful competition.[51]

Work

Thurow's underlying moral thrust is illustrated by his concept of work. Whereas laissez-faire offers a vision of individualized competition where people are driven by appetite for more and more consumption and work is always undesirable,[52] Thurow takes a social-psychological approach refining earlier reform liberal arguments. Human beings are productive tool-using creatures who are shaped by their work. His justification of more equality fits with the behavioral assumptions upon which Thurow's image of work is based. People are not lazy creatures "who must be forced to work under threat of harsh penalties for failure and the lure of large rewards for success." Rather, most people are essentially ants. They want to work—a point made by Keynes and confirmed by many opinion polls—and want to do well at it. Work often has a large cooperative element, not because competition forces people to cooperate, but because under decent conditions work is significant and satisfying. Money is not the only reward. To the extent their work environment allows, most people express their creativity at work. In an argument that begs for further development, Thurow suggests "The wants satisfied in the process of production may be more important than the wants satisfied by it." Work is associated with creativity, self-esteem, friendship, "feelings of accomplishment," and membership in communities. It also blurs simple public-private dichotomies. Work is where people achieve goals such as "[b]elonging, esteem, power, building, winning, and conquering." Brandeis' economic democracy, Keynes' reduction of the desire for superiority, and Galbraith's expansion of public consumption are more achievable if humans are viewed as producers rather than merely consumers. Then "we are no longer in the simple world of 'homo economicus.'" Efforts to increase productivity that ignore the collective component of work fail.[53] Everyone's job is not satisfying and probably no one's work is always so, but changes in the structure of work can increase satisfaction and productivity.[54]

If work is intrinsically satisfying for growing numbers of people this undermines orthodox claims that unemployment is voluntary or is caused by so-called generous welfare payments or unemployment compensation. Thurow sees voluntary unemployment as a circular argument. As Keynes also argued, large-scale unemployment is not caused by people who value leisure more than work. Such unemployment is a societal problem beyond the control of single individuals. Of course, some people are lazy and voluntary unemployment does occur, but if millions want to work and cannot find suitable jobs, a society that values work is obligated to help them. Inequality, American attitudes about the work ethic, economic efficiency, and the importance of work to individuals impose "a moral responsibility to guarantee full employment."[55] Where conservative views of motivation support the conclusion that public welfare and employment policies must fail because only necessity drives people to work, Thurow asserts these policies are necessary to justice and prosperity.

Labor is not just another factor of production but is uniquely attached to the person performing it, which gives enhanced moral significance to labor in an individualistic society. Prosperity requires that fear of starvation be replaced with other, more "humane" motivations. "[S]ecurity is more than a steady income. It is stability and knowing how one's immediate world functions." Companies that provide relative security, invest in employees, or do not readily fire them "generate group solidarity," cooperation, steeper "learning curves," and a willingness to work harder and make some sacrifices for the firm. This is important because "every industrial operation requires a substantial amount of voluntary cooperation" without which, as when "work to rule" prevails, "any industrial operation can be brought to its knees." Thurow believes internationally competitive Japanese and European firms generate this kind of loyalty. Motivation, reduced employee turnover, and training are essential to increase "soft productivity." Conversely, "[w]orkers who fear economic uncertainty and hunger thwart economic change at every opportunity." Workers, however, "want greater autonomy, challenge and personal contact." Most training occurs on the job. Wage rigidity, seniority, and refusal to fire higher paid workers and hire lower paid ones are rational responses that encourage experienced workers to train new workers, share skills, willingly accede to "technical change," and promote industrial peace. Without such security, "little or no training and learning would occur," lowering productivity.[56]

One is tempted to see an element of democracy in Thurow's picture of work but it is not economic democracy. Thurow calls for more worker control and bottom-up management but this is to increase productivity, although it would also produce more worker satisfaction and worker power. If humans are productive creatures, work shapes who we are, and "militaristic top-down decision making processes" undermine American ability to compete with "foreign firms who tap the ideas, initiative, and experience of their employees in bottom-up decision making,"[57] then more worker participation in decision making is essential. Top-heavy, autocratic management stifles workers and productivity and must be replaced by "participatory management." In part Thurow's argument for a "willingness to make workers part of the management team, to share information, and wherever possible to replace managers with workers who manage themselves" is similar to Brandeis. Increasing decision-making power on issues under workers' immediate responsibility is a regular feature of Thurow's discussions,[58] but he does not amplify how this can be done or suggest how American workers might respond. One could go in many directions with his argument, from consulting with employees to worker ownership, but Thurow does not develop any of them.

The International System

Thurow is more involved with the impact of international political economy on domestic policy than was Galbraith and much less active than was Keynes in attempting to devise international institutions for lessening this impact. Thurow's early work reflected a largely autonomous American economy, though not as much as did Galbraith's. Around 1980 Thurow began to discuss the impact of international events on domestic policy, but at that time the United States was still sufficiently autonomous to act as a locomotive for world recovery in 1982–1983. Given fundamental international changes—including the end of communism; a world-wide rise of skill-based "brainpower" industries; a new demography that consumes more government services for the elderly; the full emergence of a global economy; and the development of an international system where no one power dominates economic, political, or military relations—alone, the United States lacks the capacity to fuel world growth or protect national welfare policies.[59] Thurow's more recent work focuses on the nexus between domestic and international political economy. His two major concerns, for our purposes, are the increasing impact of an integrated world economy on the domestic political-economy and on social choices, and what he sees as inadequate American adaptation to the competitive international political economy. This second problem worsens the first.[60]

National boundaries no longer mark the scope of national social, political, and economic control. States are losing command of their domestic policy: "World economic integration has . . . outrun national economic policy-making." Domestic reform is more difficult due to slower productivity growth and increased international competition. As Keynes noted regarding the then existing gold standard, international economics complicates and obstructs domestic reform. To Thurow, increased competition has made more and more Americans vulnerable. This causes real pain, even when more people win than lose, pain that is frequently ignored for "the bottom 60 percent of" the work force. As Reich also observes, domestic wages and benefits increasingly reflect the level paid for the same skills in a worldwide market. Given capital mobility, national efforts to improve lifestyles and welfare for the majority, or to change the environment for business, can encourage corporations to move production "to those parts of the world where such benefits don't have to be paid, thereby forcing the benefits to be eliminated." The politically explosive result is that "uncoordinated national economic policies" can no longer protect workers and the domestic economy, meaning that Keynesian stimulus policy "is impossible, there are no longer mechanisms for fighting recessions." That leaves three choices: accept what results, meaning "there will be more frequent, longer, and deeper recessions with much slower recoveries," which Thurow considers impossible to justify in a democracy; reduce economic integration to the point where states can have separate national policies, which he opposes; or, encourage states to "coordinate their economic policies," including harmonizing worker benefits. Though Thurow prefers coordination and negotiation, unlike Keynes he systematically proposes few specific international reforms or the political means to achieve them. In a real sense, our first imperative remains what it has been from the start: reform American industrial structure and performance.[61]

Thurow agrees with Reich on the importance of international political economy but sees the existing system as less open than does Reich. He criticizes Reich's argument that the nationality of producing firms does not matter as long as American workers are highly productive and learning competitive new skills, and he doubts that Japanese firms in the United States hire and promote based solely on talent, or that "highest value-added products" will be made in the United States. Though not the only cause of inadequate competitiveness, changes in the international system have profound implications for the United States and world economic relations. The rise of Japan—despite recent domestic slow growth—and the European Community to relative equality with the United States means the United States is no longer able to write the rules of international trade. The new powers, especially Europe, with their different conceptions of capitalism and of the relation of government and industry, will make the "managed trade" rules about which many Americans are already complaining. The world is dividing into "quasi trading blocs" and even though the "specific outlines" of non-European trading blocs are unclear, "it is far better to accept the reality of trading blocs" and manage them so as to avoid deteriorating "into the negative-sum games of the 1930s." Problems remain, including "[m]acroeconomic coordination" especially over issues that do not threaten disaster, and lack of a "Lender of Last Resort." Contrary to some of his critics' claims, Thurow does not approve "creating regional trading blocs" but accepts trading bloc development as a reality to which theory and policy must adapt. To remain competitive one must do as others do. The United States will enter "a competitive-cooperative" relation with Japan and Germany, but to be successful in that relationship it must institute reform.[62]

Conclusions

Thurow is less directly political than the other theorists examined here, but he recognizes the interrelation of society and politics with economics. He argues that laissez-faire causes some of our problems because this ideology and its policy prescriptions ignore social context, needs, and structures. Community is an example. Thurow does not have a strong concept or detailed analysis of community but its importance is assumed throughout his work. In his most recent work, Thurow has expressed both deeper criticism of capitalism's radical individualism and his appreciation of the need for community to sustain democracy, protect capitalism, and meet human needs for inclusion. "Societies are not merely statistical aggregations of individuals engaged in voluntary exchange but something much more complicated." Looking only at individual self-interest ensures that the whole is misunderstood. "A society is clearly something greater than the sum of its parts," yet "capitalism explicitly denies the need for community." With interdependent preferences and motivation "the economy . . . becomes something quite unlike a random collection of individuals." The dominant utility-maximizing view is not wrong about individual motivation but perilously incomplete. Individuals are not alone. Society needs both individuality and "social organization" which complement not cancel one another. We are not simply separate individuals tied only by self-interested contracts, but we share common beliefs and rules that express and shape individual behavior. Membership develops a sense of trust and fairness allowing people to engage in common goals. Without it there is no basis for economic or political agreement. We also acquire a sense of responsibility to one another. "Communities, societies, and nations are designed to be mutual aid societies." Acknowledging and developing community feeling weakens the zero-sum ethic, which at least partly results from individualistic myth, making successful intervention possible. This is one reason why nations practicing even weak communitarian capitalism are becoming more productive.[63]

Capitalism "systematically underinvests" for future needs. Thurow challenges liberals and the "left" to develop a "vision" to overcome this, "so that governments" with their potential for a longer-term perspective "can once again become a messenger of the future to the present."[64] He hints at values to guide economic policies yet is less explicit about his values than the other authors here. The most significant political problem with Thurow's argument is that he does not develop either its philosophical base or explain the process by which his proposals might be realized. Repeatedly he defends pictures of active government, equality, democracy, community, and justice that are quite different from orthodox theory without sharing the moral justification for his values. Thus worker participation, which many defend in terms of community, self-fulfillment, or protection from tyranny—each of which Thurow seems to accept—is justified as ensuring more cooperation and productivity. This is not to deprecate his economic arguments but to recognize that by his own standard his argument is incomplete. Thurow correctly says value judgments are inevitable but leaves us asking by what criteria do we make them. He says circumstances should determine policy, but even "circumstance" is a slippery concept, subject to the interpretation and obfuscation he discusses elsewhere. To have linked his proposals to an explication of the values he seeks to defend would have strengthened his entire argument.

Growth is one way of helping the poor that the wealthy and powerful can embrace, but growth alone is insufficient according to Thurow and Galbraith. Thurow's emphasis on growth does not abandon traditional Democratic concern for "the Capraesque 'little guy' who wants a 'fair shake'."[65] In reemphasizing productivity and growth—not that reform liberals ever said they are unimportant—Thurow has not embraced growth as a surrogate for reform. He insists government can and should care what happens to the majority. The nature of the circumstances that he confronts, not his specific values, distinguish Thurow from earlier liberal political-economy. Bluntly, growth is a means to reform and is necessary to avert "[r]enewed class warfare."[66] For Thurow the economy is not sufficiently strong and independent to support active social reform without bitter and divisive zero-sum conflict. In the face of domestic opposition and strong international pressure basic liberal assumptions remain: the impact of the economy on domestic social-political relations is important and must be addressed; leaving things alone does not solve problems; political-social considerations are important; economics is not autonomous; democracy, equality, and community are positive values that deserve equal or greater consideration than narrowly defined economic goals; and government action can enhance these values.

"Economic battles are won by combining free markets and individual initiative with social organization." Transition to better social organization is essential but Thurow, like many reform liberals, is better at telling what must be done than developing the mechanisms to accomplish reform. "Economically what has to be done is as clear as the politics of doing it are murky." Thurow is pessimistic. Gridlock is being broken by the renascent right, but their policies will increase inequity and will slow growth. With the collapse of noncapitalist alternatives, "capitalists have been able to employ more ruthless approaches to getting maximum profits without worrying about political pressure." Thus, "what needs to happen . . . is not likely to happen" and "there is not even a glimmer of hope that those real answers will be adopted."[67] Keynes had the good fortune to be both intellectually and politically influential, having access to most levels of British government. Galbraith makes some weak suggestions about organizing for reform. Reich holds high public office. Thurow has been active in political campaigns and public persuasion but, unlike conservative economists, does not have a plan for achieving the reforms he favors. More than Keynes, Galbraith, or Reich, he relies on classic liberal faith in reason, not developing political movements to carry out his policies. This emphasis on changing opinion may reflect Thurow's worries over the difficulty of governing our society. His analysis and criticism are more radical than his policies. Like Galbraith he is a reformer not a revolutionary, and he sadly admits that change will be very difficult. But when power and economic benefits are concentrated among the top 20 or even 40 percent, it will take political organization to implement the values he seeks to justify.

6

Robert Reich: Rebuilding Liberalism, the Economic Base of Citizenship

To maintain the old order under changed conditions may be, in fact, to initiate a revolution.
—L. T. Hobhouse, *Liberalism*

ROBERT REICH (b. 1946) is a liberal critic of what is popularly seen as contemporary liberalism. Failure to develop and implement a workable public philosophy consistent with fundamental liberal values, not—as claimed by conservatives—permissiveness, profligacy, or softness on supposedly natural market relations, have made Keynesian, social, and welfare liberalism inadequate and incomplete. American liberals "are without bearings. The ideals that had guided them since the 1930s and through the postwar decades seem less clear, and the premises of public debate in recent years strangely disorienting." Contemporary liberalism is less "balanced" than New Deal liberalism, failing to give the average person a coherent and believable picture of social justice coupled with growth, mutualism, and community. Its diminished public philosophy, emphasizing "altruism" rather than "social solidarity," was "doomed to excess" because it had no standards by which to weigh and judge rival claims. Given a slow economy, accelerating international economic challenges, decaying sense of community, and superficially credible but simplistic conservative explanations of economic discontent, contemporary liberals have experienced "[p]aralysis in the face of political choice," having "no compass" to guide them, "governing principles on which they could draw," or "new vision of social solidarity." Given their failure to offer the public a "finely honed and rigorous liberal public philosophy," they have abandoned the crucial field of ideas to divisive, fear emphasizing conservative mythmaking.[1]

Before becoming Secretary of Labor in 1993 Reich taught public policy, including a course "on the role of public managers in a democracy"[2] at John F. Kennedy School of Government, Harvard University. He has a

J.D. degree from Yale. Reich's first major book, *The Next American Frontier* (1983), established him as a leading proponent of industrial policy, a position he subsequently modified. In some years he has earned more than $500,000 from his writing and lectures. In the 1970s he was an assistant to the solicitor general and director of policy planning for the Federal Trade Commission. He was founding chairman of the liberal journal *The American Prospect* (1989–1993). Thurow is a member of the same journal's editorial board and Galbraith is a member of the "Board of Sponsors." Reich was a contributing editor to *The New Republic* (1982–1993). Reich and President Clinton met as Rhodes scholars and remain friends. He served as an economic adviser during the 1992 presidential campaign and as economic coordinator during the postelection transition. Reich raises surprisingly strong passions. Like Galbraith earlier he is seen as both a model for liberals and as a danger to the republic. Laura Tyson calls him "the most important liberal of this generation." Many see him as offering the only workable solution for liberalism and as a model for the Clinton administration's opposition to Republican congressional policy dominance. One Republican member of Congress, Representative Randy Cunningham, called Reich a "Communist" supporter who "goes along with Karl Marx in many of his writings."[3]

Reich accepts core liberal values but argues they must be adapted to new and often threatening circumstances. Liberals must rearticulate their version of the American public philosophy, including reassertion of obligation, mutual responsibility, education, "equal sacrifice," expansive equal opportunity, local and national community, more participatory democracy, and active government. Radical economic individualism is dividing the United States into two separate societies. It and zero-sum conflict must be replaced with economic expansion and support for those bearing the costs of change and the transfer of low paying jobs out of the United States. Most important for those still valuing social justice and democracy, "[l]iberalism must respond to the apprehension about survival." Understanding the need for an alternative vision to economic conservatism, liberalism's "real challenge . . . is to enunciate an ideology appropriate to an era haunted by fears of survival." To do this, liberalism must substitute expansion, "fairness," "civic virtue," and democracy for the new social Darwinism.[4]

There are five interconnected themes in Reich: the importance of ideas and ideology; the continual and legitimate interaction between politics and economics; the impact of changed economic circumstances on political and social relations; the specific public policies to address these links; and the challenges of democracy. Each will be treated in this chapter.

Ideology

Ideas, especially *public ideas* about communal relations,[5] shared and expressed in public, shape thinking, awareness, motivation, expectations, and
behavior. Reich does not distinguish philosophy from ideology, or ideology
from dispositions, but focuses on ideas in action. The systems of values and
perceptions that explain reality to people are rarely consciously selected or
held. People understand the world through their shared ideas. These ideas
determine what is a problem, possible solutions, and the proper role of government in addressing whatever people decide is a problem requiring public attention. Public ideas include stories that explain but often hide reality.
Whether well-organized or "disguised, unarticulated," these often myth-
based public ideas "are the unchallenged subtexts of political discourse," setting limits on the range of argument.[6]

Ideas are central to political-economic conflict. Political-economy is not
a hard science with precise formulation of problems and clinical application
of solutions. Rather, ideas, perceptions, and beliefs interact with circumstances to produce public policy. Along with Dewey, Hobhouse, Keynes,
Galbraith, and Thurow, Reich argues part of our problem is that the ideas,
values, tales, and myths through which we explain reality often distort and
hide actual relations and possibilities. Problems are not obvious, objective,
or quietly waiting for a neutral detached solution, but are defined when an
existing situation painfully fails to meet a criterion, belief, or value. How
and by whom "choices are posed and goals tacitly accepted can make all the
difference." We are trapped by "vestigial thought" in a "mythic contest" and
"endless debate" over "two highly artificial concepts: the 'free market' and
national planning," both of which are comfortable to believers, neither of
which is viable, either of which alone could lead to disaster. Such "ideological blinders" illustrate "the power of ideology over political reality" by preventing government from assisting in the solution to real problems. As a
result, continuing and necessary government involvement in economics is
treated as "an illicit affair, hidden from public view, and thereby undermining the chances" of its earning "cultural legitimacy."[7]

These arguments reflect the distinction between principles and the policies that might fulfill principles. For Reich the public philosophies of American liberalism and conservatism share the same "four morality tales"[8] but
interpret and apply them very differently. Widely accepted interpretations
persist for long periods often with the support of people who benefit from
them. Problems emerge when "reality changes and the mythology does not."
When beliefs and resultant policy preferences resist or only superficially

accommodate change, they sabotage future success. Policies that at one time could embody and actualize traditional liberal values are now obstacles to their realization. For example, the view that government is the only coercive agent, an emphasis on the market as the sole legitimate way to solve problems, the idealization of solitary initiative and success, and a rigid distinction between government and society-market support policies that are incongruent with existing conditions. Valid in the eighteenth and parts of the nineteenth centuries, these ideas now obstruct improvement. Only changed perceptions of what is legitimate policy will allow real social-economic advance.[9]

Reich uses the term public philosophy deliberately, linking his ideas with a communitarian perspective. He asserts liberalism has and must develop a better public philosophy that emphasizes civic virtue. Civic virtue includes concern for others, adherence to the spirit of law, and "economic citizenship" as "the adhesive of social and economic life." He believes civic virtue and liberalism are compatible. Against neoclassical liberals and contemporary individualistic conservatives, who would not use public philosophy within the context of economics or political economy, Reich asserts that a public exists, as well as a public or common interest, and that public philosophy rests on the existence of real community. Public philosophy is more than a mask to allow selfish interests and temporary majorities to plunder wealthy minorities. Unlike traditional conservatives who based public philosophy[10] on natural law, Reich believes the content of public philosophy evolves, the mass public has a necessary role in generating and developing it, and it is "the source of our collective vision." It has recently been monopolized by conservatives who mold the basic parables of American discourse to their ends and interpretations. In hyperbolic terms, a truly liberal public philosophy will discourage "[a]varice" and emphasize "loyalty, collaboration, civic virtue, and responsibility to future generations. . . . common concern for, and investment in, the well-being of our future citizens," "civic responsibility" not "economic aggrandizement," and pragmatic recognition that the well-off minority has a stake in the welfare and productivity of the rest.[11]

Politics and Economics

Politics and economics, government and business are inextricably linked, according to Reich. Each inevitably and necessarily affects the other. Efforts to separate them, whether to create a pure market or pure civic relations are doomed to failure. Such efforts are prime examples of vestigial thought, of clinging to images of idealized individualism or mythic perfect communities. Both ignore reality.

Reich sees "two major realms of authority: political power and economic power." Not only is power shared between business and government, but "[e]conomics cannot be divorced from politics." This linkage means "[t]he conservative's idyllic 'free market,' unencumbered by government meddling, is a logical impossibility." Although he criticizes conducting business-government relations as usual, Reich will not "politicize every economic issue"—it is never a matter of either politics or free markets-economics, always a *chosen* combination of both—but argues "every important economic choice is by nature political," allocating costs, benefiting winners, injuring losers, and redistributing political and economic power. Policies chosen by bureaucratic and business elites in processes hardly open to public debate and scrutiny obscure political choice by hiding influence and who has influence, conceal the criterion of choice, and make economic outcomes seem inevitable. "This submergence of politics results in economic policies whose burdens and benefits are allocated in ways that many people consider unfair. . . . Efforts to submerge politics serve only to pervert it." Reich repeatedly argues we must "open up political channels" and publicly debate the extent and parameters of public-business association, what government should be doing in the economy, or risk both economic success and democracy.[12]

Reich questions the legitimacy and practicality of traditional attempts to separate public and private, especially in economic affairs. He insists that these are not watertight compartments, and that hard-and-fast distinctions between them are essentially wrong. The public and private spheres overlap, closely influence one another, and share common concerns. In terms of function, authority, and power it is often difficult to distinguish private and governmental realms. Large corporations have become political entities characterized by internal and external political relations. The private realm is not primarily economic, and most large-scale economic relations have a profound public impact and component. The choice between market and government "is falsely posed. . . . such sharp distinction . . . has long ceased to be useful." "No clear distinction exists between private and public sectors within this or any other advanced industrialized country." If "economics, foreign affairs, and social policy" are interdependent, traditional liberal bifurcation between the private as economic and the public as political is no longer adequate.[13]

This linkage between the putatively private and public is illustrated in the relationship between business and government. Business and government need one another. At the simplest level, government requires business-created resources to carry out public activities and to maintain popular satisfaction. Business needs protection and support to successfully produce and compete. Conservatives could endorse business-government interaction if it remained at this level. But there is more. In addition to mutual support government is involved in economics, business techniques and thinking shape government actions, business decisions affect civic life, and the top business and government elites share power and world outlooks. Thus a managerial mentality has come to dominate much government thinking even when it is proving less and less effective in business. The business ideology of "scientific management" encouraged top-down control in government, which in business and government disastrously separated so-called thinkers from those who carry out policy. Elites in both realms have authority and power. In both they "are often cushioned against the consequences of incompetence" and "arrogance is often endemic."[14]

The public and the private are different. This remains a vital distinction in many areas, but in political economy insistence on rigid separation obscures the interrelation between competitive pressure, economic and social inequality, and deteriorating living standards. Contemporary conservatives fail to see that their policy prescriptions are often invalid and harmful to the nation when they are followed. Reich's linkage between these traditionally opposed parts of the "social fabric" forces concern with "the future of American *society* as distinct from the American economy."[15] This concern includes the possibility of openly choosing the direction of economic change, with implications for who benefits and onto whom costs and burdens are imposed—not just the powerless and excluded as now. Reich's argument legitimates interest groups, welfare, and expanded participation in public decisions, whether economic or political.

Two further points illustrate this relation between politics and economics: the current American political-economy and Reich's claim that conservatives have failed to account for the changes that concern liberals.

The Current Economy

The validity of Reich's policy proposals depends heavily on his picture of the political-economy. The real as opposed to the imagined economy changes constantly and is closely interwoven with government, politics, and social relations. In *The Next American Economy* Reich identified three stages of American political-economics since 1870. These are the "The Era of Mobilization," ca. 1870–1920, characterized by aggregating resources and capital, overcoming problems of production, disciplining a work force, and developing large organizations; "The Era of Management, 1920–1970"; and, "Impasse, 1970–" a period of major world economic change, "paper entrepreneurialism," efforts to preserve the historic industrial structure and its social relations, and "dead-end labor." Reich added an "Era of Human Capital," emphasizing work skills—which appears in all his major work—and political choice of our future.[16] Reich later included a system of flexible production and adaptation to international pressures and opportunities. Each "era" had a different relation with government and distinct impact on the social-political structure.

"The Era of Management, 1920–1970," some of whose features Dewey identified, still governs much of our thinking. This era approximates Galbraith's technostructure, though Galbraith extends it into the 1980s. Professional management dominates large, centralized, hierarchically organized enterprises. Economics penetrates the political system. Government supports major businesses. National and corporate interest are linked, market control over large entities decreases, oligopolistic concerns cooperate and manipulate prices, and concern for the social and political impact of production and corporate dominance declines. During this period "thinkers" were separated from "doers," and industry-wide management became common, often with tacit and explicit government regulatory, spending, and research support. Top-down control efficiently organized simple, repetitive mass production. But this period had wider implications. "The logic of routine, large-scale manufacturing first shaped its original business environment and then permeated the larger social environment." It provided a bureaucratic "ideology of management control," though Reich does not discuss the role of power in growth of staff, managers, and responsibility as does Galbraith. Large organization dominated all relations, ending the reality though not the myth of the rugged competitive individual. The managerial ethic is an "inappropriate political legacy" for government. It has supplanted political debate with a myth of managerial efficiency; it has disparaged political processes and made government unable to fairly address zero-sum and resource conflict, make "hard political choices," or develop consensus; and it has encouraged business to ignore its "public responsibilities."[17]

The two earlier periods successfully responded to then current challenges and opportunities. But the world has changed. Policies, forms of business, and ideas about the nexus of polity and economy that were suitable to the "era of management" are no longer appropriate. Challenges and opportunities are different. High-volume standardized production no longer expands or sustains American prosperity. American business and political institutions have not accommodated this reality, preferring instead protectionism and myths of radical individualism, supply-side economics, and self-equilibrating markets.

What has changed? Like Keynes' argument about Britain in the 1920s, Reich says that the United States is no longer the unchallenged, dominant economic actor. Advanced technology has spread around the world, core American corporations are no longer able to set prices, many basic industries cannot compete with those of developed or increasingly developing nations, and all of these changes aggravate social tension. "[O]nce again the economic context has changed and our institutions are coming under pressure to evolve" to "high value" and customized production requiring advanced work skills. But American management has not responded adequately. Successful competition and improved standards of living require "a different form of organization" that is "far more flexible and adaptable." Since at least 1983 Reich has argued that the world is rapidly "becoming a single marketplace." More recently, with continuing integration into the international economy, "'American' industries are ceasing to exist in any form that can meaningfully be distinguished from the rest of the global economy. . . . the American economy as a whole" is not "retaining a distinct identity, within which Americans succeed or fail together." What distinguishes one nation from another and ultimately improves the standard of living is "worldwide demand for . . . skills and insights." "This . . . emerging reality" requires changes in whom government supports. To believe things can be as in the past is "vestigial thought" no longer addressing the world as it is.[18]

These changes have enormous political-social implications to which neither business nor government has adapted. As with Keynes and Thurow, Reich says international economics reaches into the domestic political economy to undermine economic and political stability. Economic changes simultaneously increase demand for a larger government role in training and educating Americans and reduce the willingness of the top 20 percent of the nation to pay for needed reforms. Leaving things alone, accompanied as in the past by quiet government support for major corporations, cannot effect a socially desirable transition. If the economic fate of the bottom 80 percent hardly affects the people who have "symbolic-analytic" skills necessary to successfully compete in the international economy, then Americans no longer succeed or fail together, and society is likely to further divide along economic lines. When "national borders no longer define our economic fates," then unwillingness to pay taxes, to sacrifice together for the common and ultimately individual interest, to provide welfare, or to acknowledge common political identity becomes greater. The very continuance of the United States as a functioning political and economic entity is at stake, as economic changes "tear at the ties binding citizens together." Unlike laissez-faire theorists who have little concern with the fate of individuals and nations, Reich claims we must talk about "national purpose" in terms of the lives and fates of fellow citizens. Given the interrelation of politics and economics the issue becomes "Are we still a society, even if we are no longer an economy?"[19]

Conservative Failure

Conservatives have missed the significance of these changes, preferring to reiterate the ideology of a triumphant, unmanaged, self-regulating market, which is superior to social and political matters. Conservatism "ignores the fundamental transformation of the world economy and society. . . . relationships between domestic poverty and stagnation of family incomes," and the relationship of these to international competitiveness.[20] As with Dewey, Keynes, and Galbraith, Reich believes that laissez-faire political-economy once constituted a reasonable statement about the world. Now it inaccurately describes reality and provides faulty and hazardous policy advice especially for democratic systems. The theory's unrealistic assumptions and prescriptions obscure the actual operation of the economy and its interrelation with politics, government, and society, producing unacceptable results that stimulate economic, social, and political breakdown. The conservative explanation of American problems—intervention and liberal permissiveness—is too simple, yet "[t]he liberal response has been notoriously unconvincing." Most prescriptions for dealing with problems "are alternative means for growing poorer."[21]

Reich's extensive criticism of the radical individualistic perspective can only be sampled. He starts with assumptions. Individual utility maximizing does not explain all behavior and pursuit of self-interest does not necessarily lead to the common good. In a criticism of public policy making that applies to conservative political economy and to efforts to remake government in a conservative image, Reich rejects tales that "people are essentially self-interested [and] . . . behave much the same way" in the market and in politics; "personal preferences are not significantly affected by politics, social norms, or previous policy decisions"; and "public good" is the result and sum of "individual preferences." Given existing conditions, alone, "private market exchanges" cannot improve society. Especially in matters of productivity and education, where investment is "necessarily social," individual decisions are frequently insufficient to make the United States as competitive as it must become. A society cannot exist "premised upon the principle of selfish interest" any more than one premised on the vain hope of "altruism and compassion." To paint these not as ideal types but as either-or choices is to massively ignore actual behavior.[22]

So called market solutions to current problems impoverish the United States and increase inequality. The myth that individual utility maximization produces optimum social good is "nonsense, or worse." By focusing on profitable transactions for managers and takeover specialists, rather than on national productive structure, competitiveness, and the people who lose from major changes, conservative theory and policy encourage the rise of a "paper economy," "paper entrepreneurialism," and "paper entrepreneurs," who profit from rearranging and manipulating the financial assets of existing enterprises rather than through creative research, improving worker-management relations, constructing new facilities or developing new processes and products. Managers possess "discretionary power to serve their own goals" and their "incentives" have been separated "from socially productive results." "[B]roader costs and . . . potential benefits" are ignored "in individual tallies of profit and loss" so that—as Dewey, Hobhouse, Keynes, Thurow, and Galbraith also argued—often "[w]hat is rational for the individual is tragically irrational for the society as whole," harming the interest, livelihood, security, and sense of community of the vast majority. Echoing Keynes' warning about the dangers when stock markets become casinos, Reich argues, "The current obsession with asset rearrangement harms productivity" in its emphasis on the short run and "the precipitate balance sheet mentality." Those with "the strongest economic stake in the long-term health of an enterprise"—low paid and immobile workers—have the least influence over these processes.[23] Moreover, major policies, such as civil rights and health and safety regulations, are not understandable in terms of individuals satisfying selfish interests. Rather, ideas and arguments about the public good and public interest mold thought, educate, and motivate people.[24]

God did not create the market in the first six days and it is not part of natural law, but "is a human artifact" that cannot be understood separate from "laws and political decisions that create it." Results are not predetermined. Numerous "equally efficient" alternative outcomes are possible.[25] A "minimalist role for government might be appropriate for" a rapidly growing economy or one "sheltered from international competition." In present circumstances the "laissez-faire approach is both naive and dangerous." Agreeing with Keynes and Thurow, Reich is concerned that economic adjustment is not automatic or even reasonably compensatory, which engenders opposition to both harmful and needed changes. Slow growth, corporations best understood as political entities, insufficient opportunities, and the actual interrelation of politics and economics make it perilous to rely on free market myths. The trickle-down theory ignores the flight of capital abroad and the growing problems of people on the bottom. Adjustment is costly, and in a partial refutation of Pareto theory, the losers are rarely the same people as the winners nor are they compensated by the winners. That adjustment will occur is an irrefutable truism, the question is whether it can be made "easier, more socially equitable, and more efficient."[26]

Reich does not attack profit making, private ownership, or the market, but—applying conservative claims about government to putatively private actions—believes current economic behavior and theory foster irresponsibility. They cause a "politics of class" and "beggar-thy-neighbor strategies" that "undermine civic virtue and ultimately reduce the prosperity and security of everyone." In three books he criticizes economic conservatism's "faith in the utility of fear and avarice." As motivators they are counterproductive though their supposed social utility is flattering to the people who profit. An economic theory emphasizing "greed and fear" rewards "clever criminals," encourages resistance to change, demoralizes "average working people," weakens national security and causes the "social fabric" to slowly unravel. This "ideology of wealth and poverty" fitted "a simple frontier economy" where one could produce without extensive social interaction, but its current manifestation in the form of "cynical indifference and opportunism" destroys the cooperative horizontally structured organizations necessary to meet contemporary conditions.[27]

The economic theory Reich criticizes emphasizes contract but says little about trust. Reich claims trust makes successful political-economic relations possible. Trust permits people to "engage in common goals" allowing an enterprise to succeed. New conditions require trust to encourage cooperation and reduce opposition to change. Trust breaks down under "opportunistic individualism" and "preemptive betrayal." Pure pursuit of self-interest is very different from the benevolent, damage-limiting market relations of market theory. Efforts at self-protection through rigid and ever more specific contracts, increased police protection, and resistance to change—as also arise in Thurow's zero-sum society—fail, and clog the system, though they are individually rational when some people cannot be trusted to abide by the spirit of rules and regulations. This lack of trust weakens civic culture and generates gridlock and the intrusive, detailed government regulation that conservatives oppose. Ever more detailed rules and regulations designed to curb evaders and cheaters cause overregulation as people try to find explicit rules for everything. Overregulation occurs also because conservatives refuse to acknowledge the necessity of close government-business cooperation and regulation. Conservatives' condemnation of government and their belief that the market can cure most social-economic problems actually cause market breakdown, red tape, and unnecessary conflict between government and business. Productivity falls, conflict and opposition to change increase, and people feel disconnected from the nation. Zero-sum conflict becomes the norm.

The "moral force" of law is undermined, further weakening enforcement and social cohesion. Much fault lies with "triumphant individuals [who] are not bound by ties of loyalty."[28]

Equality

Reich is troubled by the social-economic costs of increasing inequality. Conservatives and most liberals have failed to address the political and economic causes and impact of growing inequality. Americans are "[n]o longer . . . rising or falling together." Regulation, growth of single parent families, or the large number of baby boomers entering the economy cannot account for increasing inequality since the "mid-1970s." Unlike during earlier periods, unemployment is not the only cause of poverty. Many poor are employed full time. The growing income gap between American workers and corporate executives is already among the largest in the industrialized world, and inequality is growing most rapidly among the employed. One result is that traditional liberal emphasis on full employment is now inadequate. Although public policy in the 1980s, such as tax increases of "one-sixth" for the bottom 20 percent of taxpayers and decreases by "one-twentieth" for the top 20 percent account for some of the increase in inequality, increasing differences in level of education (which closely correlates with income) are also significant. Those most likely to increase income, leaving paper entrepreneurialism aside, were those best able to perform in the new international system. Another result of growing economic inequality is the development of a "new community," segregated according to income, accompanied by "growing inequalities of service."[29] Although Reich disregards long-standing economic segregation, increasing inequality following decades of relative decline is new.

The Horatio Alger myth, "a noble ideal," no longer fits reality. Increasingly the successful are offspring of the successful, limiting the ideal of social and economic mobility and severing "the presumed connection between high incomes and inherent worthiness" or reward for effort. The growing division within the United States is illustrated by formation of two virtually separate educational systems: one, the best in the world, trains 15 to 20 percent of the population to be symbol analysts who manipulate data and make deals; the other, for the majority, results in "17 percent of American seventeen-year-olds" being "functionally illiterate." Education for the well-off minority emphasizes four fundamental skills: "*abstraction, system thinking, experimentation,* and *collaboration.*" The majority are offered a kind of rote learning that may once have been suitable for standardized mass production but is inappropriate for effective world economic competition or active citizenship.[30]

Reich rejects classical, neoclassical, and supply-side defense of inequality as an incentive to and as a reward for success. Although social Darwinism and the survival of the fittest are no longer acceptable in their classic dress, they are "disguised within socially acceptable rhetoric," which stigmatizes the unsuccessful as lazy, unfit, or incompetent. The myth of the "Triumphant Individual" emphasizes individual conquest and reward, ignoring social and collective effort. Low taxes for the wealthy and economic discipline for the rest are called necessary to progress and effort. Arguments that workers, the poor, or the weak are fat, soft, lazy, coddled, encouraged by welfare checks to overbreed, and that anyone can find work are acceptable restatements of social Darwinism. "[T]he conservative story fails utterly to take account of the larger setting in which American poverty has persisted. . . . in large part a function of economic stagnation above."[31]

What is needed? Social justice and a strong sense of equality of sacrifice are essential. Reich discusses content but does not define these concepts. Social justice is compatible with and essential to economic growth. Common needs and "social concerns" should be "the ends that economics seeks to serve" rather than only serving immediate individual profit. Society articulates not just one priority but many "social values and a sense of civic life," including "equity, security, and participation." "A just and democratic society depends on a citizenry educated in civic responsibility" not only in the pursuit of economic prizes. Economic goals are "proximate goals," which have become "disconnected from ultimate goals and take precedence over them." Competitiveness should be measured by how Americans actually live, not by statistical averages. Reich shares the same goal as theorists whom he criticizes, raising the "standard of living" for all citizens, but he adds two elements in addition to higher productivity and more private goods and services. People are more than consumers. As do Galbraith and Thurow, he includes communal goods which people value, such as clean air. He adds a political-moral component to the standard of living, a sense that goods "are justly shared among citizens."[32] Living standards for the bottom two-thirds of the population must be improved. Closing loopholes and expanding the progressive income tax on the wealthy is necessary; the United States' taxes are "the lowest of any industrialized nation." What will these taxes finance? At one time Reich would have emphasized industrial policy. Now he focuses on educating and retraining the majority, who are increasingly unable to compete worldwide and whose living standards are either stationary or declining.[33]

The purpose of government intervention is to secure equal opportunity that is fitted to changing opportunities and circumstances. Equal opportunity is a contested concept. For Reich, defining equal opportunity as the removal of legal obstacles and the ideal of opening careers to talent is too narrow. It ignores the environment within which people operate and assumes that wants and preferences are self-generated and independent of social context and influence. Effective aid can "increase people's capacity to take active responsibility for their fate." Social insurance expands freedom. Welfare represents "mutual obligation" not charity or altruism. Effective equal opportunity weakens "class rigidities" and means everyone has a realistic chance to enter better jobs—"any talented American kid" can become a "symbolic analyst—regardless of family income or race." It requires retraining at all levels of work, nutrition programs, health care, better education, development of human capital, and infrastructure improvement. These are not welfare but "investments in our collective future." They involve our sense of nation, of belonging, and of sharing, and reveal the limits of public action in a society where economic power confers influence. Whether the fortunate minority "are willing to bear these burdens" is uncertain. "As the economic fates of Americans diverge, the top may be losing the long-held sense of connectedness with the bottom fifth, or even the bottom four-fifths, that would motivate such generosity."[34]

Community

Reich's concern with equality, common interest, "public deliberation,"[35] social insurance, civic culture, and public philosophy reflects a deeper absorption in community than many critics find in liberalism. As with Hobhouse and Dewey, but more firmly than Keynes, Thurow, or Galbraith, Reich links liberalism and community, though not communitarianism, and usually discusses community in national terms. Americans have always believed in though not invariably practiced a notion of community. The common tale of a "benevolent community" is a story about helping one another, sacrificing for the common good, expressing "community pride and patriotism. . . . generosity and compassion." The liberalism of the "New Deal . . . Fair Deal . . . Great Society" visualized the United States as "a single, national, community, bound by a shared ideal of equal opportunity, and generosity toward the less fortunate." Successful policies benefit everyone: Social Security, unemployment insurance, or tax exemptions for health insurance.[36] "The common error" of individualistic liberals and conservatives is to divide people into us and them, emphasizing conflicts of interest rather than shared heritage, "mutually rewarding encounters, or common efforts to overcome perils." Post–World War II liberals tend to see the poor, minorities, and anyone experiencing problems as victims needing help. Conservatives see them as dangerous, "unruly and exploitative," needing discipline.[37] Both ignore the "social obligation," interdependence, and responsibility that develop a sense of community. Collapsing under economic strain and weakened by hostile ideology, social cohesion is disintegrating and the national community is splintering. Wealthy, successful minorities are seceding from the United States. The majority are facing reduced circumstances and real losses. Community feeling crumbles, yet community is vital to economic and political success. "Much depends on the extent to which we consider ourselves one people whose fates are linked."[38]

Reich's individualism differs from that of classical and laissez-faire liberalism, which are satisfied if people are allowed to compete. The radical, competitive, utility-maximizing, self-activating ego, standing alone in time and space, calculating personal costs and benefits, bound only by individual valuation and voluntary contracts, is alien to his argument. The achievement of private ends is not identical with the common good. "[O]pportunistic individualism" destroys collective activity, traps us in "the dismal logic of the prisoner's dilemma" where a premium is placed on lack of cooperation and trust, and ignores how wants are formed. Individualism and community are not necessarily opposed. Reich agrees with Michael Sandel that people are never "unencumbered" but they are always "situated" in an environment that shapes and gives meaning to them. Policy can emphasize common interest, "mutual responsibility and reciprocal benefit," widening and shaping the individual's expressions of self-interest.[39] Reich frequently denies that people are only individualized utility maximizers, and he rejects a sharp dichotomy between the public and the private, clarifying the relationship between individuals and community:

> It is the *interaction* between our public and private selves that shapes the nature of our politics and the character of our economies and determines our capacity to adapt to the changing conditions we confront as a nation. It is in the balance between the two that we simultaneously preserve our individuality and cultivate our social membership.

Giving either sphere "exclusive claim to our loyalties" risks "falling victim to either mass tyranny or solipsism."[40]

American community feeling is founded on three unifying factors: a sense of shared history; economics,[41] especially a feeling of fair treatment and a willingness to postpone demands, reach accommodations, and moderate self-interest on the promise that the future will be better; and in waging the Cold War, a willingness to sacrifice individual aims in pursuit of national aims against the Soviet Union. Number three has virtually disappeared, and Reich wonders if anything can replace that lost sense of national purpose, one which was used to justify needed federal spending on common goods such as roads and education. Willingness to postpone demand is also disappearing. As global economic webs develop and American manufacturers move routine, standard production to low-wage areas, the wealthy 20 percent gain from these global ties, while most of the other 80 percent decline. The economic element remains crucial. Community and nationhood depend heavily on economic ties and benefits that are now disappearing, and our sense of shared history may be too fragile to keep us united. This threat of disintegration justifies Reich's claims about the inseparability of politics and economics, his proposals for public intervention into the economy, and his concern whether the political community can survive the breakup of strong national economic ties.[42]

Reich is critical of supply-side and laissez-faire notions that deny community. Conservative policy in the 1980s and 1990s exploited mutually supporting myths of the triumphant individual, fear of the other, mistrust of welfare, and a narrowed image of community to argue that we owe little to one another. This absence of mutual duty allows retreat into enclaves of like-minded people with similar status, bound only by comparable income, isolated from and denying existence of a national community. Such isolation aggravates divisions between the most successful who participate in the new international economy and the majority who do not. President Reagan's tales of local community disguised the creation of these "ersatz neighborhoods." With more ties to the world economic net than to fellow "citizens," even to those living in the poor town next door, this "new community" represents not a "'renaissance'" of American community feeling but its further shattering. "[G]enerosity and solidarity end at the borders of our common property values," so that benevolence, community feeling, and responsibility require little from the affluent.[43]

Although global economic forces are splitting it apart, the "economic community" can be strengthened and reinvigorated. "[C]ommunitarian values can be shown to underpin future prosperity." Conservative ideology justifies "radical bifurcation of the work force," making cooperation to improve conditions impossible. Successful entrepreneurialism needs to revise the myth of the "Triumphant Individual" that blinds us to challenges requiring "joint effort rather than individual conquest." Reich believes, as did Brandeis and Thurow, that relationships that develop within an organization are important to people, valuable "in themselves," and represent community feeling that frequently transcends "contractual agreements." Reich argues we must recognize the social costs of abandoning communities and the social-economic benefits that often accrue from keeping teams of workers together and not fearful for their futures. Yet, "at every level" American workers lack "reciprocal obligation . . . mutual trust" and "a sense of shared purpose." "Collective Entrepreneurialism," which emphasizes coordination, sharing common experience, and integrating skills into groups, can create trust and community. The relevant questions are "Who Is 'Us'?" and what can be done to create "conditions for confident engagement on joint endeavor?"[44]

Community does not mean corporatism or integration into an entity representing one's real will. It is much harder to say what it does mean, for Reich lacks a detailed analysis and blueprint for achieving community. Community involves discourse, some mutual identification and sense of membership through shared experiences and identities beyond solitary egos, accepting social obligation for benefits received, and a revival of democracy. Continued secession into enclaves could mean the end of the "'American experiment' . . . a diverse society bound together not only by its love of individual liberty but also its sense of justice." The key variable is "social membership." This requires changing the contractual approach to individualism and fostering the "deep strain of civic republicanism" that includes following the spirit of rules and recognizing local organizations, "economic cooperatives, religious groups, and community associations" that have traditionally supported the moral structure of civic relations, liberty, and training for citizenship. Reich believes that to sustain a sense of community liberals must reemphasize "equal sacrifice" for all. Contemporary policy is abandoning that essential ingredient of fairness, discouraging the willingness "to contribute rather than exploit." Cooperation develops only when people are initiated "into a culture of shared responsibility and mutual benefit." Only confidence that the costs, burdens, and benefits of change will be fairly shared—a sense of "social justice"—can reduce opposition to needed social-economic change. Such confidence arises from belief in community and belief that one has some effective input into decisions. It does not come through rational pursuit of economic utility maximization.[45]

Reich argues that mutual obligation and responsibility are based on long run, enlightened self-interest, and he defends trust, obligation, and mutual responsibility as necessary if we want growth, national well-being, or high-wage jobs. His argument for community is, in fact, a moral one, although the specific moral and ethical content are neither justified in moral terms nor spelled out in full detail. Reich offers clues as to the ethical criteria of a good society: society is not divided into heros and drones or the strong and the weak but many have untapped potential; all people have worth; equality is a positive value; government should have an active role in aiding people; and people share a common interest that transcends competitive self-interest. In some of his work, however, the ethical basis for community becomes submerged in the argument that achievement of our economic goals is contingent upon community. Community then appears to be a means to achieving economic ends rather than an end in itself.

Democracy

Reich's theory of democracy, which shares with Dewey, Hobhouse, and Brandeis a concern with the nature of democracy in an industrial society dominated by large organizations, is largely ignored by commentators and is partly detached from his economics. Community and democracy are essential to one another, with participation fostering a sense of community that supports democracy. Democracy creates conditions that open the possibility of political and economic reform. Whereas traditional and economic conservatives seek to limit and curb democracy, Reich urges wider participation. He accepts neither a conventional pluralist[46] nor an elite vision of democracy and acknowledges that private and public bureaucracy undermine community and democracy. American democracy is plagued with problems that frustrate its meaning and effectiveness. The system is complex, "noisy . . . time consuming," vulnerable to being blocked at many points. The public often wants incompatible things, leading it to see civil servants and government as ineffective and unresponsive. Democracy, however, "is also the best system for ensuring that government is accountable to its citizens" and, until recently, secured a relatively fair process for responding to and initiating change. The managerial ethic of independent, hierarchical, centralized decision making in business and government, which ignores the value of a participatory "process of political choice," has weakened democracy and political institutions. Administrators' duty is not to dictate to the public but "to sustain, even strengthen, democratic institutions."[47]

Administrative and judicial independence from the political process are a major problem, as are business appeals for aid, which are often hidden from the public. Unlike Keynes, Reich doubts that popularly elected legislatures can control public bureaucracy or ensure it is responsible. In contemporary conditions, to think otherwise "is a perilously weak argument" because bureaucrats are never automata following neutral processes or legislative mandates. Bureaucratic discretion is necessary but difficult to reconcile "with democratic values" and managerial criteria are often insufficient justification for policy in a democracy. It is impossible for either bureaucrats or judges not to have values, and the processes in which they make decisions—where "the real contours of the public and private sectors of the economy are mapped"—are "subterranean." Emphasis on results and meeting what the bureaucrats or judges perceive as needs subverts the public's ability to "deliberate." Political and bureaucratic refusal to "make explicit choices," and inequalities of power, wealth, and organization increase the ability of powerful interests to "manipulate" public perceptions and directly influence decision makers. Public servants can be made more responsible "by having regulatory agencies publish clear statements of what they intend to accomplish and how they are willing to be evaluated"; as Galbraith also proposed, by ensuring that "talented and dedicated people go into public service"; and by expanding popular participation. Whether or not the first two are adequate Reich strongly emphasizes the third possibility. Stimulating debate is crucial to this end.[48]

Reich cannot conceive of subordinating participation, by which citizens are educated and common interests are forged, to economic efficiency. In a critique of market philosophy as fundamental as Galbraith's critique of power, Reich argues that dominant administrative and economic theories ignore citizenship, the real process by which demands and interests are formed, and "disregards the role of ideas about what is good for society. . . . the importance of democratic deliberation for refining and altering such visions over time and for mobilizing public action around them." Individual ability and potential are not fixed "and immutable." Democracy does not consist of administrative entrepreneurs servicing autonomous, fully developed, individualized wants and demands. The view that represents interest solely in terms of personal wants, the public interest as "aggregation of individual interests," and democracy as a process in which people pursue individualized self-interest, is inaccurate and "normatively suspect" in ignoring "some of the most important aspects of democratic governance." These include "public deliberation over public issues and the ensuing discovery"—and creation—"of public ideas." Individualized pursuit of self-interest "may have a corrosive effect on civic life." "The tradition of democratic deliberation" has always emphasized citizen education and social good, countering the economic image of democracy and solitary pursuit of purely private good. Public debate over economic issues and demands for some protection from the effects of major economic change "cannot be suppressed in a democracy." Efforts to limit the scope of democracy to protect economic theories ultimately destroy democracy.[49]

As do Dewey and Galbraith, Reich argues that wants, preferences, and judgments are shaped, developed, upgraded, and understood in a social-political environment that conditions their formation, expression, and achievement. "Individual preferences" develop in a "social context" and "are influenced by" political, social and policy processes. Critical of public choice theory, Reich emphasizes collective formulation of ideas, interests, and preferences in consultation with others. Citizens have shared wants, preferences, *and* judgments that are formed through discussion and decision; these change their perspective, preference-ordering, and understanding of issues, problems, and solutions. Preferences have a public component and can be directed at achieving public goods. "Common interests are discovered. . . . social morality is defined and refined." But agreement is not assured. *"Deeper conflicts may be discovered."* Political action transforms actors. As in arguments from Aristotle through Jefferson and John Stuart Mill to contemporary participatory democrats, more participation can promote "civic virtue" and produce a sense of membership in society.[50] An acceptable social preference ranking[51] is possible because individuals' preferences are altered by judgments that are discovered, modified, and ranked in public discussion, not only in private.[52]

Democracy requires "an opportunity for the public to deliberate about what is good for society" through a process of "civic discovery." Participation develops and deepens social consensus and common interests, reducing zero-sum, trust-destroying behavior. People undergo social and collective learning about public possibilities, and decision makers have a "core responsibility" to facilitate that learning. A "deliberative relationship" can develop, which is "iterative and ongoing" in which citizens and bureaucrats talk and are mutually educated. Creation of community environments within which people "critically evaluate and revise what" they believe and want can weaken "passivity," strengthen "democratic institutions," and develop mandates for public policy that the individualized approach both objects to and cannot imagine.[53] "Civic discovery" assumes prior existence of community interest, rather than demonstrating it, and assumes that such interest will be refined through participation. Consensus building and development of common interest do not, however, eliminate individual interest and affiliation with other groups. Groups "are seedbeds for democratic opposition. . . . help to check state power" and provide training for citizenship.[54] Supporting individuality and separate interests, community does not require an amorphous, all-embracing consensus that would leave decision makers free to control policies.

Unlike participatory theorists such as Benjamin Barber, whose influence Reich acknowledges,[55] Reich appreciates the barriers to expanding effective participation and "nurturing social learning about public problems and possibilities." Obstacles include great difficulty of creating the time and opportunity for deliberation, the elusiveness of implementing deliberation, the potential exacerbation of community divisions, resentment by politicians, desire by bureaucrats to substitute personal vision for "public authority," and the possibility of different results if other groups or representatives had participated. Participatory dilemmas are worth facing to make government and bureaucracy more legitimate and to integrate the public into decision making. Effective public participation engenders learning in public, which "is a prerequisite to everything else." For Reich, this is the only process through which real mandates can be created. Other approaches, such as the belief leaders know what is best for the public or limiting public input, justify ignoring public demands or manipulating public opinion.[56]

Reich is unclear and strangely apolitical about mechanisms for increasing participation, urging experimentation. His is not direct democracy in any classic sense. Reich focuses on administrative processes and limited economic democracy, not on expanding participation at the expense of legislative bodies. The public will not make decisions per se but enter into dialogues with decision makers, acting to limit and legitimate their policies, critiquing proposals, offering input into determining problems, and evaluating solutions. Participation includes an "interactive process" of mutual exploration, through public meetings, public debates over proposals, workshops, hearings, and by seeking out representatives of affected and unorganized groups. This process can teach participants that there is no one unique, perfect solution, and may help develop public trust.[57]

Democracy is not just a limited decision-making procedure, lacking goals or purposes. Reich insists politics is a legitimate method for determining policy and an important part of life, not secondary to spontaneous markets. Political action changes and improves the actors themselves.[58] Democracy becomes almost a way of life, a forum within which citizens relate to one another, not only a means for making decisions. Its major feature is participation—consensus developed through discussion—not majority rule or consent. The classic democratic concern with equality is expressed in both proposals for more participation and for more substantive economic equality of opportunity. Democracy holds decision makers accountable to the public that is affected by decisions; they are made accountable by talking to people, justifying policies, and defending decisions. In the process, public deliberation comes to focus on the inevitable normative aspects of decision making. "[T]his richer notion of democracy" is designed to engage the public. Democracy does not need to be limited in order to curb popular passions, but deliberation revises the calculations of self-interest and common good, providing the "strongest bulwark against demagoguery."[59]

Reich reflects Brandeis' concern with the public effects of the methods of internal control in private enterprises. As do Brandeis and Galbraith, he applies political concepts to the activities of enterprises, reducing the public-private distinction. For Reich, democratization includes an element of economic democracy, in the form of participation in decisions at work and some degree of worker ownership. Unexamined "assumptions about the nature of work and authority" justify hierarchial, centralized control that frustrates collaboration. The "work community" is crucial to developing values such as cooperation, "privacy, equity, security, and participation" because it is here that "people experience authority most directly." Reich urges exploring "employee ownership and participation" on instrumental grounds—to increase productivity, long-term growth, worker satisfaction, and worker understanding of where their interest lies. International competition requires that "workplaces . . . become more equitable, secure, and democratic" to develop commitment to an enterprise. Participation at work includes a substantial element of team responsibility for decisions and production. Although arguing that worker ownership should become "commonplace," he does not explain the mechanisms through which it can be developed.[60]

Reich is the only one of the four economic theorists considered in this book to propose systematically expanding democracy in a way that is co-extensive with his economic proposals, but he does not explore his argument's full potential. He illustrates, however, that there is no necessary conflict between liberalism and democracy. Reich argues American democracy is endangered by faulty economic theories and failing competitiveness. Economists must accommodate to the reality of democracy and popular demand for government intervention when people suffer from market relations. Unlike conservative theorists, he would not have us strip government of power to intervene, make it less responsive, or reduce democracy. Rather we must enhance democracy. Problems of democracy can be cured only with more democracy, public involvement, and participation.

This attractive picture is neither a fully developed theory of democracy nor of the relation between democracy and policy making. Short of detail and means to achieve, these arguments are vaguer than his accompanying economic proposals. In the past "networks of economic interdependence induced the habits of citizenship." Interdependence in the United States is breaking down, weakening citizenship.[61] More participation is not the answer to the problem of symbol manipulators opting out of the system, and Reich does not claim it is. Despite his awareness of the impact of working conditions on citizenship, he does not make economic democracy the major element in his picture of democracy,[62] and participation at work is not integrated into civic participation, though like Brandeis he sees them as supplementing one another. Most other participatory democrats also fail to link these related spheres of work and citizenship. Conflict between them is possible as one's role as a participant in the work community may clash with one's civic role.[63] Reich does not analyze the tension between having elected representatives, who may feel little obligation to follow constituents' "unconsidered preferences"—as opposed to constituents' considered judgments—and trying to increase participation.[64] Moreover, the links between participatory democracy, economic change, and the international context are not fully explored. Presumably, participation gives people more control, makes them more trusting, and gives deeper insight into problems and common interests, which in turn should make people more accepting of necessary changes, but the mechanism is unclear.[65]

Role of Government

Reich sees the search for policy-relevant neutral[66] principles as futile. The market, public policy formation, and the substantive results of either process are not neutral. Wealth, organization, power, and position affect access, impact, and outcomes. Nonbiased policy administration is possible only in a framework of prior normative and allocation decisions. Lacking consensus, "in a heterogeneous society . . . ends and means are hotly contested." Determining common interest is difficult: "there is no really neutral process for defining the public interest." Institutions and decision-making structures favor "some substantive outcomes over others." Regarding industry, Reich claims, "The notion of 'neutral' policy is simply fantasy." Any decision affects future development and the mix of knowledge, skills, and resources that will flourish or wither. The problem for democratic government is not that economic policy has different impacts on different people and groups, depending on their needs and standing, but that choices among beneficiaries are rarely made explicit in industrial and trade policy. This allows decisions in these areas to be manipulated "by special interests," frustrating the possibility of achieving public economic or political consensus.[67]

The inability to formulate completely neutral public policy does not make Reich embrace the unmanaged market. The economy does not spontaneously produce neutral rules or neutral treatment in any but a superficial sense. Efficiency is not a neutral criterion. Existing law, organization, desired goals, and power mold market results. Numerous "alternative market outcomes" can be efficient "depending on the *initial* distribution of resources." Executives and corporations have great discretion and influence. Since preferences develop within a social context, and since individuals face different contexts and opportunities, allowing only individual market goals to shape results favors outcomes desired by the powerful, which may be socially or morally unacceptable.[68]

That many people no longer view markets or bureaucrats as neutral is politically significant and must be incorporated into policy making, not suppressed. One can pretend that economic changes are neutral between individuals and groups, or one can examine "the human consequences of economic change" and "invent other means for easing the adaptation." Increased democracy is one response to the impossibility of neutral public policy. If the existing policy system and its perceived major alternative—the market—do not guarantee neutrality, it is better that citizens have a significant voice in decision making by upgrading common interest and ensuring that the largest number of people possible, not just corporate and interest group leaders or top bureaucrats, have a role in determining policy.[69] Participation provides a forum in which allocation decisions can be made explicit, and costs and alternative beneficiaries debated. Opening up decision making can also make people feel that decisions are fair, increasing their willingness to accept needed changes.

Contrary to conservative rewriting of history, "[g]overnment creates the market by defining the terms and boundaries for business activity. . . . Business . . . is taking on tasks that once were the exclusive province of government." Given modern needs, "government is the principle agency by which the culture deliberates, defines, and enforces the norms that structure the market." Whether modern needs require, as he argued in the early 1980s, an industrial policy to make American corporations more competitive, or, as he urged in *The Work of Nations,* acceptance of national economic incorporation into the world economy and implementation of policies to make American workers more competitive, Reich rejects passive acquiescence in the face of threatening change. The "next frontier" is first economic but requires different social-political relations and ideas from those during early industrialization or the era of management dominance. As needed transitions will not occur spontaneously, major government involvement can help achieve our preferred futures.[70]

Given what Reich sees as the historic and current relation between government and economics—"[p]ublic and private spheres are becoming indistinguishable"—government involvement in the economy and business pressure on government are inevitable. The government-economy relation is a continuum of possibilities, not dichotomous. Even though the United States has gone through cycles of business-government interaction, with attempts to regulate business alternating with removal of constraints from and active support for business, Reich maintains that American governments have promoted business from the early years of the republic. The national government has been "an agent and a silent partner" especially for industrial planning and development, although it attempted "explicit . . . industrial management" only twice: in the 1930s in response to the Depression, and in the late 1960s with health, safety, and environmental regulation. Regulatory coordination of industries, quotas, tax breaks, tariffs, interest-free loans, government funded research and development, and so forth supported industry much more effectively than explicit and public bailouts. Although on a lower level than in most other nations, this intervention helped propel the United States into standardized, high volume production.[71]

Regardless of ideological claims to the contrary, the United States has developed an "ad hoc system of national planning," "industrial policy by default," that is "fragmented and hidden from view," "obscured," while larger questions of goals, who should benefit most, and the relation of these policies to national purposes remain unasked. Even the Reagan-Bush supply-side doctrine was a form of industrial policy, "sold to the American people" as a bargain that services for the many and taxes for the well-off would both be reduced on the promise the latter would invest more, improving everyone's welfare. Coupled with rollbacks on "health, safety, and environmental regulations," it was a coherent though erroneous and destructive industrial policy. Defense spending is very important. Pentagon support of research constitutes a "tacit industrial policy," shaping national research and resource allocation, benefiting some enterprises, and employing large amounts of scarce engineering and scientific talent. More important, we have used defense as a pretext for doing things we should not do, such as "preserve the nation's outmoded industrial base," and for doing things we should justify in terms of contribution to common benefit, such as "public-sector investment" in highways, education, student loans, and much of the space program. Although military justification failed to sanction "all that needed to be done domestically," it provided "a means of talking about our common goals, and thus legitimizing discussions about our common needs."[72]

Reich is known best for his industrial policy proposals. He argued government should play a major role in upgrading and reshaping American industry to enhance international competitiveness, and should develop policies that allow Americans to work smarter. In the early 1980s Reich said it is better to admit what we are already doing as the first step to developing an effective, "transparent," accountable, and democratic industrial policy. Failure to admit engagement in trade and industrial policy allows special interests to manipulate and abuse the situation. "Such back-door interventions undermine the democratic process." They help realize self-fulfilling prophecies that government must fail because none of them "has been viewed as part of a coherent industrial policy" or in terms of "international competitiveness." Protection was never "made . . . contingent upon an industry's willingness to restructure itself," which resulted in lost opportunities to improve competitiveness. Reich believed government should impose on "private" enterprises explicit conditions that would promote national interest, as it did with Chrysler, in exchange for aid.[73] In this, he requires less of government than Keynes who emphasized capital accumulation and direction of investment. Reich denies this is national planning, "if we take that to mean the centralized drafting of detailed blueprints for future economic management. We already have that sort of planning" by large corporations, sometimes in cooperation with government agencies. Calling industrial policy national planning is a "caricature" of "flexible and experimental" policies to foster competition. There are "too many variables" and complex networks to do without markets. But markets can be aided, shaped, and encouraged.[74]

Improvement requires "massive change in the skills of American labor" necessitating "investments in human capital" that only governments can make. Details are less important than the basis of Reich's argument. Reich claimed that public interest and common benefits exist and industrial policy is "appropriate when the public return on investment is likely to exceed the private return." Individuals and individual firms do not capture the full value of their investments in education, which have wider social impact. Return includes economic, social, and political considerations such as enhanced competitiveness; reduced pain from job loss, inability to relocate, insecurity and status loss from unemployment; maintaining the fabric of the local and national community; and ensuring the economic base for citizenship. Even if markets could manage needed improvements, costs would be unnecessarily high, produce undesirable results, and government would still be involved. "[S]ocial justice is not incompatible with economic growth, but essential to it. . . . the goals of prosperity and social justice cannot validly be separated." Costly change can be accomplished in one of two ways: weaken democracy—that is, "eliminate political organization and political access"— or "democratize" planning and ensure that change and burdens are fair.[75]

By the time Reich published *The Work of Nations* (1991) economic circumstances had changed—the Unites States could no longer control its economic borders. He embraced more of the market, abandoned industrial policy and industrial restructuring designed to sustain American firms, advocated free trade, and claimed there were few uniquely American firms. "American" corporations, purely "American" products, and a separate national economy were merging into a global economy. Helping United States corporations does not automatically help American workers. The nationality of a firm owner has limited relevance to individual Americans' welfare. Thus, as Galbraith also argued, corporate interests are no longer

identical with national interests. The central question is the value that a
nation's workers add to world economic webs in which they take part.
Increasingly the standard of living depends on the "skills and insights" that
individual Americans contribute to the world economy. Unfortunately, only
a small minority, about 20 percent, the "symbolic analysts" are equipped to
compete. The rest, often caught in eroding industries and low-skill service
work cannot maintain deteriorating living standards. Education, retraining,
investment in the bottom 80 percent and a sense of fair dealing are crucial to
whether the United States can remain a "society" even if integrated into the
world economy.[76]

Arguments that *Work of Nations* demonstrates a fundamental shift in
Reich's thinking[77] are overstated.[78] The specific policies advocated have
changed but the deeper level of principles and moral-social goals upon
which policy is based continues between his earlier and later work. In both,
economic forces dividing the nation must be addressed. Reich saw industrial policy as a means to an end: individual and national welfare and social
justice. *Work of Nations* retains emphasis on the social-political significance
of nation and national identity; however, the uniqueness of national companies and economies has disappeared due to pressure from economic
change. Nationalism needs to be expressed in new ways. Beggar-thy-neighbor nationalism is mutually destructive. The "new logic of economic nationalism" focuses on the welfare of individual people through the development
of skills necessary for global competition. It requires public investment in
infrastructure and education to ensure that Americans can compete, not
withdrawal from the world, laissez-faire, or ignoring how American companies have integrated themselves into the world economy. This "positive
economic nationalism" enhances skills and productivity and is thus not zero-
sum. It uses health care, payments, and training to encourage worker movement from old to advancing industries; sees investment in these areas as
"unambiguously public"; is compatible with some subsidies to producers;
and encourages similar development elsewhere.[79]

Broader acceptance of the market does not mean that Reich has abandoned active government. If the market does not operate as laissez-faire theory claims, there is no need to accept its social-political results. Though he
may concede more to neoclassical theory and the role of the market now
than in *The Next American Frontier or Minding America's Business,* his proposals "are not intended to comfort the defenders of laissez-faire orthodoxy"
about how to improve "the economic prospects of citizens."[80] The type of
adjustment needed is different, but he still argues that active government
can foster broad social goals and accommodation to world forces. Echoing
Keynes, Thurow, and even Galbraith, he says "I'm a free marketeer, but I'm

also a believer that the public sector has a central role." Choices are limited to "different laws designed to motivate different behavior," not to intervention or quietism.[81]

Government is not destined to fail. Past success in promoting business shows the usefulness of government economic involvement. The General Agreement on Tariffs and Trade and the International Monetary Fund powerfully promoted international trade. Postwar industries receiving the most aid and regulation—"[a]erospace, aircraft, telecommunications, agriculture, pharmaceuticals, and biotechnology"—are among the most successful industries. Reich does not claim government is always effective; some failures are due to following industry's goals and organization patterns. Reversing conservative ideology, however, he puts the burden of proof on those who argue there is no need for active government to address the social-economic problems generated by conservative political-economic ideology and policy. Government does not have the knowledge or means to run the economy—business must do that—but it is responsible for creating conditions that attract good investment, investing in risky, expensive knowledge-generating projects, and coordinating the investments and social policy that are essential to reform.[82]

Government can also more successfully carry out traditional duties. In a theme reflected early in the Clinton presidency's proposals on education, Head Start, employment, infrastructure, and health care, Reich argues that money spent on "health and education are investments in America's future" every bit as much as (if not more than) money spent on factories and equipment. Only infrastructure and worker skills are immobile and unique to a nation. They attract foreign investment and promote competitiveness. Government has "'an extraordinarily important role . . . in the future productivity of the bottom 80 percent.'" Declining "public investment" spells deep trouble for future growth and citizen satisfaction. Private utility maximization cannot fully perform these tasks; even Adam Smith accepted a government role. Yet, public investments deeply "affect our future capacity to produce."[83] The best way to address government weaknesses is to open up decision making, encourage a popular sense that decisions are fair, and expand participation. Coupled with Reich's argument for "transparent" public policy making[84] this counters conservative claims that government must be stripped of its power, democracy curbed, and more things made "private" in a supposedly neutral market. Reich claims it is also good economic policy.

Too many policy makers tend to "view the world through the eyes of bankers and traders . . . prone to sacrifice the real to the symbolic and the present to the future." They confuse ends and means, proximate and ultimate goals, immediate financial success with long term structural adaptation. Economic success is defined as lower inflation or a strong currency, not the physical, civic-moral, or public goods that comprise welfare.[85] In a reversal of conservative claims that liberals sacrifice the future for the present, Reich asserts that maintaining current policies and beneficiaries will not meet long-term needs or produce acceptable living standards for the majority. Thus the market is not the sole legitimate means for determining our collective future. The United States must choose its future. Politics and democracy have a significant role in defining the kind of economy and society we want, and trying to create political and social institutions to "cope with . . . centrifugal" international economic forces that impair the economic base of citizenship. United States capitalism is not the only or the most popular possibility. "East-Asian neo-mercantilism" and "European social-democratic" models challenge comfortable illusions about sustaining sharp distinctions between economy and polity. Whatever path we choose, and it is always a matter of choice, government will be involved.[86]

Conclusions

Given current usage, Reich's linkage of liberalism and community is problematic, and Reich's incomplete discussion of either freedom or individuality—both central liberal values—makes it even more so. Liberalism, however, is multifaceted and evolving, and cannot mean only one thing. It is unimportant whether Reich is called a neo-liberal[87] or whether he is seen as fitting the pattern of New Deal liberalism.[88] Reich insists that positive government is necessary to confront problems caused by economic growth and change, while preserving values of democracy and social cohesion. There will be no just or successful solutions without a large government role. Reich is part of the liberal tradition and supports values and relations many liberals find compelling and even essential to meaningful liberalism—empowering workers, reforming political-economy, political participation, education, reducing job insecurity. Reich's communitarianism values individualism and supports pluralism. He does not accept Barber's[89] lack of economics. His more modest model contends that neither individuals nor beliefs develop in isolation, but groups shape personality, belief, and world outlook. In short, the group is essential to the development of wants, personality, and economic productivity. People and policy must be understood within their context. There are no isolated selves, and politics and economics overlap with one another. Ideas about what is good or desirable shape behavior and self-interest. In political economy each term modifies and shapes the other. Even here Reich is in the tradition of Hobhouse, Dewey, Keynes, and Galbraith.

Reich is passionately concerned with the crumbling middle class and millions of unskilled and underskilled workers who cannot compete well. Like Keynes' support for the World Bank and International Monetary Fund, Reich's economic analysis raises the political question whether or not the United States and other nation states can survive as unified societies with distinctive social policies. Reich does not address the full implications of the withdrawal of symbol manipulators from the rest of society, the division into an affluent minority and an increasingly threatened majority, and the weakening of ties between citizens. Deepening divisions between symbol analysts and the rest could lead to a destructive politics of class and class conflict. Active government, positive economic nationalism, defense of political sovereignty, ability to tax, and effective social welfare programs may not survive the new capacity of the most successful members of the community to tap into the international system for resources to pursue their own economic and social ends. Reich does not discuss power, but these people have power, in the sense that their skills and resources are needed and in their ability to transfer resources outside the nation. In short, why should they pay taxes when they do not need their fellow citizens, especially when it is possible to manipulate popular feelings of nationalism?[90] Industrial policy could have helped forge a sense of common national purpose and need, but national industrial policy is no longer an option. Reich's problem is that of all liberals and social democrats: given factor price equalization, are relatively full employment, attractive living standards, a sense of security, and social justice possible in a free-trade, open system? There are no ready answers. Reich's incomplete specification of coalitions for change would be less troublesome if he had consistently developed the morally relevant assumptions in his work—that all people have ability that can be developed, social justice is possible and government has a central role in its attainment, equality is valuable, and increased participation fosters development, social justice, and equality—on which his proposals are often based. Reich is aware of some of these problems and seems to hope that symbol manipulators will realize their duty to the rest of society, but he is not sanguine. The United States may yet become "a microcosm of the world."[91]

7

Issues

Every man will submit with becoming patience to evils which he believes
arise from the general laws of nature. . . .
—Thomas Robert Malthus, *An Essay on the Principle of Population*

Energy and self-dependence are . . . liable to be impaired by the absence
of help, as well as by its excess.
—John Stuart Mill, *Principles of Political Economy*

It is very hard to recognize that new realities force the creation of new
virtues—new procedures, new rules, and new institutions.
—Lester Thurow, *Head to Head*

PREDICTIONS OF THE IMMINENT DECLINE of liberalism have been
common for decades.[1] Liberalism, however, is not a platoon of unchanging
policies, but an array of continuing *principles* that are embodied in evolving
policies and adapted to changing circumstances. The theorists in this book
illustrate that liberalism is capable of reinvigoration and adaptation. They
insist that political-social values and moral discourse are integral to political economy—not determined by spontaneous market operation—and that
active government is necessary to democracy and to economic well-being.
Such arguments have transformed the liberal democratic understanding of
freedom, individualism, and liberal equality, as well as of the relations
between individual and community, public and private, economics and
democracy. Reform arguments and recommendations have shaped public
policy affecting hundreds of millions of people, and, in the case of Keynes,
world order itself. Whether or not one agrees with Galbraith that Keynes
saved capitalism, reform liberals have attempted to interpret and apply liberal principles to altered circumstances, believing that they are protecting
basic values, past gains, and future possibilities—and in the process criticizing conservatives and conventional liberals. Most of these theorists are
not philosophers[2] but activists comfortable with ideas, who apply principles

and values to public problems and policy. While usually avoiding technical philosophy, they offer principled alternative answers, as against market ideology, to their contemporary problems. Liberalism, however, must address a number of dilemmas and criticisms if it is to prepare itself for twenty-first-century conditions. Debate over these issues is grounded in philosophical and ideological differences, but it is argued at the level of policy preferences and implementation. It involves interrelated pictures of democracy, human motivation, freedom, community, and location and meaning of power; and such fundamental questions as whether capitalism is self-stabilizing, what standards should determine distribution, whether policy can be neutral, and what are appropriate relations among polity, society, and economy. These issues have been discussed in previous chapters. Here we examine reform liberals' general response to criticisms and problems.

Measured by current influence on policy, reform liberals are losing the battle for public opinion in contemporary politics. Liberals such as Galbraith, Thurow, and Reich have been less successful than conservative critics in capturing public understanding of liberalism and in explaining the purpose and role of government. Their difficulties on this point have allowed conservatives to demonize liberalism and to define such liberal values as freedom and individualism for their own purposes. Although economic values and assumptions are not the only causes of disquiet, they shape pictures of many legitimate public policies. In this environment, changed economic realities cause social-political problems and discontents that are used—in the name of traditional values—to attack policies that reform liberals insist can fulfill historic values and principles. Contemporary proposals to reduce health protection, worker safety protection, business regulation, job training programs, income and security programs, federal support for education, funding for the arts and public broadcasting, environmental protection, or energy conservation research are based on the assumption that there are only private purposes and government spending harms freedom, produces no net gain, and by definition is more wasteful than private spending. Reform liberals dissent vigorously. Even if they are not currently defining legitimate public policy and a role for government, reform liberals offer the only widely accepted option in the context of liberal-democratic society. Conservative ascendance and its destruction of the resources necessary for active government may be permanent or temporary, but reform liberalism remains (as it has for one hundred years) the main alternative to the philosophy of leaving the economy and social-economic relations alone.

Democracy

Democracy is commonly considered the most complex problem for liberalism. The relation between liberalism and democracy has been problematic and at times hostile but never simple. Seeming conflicts between protecting individualism, individual rights, and property (on the one hand) versus participation, an active public role in the economy, the majority principle, and equality (on the other hand) have provoked generations of debate. Liberal failure to accommodate democracy is often cited by critics of liberalism. Jefferson's emphasis on majority rule and minority rights summarizes this tension. But asserting that a dilemma exists is itself problematic, because there is no single relation between democracy and liberalism, just as there is no single concept of liberalism or democracy.

The historical picture of the relation between liberalism and democracy is mixed, in part because liberalism developed before modern concepts of democracy did. Until the late nineteenth century, economic liberals were often indifferent or hostile to democracy. The classic statements of economic liberalism by Adam Smith and David Ricardo do not mention democracy, and Ricardo's economics is largely incompatible with democracy. In a continually recurring argument in early liberal political-economy, Thomas Robert Malthus opposed expanding political participation until the working classes accepted his economic theory, which founded their—and all other persons'—position in natural laws and God-given rules of property, so that nothing could be done to better their condition until they produced fewer children. Utilitarianism was mixed. Bentham eventually accepted the need for enlarging suffrage, but James Mill proposed limiting it to the middle class. Social Darwinism opposed expanding the meaning or content of democracy. William Graham Sumner argued that, if one favors democracy, one must support the system of laissez-faire capitalism on which it is based and avoid any public intervention in the market. This claim is mirrored in the work of more contemporary conservative liberals such as F. A. Hayek and Milton Friedman. On the other hand, Thomas Jefferson proposed nearly universal, white male suffrage and some direct democracy. John Stuart Mill feared mass society and was willing to give more votes to intellectuals, yet he would have extended the vote to the working class and was the first major male theorist to argue for women's suffrage. In the United States, in our century, John Dewey and Louis Brandeis defended what can be called economic democracy.

Many claims are made about the relation between liberalism and democracy: the connection is weak or nonexistent;[3] democracy is dangerous to liberal political-economy; liberalism has an inadequate image of democracy; and, the position taken by liberals in this book, liberalism and democracy are closely related and mutually reinforcing.[4] This section briefly examines the second and third arguments.

Two[5] standard, contemporary, economics-related criticisms are leveled against liberal political-economy and democracy[6] and against liberalism in general. For want of better terms these may be identified with laissez-faire political-economy on the "right" and with demands for more democracy on the "left." The laissez-faire criticism has an affinity to traditional arguments, found in sources as early as Aristotle, that democracy is a threat to property and culture. It argues[7] that current forms of democracy allow excessive influence to the mass public represented by greedy special interests who use their power to rob and plunder the well-off. The welfare system and Keynesian economics are primary targets of this criticism. Democracy and liberal economics, especially Keynesian, are seen as a fatal combination incapable of limiting destructive economic intervention: "Democratic political processes are inherently myopic" and "short-sighted." According to F. A. Hayek, democratic government "should be limited" more than any other. As with Sumner, conservative theorists such as Milton Friedman assert democracy is impossible without their version of free markets: George Gilder argues, "Markets provide the ultimate democracy"; and Hayek asserts that "only within this system democracy is possible." Therefore the market must be left alone. To expand democracy into "previously non-politicized [market] areas of interaction" is perverse, according to James Buchanan. Hayek summarizes this position: "It is therefore necessary to restrain these powers to protect democracy against itself."[8] But while democracy must be limited to protect it against inherent excesses, the same argument does not apply to markets.

By "left" I mean the democratic "left,"[9] a mixed group of critics who tend to identify laissez-faire with liberalism. They argue that liberalism has a thin theory of democracy and is often hostile to democracy. Liberalism is insufficiently democratic, tolerates and often subserves economic power, allows capital to dominate, undermines community, and/or inadequately supports participation. Liberalism thus marginalizes[10] democracy. Michael Harrington, Benjamin Barber, and C. B. Macpherson exemplify theorists with this perspective. Harrington claims that liberals such as Galbraith ignore the "strong evolutionary trend toward subordinating the social good to private purpose." Liberalism fails to appreciate the role of participation in planning, supports a version of welfare that does not challenge capitalism, and supports a form of egalitarianism that fails to redistribute wealth, income, and power.[11] Barber focuses on points of opposition between liberal theory and democracy. Individualism and excessive emphasis on the private at the expense of the community make people apolitical, erode public interaction and relations in public, and dismantle "institutions that promote community life and active political citizenship." Barber proposes replacing this limited theory with "strong democracy," which stresses citizenship, participation, and community, leaving the role of representation unexplored.[12] Macpherson's criticism is even stronger. Liberal democracy has heretofore depended on a market model of narrow self-interested utility maximizers. Directly contradicting conservative claims about excessive democratic interference with the autonomous market, Macpherson asserts that liberal economics removes "political decisions from any democratic responsiveness." The liberal focus on economics creates possessive individualism, elevates economics above politics and community, nourishes inequality, and undermines democratic values that cannot function in an economic system fostering inequality. "[A] more equitable and humane society requires a more participatory system," which in turns calls for "a great reduction of the present social and economic inequality."[13]

It is doubtful that both criticisms of liberalism and democracy can be correct, though each contains telling arguments. Their validity or invalidity depends on conflicting starting pictures of democracy and of liberalism.[14] If democracy is simply a procedure for selecting governors, has no substantive content, and, along with politics, is secondary and epiphenomenal to an underlying economic reality, then there is little need for widespread participation, extensive equality, or an active role for majorities. Conflict between democracy and liberalism applies most strongly, therefore, to laissez-faire theory and policy—to the extent that the latter is still liberal. On the other hand, if democracy requires extensive participation, has a goal or such substantive purposes as social justice, freedom, popular control, and community, or is valuable in itself, it may require more equality, more public input, and more severe restraints on private economic power—all of which are compatible with reform liberalism. Brandeis, Dewey, Reich, and to some extent Galbraith and Thurow illustrate that liberalism can go quite far in addressing some of the criticisms made by the democratic left; and each theorist has serious disagreements with critics from the laissez-faire perspective.

This book has presented several approaches to democracy, each richer than the one contained in laissez-faire theory, and none claiming that the market embodies the essence of democracy or that democracy must be limited to protect market values. All seven reform liberals see a close reciprocal interaction between liberalism and democracy, and each denies that any inherent conflict exists between democracy and efficiency. Dewey insisted that democracy is the liberal method of change. Brandeis, Dewey, and Reich have the most expansive concepts, calling for more participation and for partial economic democracy. Keynes focused on protecting existing democratic systems, acted as though the extent of democracy had been settled, and did not discuss enlarging popular participation in political and economic decisions. Despite being a co-founder and one-time chair of Americans for Democratic Action—and more nearly a social democrat than any of the others—Galbraith focuses on the impact economic power and inequality have on existing and slightly expanded democratic practices, rather than exploring how a democratic economy can be achieved or how it could function. Faced with concentrated power and contented interests, he hopes many small reforms are possible. Reich dreams the big dream: direct participation—which Galbraith fears will co-opt people if limited—is possible and necessary. Still Reich does not explore the full meaning of participation in every aspect of political-economy. Thurow wants to strengthen the conditions for democracy, which, as with Dewey, he sees as growing increasingly inhospitable to real democracy; but he proposes little expansion in the functional scope of democracy. This limitation is troublesome since the theorists whom these writers chiefly criticize propose to curtail contemporary democratic practices and institutions to protect their image of free markets.

These purposes do not exhaust reform liberals' relation to democracy. Democracy is a bundle of elements, including freedom, equality, participation, and decisions about the areas of life to which they apply. Equality and freedom are essential components of democracy; but as with everything else discussed in this book deep, policy-related controversies rage over their meaning and application. The content we assign to them shapes class relations, justifies one power distribution as opposed to another, draws boundaries and links between public and private spheres and duties, and partly defines the legitimate role of government. Democracy is more than an elective procedure, but reform liberals (with Keynes partly excepted) apply it in varying degrees to social and economic relations. Dewey, Brandeis, Reich, and possibly Galbraith would agree with Macpherson that it is also a way of life, though not the same way of life as his.

If reform arguments about equilibrium, power, and organization are even partly valid, the laissez-faire model leaves much of the economy—and related social-political relations—under the control of private interests answerable only to themselves. In contrast, assurance of employment, welfare minimums, attempted limits on private economic power,[15] and expansion of equality and freedom can support democratic growth. Thus, while reform economists do not actively expand democracy as a political system, their economics is democratizing without always being democratic.[16] Whereas in the name of economic theory laissez-faire limits democracy by curbing participation, government, and government responsiveness, reform liberalism enhances the possibility for expanding democracy. For Dewey, Hobhouse, Brandeis, Reich, and (to some extent) Galbraith, the way to control government is to make it more democratic and responsive. Although much has gone wrong, and many liberals have come to defend the comfortable, liberalism has "wished to democratise the benefits of economic processes."[17] Most varieties of liberals admit this as a principle, although they passionately disagree over meaning and implementation. For reform liberals, more economic equality and public intervention to promote equality and to improve life-chances can prevent democracy from becoming, in J. S. Mill's phrase about unchallenged ideas, a shell and dry dogma unable to protect its basic values or adapt to new challenges.

Thus the first concern has been to protect broadly understood political, social, and economic conditions for the possibility of democracy. Given current problems and the small likelihood of transforming people in the short run, these theorists ask what needs to be done now. This helps explain why they discuss democracy more in terms of goals than in terms of mechanisms to achieve them. Open elections, equal votes, free speech, and representative institutions are assumed without question but are considered not to be enough. One theme has been constant: Ignoring economic stability and impact courts disaster. There is little hope for democracy, community, or civic virtue when people are afraid or struggling for economic survival. Economic insecurity, growing inequality, perceived social injustice, and a status quo in which some people use economic power to control the lives of many others endanger democracy. They engender and magnify zero-sum conflict,[18] discredit trust and cooperation, and encourage people to embrace undemocratic or potentially undemocratic alternatives.

Claims of inevitable conflict between liberalism and democracy are simply wrong, since they identify laissez-faire as synonymous with liberalism. The theorists examined in this book see democracy as having substantive ends. They agree with Thurow that "In a political democracy, greater economic equality may be necessary to preserve political equality." As early as 1888, Dewey argued that economic democracy is essential to political democracy; and Strum asserts—in a proposition that fits Dewey and Galbraith—that Brandeis applied Jefferson to "the industrial era."[19] Combined with Brandeis' condemnation of industrial absolutism, and the profound worry—by Dewey, Galbraith, and Reich—that growth of large organizations decreases popular control, this can serve to defend a worker share in business decision making.[20] Although Keynes and Galbraith do not discuss democratic participation in economic decisions, and Thurow only alludes to it, their arguments about power, against the autonomy and self-correcting nature of the economy, and in favor of an active government role[21] weaken claims that the market is democratic or that buying and selling define and protect one's interests. Thus, reform liberal economics does not exclude public participation but allows attempts at more popular control over the economy. None of these seven theorists calls for mass political quietism.

Much is missing. There is little discussion of the practice of democracy or of employing democratic organization to attain economic ends. Strengthened democracy requires both more, and more effective participation[22] and greater economic equalization. Only Brandeis, Hobhouse, Dewey, and Reich recognize the advantages of expanded participation that Jefferson or J. S. Mill claimed: developing active intelligent citizens, expanding appreciation of community needs, and creating means for resisting oppression. All argue that democracy requires economic stability, more nearly full employment, and more equality; but with the exception of Brandeis, Dewey, and (to some extent) Galbraith, on power, they do not connect this to citizenship, expanding choice in politics, or increasing resources for participation. They hardly discuss majority rule, despite their emphasis on majority well-being as opposed to profits for a few, and they have not worked out the interrelation between participation and representation. Arguments that the gap between corporation and government is smaller than in conventional theory, and that corporate officials hold real power over workers, the public, and government, can support economic democracy but it and other means for addressing private power are underdeveloped and often unexplored by the later theorists. Although international economic competition affects domestic control over work, welfare policy, and even, potentially, democracy due to growing economic inequality—arguments Keynes made in the early 1940s—the recent theorists do not question how more participation relates to or is affected by international economics.

The argument that liberalism has a weak picture of democracy is partly valid. But liberalism has evolved, and reform liberalism, despite lacking a complete theory of democracy comparable to its political economy, complicates and enriches the picture. Such a critique presupposes an image of democracy in need of specification and frequently ignores the contribution reform liberalism makes to expansive democracy. Moreover, there are hints and directions that can yet be taken. Development of Brandeis' argument for more democracy as a partial answer to corporate power would go far toward meeting this problem. Brandeis and Reich support more participation and a form of economic democracy conceived of mainly as sharing in decision making. But there is more. Reform liberals focus on economic reforms that encourage greater equalization, reduce private power, and promote freedom. The farther liberalism moves from an individualized, utility-maximizing model, the easier it becomes to embrace participation and equalization, in addition to traditional components of democracy such as freedom and consent. Reform liberals' strongest association with democracy has been to enhance the social-economic and political-economic conditions within which democracy can flourish. From within liberalism, these liberals criticize and reject the economic theory on which the laissez-faire version of democracy is based and stand closer to the democratic "left" than to traditional economic liberalism. They show that conflict between liberalism and democracy is unnecessary if both are generously interpreted. Urging a narrowing of the traditional gap between public and private, arguing for equality or full-employment policies that increase bargaining power, and claiming that economic dislocation undermines democracy, they emphasize that it is foolish and dangerous in a democracy to demand that people subordinate themselves to an economic theory. In this regard, reform liberalism justifies more democracy than is currently practiced in the United States or Britain. The picture of democracy becomes clearer in the context of political economy, community, and the role of government.

Political-Economy

One of the most common criticisms of liberalism is that it focuses excessively on economics and economic growth; believes growth can solve or eliminate problems of social justice, equity, and obligation; and substitutes growth for community and citizenship.[23] That is a straw person. It is laissez-faire ideology that insists politics and economics are separate, and that asserts economic considerations are superior to politics and social relations. When William Graham Sumner, David Stockman, sometimes Newt Gingrich, and F. A. Hayek are reduced to their essentials, they claim that natural economic forces ensure that things work as well as is possible. When applied to policy, this tenet allows private forces virtually unrestrained latitude to pursue their economic self-interest, which is assumed to ensure maximum growth and freedom for the polity as a whole. Nearly seventy years of activist public policy is dismissed as an organized assault on individual responsibility and market society, justifying claims that problems such as deficits, crime, inflation, illegitimacy, bad education, laziness, and slow growth are direct consequences of government intervention and welfare. Beyond a few fundamentals, including defense and (perhaps) monetary policy, whatever needs doing is done better by the market.

Reform liberals insist that divorcing politics from economics violates reality. Economic relations are important both as obstacles and as supports to freedom and individual development, and this necessitates that they be addressed. Destructive economic impacts on social-political relations, which have their own validity separate from economics, can be remedied in part by public intervention. Economic theories and proposals are politically relevant because they color perceptions of issues and permissible solutions. They shape understanding of, determine duties for, and set limits to government. The claim that economics contains many elements ascribed to politics, and the political content in many seemingly private relations—large organizations that act as political entities, the connection between political and economic power, and the public impact of business decisions have been discussed—spills over into politics and society. Reform liberals do not apologize for emphasizing economics and economic activities, because they do not insist on an unyielding distinction between politics and economics. Rather, they insist that economics has a deep impact on social and political life that is often ignored by conservative critics.

Growth is essential, yet it is not the sole or overriding concern. It is instrumental and does not substitute for equity, community, social justice, morality, or more equality—though under the right circumstances it may foster them. Galbraith and Keynes assume that there is a public, and they insist that we are rich enough to satisfy public needs and aid those left behind by increased output. Keynes saw economics as serving higher ends, and so do Galbraith and Reich. Reich and Thurow insist on growth with equity and some degree of redistribution. This reflects a picture of human motivation different from either laissez-faire liberalism or communitarian and civic republican arguments. Self-interest is broader and more integrated into communal relations than in the first theory which cannot explain patriotism, self-sacrifice, civic pride, or extensive cooperation. Reform liberals have some sympathy for communitarian and civic republican approaches, but they claim that both tend to neglect economic relations, economic power, the impact of economics on politics, and the objective basis for conflict. Hope that a communitarian focus and civic virtue can replace large parts of self-interested behavior may be a desirable goal, but it does not address the concerns of people currently living under stress, nor does it solve the problems that obstruct progress toward a more equitable society.

Criticism of laissez-faire political-economy is the key to reform liberal values and policy proposals. Socialism aside, reform liberalism has for a century been the main alternative to varying forms of social Darwinism. From Hobhouse's attack on evolutionary political economy and his argument that no part of society stands separate from the rest; through Brandeis and Dewey on power and organization; through Keynes about the impact of deliberate human decisions on welfare, and his denial that natural, self-stabilizing economic forces exist; through Galbraith on power, public needs and lack of individualistic competition in a significant part of the economy; to Reich's criticism of opportunistic individualism and its failure to protect people in the future; and to Thurow's analysis of zero-sum conflict and the dangers of a clash between capitalist inequality and democratic equality; as well as their shared doubt that capitalism stabilizes itself or that an essentially benign invisible hand ensures things work for the best, each theorist rejected the leave things alone philosophy. That theory is an inaccurate picture of reality, makes bad policy recommendations, protects power, and results in unacceptable and unnecessary suffering, dislocation, and conflict.

Rejecting the economic philosophy of laissez-faire, reform liberals necessarily reject the political and moral theory based on it. The market is not the preeminent institution, and natural economic forces do not determine political possibility. Economic disequilibrium and depression are normal, demanding choice and a conscious human role in shaping and determining social, political, and economic institutions and relations. If everything that results from self-interest in markets need not be accepted, moral choice—deciding which possibility is better—re-enters. Laissez-faire policies can, therefore, be modified or abandoned when they are perceived as an obstacle to basic goals. Reform liberals agree with Keynes that existing theory disregards "social detail" and runs the risk of "war, until those who are economically weakest are beaten to the ground."[24] Even if government intervention does not improve the economy, though they believe it does, it can achieve desired public goals and help protect democracy and society from instability, class war, zero-sum conflict, and despair.

While simultaneously agreeing that intervention is necessity, and accepting the value of markets[25] and private ownership, these theorists propose different types of intervention and regulation. None is a so-called welfare liberal—providing services and money without imposing some obligation on the part of the recipient—even if welfare is necessary to ensure a minimum level of subsistence from which people can develop. Welfare is an often necessary though second-best solution when we leave things alone or fail to intervene properly.[26] Conversely, reform liberals provide significant support for redistribution and social justice, as distinct from welfare policy. Only Brandeis wanted smaller-scale production. Dewey, like Galbraith, accepted organization and large size even though he did not like them. Each insists that the economy is embedded in, affects, and is inseparable from the social-political environment, but politics and economics are most closely linked in Galbraith.[27] With varying degrees of approval, Galbraith, Reich, and Thurow accept Keynesian-type aggregate demand stimulation. Galbraith is most critical that such policy neglects public needs, lacks strategy and goals beyond creating more production, and leaves the role of the state and economic power largely unchanged.[28] Reich also criticizes traditional liberal approaches. He and Thurow agree that such policy is now insufficient; and both emphasize public leadership in reshaping the economy, with Reich more concerned with social-political relations. Of the last three, Thurow has the most orthodox belief that the market can address issues such as environmental problems if the government properly structures incentives. Markets alone do not solve such problems.

Despite this open acknowledgment of the link between politics and economics, reform liberals today have less influence in shaping policy than do conservatives. Emphasizing existing conditions, actual markets, and the task of accommodating theory to reality, the complexity of the reform liberal world makes simple slogans irrelevant, yet these can provide comfort and political advantage. In contrast, reform liberals ask people to tolerate ambiguity. Distinctions are often blurred. Government economic involvement is not necessarily good or bad; it is just necessary. Deciding whether we need more or less depends on a changing political-economic-social environment, on legitimate goals, and on shifts in power—not on immutable economic laws. Answers to problems do not claim divine or natural sanction, or perpetuity; they only claim that they may work until conditions again change, at which point new answers will be required. This view applies also to freedom.

Freedom

Freedom is the core of liberalism. Having criticized laissez-faire political economy's picture of freedom as right of contract, government leaving people alone, and using one's resources as one chooses—if the market allows—reform liberals argue for a broader and historically contingent freedom. Freedom, its required institutional setting, and perceptions of how far it extends have changed and developed over time, and a single abstract principle or policy formulation cannot capture its meaning or significance.[29] Laissez-faire theory is oddly unconcerned with the actual situation. As long as formal procedures are satisfied, the market protects and embodies freedom regardless of actual outcomes. Reform liberals take an essentially consequentialist position. While valuing freedom as good, they also ask what is the purpose of freedom. Why do people want freedom? What can serve those purposes? They argue that it is necessary to examine the conditions under which people can experience freedom—that is, realize their potential, actualize what they are allowed to do, or achieve their purposes—rather than exclusively guarding against government coercion. They measure freedom in terms of actual situations, how people perceive their circumstances, and what their effective opportunities are. Under many conditions,[30] intervention can enhance freedom, by recognizing that freedom has other dimensions than government interference or noninterference. Judging whether this fundamental addition to traditional liberalism is reasonable or not turns in part on one's conception of the obstacles to freedom. For reform liberals, formal legal freedom is the necessary first step; but functional enjoyment of freedom is thwarted by conditions such as poverty, unnecessarily unequal power, few desirable choices, and excessive hierarchy at work. In addition to upholding traditional liberal political freedoms, civil rights, anti-discrimination (Brandeis and the last three), and sometimes affirmative action (Galbraith, Thurow, and Reich), reform liberal policy supports[31] increased economic democracy, minimum standards to help actualize formal freedom,[32] macrolevel intervention and regulation, full employment, and welfare.

The claim that one cannot expand freedom through intervention or by limiting the economic freedom of another—because freedom consists of lack of force and of using one's resources as one chooses—is a metaphysical belief, not a statement about reality or something we systematically practice. The legitimacy of intervention opens the possibility of positive freedom. Reform liberal theorists emphasize that *"external circumstances"* and *"capacities to act* within those circumstances"—according to Berlin, "what doors, and how many, are open"[33]—determine one's actual freedom, requiring protection against private power, lack of opportunity, and economic disaster, as well as provision of basic resources. For Hobhouse and Dewey (and with elements in Brandeis, Keynes, and Galbraith), freedom contains an element of autonomy and self-development, conceived of as more extensive realization of one's potential and at least partly self-chosen ends within a social-political context that actively supports individual endeavor. While not imposing any external criterion or guide as to one's real self, real purpose, or standard of achievement, this conceptualization is a step toward positive freedom. Reform liberals therefore accept a limited notion of positive freedom,[34] while criticizing the mechanical systems and quasi-determinism of classical liberal and laissez-faire political economy. Positive freedom does not mean achieving one's real end, whether or not one recognizes it; rather, it emphasizes outcomes and formal procedures. For these theorists it means ensuring minimum resources to protect people, including "the freedom that social insurance allows,"[35] from necessity that otherwise might force them to serve as the means to someone else's ends, despite their formal freedom. Thus Brandeis defended industrial democracy; Keynes supported fuller employment; and Galbraith promoted labor unions, a regular paycheck, and guaranteed minimal social goods as means to help ensure freedom and un-coerced choice.[36]

Individualism and Community

Classic theory started with the separate, distinct individual—an image strongly defended by contemporary laissez-faire theorists, who argue that community is the temporary coincidence of individual self-interest.[37] Crit-ics across the political spectrum, from Burkean conservatives through vari-ous types of communitarians to neo-Marxists, condemn all liberals and all forms of liberalism for inadequate or harmful concepts of individuals, com-munity, and their interaction. They maintain that an atomistic image of individuals lies at the heart of all liberalism, and they counter it with the assertion that dignity, development, mutual needs, justice, and spiritual well-being require strong community, solidarity with others, and, according to some, participation in community affairs.

The conservative theorist Russell Kirk argues that emphasizing self-interest and economic abstractions undermines community, common inter-est, and the myths that give meaning to lives.[38] From a different perspective, Benjamin Barber claims that liberals define individualism in a way that nec-essarily conflicts with community and with humanity's social being. "Alone-ness" characterizes liberal humanity. People are separate, apart, lonely, and solitary. Individualism destroys community and leaves "individuals cut off not only from the abuses of power but from one another. . . . easy targets for authoritarian collectivism."[39] Some claim that individualism precludes commu-nity. Introducing concern for the social context in which interest is defined or acknowledging people's social nature ruptures the liberal system and its "almost willful blindness" in believing people "are atoms of will" uninflu-enced by their environment.[40] Michael Walzer summarizes several criti-cisms: society is fragmented; people are encumbered; the liberal picture of voluntary association is inadequate; and numerous groups have great sig-nificance for people.[41]

Such criticism fits parts of liberalism but is inapplicable to reform lib-eralism. Liberals have a long tradition of concern for community and com-munal relations—a tradition that the theorists in this book reinforce. Mean-ings attached to individual and community have changed over the last 300 years. Reform liberals have moved away from and repudiated the philoso-phy of self-interest and its atomistic individualism. Individuals do not form preferences in isolation. Rather, people depend on and are deeply influenced

by others, circumstances and environment are critical, and we cannot satisfy individuality by leaving people alone to compete. What is individually
rational or profitable may be irrational or harmful for groups and nations.
Moreover, ideals of community and association must be alloyed with attention to the social and economic environment.[42] Reform liberals often emphasize the cooperative nature of life, of social relations, and of the economy. Hobhouse, Dewey, and Reich[43]—in his discussion of public ideas,
public philosophy, and civic virtue—are closest in spirit to communitarian
theory, but they see no conflict between community and liberalism. Hobhouse emphasized interdependence and social well-being, using the language of organic society. Dewey, Galbraith, and Thurow stress that traditional individualism ended with the development of a corporate perspective
in which individuals adopt the outlook of the group, often subordinating
seemingly individual interests to group interests. Dewey, Brandeis, and
Reich argue that community and democracy are necessary to each other.
Without exception, each calls for a revamped individualism that recognizes
and protects individuality while abandoning obsolete and counterproductive notions of solitary, competitive individualism. Thurow emphasizes
learning curves and, along with Brandeis and Reich, the cooperative aspects
of production. For Dewey, Keynes, Galbraith, and Reich, common good
embraces more than private consumption; and each theorist wants to expand
public goods. Brandeis' workplace democracy and Thurow's association of
the workplace with values other than money making raise the possibility
that work could form the basis for satisfying community relations. Galbraith,
Dewey, Thurow, and Keynes acknowledge that public and private or individual and community interests can clash, and the first two argue that only
government can protect public interest against powerful private actors. Galbraith's emphasis on social balance assumes community and common interest, as well as the prospect that conflict between private and community
goods and services can be settled. Thurow's zero-sum conflict is a problem
because the United States lacks community feeling, and dominant modes
of individualism militate against cooperation.

These arguments do not constitute a developed theory of community,
or a theory of how individuality is realized in strengthened communities;
but their concern with communal relations and public ideas is very different from critics' pictures of liberalism. As a group, these liberals are stronger
at criticizing and redefining individualism to allow a community orientation than at specifying community. Dewey, Brandeis, and Reich offer the
most concrete suggestions for achieving community. With the partial exception of Keynes and Reich, the last four see community in national terms,
letting slip the opportunity to develop personality or political action on the

economy at the local level. Community, however, is more than a warm and fuzzy feeling. Individual and community are not dichotomous, and individual and common good are compatible and mutually reinforcing. Laissez-faire's rigid boundaries between individual and community disappear, but individuals are not enveloped into community as some communitarians suggest. Individuality is the key. Reform liberal theorists stress individuality— achieving more of one's ends and interests; developing personality; escaping as many constraints as possible; being different, if that is what one wishes— as opposed to the philosophy of individualism, which asserts that pursuit of private self-interest through market competition is the sum of common good, and which is unconcerned with the feelings or experiences of individual people. Conditions for individualism have altered with organizational growth, economic change, and concentration of economic power; so preservation of individuality requires new means, at least some of which necessitate intervention. Of course, tension remains between individual and community. People continue to pursue economic self-interest, but individuality is not exclusively gratified by consumption. This image is not simply a compromise between laissez-faire and community, since reform liberals insist that reality cannot be divided into a choice of one or the other. Instead, they offer a picture of individuals acting in a supporting environment that suggests, transforms, and helps attain individual and common goals and interests.

Public-Private

Economics-politics, private-public, and business-government are different ways of talking about dualities between a sphere of primarily particular and one of essentially communal relations. Pictures of individualism, community, and the interaction of politics and economics shape a theory's image of public and private. Reform liberals see a complex relation. As with many issues there are two broad categories of criticism. Contemporary laissez-faire theorists criticize liberals for breaching the public-private distinction and allowing government to interfere in private matters. Calling economic decisions and relations voluntary and self-interested, yet system-sustaining and constitutive of whatever common good is possible, these critics assimilate such decisions and relations to the private. Others claim liberalism divides people by emphasizing only the private. For Barber, market emphasis precludes many public decisions and leaves too much of life under the control of so-called autonomous forces, which disguise manipulation and private power.[44]

No theory or polity folds all public matters into private relations nor claims that every thought and action are subject to public scrutiny—though some libertarians come close to the first and Mao may have contemplated the second. Much depends on one's conception of the separation between private and public: what one includes and excludes, where one draws the line, and how public and private responsibilities blend into one another. A theory could not remain liberal and assimilate private to public, but the classic and especially the laissez-faire specification of public-private is not the only possibility, nor are public and private completely dichotomous. The public-private nexus is not the point where people impinge on one another, but the point where one sees a legitimate or illegitimate impact. Looking at self-interested intentions, laissez-faire makes all legal market transactions part of the private; in contrast, reform liberalism emphasizes effects of economic decisions and refuses to reduce all goods to private goods. When results are broad or deleterious they take on a public character. Moreover, the private and privacy are not coextensive. One may properly demand privacy in a public forum, as when using a pay phone or with public data banks. Private refers to the arena of formal, defined self-regarding actions, and to that which is restricted or belongs to identifiable persons[45]—although what specifically is included under this heading is disputed. Privacy has many, sometimes conflicting meanings most of which center on autonomy, freedom from intrusion, and control over information about oneself.

Much policy controversy revolves around the question of what is public versus what is private. Conflicts over health care and Medicaid, taxes, smoking in public, welfare, abortion, school lunches, even unemployment compensation, ultimately reflect disputes over what is a private matter or responsibility and what is a legitimate public concern. Debate includes how far private or self-regarding behavior can affect others before it may reasonably be considered public. During much of the nineteenth century, wife beating was largely deemed a private matter. Today that is not so. One smoking fireplace is not a problem; thousands can foul the air. One business failure in a prosperous economy has little impact; thousands during a recession encourage social discontent. Many conservatives claim that air pollution and discrimination should be settled by the market. No one says that every unfavorable market outcome requires a public solution, but United States policy currently defines unemployment and unsafe products as public issues.

Given private power and the deep social-political impact of economic decisions, reform liberals oppose declaring most parts of the social-economy private. In altering traditional liberal images of the relation of politics and economics, freedom, individualism, community, and power, theorists in this book challenge core market ideology by modifying its separation between private and public spheres, broadening the areas of public concern and the range of legitimate means to address these. For reform liberals, the distinction between private and public is less clear and less tight than in traditional theory. Rather, the line is fluid, shifting, and sometimes blurred. Public involves more than government. Many putatively private areas—market, poverty, work conditions, some social connections, economic relations, discrimination—have a large social component and a substantial political impact. Important private concerns remain, but the economy is not the realm of purely private behavior, and the private arena is not exclusively or even primarily business or the economy. Moreover, the boundary between public and private shifts with changes in technology, in economic and political organization, in expectations, and in international relations.[46] Galbraith's *Affluent Society,* which contrasts private affluence and public squalor, identifies overemphasis on private consumption as a major cause of social problems and thus widens the sphere of the public without quite defining it. Galbraith's bureaucratic symbiosis, private power and business influence on government, or Reich's emphasis on the similarities between business and government bureaucracies, also bridge the public-private gap. Arguments by Dewey, Reich, and Thurow on education and by Brandeis on oppressive work conditions, which he says undermine one's ability to act as a free, consenting, democratic citizen, illustrate their shared belief that ostensibly private behavior has a deeper impact than is captured by markets.

Democracy is also affected. Traditional identification of "private" with market relations and "public" with coercive government has limited the extent of democratic activity. A broad conceptualization of the private curtails participation, citizenship, and democratic determination of policy. For example, Galbraith argues that advertising and commercial glorification of private consumption weaken regard for the public and for the common interest.[47] By reducing the gap between public and private, reform liberals potentially open more areas to democratic decision making. Because the content of the public is dealt with indirectly—usually in the course of addressing specific policy problems—the public is not fully defined. Reform liberals have a narrower public arena than do some proponents of participatory and communitarian theory; but when the public arena is seen as a key shaper of people and as the area of common interest, an enriched notion of public activity becomes possible.

Modification of the traditional liberal separation between public and private is related to power. If some economic actors have power—to buy acquiescence, to threaten workers or to induce government to accede to their needs, wants, and demands—this drastically weakens any hard-and-fast distinction between private and public. These are not either-or relations.

Power

Reform liberals reincorporate power into political economy. As befits all liberals, reform theorists are deeply worried about power; but unlike classic and laissez-faire liberals, they include private economic power in their concerns. Where traditional liberals focus on force, fraud, and coercion, reform liberals expand the meaning and sources of power, thereby enlarging the range of relations in which power can figure. They view claims that power dissolves in the market as gross and dangerous simplifications of what people actually experience. The economy is not innocent of power like the Lockean state of nature. In classic liberal terms, popular control and distinctions between state and society, and between market and government have broken down. If the traditional area of protection for the individual and for individual freedom can be a danger to historic liberal values, the conservative-libertarian identification of the market with freedom and its linkage between market and society breaks down, and government ceases to be the only threat. Individuals are generally powerless, but some individuals and many organizations have power. Work conditions and poverty frequently exert severe restraint—if not coercion—over individual behavior, because people often needlessly lack feasible alternatives. Power is not a dichotomous relation. There are degrees of power and vulnerability, and, as with obstacles to freedom, use and experience of power are shaped by existing circumstances.[48]

Reform liberals employ many examples of power as control and changing behavior: coercion,[49] force, manipulation, psychological restraint, preventing people from acquiring the means to act, exclusion of alternatives, taking advantage of others' desperate circumstances or vulnerability, implementation of policies that harm one class for the benefit of another, purchasing conformity, and shaping attitudes and beliefs to preclude other options, a concept that borders on hegemony. Unequal power undermines one's ability to act as a full, free citizen and is often unjust. Galbraith argues—and Dewey and Brandeis ("industrial absolutism") agree—that unequal power exists in market and other "voluntary" relations when business can influence or affect people, their lives, and concepts of welfare to conform to corporate interests. Keynes and Galbraith argue that making capital abundant would end capitalists' ability to exploit its scarcity value. Dewey, Brandeis, and Galbraith see power in wielding control over one's livelihood, especially when jobs are scarce.[50] If power includes not just coercion, but also influence, manipulation, and foreclosure of possibilities, it affects effective freedom and may be made subject to a wider range of public interventions in social-economic relations.

Empowering people is not often associated with liberalism. Even though they do not use the phrase, reform liberals propose to empower people by reducing constraints and expanding their ability to act. The issue of empowerment has moved from academic writing to partisan debate. Everyone wants to empower people, which raises two immediate questions: what does empower mean, and how can it be done? Contemporary conservatives such as Newt Gingrich propose to empower people by means that reform liberals insist reduce people's control: by curtailing government, expanding individualistic competition, reducing public services, and allowing the market to determine all benefits and rewards. The presence in the market of unequal power casts doubt on that enterprise. Participatory theorists favor increasing local and sometimes industrial democracy—a project that reform liberals can accept if it is accompanied by reduced concentrations of economic power and inequality. Given their assumptions about economy and polity, reform liberals make a number of proposals that may increase people's influence and control over events relevant to their own lives—without, however, claiming that power will ever be made equal. If redistribution and more equality—though less than socialists advocate—are empowering, continual rejection of the classical and neoclassical justifications of inequality and demands for more equality lead to that end. Other elements include social justice or at least social equity; efforts to limit the power of large organizations; and for Brandeis and Galbraith public support of smaller producers and use of government to redress unequal bargaining power. Emphasizing full employment, greater equality, and welfare lessens the costs of leaving painful situations or the need to take any offer of work or charity, regardless of attached conditions. Each argument directly or indirectly addresses inequality of power in attempting to provide people with means to achieve their ends and resist undesirable or harmful demands.

This forceful critique of power weakens market claims and allows government to intervene to curb and rechannel power, as it does in instances of explicit coercion, but it does not supply an answer to the fundamental issue of unequal power. Reform liberals confront just the periphery of property's coercive potential, accept the legitimacy of private ownership of the means of production, and emphasize convincing people to change, which allows only partial reform of power relations. Given their criticisms, these theorists need to attack power with more vigor and at its source. With few exceptions they offer inadequate proposals for how to implement institutional control over power. If one believes markets prevent the use of power, the institutional answer is simple: allow markets free reign and expand their scope. If one believes civic virtue born in local democracy or electronic meetings can overcome all obstacles, corporate power is not directly relevant to social and political life. Reform liberals take a more complex view, in which there are no final answers. Neither market nor government will dominate. Both are problems. In shifting patterns of equipoise, each is a partial solution to the other. Galbraith believes that communitarian democracy is probably too weak to challenge the power of large organizations. If so, the major hope for improving society lies in changing public opinion and the social-economy, and in placing the correct people into public office.

Neutrality

Liberals have increasingly debated whether liberalism is or should be characterized by public neutrality, especially with regard to individuals' moral ends or notions of the good life.[51] Reform liberals indirectly challenge arguments for neutrality when these arguments are taken literally. While neutrality about ultimate values may be possible, several of the theorists we have discussed consider it impossible to be neutral about some values. More importantly, ends and values are affected by and embodied in public policy, which often has differential impacts on people. Achieving some moral ends requires changes in policy or in publicly supplied, supplemented, or tolerated resources. If a decision to help people realize their ends is made, neutrality ceases. Organizational links to government and economic policy, especially, undermine neutrality claims. Moreover, if government must be neutral about ultimate moral ends, all power holders must be neutral. Thus neutrality claims must confront how embedded people are, who has power, and what is the meaning of power.

Given inequalities of power, status, influence, education, position, and resources, an expanded government role is related in two senses to neutrality: laissez-faire policy has a superficial similarity to neutrality, but reform theorists deny the market is neutral between people; and public policy can be formally neutral if one means identical treatment when each is similarly able to pursue moral ends. Gains and losses from public policy, however, are not even. If policy cannot be fully neutral, government cannot be merely negative, defending property and the market and getting out of the way. Doing nothing[52] or continuing existing policies is a choice to profit beneficiaries of the status quo. This may be acceptable, but when confronted with significant problems or major public discomfort or dissatisfaction, the status quo does not have a privileged position. For example, the four later theorists attack both deliberate deflation and fighting inflation with policies that cause unemployment, asserting that they are not natural, just, or neutral.

Denying policy neutrality does not mean there are no rules and that anything is acceptable. Reform liberals stress criteria that many people who emphasize neutrality accept: avoiding capricious and arbitrary policy; discussing differences; equity; fairness; and emphasis on public and impersonal judgments (not preferences). Eliminating the hope for neutral policy means one cannot avoid recognizing, by hiding behind claims that markets produce equitable or optimal outcomes, the choices one makes.

Policy conflicts over such issues as budgets, welfare, and regulation are grounded in philosophical differences. Neutral policy is possible only within an accepted normative framework. That is not our situation. Governments and the public have no choice but to choose who benefits from public policy, justifying more democracy to ensure citizen deliberation over ends and means. Choices about ends served, values celebrated or denied, and resource distribution are intrinsic to policy making. As noted by Keynes, whose political economy "brought back the moral problem that *laissez-faire* theory had abolished,"[53] denying determinism justifies trying to shape the political-economy to fit goals and moral beliefs. It is necessary to discuss and determine purposes and values—Dewey and Reich see this as one goal of participation—because goals are neutral only within an already accepted political-social-economic-moral structure.[54]

Government

One's picture of public problems and government capabilities shapes what one expects government to do. The arguments in this book support expanding government's role. However, people who believe that society and/or markets are orderly, order producing, and competent to achieve goals often assigned to politics, usually conclude that government should have a small role. Classical, neoclassical, and laissez-faire liberals mistrust and attempt to constrict the role, power, and importance of government. In contemporary public debate, this image assumes that spontaneous markets and self-interested marketlike behavior are the fundamental social reality, reflect essential human nature, and drastically reduce the need for government. The current congressional Republican claim that intervention, welfare, and regulation always fail[55] and show contempt for the mass public—often accompanied by an invocation of the "nanny state" to ridicule such policies—reflects these deeper assumptions about order, freedom, and human nature. Proposed cutbacks in regulation, education, welfare, environmental protection, and health and safety policy, are (in Dewey's and Galbraith's language) remarkably congruent with the interests of the powerful and contented. Conversely, academic discussion of liberal government is dominated by a Lockean laissez-faire paradigm that is not an accurate picture of contemporary liberal concepts of the role of government although it does provide a convenient focus for criticism. Here we reach the central, century-old, mainstream political-economic policy dispute that rages in reasonably democratic capitalist states. Beyond all the rhetoric, criticism, and proposals stand basic, significantly different pictures of how people relate to and interact in and with society, what civil society can achieve, and, therefore, the permissible role for government.

The fashionable image of liberalism that identifies it with bureaucracy and big government is partly correct but ignores why public responsibilities have expanded and what institutions can meet those needs. As even Herbert Stein has indicated, one cannot judge the impact of government by its size, but only by the purpose one assigns to it.[56] Reform liberals' picture of the purpose of government differs from that of their critics. Government's role and power have grown because the mechanisms of community, market, and night watchman government—crafted under largely agricultural small-property-owning conditions, and (in the United States) effective equality for white males—proved incapable of protecting individuals or meeting individual and group needs in urbanized, industrial, large-organization society. For reform liberals, government is not inherently bad, not always oppressive, not the natural enemy or primary obstacle to the good life. Active government is flawed but indispensable. It is a conclusion based on circumstances, not a principle; a sometimes means to desirable ends, not an end in itself. Active government draws on the same values as eighteenth- and nineteenth-century arguments for limited government, but it recognizes new forces that endanger individuals—forces that may be modified by public action. Government, therefore, can be a positive agent, but only if it is democratic.

The enlarged role reform liberalism assigns to government follows from reevaluation of the capacity of government now that it is democratic; from arguments about economic power, neutrality, economic breakdown, and instability; from appreciation of government's actual role even under ostensibly laissez-faire regimes; and from developing concepts of freedom. Reform liberals are of course apprehensive about possible abuse of power; but given these understandings, and their rejection of self-adjusting markets, they see much less government economic abuse than do laissez-faire and libertarian critics. Unlike them, reform liberals do not define intervention and welfare provision as freedom-destroying abuses of power. Much of what critics see as abuse, the theorists in this book see as necessary to expand freedom and equality, curtail private power, and preserve the system from economic turmoil, injustice, or damage.

For these liberals, the question is never seen in absolute terms that require or forbid involvement, but rather what and whose ends are served. To prohibit government from an active role is to surrender to instability and private power. Market failure does not automatically justify government action, but it lends a presumption to more active government. Expanding the public role in political economy seeks three ends: to maintain, stabilize, and expand the economy; to support desirable social-political institutions when threatened by economic problems or relations; and to achieve positive individual and social ends. The earliest reform theorists were less concerned with the first aim, stabilizing the economy, than with remedying the social-political impact of economic relations. Following possibilities that Keynes opened, reform liberals such as Reich, Thurow, and Galbraith argue that active government and economic efficiency are necessary to one another to save capitalism and to make the market function better, but they do not limit government to that purpose. The second and third aims are prominent throughout their work.

The second purpose (supporting desirable social and political institutions) is related to the first and follows from the reform liberal understanding of the interrelation of politics and economics. As the social-political dilemmas of formerly communist countries again remind us, economic discontent is a powerful source of dissatisfaction with a political system. One recurring theme has been reform liberals' deep apprehension—which has no systematic counterpart in conservative political economy—over the impact of economic insecurity and dislocation on politics and society. Their continuing purpose is to expand people's sense of security, predictability, and control in everyday life. Personal insecurity is individually and socially devastating, particularly when people no longer believe that it "spring[s] from nature."[57] Again, pure economic efficiency is not the only criterion. It is supplemented by attention to threatened living standards, popular feelings of inequitable treatment, the position of people who do not win from economic change, unemployment, increased inequality, lessened opportunity, and the inability to cooperate for a common good—all of which threaten the social fabric, democracy, and liberal values. Economic and political needs coincide because economic problems requiring public intervention often engender political-social conflict. Intervention can preserve and even expand basic values while weakening demands for radical alterations of the political-economic system. The corollary is that economic relations often manifest political behavior such as control, constraint, and superordinate and subordinate positions. Claims about oppressive work environments, bureaucratic behavior, organization, close links between public and private, manipulation, and power illustrate how the "private" sector contains extensive relations usually ascribed to politics. People therefore need many of the protections and opportunities that liberalism requires in the polity, legitimating government involvement.

The third purpose (achieving positive ends) is the most controversial. Concentrating on government action only in terms of market failure or response to market excess emphasizes a narrow slice of public activities that relate to or interact with economics, such as macroeconomic Keynesian demand management to maintain employment or growth, or to rectify problems such as pollution. Although Keynes emphasized stimulating aggregate demand and increasing total production and employment—he cared that people were employed, not what they produced—this was a necessary first step, not an end in itself. For Brandeis, Dewey, Hobhouse, Keynes, Galbraith, Reich, and (to a lesser extent) Thurow, market failure is not the only circumstance that warrants use of government. Positive ends, such as opening more opportunities, serving important common purposes, and providing public goods, can be achieved only through active government. Justifying a positive role for government in economic relations—positive in that goals are unattainable by simply leaving people alone—claims that achieving common services and social ends such as freedom, equality, equity, and an improved quality of life require public action. In pursuing these goals, government is imperfect but indispensable.

Calls for an expanded public role must contend with the influential argument that economic theory proves government must fail in all attempts at regulation and intervention.[58] The theory of government failure is the conservative counterpart to and intended refutation of all three justifications for active government. Reform liberals reject conservative dogma that self-interest and economic laws doom government intervention to failure. That metaphysical claim ignores power and individual people and is immune to evidence of past success[59] because long-run market outcomes *must* be better than intervention (a claim that has been disputed throughout this book). To depend on the market to redress problems and to actualize social goals is to depend on a useful but for these purposes more imperfect instrument than government and public action. Possible government failure does not justify tolerating bad conditions, doing nothing, or pretending that the market operates optimally. For the theorists in this book, critics are snapping at shadows while ignoring the substance of private power and the actual conditions of life experienced by millions. Economic laws do not decree that government will make things worse. A market that often produces disorder and that requires intervention and regulation to perform well is a limited substitute for government. Whether the issue is protecting the weak and future generations, maintaining conditions favorable to democracy, redressing power imbalances, maintaining Galbraith's social balance, reducing poverty, or encouraging an environment within which people can achieve individuality, these arguments extend beyond market failures and imperfections. They employ government not only to pursue economic objects, but subordinate purely economic goals, such as increased production as the highest end, to social and political purposes. Discussion is often contained in specific arguments, as with the claim that monetary policy fails and is hostile to social justice, but always incorporates political-social concerns into economic debate.

Perhaps due to their roots, classical liberalism and modern liberalism never developed a complete theory of the function and justification of either government or state.[60] For classical liberalism, protection of society and individual rights delineated the proper role of government. For laissez-faire liberalism, the economy sets the duties and limits of government. In both cases government is derivative, subordinate, and secondary to seemingly autonomous "social" relations. Given its image of power and the interrelation of politics and economics, reform liberalism is more politically aware but lacks a clear theory of the state, institutions, politics, and government. Unlike laissez-faire, which has an explicit political theory—government and democracy must be limited because they link self-interested behavior to power—reform liberal political concepts and methods are underdeveloped. Everyone agrees with Keynes that political economy needs "a new conception of the possible functions of government,"[61] and these are spelled out. But the next step, organization, is not. This is unfortunate, given the weight that reform liberals place on government, simultaneously needing it and retaining traditional liberal fear of government. At the level of principle rather than example, they often do not address conservative claims about government failure. Moreover, reform theorists often do not draw links between what their political economy allows and the social-political means, mechanisms, and changes in opinion necessary to accomplish these reforms, fit them into existing institutions,[62] or operate new functions. Thurow admits the last point. Reform theory about politics and government structures is at best implicit. Rather than discussing political organization or coalition building, (neither do conservative critics) they rely on pluralism, electoral politics,[63] and educating public opinion to develop consensus for change. When it obtains its ends, contemporary reform liberalism often does not analyze or address the struggle that develops over government involvement nor does it reshape politics to the new reality it helped create. Conversely, by keeping open options that other theories close, reform liberalism contains much that encourages and little that prevents participation in government involvement in the economy.[64]

Conclusions

Reform liberals see different problems and solutions from those seen by laissez-faire liberals. They are more concerned with individual lives, feelings, fears, what people face, and the common good—and less wedded to theory or to making reality conform to theory. This permits a larger role for government. Goals other than the "free" play of market forces, and results other than "private" economic gains are important and relevant. Power, instability, and unequal access to government ensure that leaving markets alone will not foster equality or democracy. Results include impact on democracy, social structure, political relations, and traditional liberal values. Market theory—whether monetarism, supply-side economics, or rational expectations—does not overturn reform arguments, because reform liberals present an alternative and equally normative picture in which the market and limited notions of economic efficiency are not the arbitrator of values and relations, and in which political-social-moral factors are legitimate components of decision making for the economy. Conservatives argue that this position caused what they call the failed policies of the past, but reform liberals argue that conservatives are returning to their own failed policies and the ensuing social-political traumas that reform liberals then attempted to solve. From the beginning, reform liberals have insisted that leaving the economy alone is a recipe for failure because nostalgia for an idealized theory or past disguises power and earlier disorders and neglects the full scope of human needs, ensuring that real problems are ignored.

All of the theorists we have examined are reformers, not revolutionaries.[65] Each is engaged with tangible and immediate problems of political and social economics. Part of their problem is that, in a deeply politicized debate, they are not political enough. Brandeis, Reich, Thurow, and Galbraith discuss and are more involved in politics—and better understand obstacles to reform—than Hobhouse, Dewey, or Keynes. Emphasizing goals, none has an action plan to gain control of government, though Dewey saw his education for democracy proposals as crucial to reform. Reason and education can chip away at the foundation of other arguments, convince people that existing ideas and practices are harmful and incomplete, and offer alternatives. While focusing on changing opinion—even if arguments read by millions have an uncertain impact on politics and society[66]—on education, convincing decision makers, and sometimes on participatory democracy, they scarcely discuss the means or political organization needed to accomplish their ends. Galbraith embodies that approach: politics and economics are closely related; conditions are never ideal; and action is shaped by what is possible; but many radicals ignore fiscal and economic limits to change.[67] Quite often reform liberals are incisive and indeed radical in their critique and analysis but not nearly so trenchant in their recommendations, hoping instead that small changes can produce major results. Even Galbraith does not attack the structure of power relations. The slight edge of radicalism in Brandeis, Dewey, and Hobhouse is not present in Galbraith, Keynes, Thurow, and Reich, who are willing to preserve more existing social-political relations in the economy.

Critics tend to view people who are eager to expand rights or who are dismayed by economic dislocation or the plight of those with few resources as soft-hearted (and soft-headed) idealists. But reform liberals are not Panglossian. Given their perceived realities of power, opinion, and entrenched interests these liberals think no other course but sometimes gradual, and sometimes more basic reform is possible, especially if one cares what happens to individuals. They may be sad, frustrated at, and even pessimistic about the consequences of society's willingness to place laissez-faire ideology ahead of what is happening in the political economy, but they insist that much needs to be made better. Unlike their chief rivals, they have no faith in natural systems of economic relations that are assumed to maximize freedom and ensure that things work out for the best, regardless of the fate of individuals. They do not demand that people who are injured by change or the status quo be politically quiet on the pretense that politics and economics are separate. Active government is crucial to, not dichotomous with, the market and freedom. Reducing government solves few or no major problems. Vigorous government does not entail extreme political or economic transformation. Absolute political or moral claims are irrelevant to real conditions. Ending private property or capitalism, instituting massive planning,[68] changing constitutions, or instituting government ownership of the means of production are unnecessary and harmful. Rather, material and spiritual well-being are interrelated, and material prosperity provides resources for individuality, experimentation, and moral improvement. Reform liberals are anxious for both preservation and change, as opposed to radical conservatives who seek to return public economic and welfare policy to pre–World War I relations that Keynes insisted had been permanently changed. In terms of maintaining basic values, opposing the exercise of private power, and preserving the political system from economic disequilibrium, reform liberals personify the essence of Burke's conservatism—reform to preserve—though they would reform much more than he ever dreamed.

Today, reform liberalism offers a workable option for people dissatisfied with increasing economic inequality, hostility to public responsibility for social-economic conditions, and rejection of limits to economic power, together with their potential social-political conflicts. The issues and problems in this book raise fundamental questions that lie at the heart of reform liberalism's relevance to modern problems. Reform liberals have three central messages for today: politics and economics are closely related; active government is essential to political and economic stability, economic efficiency, and competitiveness; and in contemporary conditions, democracy, freedom, and equality require active government.[69] Many unrealized possibilities remain. The primary weaknesses are an unfinished theory and practice of democracy, and a tendency to not develop the means and organization needed to achieve liberal ends. If the market operates as portrayed in this book, if power resides in economic relations, and if large organization is as significant as several authors claim, these realities raise profound and disturbing issues for democracy, democratic control of government, and the possibility of popular control over significant parts of our lives— questions the authors we have discussed do not fully answer. But participatory theorists, civic humanists, and (especially) market-first theorists have even less satisfactory answers. By insisting on the importance of the economic in politics and of choice in political economy, reform liberals open the possibility of confronting economic power and inequality better than does an exclusive focus on either economics or politics. Reform liberalism may not be a model, but it offers a pattern and principles by which to confront our dilemmas. Reform liberalism is a positive, "entirely nonutopian"[70] approach to public life according to which policy must avoid ideological rigidity and must understand the pressures on and desires of people in situations that are often beyond individual control. In the contest for the soul of liberal democracy at the end of the twentieth century and continuing into the twenty-first, reform liberalism is the major alternative to the increasingly dominant market approach to public life. Choosing between these and other possibilities is not just a matter of testing which works "best" but deciding which of many possible ends correspond to the principles, values, and goals that shape what is seen as "best." As always the contest is one of ideas.

Notes

PREFACE

1. With apologies to Robert L. Heilbroner, *The Worldly Philosophers* (New York: Simon & Schuster, 1980).

2. Despite their frustrations with legislators, colleagues, and subordinates, public experience may have shaped their belief that government can be effective; or a prior belief that government can be effective may have led them into government service.

3. Unions are seen as special interests, while business is not; welfare for the poor is bad, while welfare for the rich is not or is ignored. Reform liberals insist that one must look at all claimants to and beneficiaries of government support.

4. Walter Shapiro, "The Party's New Soul," *Time* 132 (July 25, 1988): 17–19; Jonathan Rabinovitz, "Liberal Coalition Has Biggest Victory," *New York Times* (September 20, 1994), p. A15.

5. The values quote is from Melville J. Ulmer, "The War of the Liberal Economists," *Commentary* 76 (October 1983): 54. See also Urs Schoettli, "The State of Liberalism—Challenges from Left and Right," *Contemporary Review* 248 (1986): 79–85; Philip Green, "In the American Tradition: A Few Kind Words for Liberalism," *The Nation* 255 (September 28, 1992): 309ff; Elliott Abrams, in "What Is a Liberal—Who Is a Conservative: A Symposium," *Commentary* 62 (September 1976): 34–35.

6. Conrad P. Waligorski, *The Political Theory of Conservative Economists* (Lawrence: University Press of Kansas, 1990), pp. 14–16, 19–21; Robert L. Heilbroner, "Economics and Political Economy: Marx, Keynes, and Schumpeter," *Journal of Economic Issues* 18 (September 1984): 689, 693; Charles R. Morris, *A Time of Passion: America, 1960–1980* (New York: Penguin, 1986), p. ix; James Burke, *The Day the Universe Changed* (Boston: Little, Brown, 1985), pp. 11, 308–12, 326; J. Philip Wogaman, *The Great Economic Debate: An Ethical Analysis* (Philadelphia: Westminster Press, 1977), pp. 155–61; Joseph A. Schumpeter, *The Great Economists: From Marx to Keynes* (New York: Oxford University Press, 1951), p. 268; Thomas Sowell, *A Conflict of Visions: Ideological Origins of Political Struggles* (New York: Quill, 1987); Joan Robinson, *Economic Philosophy* (Harmondsworth, U.K.: Penguin, 1962), p. 19; Dudley Dillard, *The Economics of John Maynard Keynes: The Theory of a Monetary Economy* (New York: Prentice-Hall, 1948), p. 52; Michael Freeden, *The New*

Liberalism: An Ideology of Social Reform (Oxford: Clarendon Press, 1978), pp. 247–50; Steven Kelman, "Why Public Ideas Matter," in Robert B. Reich, ed., *The Power of Public Ideas* (Cambridge, Mass.: Harvard University Press, 1988), pp. 31–53; Carol Leutner Anderson, "Economics and Metaphysics: Framework for the Future," *Review of Social Economy* 40 (1982): 199–226; Homa Katouzian, *Ideology and Method in Economics* (New York: New York University Press, 1980), p. 140.

7. Waligorski, *Political Theory of Conservative Economists*, pp. 3–5, 14–17.

8. Cf. Michael Freeden, "A Non-Hypothetical Liberalism: The Communitarianism of J. A. Hobson," and oral comments, American Political Science Association, September 3, 1993. Within this book—even when they are "philosophical"—Dewey, Hobhouse, and Keynes are policy related.

9. Waligorski, *Political Theory of Conservative Economists*, op. cit.

CHAPTER 1. THEMES

1. Francis Fukuyama, "The End of History?" *National Interest* 16 (Summer 1989): 3–18; Francis Fukuyama, "A Reply to My Critics," *National Interest* 18 (Winter 1989/90): 21–28; Robert Heilbroner, "The Triumph of Capitalism," *New Yorker* 64 (January 23, 1989): 98–109; Robert Heilbroner, *21st Century Capitalism* (New York: W. W. Norton, 1993). After the Cold War, religion, nationalism, statism, and traditionalism remain. John Kenneth Galbraith, *The Good Society: The Humane Agenda* (Boston: Houghton Mifflin, 1996), and Lester C. Thurow, *The Future of Capitalism: How Today's Economic Forces Shape Tomorrow's World* (New York: William Morrow, 1996), agree that socialism is dead, but its demise presents new challenges to capitalism.

2. Benjamin Barber, *Strong Democracy: Participatory Politics for a New Age* (Berkeley: University of California Press, 1984); Terrence E. Cook, *The Great Alternatives of Social Thought: Aristocrat, Saint, Capitalist, Socialist* (Savage, Md.: Rowman & Littlefield, 1991); Roger King, *The State in Modern Society: New Directions in Political Sociology* [chapter 8 by Graham Gibbs] (Chatham, N.J.: Chatham House, 1986), pp. 81–99; Don Lavoie, "Democracy, Markets, and the Legal Order: Notes on the Nature of Politics in a Radically Liberal Society," in Ellen Frankel Paul, Fred D. Miller, Jr., and Jeffrey Paul, eds., *Liberalism and the Economic Order* (Cambridge: Cambridge University Press, 1993), pp. 103–20; C. B. Macpherson, *The Life and Times of Liberal Democracy* (Oxford: Oxford University Press, 1977); C. B. Macpherson, *The Political Theory of Possessive Individualism: Hobbes to Locke* (Oxford: Clarendon Press, 1962); D. J. Manning, *Liberalism* (New York: St. Martin's Press, 1976), pp. 97–98, 140; William M. Sullivan, *Reconstructing Public Philosophy* (Berkeley: University of California Press, 1986). Charles Lindblom, *Politics and Markets: The World's Political-Economic Systems* (New York: Basic Books, 1977), p. 45, sees elements of liberalism carrying into "twentieth-century reformism," but they are separate.

3. Cf. John Dewey, *Liberalism and Social Action* (New York: Capricorn Books, 1963); John Kenneth Galbraith, *The New Industrial State,* 4th ed. (Boston: Houghton Mifflin, 1985), p. 225; John Maynard Keynes, *The Collected Writings of John Maynard Keynes,* edited by Donald Moggridge, vol. 9, *Essays in Persuasion* (London: Macmillan, 1972), pp. 295–306; Robert B. Reich, *Tales of a New America: The Anxious Liberal's Guide to the Future* (New York: Vintage Books, 1987); Robert B. Reich, *The Resurgent Liberal (And Other Unfashionable Prophecies)* (New York: Vintage Books, 1991); Michael Davis, "Liberalism and/or Democracy?" *Social Theory and Practice* 9 (Spring 1983): 51–72; Russell Hardin, "Liberalism: Political and Economic," in Paul, Miller, and Paul, eds., *Liberalism and the Economic Order,* pp. 212–44; H. J. McCloskey, "The Problem of Liberalism," *Review of Metaphysics* 19 (1965): 248–75; Ronald D. Rotunda, "The 'Liberal' Label: Roosevelt's Capture of a Symbol," *Public Policy* 17 (1968): 377–408; Urs Schoettli, "The State of Liberalism—Challenges from Left and Right," *Contemporary Review* 248 (1986): 79–85. M. Francis, "A Case of Mistaken Paternity: The Relationship Between Nineteenth-century Liberals and Twentieth-century Liberal Democrats," *Australian Journal of Politics and History* 31 (1985): 282–99, argues that there is little continuity between nineteenth-century liberals and modern liberal democrats.

4. One can also add tolerance, consent, and hope about human possibility. Cf. lists in David P. Barash, *The L Word: An Unapologetic, Thoroughly Biased, Long-Overdue Explication and Celebration of Liberalism* (New York: William Morrow, 1992), pp. 45–51, 168, 209, 210; Michael Freeden, *The New Liberalism: An Ideology of Social Reform* (Oxford: Clarendon Press, 1978), pp. 22–23, 44, 158–69; Michael Freeden, "A Non-Hypothetical Liberalism: The Communitarianism of J. A. Hobson," paper and oral presentation at the American Political Science Association, September 3, 1993; Patrick M. Garry, *Liberalism and American Identity* (Kent, Ohio: Kent State University Press, 1992), pp. 34–35; Peter M. Lichtenstein, "Some Theoretical Coordinates of Radical Liberalism," *American Journal of Economics and Sociology* 43 (1984): 333; Manning, *Liberalism,* pp. 13, 78; Massimo Salvadori, *The Liberal Heresy: Origins and Historical Development* (London: Macmillan, 1977), pp. 9–12, 22–29; J. Salwyn Schapiro, *Liberalism: Its Meaning and History* (Princeton, N.J.: D. Van Nostrand, 1958), pp. 17–25, 89–90; Conrad Waligorski and Thomas Hone, *Anglo-American Liberalism: Readings in Normative Political Economy* (Chicago: Nelson Hall, 1981), pp. 12–19.

5. I am not equating liberalism with economics. Macpherson, *Life and Times of Liberal Democracy,* p. 2, notes that hitherto "the market view" has been assimilated into liberalism and liberalism into capitalism.

6. Thomas Paine, *Political Writings* (Franklin Center, Pa.: Franklin Library, 1978), p. 5. Yet in *Rights of Man* he proposed replacing the Poor Law with a simple welfare system that included family allowances, education, small payments to needy aging workers, and employment for the poor in major cities. Ibid., pp. 580–93.

7. For Galbraith, see John Kenneth Galbraith Collection at the John F. Kennedy Presidential Library, Boston, Massachusetts, Box 103, "Youth in the Social Context: The Basic Impact of Urbanization," p. 3.

8. John Locke, *The Second Treatise of Government*, in *Two Treatises of Government* (New York: Mentor Books, 1965), paragraphs 27–29, 45–50, 85, 94, 124, 127.

9. I examined this argument in an earlier book. See Conrad P. Waligorski, *The Political Theory of Conservative Economists* (Lawrence: University Press of Kansas, 1990). *Laissez-faire* is a convenient term for a particular approach to theory, moral responsibility, and policy. Broad and not completely accurate, it reflects a central political tenet shared by diverse groups who oppose arguments that the market is not self-stabilizing and that government has a legitimate role in economic regulation. The term *laissez-faire* is used by some theorists in this book.

10. On classical and neoclassical theory, see James A. Caporaso and David P. Levine, *Theories of Political Economy* (Cambridge: Cambridge University Press, 1992), pp. 33–54, 79–99.

11. Dewey, *Liberalism and Social Action*, pp. 6–9, identifies "The importance attached to the right of property," the redefinition of liberty to "subordinate political to economic activity," and the attachment of natural law to "production and exchange" as major laissez-faire borrowings from and modifications of Locke. See also L. T. Hobhouse, *Liberalism* (London: Oxford University Press, 1964), pp. 32–34.

12. John A. Hall, *Liberalism: Politics, Ideology and the Market* (Chapel Hill: University of North Carolina Press, 1987), pp. 37–46; O. H. Taylor, *Economics and Liberalism: Collected Papers* (Cambridge, Mass.: Harvard University Press, 1955), p. 97; Adam Smith, *An Inquiry into the Nature and Causes of the Wealth of Nations* (New York: Modern Library, 1937, 1965), pp. 384–85. Smith saw public benefits from education and argued that government has a duty to pay "some attention" to the educational needs of the majority. Ibid., pp. 734–36.

13. Among other sources see Sidney Blumenthal, *The Rise of the Counter-Establishment: From Conservative Ideology to Political Power* (New York: Times Books, 1986); Caporaso and Levine, *Theories of Political Economy*, pp. 34–44; Sidney Fine, *Laissez-Faire and the General Welfare State: A Study of Conflict in American Thought 1865–1901* (Ann Arbor: University of Michigan Press, 1956); Waligorski, *Political Theory of Conservative Economists*.

14. Many other names are possible. Not all are synonymous, but each refers to liberal alternatives to classical and laissez-faire liberalism that maintain the essentials of liberalism while changing policies perceived to be no longer viable. Cf. "new liberalism" (which is not so new after a century), Freeden, *New Liberalism*; and Jeffrey H. Birnbaum, "Brave New Liberalism," *Business Month* 132 (October 1988): 48–53; Keynes, *Collected Writings*, vol. 9, p. 305; "renascent liberalism," Dewey, *Liberalism and Social Action*, p. 87; "humane liberalism," John Dewey, "The Future of Liberalism or the Democratic Way of Change," in John Dewey, Boyd H. Bode, and

T. V. Smith, *What Is Democracy? Its Conflicts, Ends and Means* (Norman, Okla.: Cooperative Books, 1939), p. 9; "liberal progressivism," Michael Williams, "Liberalism and Two Conceptions of the State," in Douglas MacLean and Claudia Mills, eds., *Liberalism Reconsidered* (Totowa, N.J.: Rowman & Allanheld, 1983); "radical liberalism," Lichtenstein, "Some Theoretical Coordinates of Radical Liberalism"; "progressive liberals" and "pragmatic liberalism," Charles Anderson, *Pragmatic Liberalism* (Chicago: University Press of Chicago, 1990), p. 138 and passim; "resurgent" liberalism, Reich, *The Resurgent Liberal*; "social liberalism," J. G. Merquior, *Liberalism: Old and New* (Boston: Twayne, 1991), pp. 104, 146; Schapiro, *Liberalism*, p. 37; "communitarian liberal," Alan Ryan, "Communitarianism: The Good, the Bad, & the Muddly," *Dissent* 36 (1989): 350; "egalitarian liberals," Michael J. Sandel, "The Political Theory of the Procedural Republic," in Robert B. Reich, ed., *The Power of Public Ideas* (Cambridge, Mass.: Harvard University Press, 1988), p. 113.

For varied use of "reform liberal," see Waligorski and Hone, *Anglo-American Liberalism*, pp. 7–10; Kenneth M. Dolbeare and Patricia Dolbeare, *American Ideologies* (Chicago: Markham, 1973), pp. 86ff; Kenneth R. Hoover, *Ideology and Political life* (Belmont, Calif.: Wadsworth, 1994), pp. 81–105; Philippa Strum, *Brandeis: Beyond Progressivism* (Lawrence: University Press of Kansas, 1993), p. 6.

15. Dewey, *Liberalism and Social Action*, pp. 21, 7.

16. Reich is not a credentialed economist, but he has written and taught extensively on political and economic aspects of public policy.

17. I owe this phrase to Kenneth Dolbeare.

18. Dewey, Hobhouse, Keynes, Galbraith, and (to a limited extent) Thurow agree that laissez-faire was appropriate in the circumstances of its birth, but they argue that these circumstances no longer exist.

19. John Dewey, *Freedom and Culture* (Buffalo, N.Y.: Prometheus Books, 1989), p. 50; Dewey, *Liberalism and Social Action*, p. 54 [see also pp. 47–48, 55]; L. T. Hobhouse, *Democracy and Reaction* (Brighton, U.K.: Harvester Press, 1972), p. 219. Cf. D. A. Lloyd Thomas, "The Justification of Liberalism," *Canadian Journal of Philosophy* 2 (1972): 214 ["The change from a laissez-faire view of the role of the state . . . to a much more so-called 'interventionist' view . . . involves no change of principle. . . . The change has been in those practices thought more desirable for the state to uphold."]. Cf. Alfonso J. Damico, *Individuality and Community: The Social and Political Thought of John Dewey* (Gainesville: University Presses of Florida, 1978), p. 67; Robert Eccleshall, "When is a 'Liberal' Not a Liberal?" *Contemporary Review* 232 (April 1978): 188; Garry, *Liberalism and American Identity*, p. 87; Don Herzog, "Up Toward Liberalism," *Dissent* 36 (1989): 359; Arthur Schlesinger, Jr., "The Challenge of Abundance," *Reporter* 14 (May 3, 1956): 8–11; Freeden, *New Liberalism*, pp. 4, 44, 22, 158–69; Hall, *Liberalism*, pp. 2, 36; Taylor, *Economics and Liberalism*, pp. 110–11, 173. Cf. John Maynard Keynes, *The Collected Writings of John Maynard Keynes*, edited by Donald Moggridge, vol. 7, *The General Theory of*

Employment Interest and Money (London: Macmillan, 1973), p. xxiii, for his "long struggle of escape" from the older ideas.

20. Garry, *Liberalism and American Identity*, pp. 5–6, criticizes contemporary liberalism for overemphasizing economics, linking it with "money liberalism," which sees people "strictly as economic actors." This criticism equates laissez-faire with liberalism, slights the historic roots of liberalism, and if taken literally reads the authors in this book out of liberalism. On p. 40 he notes, however, that American liberalism has consistently addressed the problems of people on the bottom against "the economic elite."

21. Michael Williams, "Liberalism and Two Conceptions of the State," in MacLean and Mills, eds., *Liberalism Reconsidered*, p. 126.

22. Hobhouse, *Liberalism*, p. 58, sees John Stuart Mill as a bridge from "the old" to "the new liberalism." Cf. Merquior, *Liberalism*, p. 62.

23. Rotunda, "The 'Liberal' Label"; Ronald D. Rotunda, *The Politics of Language: Liberalism as Word and Symbol* (Iowa City: University of Iowa Press, 1986), pp. 40–42, 70–73; Richard P. Adelstein, "'The Nation as an Economic Unit': Keynes, Roosevelt and the Managerial Ideal," *Journal of American History* 78 (1991): 160–87. Rotunda finds evidence that limited non-laissez-faire use of *liberal* occurred as early as 1916 in the United States.

24. This book focuses on the economic heart of modern liberalism. Some issues of concern to contemporary liberals (including Galbraith and Reich), such as civil rights, are not discussed. As there is no single "liberal" agenda or dimension, reform liberalism is not "cultural" liberalism. Reform liberalism and the cultural and social movements of the last twenty-five years certainly may be compatible—especially in Galbraith and Reich—and they may even overlap in some circumstances. The women's movement, for example, as the latest development of the impulse toward freedom and equality, and to the extent it questions traditional individualism, postulates some communal goals, and defends more participation, shares much with theorists in this book. But this book is about political economy and only occasionally touches on other topics.

25. Robert Skidelsky, *John Maynard Keynes*, vol. 2, *The Economist as Saviour* (New York: Penguin Press, 1994), pp. 134, 223. Yet on pp. 223–24, the author notes that similarities existed. Cf. Robert Skidelsky, "Keynes and the Reconstruction of Liberalism," *Encounter* 52 (April 1979): 31.

26. Strum, *Brandeis*, p. 6; Robert B. Westbrook, *John Dewey and American Democracy* (Ithaca, N.Y.: Cornell University Press, 1991), p. 46 n. 16, views Hobhouse's "new liberalism" as being "quite similar to Dewey's postidealist social philosophy." Yet Dewey does not see links between American and British liberalism in the early twentieth century. Dewey, *Liberalism and Social Action*, p. 21.

27. Freeden, *New Liberalism*, pp. 128, 130; Merquior, *Liberalism*, p. 147.

28. Roosevelt quoted by Reich, *The Resurgent Liberal*, pp. 249, 229–30; John W.

Jeffries, "The 'New' New Deal: FDR and American Liberalism, 1937–1945," *Political Science Quarterly* 105 (1990): 397–418.

29. The quotes are from Alpheus Thomas Mason, *Security Through Freedom: American Political Thought and Practice* (Ithaca, N.Y.: Cornell University Press, 1955), pp. 85–86. See also Thomas Balogh, *The Irrelevance of Conventional Economics* (New York: Liveright, 1982), p. 4; Merquior, *Liberalism*, p. 5; Garry, *Liberalism and American Identity*, p. 69; Robert Skidelsky, "Keynes and the Left," *New Statesman and Society* 6 (April 16, 1993): 16–17; Barash, *The L Word*, pp. 50–51; Theda Skocpol, "The Legacies of New Deal Liberalism," in MacLean and Mills, eds., *Liberalism Reconsidered*, p. 97.

30. George Will argues that " 'back to 1900' is a serviceable summation of the conservatives' goal . . . to reverse many results of the liberal project first formulated around the turn of the century." "Fringe Is Marginal No More," *Morning News of Northwest Arkansas* (January 1, 1995), p. 9D.

31. Hobhouse, *Liberalism*, p. 41.

32. This strips the market of some of its philosophical—indeed mythical—ramparts. If the market is not a natural, freestanding system that reflects elemental human impulses, intervention is not automatically illegitimate.

33. I owe this concept to Kenneth Hoover.

34. Keynes came closest to placing economics first, emphasizing "a technical solution" (Adelstein, "Nation as an Economic Unit," p. 160) as the alternative to radical political change; but he, too, stressed autonomous noneconomic values.

35. Dewey, *Liberalism and Social Action*, p. 48.

36. Waligorski, *Political Theory of Conservative Economists*, pp. 76–79.

37. Ronald Dworkin, "Neutrality, Equality, and Liberalism," in MacLean and Mills, eds., *Liberalism Reconsidered*, pp. 1–11; Larry Siedentop, "Two Liberal Traditions," in Alan Ryan, ed., *The Idea of Freedom: Essays in Honour of Isaiah Berlin* (Oxford: Oxford University Press, 1979), p. 153.

38. How we define democracy is critical in determining its relation to one or another form of liberalism.

39. As one finds in John Stuart Mill, *Considerations on Representative Government*, chapter 3.

40. Reich, *Tales of a New America*, p. 145.

41. Keynes, *Collected Writings*, vol. 9, p. 375.

42. Louis Brandeis, in Alfred Lief, *The Brandeis Guide to the Modern World* (Boston: Little, Brown, 1941), p. 85.

43. Cf. Robert A. Dahl, *Democracy, Liberty and Equality* (Oslo: Norwegian University Press, 1986), p. 103.

44. Waligorski, *Political Theory of Conservative Economists;* Michael Wines, "White House Links Riots to Welfare," *New York Times* (May 5, 1992), pp. A1, 12; George Will, "Fringe Is Marginal No More."

45. Cf. Mason, *Security Through Freedom*, pp. 83–85; James Ronald Stanfield, "The Dichotomized State," *Journal of Economic Issues* 25 (September 1991): 771–72; John A. Hall, "Classical Liberalism and the Modern State," *Daedalus* 116 (Summer 1987): 102–3; Garry, *Liberalism and American Identity*, p. 97.

46. Alan Wolfe, "Dispassionate Romantic" [review of Alan Ryan, *John Dewey and the High Tide of American Liberalism*] *Civilization* 2 (July–August 1995): 83.

47. Cf. Loren J. Okroi, *Galbraith, Harrington, Heilbroner: Economics and Dissent in an Age of Optimism* (Princeton, N.J.: Princeton University Press, 1988), p. xiii: "what unites them is not any nearly perfect congruence of their theories, but rather their steadfast refusal to consider economic issues in isolation from the social world . . . [and] awareness of economic events as phenomena enmeshed in the flux of historical change."

CHAPTER 2. BEGINNINGS

1. Alfonso J. Damico, *Individuality and Community: The Social and Political Thought of John Dewey* (Gainesville: University Presses of Florida, 1978), p. 7; John Kenneth Galbraith, "Ideology and Economic Reality," *Challenge* 32 (November–December, 1989): 5. Cf. L. T. Hobhouse, *Liberalism* (London: Oxford University Press, 1964), pp. 30–31.

2. Many problems discussed by John Dewey, *Individualism Old and New* (New York: Minton, Balch, 1930), continue to resonate at the end of the twentieth century: alienation, growing division between the well-off and the poor, school troubles, insistence on enforcing older value-related policies in changed circumstances, greed, individual powerlessness when faced with concentrated economic power, and narrow economic valuation.

3. Quotes are from Felix Frankfurter, "Mr. Justice Brandeis and the Constitution," in Felix Frankfurter, ed., *Mr. Justice Brandeis* (New Haven, Conn.: Yale University Press, 1932), p. 60; Dewey, *Individualism Old and New*, p. 16. Cf. John Dewey, *Freedom and Culture* (Buffalo, N.Y.: Prometheus Books, 1989), pp. 13–14, 58, 62.

4. John Dewey, *Liberalism and Social Action* (New York: Capricorn Books, [1935] 1963), pp. 20, 87, 54–55, 32, 39, 47–48, 75. Cf. Dewey, *Individualism Old and New*, p. 93; Damico, *Individuality and Community*, pp. 71, 67; Robert B. Westbrook, *John Dewey and American Democracy* (Ithaca, N.Y.: Cornell University Press, 1991), pp. 430–32.

5. L. T. Hobhouse, *Democracy and Reaction* (Brighton, U.K.: Harvester Press, 1972), pp. 65, 67.

6. As quoted in Michael Freeden, *The New Liberalism: An Ideology of Social Reform* (Oxford: Clarendon Press, 1978), p. 253.

7. Hobhouse, *Democracy and Reaction*, pp. xii, xviii, 164–65, 217–18. Cf. Hob-

house, *Liberalism,* pp. 25, 31, 46, 58, 115. The crucial role of conditions, circumstances, and situation is a theme in L. T. Hobhouse, *Social Evolution and Political Theory* (New York: Columbia University Press, 1911).

8. Max Lerner, "The Social Thought of Mr. Justice Brandeis," in Frankfurter, ed., *Mr. Justice Brandeis,* pp. 9, 14; Brandeis as quoted in Philippa Strum, *Brandeis: Beyond Progressivism* (Lawrence: University Press of Kansas, 1993), p. 138.

9. Dewey, *Individualism Old and New,* pp. 36, 54–55; Dewey, *Freedom and Culture,* pp. 51, 122. Cf. Lerner, "Social Thought of Mr. Justice Brandeis," pp. 20, 42.

10. Hobhouse, *Social Evolution and Political Theory,* p. 194.

11. Dewey, *Individualism Old and New,* pp. 168, 115; Dewey, *Liberalism and Social Action,* pp. 28, 26–27, 39; Hobhouse, *Democracy and Reaction,* p. xxiv.

12. Dewey, *Individualism Old and New,* pp. 90–93, 51; Dewey, *Liberalism and Social Action,* p. 61; Hobhouse, *Liberalism,* pp. 84, 86. Cf. Hobhouse, *Democracy and Reaction,* pp. 145–46. Cf. Lerner: Economic individualism "is not to be confused with ethical and psychological individualism" ("Social Thought of Mr. Justice Brandeis," p. 42).

13. Dewey, *Liberalism and Social Action,* pp. 41–43, 48; Dewey, *Individualism Old and New,* pp. 28, 33, 42, 72; Louis D. Brandeis, "Industrial Democracy" [testimony before the United States Commission on Industrial Relations, 1915], excerpts in Walter E. Volkomer, ed., *The Liberal Tradition in American Thought* (New York: Capricorn Books, 1969), p. 293.

14. As quoted in Strum, *Brandeis,* p. 47; Hobhouse, *Social Evolution,* p. 94; Dewey, *Individualism Old and New,* pp. 53, 168, 81.

15. Dewey, *Liberalism and Social Action,* p. 90.

16. Hobhouse, *Liberalism,* pp. 67, 41; Hobhouse, *Social Evolution and Political Theory,* pp. 87, 29–30. Freeden, *The New Liberalism,* p. 71, quotes Hobhouse on "a kind of partnership between the individual and community." Cf. Strum, *Brandeis,* pp. 2, 116–17; Freeden, *The New Liberalism,* pp. 67–68, 70; Dewey, *Liberalism and Social Action,* p. 85, on interrelations and interdependence.

17. Hobhouse, *Liberalism,* pp. 16–29, 50–51, 78; Hobhouse, *Social Evolution and Political Theory,* pp. 189–90, 200. The quote is from L. T. Hobhouse, *The Elements of Social Justice* (New York: Henry Holt, 1922), p. 90. Cf. ibid., pp. 58–65.

18. Dewey, *Freedom and Culture,* p. 14; Dewey, *Liberalism and Social Action,* p. 48; Hobhouse, *Liberalism,* pp. 50–51, 34.

19. Dewey, *Liberalism and Social Action,* pp. 32–37, 48; John Dewey, "The Future of Liberalism or the Democratic Way of Change," in John Dewey, Boyd H. Bode, and T. V. Smith, *What Is Democracy? Its Conflicts, Ends and Means* (Norman, Okla.: Cooperative Books, 1939), p. 8; Dewey, *Freedom and Culture,* p. 130.

20. Hobhouse, *Liberalism,* p. 75; Hobhouse, *Elements of Social Justice,* p. 80; Hobhouse, *Democracy and Reaction,* pp. 37–38, 213, 215–18. Cf. ibid., p. 215: "The starving man is nominally free to take or reject the last loaf of bread, but in reality he acts

under constraint. . . . The actual freedom of choice is in all contracts a variable quantity. The two parties are seldom on equal terms."

21. Cf. Dewey, *Individualism Old and New,* p. 132, arguing that workers are treated literally as "hands," not minds, to "execute plans which they do not form." This is also an early reference to working smarter—a goal that Thurow and Reich promote.

22. Brandeis, in Volkomer, *Liberal Tradition in American Thought,* pp. 288–96; Philippa Strum, ed., *Brandeis on Democracy* (Lawrence: University Press of Kansas, 1995), pp. 84, 91; Alfred Lief, ed., *The Brandeis Guide to the Modern World* (Boston: Little, Brown, 1941), pp. 85, 108; Louis D. Brandeis, *The Curse of Bigness: Miscellaneous Papers* (New York: Viking, 1935), p. 39; Lerner, "Social Thought of Mr. Justice Brandeis," pp. 39–40, 195 n. 29; Strum, *Brandeis,* pp. 7–8, 26. Cf. John Dewey, *The Political Writings* (Indianapolis: Hackett, 1993), p. 123: "Older divisions of master and subject class tend to reinstate themselves in a subtle form."

23. Westbrook, *John Dewey and American Democracy,* pp. 37–38, 43–46, 56 n. 16, 435; Dewey, *Liberalism and Social Action,* p. 27; Dewey, *Freedom and Culture,* p. 33; Damico, *Individuality and Community,* p. 83; Hobhouse, *Elements of Social Justice,* pp. 49–50, 83; Hobhouse, *Social Evolution and Political Theory,* pp. 203–4; Brandeis, in Volkomer, *Liberal Tradition in American Thought,* p. 294.

24. Brandeis, in Volkomer, *Liberal Tradition in American Thought,* p. 292; Lief, *Brandeis Guide to the Modern World,* p. 30; Lerner, "Social Thought of Mr. Justice Brandeis," p. 131; Dewey, *Individualism Old and New,* pp. 131–32. Seventy years later, Thurow could still refer to "militaristic top-down decision-making processes . . . in many American firms." Lester C. Thurow, *The Zero-Sum Solution: Building a World-Class American Economy* (New York: Simon & Schuster, 1985), p. 129. Charles Lindblom, *Politics and Markets: The World's Political-Economic Systems* (New York: Basic Books, 1977), p. 47, notes that "most gainfully employed people in fact spend their working hours in an authority system" that is not conducive to freedom. As did Dewey, Brandeis believed that people can be educated, and argued that democracy requires a high educational standard. Lief, *Brandeis Guide to the Modern World,* pp. 73, 36.

25. Strum, *Brandeis on Democracy,* pp. 91–92; Brandeis, in Volkomer, *Liberal Tradition in American Thought,* p. 294; Strum, *Brandeis,* pp. 34, 38–39; Lief, *Brandeis Guide to the Modern World,* pp. 94–97; letter to Robert W. Bruere, February 25, 1922, as quoted in Donald R. Richberg, "The Industrial Liberalism of Mr. Justice Brandeis," in Frankfurter, ed., *Mr. Justice Brandeis,* p. 135; Frankfurter, "Mr. Justice Brandeis and the Constitution," p. 72.

26. Brandeis, in Volkomer, *Liberal Tradition in American Thought,* p. 292; Strum, *Brandeis on Democracy,* p. 60; Lief, *Brandeis Guide to the Modern World,* p. 30; Strum, *Brandeis,* pp. 158–61; Brandeis, *Curse of Bigness,* p. 35.

27. Strum, *Brandeis,* p. 96; Brandeis, in Volkomer, *Liberal Tradition in American Thought,* p. 294. Galbraith also emphasizes the compensatory role of government in situations where people have unequal power.

28. Strum, *Brandeis,* pp. 3, 8.

29. Dewey, *Liberalism and Social Action,* pp. 30–31, 85; Dewey, *Political Writings,* pp. 63, 121–23; Dewey, *Freedom and Culture,* pp. 49–53, 58, 97; Westbrook, *John Dewey and American Democracy,* p. 224. Cf. Dewey, *Individualism Old and New,* p. 131.

30. Westbrook, *John Dewey and American Democracy,* pp. 315–17, 547–59.

31. Dewey, *Freedom and Culture,* p. 122.

32. Hobhouse, *Elements of Social Justice,* p. 225; Hobhouse, *Liberalism,* pp. 116–17, 72, 126; Hobhouse, *Democracy and Reaction,* pp. xvii, xxvi–xxvii, 138, 222, 148–51; Hobhouse, *Social Evolution and Political Theory,* pp. 140–43, 148.

33. Dewey, *Liberalism and Social Action,* p. 58. The later economists agree with Dewey on this point.

34. Dewey, *Individualism Old and New,* pp. 103, 54–55; Dewey, *Freedom and Culture,* pp. 12–15, 51, 54; Dewey, *Liberalism and Social Action,* pp. 36, 57. Cf. Dewey, *Individualism Old and New,* p. 158: "Imagine a society free from pecuniary domination, and it becomes self-evident that material commodities are invitations to individual taste and choice, and occasions for individual growth." Dewey discussed corporate culture throughout *Individualism Old and New.*

35. Lief, *Brandeis Guide to Modern Life,* pp. 36–37, 83–84; Lerner, "Social Thought of Mr. Justice Brandeis," pp. 21, 23–24, 34–35; Strum, *Brandeis on Democracy,* p. 119; Nelson L. Dawson, "Louis D. Brandeis, George Gilder, and the Nature of Capitalism," *Historian* 47 (November 1984): 81–82.

36. Hobhouse, *Liberalism,* pp. 41, 50–51; Dewey, *Liberalism and Social Action,* p. 38.

37. Dewey, *Liberalism and Social Action,* p. 7–9, 33, 26–27; Dewey, *Political Writings,* p. 177.

38. Dewey, *Liberalism and Social Action,* pp. 7–8, 33; Hobhouse, *Social Evolution and Political Theory,* p. 197. Brandeis rejected natural law claims regarding the political economy, asserting that government has a right to pass social legislation and modify property rights, but he did not elaborate on this argument, unlike Hobhouse and Dewey. For all three, rights are based on individual development, on impact on people in concrete situations, and on community good.

39. Hobhouse, *Democracy and Reaction,* pp. 84–86.

40. Brandeis, Dewey, Keynes, Galbraith, Thurow, and Reich agree that laissez-faire theory is unconcerned about individuals.

41. Hobhouse, *Democracy and Reaction,* pp. 87–89, 93; Hobhouse, *Social Evolution and Political Theory,* pp. 9–10, 22–24, 28.

42. Dewey, *Liberalism and Social Action*, pp. 31–32; Dewey, *Individualism Old and New*, p. 88.

43. Lerner, "Social Thought of Mr. Justice Brandeis," pp. 29, 31–32, 36–37; Dawson, "Brandeis, Gilder, and the Nature of Capitalism," p. 75.

44. Brandeis, in Volkomer, *Liberal Tradition in American Thought*, pp. 291–95; Strum, *Brandeis*, pp. 68, 88; Hobhouse, *Liberalism*, pp. 77–78; Dewey, *Liberalism and Social Action*, pp. 36, 63–64; Hobhouse, *Democracy and Reaction*, p. 217; Hobhouse, *Elements of Social Justice*, pp. 181, 183; Dewey, *Freedom and Culture*, p. 127; Dewey, *Individualism Old and New*, p. 87.

45. Lief, *Brandeis Guide to the Modern World*, p. 54; Hobhouse, *Democracy and Reaction*, pp. 215–18; Hobhouse, *Liberalism*, p. 24; Hobhouse, *Social Evolution and Political Theory*, p. 47; Dewey, *Liberalism and Social Action*, pp. 37–38; Dewey, *Individualism Old and New*, p. 115.

46. Keynes' *General Theory* was published in 1936. Although some economists were familiar with its central argument before that time, it did not affect policy in the United States until later. Cf. John Kenneth Galbraith, "How Keynes Came to America," *Economics Peace and Laughter* (New York: Signet, 1971), pp. 44–56. Keynes thought Brandeis' emphasis held more promise than did some New Deal proposals. John Maynard Keynes, *The Collected Writings of John Maynard Keynes*, edited by Donald Moggridge, vol. 21, *Activities 1931–1939, World Crisis and Policies in Britain and America* (London: Macmillan, 1982), p. 320.

47. Lief, *Brandeis Guide to the Modern World*, pp. 19, 22; Strum, *Brandeis*, pp. 35–36, 86, 153, 131; Richberg, "Industrial Liberalism of Mr. Justice Brandeis," pp. 127–39.

48. Brandeis believed that trusts prefigured socialism, but he was uninterested in socialism itself.

49. Dewey, *Individualism Old and New*, pp. 42, 119–20, 116, 131; Lief, *Brandeis Guide to the Modern World*, pp. 52–53; Dawson, "Brandeis, Gilder, and the Nature of Capitalism," p. 73; Hobhouse, *Liberalism*, pp. 54, 87, 90–91, 108–9; Dewey, *Liberalism and Social Action*, pp. 88–90; Hobhouse, *Democracy and Reaction*, pp. 217, 219. Cf. Damico, *Individuality and Community*, pp. 74–77.

50. Hobhouse, *Democracy and Reaction*, p. xviii; Hobhouse, *Liberalism*, p. 51; Dewey, *Individualism Old and New*, p. 144; Frankfurter, "Mr. Justice Brandeis and the Constitution," p. 65.

51. Cf. Westbrook, *John Dewey and American Democracy*, pp. 316–17.

52. Hobhouse, *Social Evolution and Political Theory*, pp. 188–89; Dewey, *Individualism Old and New*, p. 89; Hobhouse, *Liberalism*, pp. 78, 76, 83, 92. Hobhouse advocated adoption of a "civic minimum wage," Hobhouse, *Elements of Social Justice*, p. 158.

53. Dewey, *Freedom and Culture*, pp. 53, 58; Lief, *Brandeis Guide to the Modern*

World, p. 85; Strum, *Brandeis,* pp. 47, 146; Dawson, "Brandeis, Gilder, and the Nature of Capitalism," pp. 79–81.

CHAPTER 3. JOHN MAYNARD KEYNES

1. Theoretical influence aside, chronologically, Keynes overlaps Brandeis, Dewey, and Hobhouse on one side and Galbraith on the other. He met Brandeis and Galbraith.

2. Cf. Robert Skidelsky, *John Maynard Keynes,* vol. 2, *The Economist as Saviour* (New York: Penguin Books, 1994), pp. 572–624, especially p. 583, about the "economic theology" in the "war of opinion among economists" over Keynes' *General Theory.*

3. For some of these criticisms, see Conrad P. Waligorski, *The Political Theory of Conservative Economists* (Lawrence: University Press of Kansas, 1990), pp. 105–6, 140, 232.

4. Cf. Benjamin Barber, *Strong Democracy: Participatory Politics for a New Age* (Berkeley: University of California Press, 1984), p. xiv; C. B. Macpherson, *The Life and Times of Liberal Democracy* (Oxford: Oxford University Press, 1977), p. 92, claims that Keynesian policy sustains "the capitalist order" by removing decisions from "democratic responsiveness" to "experts" who "could save the system"; Leonard Silk, *The Economists* (New York: Avon, 1976), p. 225.

5. Bruce Bartlett, "Keynes as a Conservative," *Modern Age* 28 (1984): 128–33. Macpherson agrees. Growing focus on Keynes' tenuous relation to Edmund Burke also tames progressive elements in Keynes. Keynes saw the "implications" of his theory, as opposed to his values, as "moderately conservative" in meeting demands for change while maintaining the essentials of capitalism. John Maynard Keynes, *The Collected Writings of John Maynard Keynes,* edited by Donald Moggridge, vol. 7, *The General Theory of Employment Interest and Money* (London: Macmillan, 1973), p. 377. Many conservatives say that Keynes subverted these essentials.

6. Robert Lekachman, "The Radical Keynes," in Robert Skidelsky, ed., *The End of the Keynesian Era: Essays on the Disintegration of the Keynesian Political Economy* (New York: Holmes & Meier, 1977), pp. 59–66; Robert Lekachman, *Keynes' General Theory: Reports of Three Decades* (New York: St. Martin's Press, 1964), pp. 5–8; Hyman P. Minsky, *John Maynard Keynes* (New York: Columbia University Press, 1975), p. v; John Barraclough, "The Keynesian Era in Perspective," in Skidelsky, ed., *The End of the Keynesian Era,* p. 110; Paul L. Sweezy, "Keynes as a Critic of Capitalism," *Monthly Review* 32 (April 1981): 33–36.

7. Joan Robinson, "What Has Become of the Keynesian Revolution?" in Milo Keynes, ed., *Essays on John Maynard Keynes* (Cambridge: Cambridge University Press, 1974), p. 128. In his attempt to preserve much of the old world in the midst

of a new one, Keynes was "the representative political thinker of the interwar period." Peter F. Drucker, *Men, Ideas and Politics* (New York: Harper & Row, 1971), p. 235.

8. Cf. Alan Bullock and Maurice Shock, eds., *The Liberal Tradition: From Fox to Keynes* (London: Adam & Charles Black, 1966), especially p. L; Skidelsky, *John Maynard Keynes*, vol. 2, p. xv; Robert Skidelsky, "Keynes and the Reconstruction of Liberalism," *Encounter* 52 (April 1979): 29–39; J. G. Merquior, *Liberalism: Old and New* (Boston: Twayne, 1991), p. 115: "the economist redesigning political economy became the main reference of liberalism rebuilt." Cf. Robert Lekachman, *The Age of Keynes* (New York: Random House, 1966), p. 162. The late Lord Richard Kahn—Keynes' student, associate, friend, and literary executor—said a focus on liberalism, the relation of politics and economics, and uncertainty is the proper way to approach Keynes' political-economy. Author's interview with Lord Kahn, October 16, 1980.

9. This is widely accepted. Seymour E. Harris, *The New Economics: Keynes' Influence on Theory and Public Policy* (New York: Knopf, 1947), p. 282; Elizabeth Johnson, "John Maynard Keynes: Scientist or Politician?" *Journal of Political Economy* 82 (1974): 99–111; Elizabeth S. Johnson and Harry G. Johnson, *The Shadow of Keynes: Understanding Keynes, Cambridge and Keynesian Economics* (Chicago: University of Chicago Press, 1978), p. 18; Minsky, *John Maynard Keynes*, p. 145; D. E. Moggridge, *Keynes* (Glasgow: Fontana/Collins, 1976), p. 155; Robert Skidelsky, *John Maynard Keynes*, vol. 1, *Hopes Betrayed 1883–1920* (New York: Viking, 1986), p. 154; author's interview with Lord Kahn.

10. John Maynard Keynes, *The Collected Writings of John Maynard Keynes*, edited by Donald Moggridge, vol. 9, *Essays in Persuasion* (London: Macmillan, 1972), pp. 295, 303, 332; Keynes, *Collected Writings*, vol. 7, p. 381; John Maynard Keynes, *The Collected Writings of John Maynard Keynes*, edited by Donald Moggridge, vol. 2, *Economic Consequences of the Peace* (London: Macmillan, 1971); Wayne Parsons, "Keynes and the Politics of Ideas," *History of Political Thought* 4 (Summer 1983): 367–92; Peter A. Hall, "Keynes in Political Science," *History of Political Economy* 26 (1994): 137–53. Cf. the discussion of dual leadership in Charles Lindblom, "The Market as Prison," *Journal of Politics* 44 (1982): 324–36, and in Charles Lindblom, *Politics and Markets: The World's Political-Economic Systems* (New York: Basic Books, 1977), pp. 173–75 and passim. Keynes, too, sometimes attempted to separate politics and economics. See John Maynard Keynes, *The Collected Writings of John Maynard Keynes*, edited by Donald Moggridge, vol. 25, *Activities 1940–1944, Shaping the Post-War World: The Clearing Union* (London: Macmillan, 1980), p. 268.

11. Keynes, *Collected Writings*, vol. 9, p. 125, 294; John Maynard Keynes, *The Collected Writings of John Maynard Keynes*, edited by Donald Moggridge, vol. 27, *Activities 1940–1946: Shaping the Post-War World: Employment and Commodities* (London: Macmillan, 1980), p. 260.

12. Keynes, *Collected Writings*, vol. 9, pp. 322–25; James R. Crotty, "Keynes on the Stages of Development of the Capitalist Economy: The Institutional Foundation of Keynes's Methodology," *Journal of Economic Issues* 24 (1990): 761–80. Keynes believed that a good economist "must study the present in the light of the past for the purposes of the future." John Maynard Keynes, *The Collected Writings of John Maynard Keynes*, edited by Donald Moggridge, vol. 10, *Essays in Biography* (London: Macmillan, 1972), pp. 173–74.

13. Keynes, *Collected Writings*, vol. 2, pp. 6, 11–13, 161; John Maynard Keynes, *The Collected Writings of John Maynard Keynes*, edited by Donald Moggridge, vol. 4, *A Tract on Monetary Reform* (London: Macmillan, 1971), p. 6; Keynes, *Collected Writings*, vol. 9, pp. 61–66, 69; Skidelsky, *John Maynard Keynes*, vol. 2, p. 263.

14. John Maynard Keynes, "National Self-Sufficiency," *Yale Review* 22 (1933): 760–61.

15. Keynes, *Collected Writings*, vol. 27, pp. 444–45; Keynes, *Collected Writings*, vol. 7, p. 3.

16. Referring to "The End of Laissez-Faire," Skidelsky criticizes Keynes for failing to "develop any sustained critique. . . . He lumps together, in briefest summary, objections to *laissez-faire* which may be philosophical or merely practical . . . moral objections . . . and objections which stem from changed techniques of production" [Skidelsky, *John Maynard Keynes*, vol. 2, p. 225]. But there is more to consider. Keynes would have supported earlier laissez-faire. His discussion of its shortcomings is found throughout his work, including *The General Theory* and in Treasury memos on the postwar world. Cf. Skidelsky, *John Maynard Keynes*, vol. 2, pp. 219–20, where Keynes gives "a powerful critique," and Keynes, *Collected Writings*, vol. 9, pp. 300–301.

17. Keynes, *Collected Writings*, vol. 9, pp. 284–85; Keynes, *Collected Writings*, vol. 7, p. 3. The most concise statement is given in Keynes, *Collected Writings*, vol. 9, pp. 287–88. Cf. Keynes, *Collected Writings*, vol. 7, pp. xxi; Keynes, *Collected Writings*, vol. 10, p. 262. It was not the great economists but popularizers who virtually created laissez-faire ideology. Keynes, *Collected Writings*, vol. 9, pp. 277–82.

18. John Maynard Keynes, *The Collected Writings of John Maynard Keynes*, edited by Donald Moggridge, vol. 13, *The General Theory and After, Part 1, Preparation* (London: Macmillan, 1973), p. 406; John Maynard Keynes, *The Collected Writings of John Maynard Keynes*, edited by Donald Moggridge, vol. 20, *Activities 1929–1931: Rethinking Employment and Employment Policy* (London: Macmillan, 1981), pp. 221, 474, 83; John Maynard Keynes, *The Collected Writings of John Maynard Keynes*, edited by Donald Moggridge, vol. 21, *Activities 1931–1939, World Crisis and Policies in Britain and America* (London: Macmillan, 1982), p. 91; Keynes, *Collected Writings*, vol. 9, pp. 90–91. See also Keynes, *Collected Writings*, vol. 27, p. 444.

19. Keynes, *Collected Writings*, vol. 13, pp. 491, 406; Keynes, *Collected Writings*, vol. 25, pp. 21–22; Keynes, *Collected Writings*, vol. 9, p. 205; Keynes, *Collected Writings*,

vol. 7, pp. 249–50; Keynes, *Collected Writings,* vol. 20, p. 221. Cf. Keynes, *Collected Writings,* vol. 13, pp. 485–92.

20. John Maynard Keynes, *The Collected Writings of John Maynard Keynes,* edited by Donald Moggridge, vol. 14, *The General Theory and After* (London: Macmillan, 1973), p. 26; John Maynard Keynes, *The Collected Writings of John Maynard Keynes,* edited by Donald Moggridge, vol. 29, *The General Theory and After: A Supplement* (London: Macmillan, 1979), pp. 101–2.

21. Peter Clarke, "Keynes in History," *History of Political Economy* 26 (1994): 126–27; R. F. Harrod, *The Life and Times of John Maynard Keynes* (Harmondsworth, U.K.: Penguin Books, 1972), pp. 535–36; Skidelsky, *John Maynard Keynes,* vol. 2, p. 31.

22. Keynes, *Collected Writings,* vol. 7, pp. 6, 267; Keynes, *Collected Writings,* vol. 13, pp. 129, 180–200, 315–17, 360, 390, 392.

23. Keynes, *Collected Writings,* vol. 9, pp. 218–23, 235, 208–11; Keynes, *Collected Writings,* vol. 13, pp. 180–200, 360–61; Keynes, *Collected Writings,* vol. 20, pp. 280, 72.

24. Keynes, *Collected Writings,* vol. 13, p. 349; Keynes, *Collected Writings,* vol. 7, pp. 30–31; John Maynard Keynes, "The Post-War National Income," June 25, 1943, Public Record Office, London, Treasury File T247/78. James A. Caporaso and David P. Levine, *Theories of Political Economy* (Cambridge: Cambridge University Press, 1992), pp. 100–124; Dudley Dillard, *The Economics of John Maynard Keynes: The Theory of a Monetary Economy* (New York: Prentice-Hall, 1948), p. 213; Skidelsky, *John Maynard Keynes,* vol. 2, pp. 498–99.

25. Cf. Peter Clarke, *Liberals and Social Democrats* (Cambridge: Cambridge University Press, 1978), p. 271; D. E. Moggridge, "The Influence of Keynes on the Economics of his Time," in Milo Keynes, ed., *Essays on John Maynard Keynes,* pp. 77–78.

26. John Maynard Keynes, *The Collected Writings of John Maynard Keynes,* edited by Donald Moggridge, vol. 8, *A Treatise on Probability* (London: Macmillan, 1973), pp. 50, 445; Keynes, *Collected Writings,* vol. 7, pp. 144–50; Keynes, *Collected Writings,* vol. 13, pp. 395, 486–92; Keynes, *Collected Writings,* vol. 10, p. 262; Keynes, *Collected Writings,* vol. 14, pp. 113–23. Cf. Keynes, *Collected Writings,* vol. 27, p. 445; author's interview with Lord Kahn; Skidelsky, *John Maynard Keynes,* vol. 2, pp. xxiv, xxviii, 616–18; Athol Fitzgibbons, *Keynes's Vision: A New Political Economy* (Oxford: Clarendon Press, 1988), pp. 80–83, 108.

27. John Maynard Keynes, *Collected Writings of John Maynard Keynes,* edited by Donald Moggridge, vol. 1, *Indian Currency and Finance* (London: Macmillan, 1971); John Maynard Keynes, *Collected Writings of John Maynard Keynes,* edited by Donald Moggridge, vol. 26, *Activities 1941–1946, Shaping the Post-War World: Bretton Woods and Reparations* (London: Macmillan, 1980), pp. 9–23; John Maynard Keynes, *The Collected Writings of John Maynard Keynes,* edited by Donald Moggridge, vol. 24, *Activities: 1944–1946, The Transition to Peace* (London: Macmillan, 1979), pp. 605–24.

28. Minsky, *John Maynard Keynes*, p. 61.

29. Keynes, *Collected Writings*, vol. 10, p. 447; Keynes, *Collected Writings*, vol. 2, p. 1; Keynes, *Collected Writings*, vol. 9, pp. 3, 63–65; John Maynard Keynes, *The Collected Writings of John Maynard Keynes*, edited by Donald Moggridge, vol. 18, *Activities 1922–1932, The End of Reparations* (London: Macmillan, 1978), pp. 83–84.

30. Keynes, *Collected Writings*, vol. 9, pp. 129, 59–75; John Maynard Keynes, *The Collected Writings of John Maynard Keynes*, edited by Donald Moggridge, vol. 19, part 2, *Activities 1922–1929* (London: Macmillan, 1981), pp. 638–39; John Maynard Keynes, *The Collected Writings of John Maynard Keynes*, edited by Donald Moggridge, vol. 6, *A Treatise on Money*, vol. 2, *The Applied Theory of Money* (London: Macmillan, 1971), p. 346.

31. Keynes, *Collected Writings*, vol. 9, pp. 224, 129–135; Keynes, *Collected Writings*, vol. 24, p. 621; John Maynard Keynes, *The Collected Writings of John Maynard Keynes*, edited by Donald Moggridge, vol. 5, *A Treatise on Money*, vol. 1, *The Pure Theory of Money* (London: Macmillan, 1971), p. 244; John Maynard Keynes, *The Collected Writings of John Maynard Keynes*, edited by Donald Moggridge, vol. 22, *Activities: 1939–1945, Internal War Finance* (London: Macmillan, 1978), p. 123. Cf. his famous giraffes example in Keynes, *Collected Writings*, vol. 9, pp. 283–85; John Maynard Keynes, *The Collected Writings of John Maynard Keynes*, edited by Donald Moggridge, vol. 28, *Social, Political and Economic Writings* (London: Macmillan, 1982), pp. 22, 28–29.

32. Keynes, *Collected Writings*, vol. 9, pp. 300–301; Keynes, *Collected Writings*, vol. 7, p. 380.

33. Keynes, *Collected Writings*, vol. 7, pp. 83–84, 155, 320; Keynes, *Collected Writings*, vol. 9, pp. 274–75, 291–93, 117, 128, 235, 373, 375, 379, 390–91, 394, 422; Keynes, *Collected Writings*, vol. 20, pp. 287–89. Cf. Keynes, *Collected Writings*, vol. 9, pp. 287–88: "The world is *not* so governed from above that private and social interest always coincide. It is *not* so managed here below that in practice they coincide. It is *not* a correct deduction from the principles of economics that enlightened self-interest always operates in the public interest. Nor is it true that self-interest generally *is* enlightened."

34. See John Locke, *Second Treatise of Government*, in *Two Treatises of Government*, edited by Peter Laslett, (New York: Mentor Book, 1965), paragraphs 182–83, 196; Keynes, *Collected Writings*, vol. 2, p. 142; Keynes, *Collected Writings*, vol. 9, p. 377.

35. Keynes, *Collected Writings*, vol. 4, p. 56; Keynes, *Collected Writings*, vol. 7, pp. 379–80; Keynes, *Collected Writings*, vol. 21, pp. 87–90; John Maynard Keynes, "Post-War Employment," February 14, 1944, Public Record Office, London, Treasury File T.247/80.

36. Keynes, *Collected Writings*, vol. 9, pp. 291–93.

37. Keynes, *Collected Writings*, vol. 9, p. 292–94. The quote continues: "Our

problem is to work out a social organisation that shall be as efficient as possible without offending our notions of a satisfactory way of life."

38. Keynes, *Collected Writings*, vol. 9, p. 305; Keynes, *Collected Writings*, vol. 28, p. 29.

39. "Economic Possibilities for Our Grandchildren," Keynes, *Collected Writings*, vol. 9, pp. 321–32, is almost lighthearted; but all his speculation about the future is not playful. Though Keynes worked on the essay for two years, it is not *a* or *the* fundamental part of his work. He discussed the future in "The End of Laissez-Faire," *The General Theory*, and much work during World War II, including "How to Pay for the War" as well as memoranda and policy proposals dealing with domestic and international policy.

40. Keynes, *Collected Writings*, vol. 28, pp. 32–33; Keynes, *Collected Writings*, vol. 7, p. 376; Keynes, *Collected Writings*, vol. 9, p. 299.

41. Keynes, *Collected Writings*, vol. 9, pp. 293, 232, xviii, 126, 335, 380; Keynes, *Collected Writings*, vol. 28, p. 343; cf. Keynes, *Collected Writings*, vol. 6, pp. 345–46, and Keynes, *Collected Writings*, vol. 20, pp. 321–22.

42. Keynes, *Collected Writings*, vol. 28, p. 34; Keynes, *Collected Writings*, vol. 9, p. xviii.

43. Keynes, *Collected Writings*, vol. 9, pp. 327–29.

44. Skidelsky, *End of the Keynesian Era*, p. 8, says that Keynes believed the age of plenty had arrived. Heilbroner says that Keynes thought it would take only one generation. Robert L. Heilbroner, "Economics and Political Economy: Marx, Keynes, and Schumpeter," *Journal of Economic Issues* 18 (September 1984), p. 683. Both see Keynes as being more optimistic than he actually was.

45. Keynes, *Collected Writings*, vol. 27, pp. 260–61; Keynes, *Collected Writings*, vol. 24, p. 411. Galbraith's *Affluent Society* addresses some of these concerns.

46. Keynes, *Collected Writings*, vol. 9, p. 331.

47. Keynes, *Collected Writings*, vol. 9, pp. xviii, 331, 326; Keynes, *Collected Writings*, vol. 13, p. 348; Keynes, *Collected Writings*, vol. 7, p. 220.

48. Keynes, *Collected Writings*, vol. 9, pp. 331, 326; Keynes, *Collected Writings*, vol. 27, pp. 269, 393, 445.

49. Keynes, *Collected Writings*, vol. 9, p. 326.

50. Keynes, *Collected Writings*, vol. 9, p. 325–26.

51. Keynes, *Collected Writings*, vol. 7, pp. 221, 374, 376; Keynes, *Collected Writings*, vol. 9, p. 293. Johnson and Johnson are wrong in asserting that Keynes believed a job for everyone would ensure a happy society. Johnson and Johnson, *Shadow of Keynes*, p. 217. Compare John Stuart Mill: "the best state for human nature is that in which, while no one is poor, no one desires to be richer, nor has any reason to fear being thrust back, by the effort of others to push themselves forward." The goal is to "cultivate freely the graces of life." John Stuart Mill, *Principles of Political Economy* (Harmondsworth, U.K.: Penguin Books, 1970), Bk. IV, ch. vi, pp. 114–15.

52. Rentier capitalism was a "transitional phase which will disappear when it has done its work." Keynes, *Collected Writings*, vol. 7, p. 376.

53. Keynes, *Collected Writings*, vol. 14, p. 378; Keynes, *Collected Writings*, vol. 7, p. 376; Keynes, *Collected Writings*, vol. 9, pp. 292, 293.

54. Keynes, *Collected Writings*, vol. 7, pp. 221, 375–76, 320. Cf. Keynes, *Collected Writings*, vol. 27, p. 322.

55. Keynes, *Collected Writings*, vol. 7, pp. 376, 164, 378; Keynes, *Collected Writings*, vol. 21, p. 500; John Maynard Keynes, *Collected Writings*, edited by Donald Moggridge, vol. 19, part 1, *Activities 1922–1929: The Return to Gold and Industrial Policy* (London: Macmillan, 1981), pp. 219–23.

56. Cf. "semi-autonomous bodies" in Keynes, *Collected Writings*, vol. 9, p. 288.

57. Keynes, *Collected Writings*, vol. 27, pp. 326, 352; John Maynard Keynes to G. Guindey, March 28, 1945, Public Record Office, London, Treasury File T.247/99.

58. Cf. (among many others) Keynes, *Collected Writings*, vol. 9, pp. 146–47, 235, 311, 376, 390, 394, 396, 399; Keynes, *Collected Writings*, vol. 5, pp. 152–53; Keynes, *Collected Writings*, vol. 21, pp. 499–500; Keynes, *Collected Writings*, vol. 7, p. 33. Johnson and Johnson, *Shadow of Keynes*, p. 28, limit social justice to the issue of unemployment. Skidelsky, *John Maynard Keynes*, vol. 2, p. 16, more accurately focuses on "unanticipated disturbances to existing economic relations," yet these are related to life chances.

59. Keynes, *Collected Writings*, vol. 19, part 2, p. 639; Keynes, *Collected Writings*, vol. 9, p. 311; Keynes, *Collected Writings*, vol. 21, p. 500.

60. Cf. Keynes, *Collected Writings*, vol. 9, pp. 146, 166, 218–29, 235, 394, 399; Keynes, *Collected Writings*, vol. 6, pp. 245–46, 264–65. Keynes, *Collected Writings*, vol. 20, pp. 70–71, 295, 590–91; Keynes, *Collected Writings*, vol. 13, p. 392. Lord Kahn said social justice did not need to be defined, since it seemed obvious: first end unemployment and the damage it causes. Author's interview with Lord Kahn.

61. "Post-War Employment," February 14, 1944, Public Record Office, London, Treasury File T.247/80; Keynes, *Collected Writings*, vol. 29, p. 235.

62. Robert E. Lane, "Market Justice, Political Justice," *American Political Science Review* 80 (1986): 396.

63. Waligorski, *Political Theory of Conservative Economists*, pp. 135–37.

64. Keynes, *Collected Writings*, vol. 9, pp. 376–77. Cf. p. 311, "The political problem of mankind is to combine three things: economic efficiency, social justice, and individual liberty."

65. Fitzgibbons, *Keynes' Vision*, p. 184; Johnson and Johnson, *Shadow of Keynes*, p. 217; Robert Skidelsky, "Keynes and the Left," *New Statesman and Society* 6 (April 16, 1993): 17; Skidelsky, "Keynes and the Reconstruction of Liberalism," p. 31; Skidelsky, *John Maynard Keynes*, vol. 2, pp. 8, 223, 233; Harrod, *Life and Times of John Maynard Keynes*, p. 391; author's interview with Lord Kahn.

66. Keynes, *Collected Writings*, vol. 7, pp. 33, 324, 372–74. Cf. Keynes, *Collected Writings*, vol. 9, pp. 410; Keynes, *Collected Writings*, vol. 14, pp. 16, 132; John Maynard Keynes to J. T. Sheppard, February 15, 1946, where he argues that unwillingness to admit one man is better than another is harmful to the country, Sheppard Papers, file Sh 6.13, King's College Library, Cambridge University.

67. Despite the crucial role of working-class spending in maintaining demand, Keynes did not advocate major redistribution. But he favored some. "How to Pay for the War," Keynes, *Collected Writings*, vol. 9, pp. 367–439, says that tax and subsidy policy should help those most in need. On p. 399, he refers to "considerable redistribution." Once investment opportunities begin to dry up, consumption must be emphasized through tax policy, "discouragement of investment and a redistribution of the national wealth." Keynes, *Collected Writings*, vol. 27, p. 360. See also p. 324.

68. Keynes, *Collected Writings*, vol. 20, pp. 11–14.

69. Keynes, *Collected Writings*, vol. 10, p. 445; Keynes, *Collected Writings*, vol. 9, pp. 268–69.

70. Keynes, *Collected Writings*, vol. 14, pp. 300, 297; Keynes, *Collected Writings*, vol. 7, p. xxiii; letter to Archbishop of York, December 3, 1941, Keynes Papers, Box 21, Kings College Library, Cambridge University. Cf. Keynes, *Collected Writings*, vol. 9, pp. 268–69; Joan Robinson, *Economic Philosophy* (Harmondsworth, U.K.: Penguin Books, 1962), p. 72.

71. Keynes, *Collected Writings*, vol. 9, p. 329; cf. p. xviii.

72. Keynes, *Collected Writings*, vol. 19, part 2, p. 648.

73. Keynes, *Collected Writings*, vol. 4, p. 65. The often-ignored remainder of the quote is: "Economists set themselves too easy, too useless a task if in tempestuous seasons they can only tell us that when the storm is long past the ocean is flat again." Cf. Keynes, *Collected Writings*, vol. 6, p. 141. Robert Chernomas, "Keynes on Post-Scarcity Society," *Journal of Economic Issues* 18 (1984): 1007–26, claims Keynes' interest was essentially long run.

74. As opposed to personal interest in history and book collecting; desire to maintain and perpetuate British tradition; and recommended public support for the arts, education, slum clearance, international organization, and planning.

75. Keynes, *Collected Writings*, vol. 20, pp. 126–27.

76. Laissez faire is ultimately unconcerned with *achieving* the future. Its supposed emphasis on the future conflicts with its individualism and disregards specific individuals. *Belief* that the system is natural and will work out best if left unaided is compatible with an organic model, not individualism.

77. Keynes, *Collected Writings*, vol. 6, p. 141; Keynes, *Collected Writings*, vol. 20, p. 120; Keynes, *Collected Writings*, vol. 7, pp. 221–22; Keynes, *Collected Writings*, vol. 13, p. 199. Circumstances were crucial. Cf. Keynes, *Collected Writings*, vol. 24, p. 597 for [1945] "responsibilities of cautious statesmanship towards the future."

78. Waligorski, *Political Theory of Conservative Economists*, pp. 101–25.

79. Keynes' economics are called incompatible with democracy because democracy requires either more participation and expansion into economics *or* less.

80. He came closest in *How to Pay for the War*. Keynes, *Collected Writings*, vol. 9, pp. 367–428.

81. Cf. Fitzgibbons, *Keynes's Vision*, p. 171; Skidelsky, *John Maynard Keynes*, vol. 2, pp. 227–28.

82. Keynes, *Collected Writings*, vol. 19, part 2, pp. 638–39.

83. Keynes, *Collected Writings*, vol. 21, p. 281; Keynes, *Collected Writings*, vol. 20, pp. 64, 221–23; Keynes, *Collected Writings*, vol. 6, p. 346; Keynes, *Collected Writings*, vol. 27, p. 374. Cf. Keynes, *Collected Writings*, vol. 18, p. 366, on the impact of German deflation in 1932.

84. Keynes, *Collected Writings*, vol. 9, p. 288; Keynes, *Collected Writings*, vol. 13, p. 199. He sought an alternative between doing nothing and adopting totalitarianism. Cf. Keynes, *Collected Writings*, vol. 28, p. 22.

85. Keynes, *Collected Writings*, vol. 21, pp. 81–92, 497; Keynes, *Collected Writings*, vol. 7, p. 377; Keynes, *Collected Writings*, vol. 22, p. 155; Keynes, *Collected Writings*, vol. 9, pp. 113–14. Collective action to protect individual initiative and freedom was a common theme of his in the 1930s.

86. Waligorski, *Political Theory of Conservative Economists*, p. 116.

87. Keynes, *Collected Writings*, vol. 7, p. 269; Keynes, *Collected Writings*, vol. 9, pp. 287, 311, 376–77, 380; Keynes, *Collected Writings*, vol. 22, pp. 123, 139; Keynes, *Collected Writings*, vol. 21, p. 493; Keynes, *Collected Writings*, vol. 28, pp. 16, 18, 25–29, 380; Harrod, *Life and Times of John Maynard Keynes*, p. 570.

88. Maurice Cranston, "Keynes: His Political Ideas and Their Influence," in A. P. Thirlwall, ed., *Keynes and Laissez-Faire: The Third Keynes Seminar at Canterbury 1976* (London: Macmillan, 1978), pp. 100–115.

89. Keynes, *Collected Writings*, vol. 9, pp. 302, 125. See Keynes, *Collected Writings*, vol. 22, p. 123, for deferred pay as "compulsion" that can "enlarge liberty."

90. Fitzgibbons, *Keynes's Vision*, pp. 172–73, 182, 184, claims that Keynes opposed political equality, accepted it as a matter of expediency and that his egalitarianism "was only a means rather than an end." The first statement is unsupported, and the second and third, if correct, apply to many liberals.

91. Keynes, *Collected Writings*, vol. 21, pp. 90–92; Keynes, *Collected Writings*, vol. 22, p. 304; Keynes, *Collected Writings*, vol. 25, pp. 269–70.

92. Keynes, *Collected Writings*, vol. 9, pp. 34–35.

93. Keynes, *Collected Writings*, vol. 22, p. 246; Keynes, *Collected Writings*, vol. 28, p. 94; Keynes, *Collected Writings*, vol. 7, p. xxi; Keynes, *Collected Writings*, vol. 25, p. 204.

94. Keynes, *Collected Writings*, vol. 9, p. 225; John Maynard Keynes, *The Collected Writings of John Maynard Keynes*, edited by Elizabeth Johnson, vol. 15, *Activ-*

ities 1906–1914: India and Cambridge (London: Macmillan, 1971), pp. 84, 87.

95. Cf. Joseph A. Schumpeter, *Capitalism, Socialism and Democracy* (New York: Harper & Row, 1976), pp. 270–73, 295.

96. Keynes, *Collected Writings,* vol. 9, pp. 33–34; Keynes, *Collected Writings,* vol. 24, p. 548.

97. Keynes, *Collected Writings,* vol. 9, pp. 34–35; Keynes, *Collected Writings,* vol. 20, p. 262; John Maynard Keynes, *The Collected Writings of John Maynard Keynes,* edited by Donald Moggridge, vol. 17, *Activities: 1920–1922: Treaty Revision and Reconstruction* (London: Macmillan, 1977), p. 427; Keynes, *Collected Writings,* vol. 28, p. 36.

98. Cf. Waligorski, *Political Theory of Conservative Economists,* pp. 105–6; Johnson and Johnson, *Shadow of Keynes,* pp. 26, 70, 165–66; 217; Moggridge, *Keynes,* pp. 128–29; Skidelsky, "Keynes and the Reconstruction of Liberalism," p. 35. Fitzgibbons, *Keynes's Vision,* pp. 173–77, sees structural similarities between Plato and Keynes, who he says preferred a Guardian-like class. But there is no philosopher king in Keynes making Guardians redundant.

99. Robert Dahl, *Democracy, Liberty and Inequality* (Oslo: Norwegian University Press, 1986), pp. 92–94. See Rodney Barker, *Political Ideas in Modern Britain* (London: Methuen, 1978), pp. 138–39, quoting Harold Laski: " 'A democracy . . . must, if it is to work, be an aristocracy by delegation.' "

100. Keynes, *Collected Writings,* vol. 21, pp. 84–92, 131–32; Keynes, *Collected Writings,* vol. 20, p. 27; Keynes, *Collected Writings,* vol. 9, p. 302. On parties see Keynes, *Collected Writings,* vol. 9, pp. 295–96. Banking policy should be insulated from "democratic control and . . . parliamentary interference," though perhaps less than it was at the time. Keynes, *Collected Writings,* vol. 21, p. 131; Keynes, *Collected Writings,* vol. 15, p. 160. Being an "expert" did not ensure expertise; Keynes, *Collected Writings,* vol. 20, p. 515.

101. Keynes, *Collected Writings,* vol. 7, p. 383.

102. Keynes, *Collected Writings,* vol. 9, pp, 296, 302.

103. Keynes, *Collected Writings,* vol. 21, p. 500; Keynes, *Collected Writings,* vol. 7, pp. 267, 269; Keynes, *Collected Writings,* vol. 9, pp. 376–77.

104. Keynes, *Collected Writings,* vol. 9, p. 332. Keynes saw this as a "humble" role.

105. Keynes, *Collected Writings,* vol. 28, pp. 341–49; Keynes, *Collected Writings,* vol. 9, p. 288.

106. Keynes, *Collected Writings,* vol. 21, p. 87–88, 90–91. Cf. Keynes' letter to Hayek, June 28, 1944, in Keynes, *Collected Writings,* vol. 27, pp. 386–88.

107. John Maynard Keynes, proposed "Introduction" to proposals for an international currency union, March 22, 1943, Public Record Office, London, Treasury File T.247/30A; Keynes, *Collected Writings,* vol. 25, pp. 207–8.

108. Keynes, *Collected Writings,* vol. 28, p. 29; Keynes, *Collected Writings,* vol. 9, pp. 305, 308–11; Harrod, *Life and Times of John Maynard Keynes,* p. 444; Keynes, *Col-*

lected Writings, vol. 19, part 2, p. 648; Skidelsky, *John Maynard Keynes,* vol. 2, p. 223.

109. Like John Stuart Mill, Keynes "felt that there was too little organised sympathy for attempts to make the private property system *work better.*" Keynes, *Collected Writings,* vol. 21, p. 493.

110. Keynes, *Collected Writings,* vol. 9, p. 298–99.

111. Keynes, *Collected Writings,* vol. 7, p. 374.

112. Keynes, *Collected Writings,* vol. 7, pp. 33, 162; Keynes, *Collected Writings,* vol. 9, pp. 222–23. Cf. Keynes, *Collected Writings,* vol. 9, p. 286; Chernomas, "Keynes on Post-Scarcity Society," p. 1018.

113. See especially Keynes, *Collected Writings,* vol. 27, p. 384; Keynes, *Collected Writings,* vol. 28, pp. 35–36; Keynes, *Collected Writings,* vol. 9, pp. xviii, 123–24; Keynes, *Collected Writings,* vol. 13, pp. 470, 492.

CHAPTER 4. JOHN KENNETH GALBRAITH

1. Irving Kristol, "Professor Galbraith's 'New Industrial State'," *Fortune* 76 (July 1967): 90. It is quoted in Charles H. Hession, *John Kenneth Galbraith and His Critics* (New York: New American Library, 1972), p. 159. From a different political perspective, Michael Harrington considered *The New Industrial State* "one of the most significant works of social thought in a generation." Michael Harrington, "Liberalism According to Galbraith," *Commentary* 44 (October 1967): 77. Conservative writers are usually less enthusiastic. George Stigler considers it "shocking that more Americans have read *The Affluent Society* than *The Wealth of Nations.*" George Stigler, "The Intellectual and the Marketplace," in Adrian Klaasen, ed., *The Invisible Hand* (Chicago: Gateway Editions, 1965), p. 34.

2. *The Affluent Society* sold nearly 1.5 million copies. Peggy Lamson, *Speaking of Galbraith: A Personal Portrait* (New York: Ticknor & Fields, 1991), p. 137.

3. Author's interview with Galbraith, October 26, 1992. Cf. his self-identification with the "liberal Left" in J. K. Galbraith, "The Death of Liberalism," *Observer* (March 26, 1989), pp. 33–34. Compare this with Keynes' "liberal socialism."

4. John Kenneth Galbraith, "The State of Liberalism" [address at the annual Roosevelt Day dinner, January 31, 1959], pp. 5, 11, John Kenneth Galbraith Collection, Box 107, John F. Kennedy Presidential Library, Boston.

5. Loren J. Okroi, *Galbraith, Harrington, Heilbroner: Economics and Dissent in an Age of Optimism* (Princeton, N.J.: Princeton University Press, 1988), pp. 35, 111.

6. See especially, John Kenneth Galbraith, *American Capitalism: The Concept of Countervailing Power,* rev. ed. (Boston: Houghton Mifflin, 1956) p. x.

7. John Kenneth Galbraith, *The Affluent Society,* 2d ed. (New York: New American Library, 1969), p. 51.

8. John Kenneth Galbraith, "Wealth and Poverty," [address delivered to meeting of the National Policy Committee on Pockets of Poverty, December 13, 1963],

John Kenneth Galbraith Collection, Box 19; Galbraith, "The State of Liberalism," pp. 1, 3; Galbraith, *Affluent Society*, pp. 87–88, 98, 149–50; John Kenneth Galbraith, *Economics and the Public Purpose* (Harmondsworth, U.K.: Penguin Books, 1975), p. 247. Cf. Galbraith, *Affluent Society*, pp. 35–41, 150–51; Galbraith, *American Capitalism*, pp. 52–56. Galbraith says anti-trust policy supports the status quo and is too limited to address power.

9. John Kenneth Galbraith, *Economics, Peace and Laughter* (New York: Signet, 1971), p. xi; Galbraith, *Affluent Society*, pp. xvi–xvii; John Kenneth Galbraith, *Economics in Perspective: A Critical History* (Boston: Houghton Mifflin, 1987), p. 299; John Kenneth Galbraith, *The New Industrial State*, 4th ed. (Boston: Houghton Mifflin, 1985), pp. xii–xviii. Cf. Okroi, *Galbraith, Harrington, Heilbroner*, pp. 41–42, 77.

10. Galbraith, *Affluent Society*, p. 45; Galbraith, *New Industrial State*, pp. 334, 8; Galbraith, *American Capitalism*, p. ix; Galbraith, *Economics in Perspective*, pp. 298–99; John Kenneth Galbraith, "A New Treatise on Political Economy: Prospectus," "Introduction" [unpublished, early 1950s], pp. 2–3, John Kenneth Galbraith Collection, Box 96.

11. Galbraith, *Economics and the Public Purpose*, p. 43 n. 9; Galbraith, *Economics in Perspective*, p. 299; John Kenneth Galbraith, "Economic Perceptions and the Farm Policy" [1953], pp. 10–11, John Kenneth Galbraith Collection, Box 99.

12. John Kenneth Galbraith, *The Voice of the Poor: Essays in Economic and Political Persuasion* (Cambridge, Mass.: Harvard University Press, 1983), pp. 11–14; John Kenneth Galbraith, "The Relation Between Economic *and* Political Development" [draft statement submitted October 22, 1951], p. 4, John Kenneth Galbraith Collection, Box 46, National Planning Association File. See also John Kenneth Galbraith, "Economic Development: Engine of Democracy," *New York Times* (August 25, 1987), p. A21.

13. Galbraith, *Affluent Society*, p. 42; Galbraith, *American Capitalism*, p. 9; John Kenneth Galbraith, "The Way up from Reagan Economics," *Harvard Business Review* 60 (July–August 1982): 6–8, 12; John Kenneth Galbraith, *The Culture of Contentment* (Boston: Houghton Mifflin, 1992). See also John Kenneth Galbraith, "Economics as a System of Belief," in Galbraith, *Economics, Peace and Laughter*, pp. 44–55.

14. Galbraith, *Economics, Peace and Laughter*, pp. 59–60; John Kenneth Galbraith, "Ideology and Economic Reality," *Challenge* 32 (November–December 1989): 4–9; John Kenneth Galbraith, *A Life in Our Times: Memoirs* (New York: Ballantine Books, 1981), pp. 28–29, 49–50; Galbraith, *Culture of Contentment*, p. 22; Galbraith, *Economics in Perspective*, pp. 113, 284–86; John Kenneth Galbraith, "The Wealth of the Nation" [review of Samuel Bowles, David Gordon, and Thomas E. Weisskopf, *Beyond the Waste Land: A Democratic Alternative to Economic Decline*], *New York Review of Books* 30 (June 2, 1983): 3–6; Galbraith, *Economics and the Public Purpose*, p. 12. This is Galbraith's most complete book, summarizing and adding to his pre-

vious work.

15. Galbraith, *American Capitalism,* p. 24. Cf. "social nostalgia" in John Kenneth Galbraith, *The Liberal Hour* (New York: Mentor, 1960), pp. 105–16; Galbraith, *Culture of Contentment,* p. 82.

16. John Kenneth Galbraith, "Time and the New Industrial State," *American Economic Review: Papers and Proceedings* 78 (May 1988): 373.

17. Cf. John Kenneth Galbraith, *The Great Crash, 1929* (Harmondsworth, U.K.: Penguin Books, 1975); John Kenneth Galbraith, *Money: Whence It Came, Where It Went* (Boston: Houghton Mifflin, 1975); John Kenneth Galbraith, *A Journey Through Economic Time: A Firsthand View* (Boston: Houghton Mifflin, 1994); Galbraith, *Economics in Perspective.* For long discussions of economic history, see Galbraith, *Affluent Society,* and John Kenneth Galbraith, *The Age of Uncertainty* (Boston: Houghton Mifflin, 1977). Galbraith believes that historical analysis enables him to understand the origins and development of thinking and conventional wisdom, when arguments made sense in their setting before changing conditions rendered them obsolete.

18. Galbraith, *Culture of Contentment,* p. 1; Galbraith, *Economics and the Public Purpose,* p. 43 (cf. pp. 61, 195–96); Galbraith, *Affluent Society,* pp. 50, 122–23, 219–20. Cf. Galbraith, *New Industrial State,* p. 424; Galbraith, *Economics, Peace and Laughter,* p. 15; Galbraith, *Life in Our Times,* p. 125. This is the theme of Keynes' "Am I a Liberal"; see John Maynard Keynes, *The Collected Writings of John Maynard Keynes,* edited by Donald Moggridge, vol. 9, *Essays in Persuasion* (London: Macmillan, 1972), pp. 295–306.

19. Author's interview with Galbraith. Compare with John S. Gambs, *John Kenneth Galbraith* (Boston: Twayne, 1975), pp. 38, 113–14. Galbraith has come to accept "practical judgment" as a guide. John Kenneth Galbraith, *The Good Society: The Humane Agenda* (Boston: Houghton Mifflin, 1996), pp. 14–22.

20. Galbraith, *Economics and the Public Purpose,* p. 9; John Kenneth Galbraith, *The Anatomy of Power* (Boston: Houghton Mifflin, 1983), pp. 145, 140; Galbraith, *Voice of the Poor,* pp. 65–67.

21. Galbraith, *Economics, Peace and Laughter,* pp. 60, 69–75; Galbraith, *New Industrial State,* p. 226. Cf. Galbraith, *Economics and the Public Purpose,* pp. 150–53; Galbraith, *Anatomy of Power,* p. 147; John Kenneth Galbraith, *How to Control the Military* (New York: Signet, 1969), pp. 39–41.

22. Hession, *Galbraith and His Critics,* pp. 128, 149; Galbraith, *New Industrial State,* p. 226.

23. Galbraith, *Economics and the Public Purpose,* pp. 29–33, 150; Galbraith, *Economics, Peace and Laughter,* p. 68.

24. Galbraith, *Economics and the Public Purpose,* pp. 54–56, 60–66, 82, 93, 108–9, 146–49, 195–99; Galbraith, *Anatomy of Power,* pp. 138–39; Galbraith, *New Industrial State,* pp. 4–6, 13–20, 178, 218–19. Galbraith often mentions his World War

II experience in attempting to enforce price controls, when he claims that large corporations were relatively easy to regulate because they had substantial control over prices and markets, whereas small firms were much harder to control because of their own lack of influence over prices.

25. Galbraith, *Culture of Contentment*, p. 134. Galbraith, *New Industrial State*, pp. 74, 140–46, 155, 169–73 and passim; Galbraith, *Economics and the Public Purpose*, pp. 98–104. Cf. David H. Ciscel, "Galbraith's Planning System as a Substitute for Market Theory," *Journal of Economic Issues* 18 (1984): 411–18; Gambs, *John Kenneth Galbraith*, p. 68.

26. Galbraith, *Economics and the Public Purpose*, pp. 43, 59–62, 71–93, 146–49, 195–99, 239–40, 268, 270–82; Galbraith, *New Industrial State*, p. 62. Cf. John Kenneth Galbraith, "Interview: The Anatomy of Power," conducted by Richard D. Bartel, *Challenge* 26 (July–August 1983): 32.

27. Galbraith, *Voice of the Poor*, p. 42; Galbraith, "Time and the New Industrial State," p. 373; Galbraith, "Ideology and Economic Reality," pp. 8–9; author's interview with Galbraith.

28. Cf. Milton Friedman, *Capitalism and Freedom* (Chicago: University of Chicago Press, 1962), pp. 14–15; Friedrich A. Hayek, *The Road to Serfdom* (Chicago: University of Chicago Press, 1972), pp. 45–46, 104, 144–45; James M. Buchanan, *Liberty, Market and State: Political Economy in the 1980s* (New York: New York University Press, 1986), p. 272; Thomas Sowell, *A Conflict of Visions: Ideological Origins of Political Struggles* (New York: Quill, 1987), pp. 128, 141; Galbraith, *Anatomy of Power*, p. 140; Albert O. Hirschman, *The Passions and the Interests: Political Arguments for Capitalism Before Its Triumph* (Princeton, N.J.: Princeton University Press, 1977).

29. Okroi argues that Galbraith is on stronger ground in his discussion of corporate influence on government, bureaucracy, and culture than he is—given a fairly significant role for competition—in his discussion of manipulation of consumers. Okroi, *Galbraith, Harrington, Heilbroner*, pp. 83–88. For a summary of criticisms of the new industrial state, see Hession, *Galbraith and His Critics*, pp. 158–94.

30. John Kenneth Galbraith, "Countervailing Power" [paper read at the American Economic Association, December 28, 1953], John Kenneth Galbraith Collection, Box 104; Galbraith, *New Industrial State*, p. xviii; Galbraith, *American Capitalism*, p. 28; Galbraith, *Economics and the Public Purpose*, pp. 282–83. Cf. ibid., pp. 22–23; Galbraith, "Time and the New Industrial State."

31. Galbraith, *American Capitalism*, pp. 24, 27, 30; Galbraith, *Economics and the Public Purpose*, p. 24; Galbraith, *Anatomy of Power*, pp. 12, 119–20, 140–41; Galbraith, *Affluent Society*, pp. xi–xvi; John Kenneth Galbraith, *Annals of an Abiding Liberal* (Boston: Houghton Mifflin, 1979), p. 354.

32. *Anatomy of Power* is Galbraith's most complete analysis but he discusses power throughout his work. See Galbraith, *Economics and the Public Purpose*, pp. 19,

22, 108; Galbraith, *Annals of an Abiding Liberal,* p. 355; Galbraith, *Anatomy of Power,* pp. 19, 47, 160; Galbraith, *American Capitalism,* p. 61. Galbraith does not specify how one determines the goals a person "would normally pursue."

33. Galbraith, *Anatomy of Power,* pp. 4–5, 14–23.

34. Galbraith and Thurow criticize conventional economics for ignoring advertising as a means of manipulation, claiming that this neglects the impact of social environment on belief formation. Cf. Galbraith, *Affluent Society,* pp. 141–42, 198–99; Galbraith, *Economics and the Public Purpose,* p. 150; Lester C. Thurow, *Dangerous Currents: The State of Economics* (New York: Vintage Books, 1983), pp. 175, 219–20.

35. Galbraith, *Anatomy of Power,* pp. 5–6, 24–38, 139; Galbraith, "Interview: The Anatomy of Power," pp. 27, 30.

36. Galbraith, *Anatomy of Power,* pp. 5, 14–23, 47–53.

37. Charles Lindblom, "The Market as Prison," *Journal of Politics* 44 (1982): 324–36; Charles Lindblom, *Politics and Markets: The World's Political-Economic Systems* (New York: Basic Books, 1977). On p. 307 of *Politics and Markets,* Lindblom refers to the "Duality of Leadership."

38. This theme first appeared in *American Capitalism* and is developed in *The New Industrial State,* especially on pp. 167–86; in *Anatomy of Power;* and in *Economics and the Public Purpose,* especially on pp. 173–84 and 216–28. The quote is from *Economics and the Public Purpose,* p. 228. Galbraith identifies Lindblom as one of the people who influenced him. Galbraith, *Anatomy of Power,* p. xiv.

39. Galbraith, *Life in Our Times,* p. 528; Galbraith, *Economics and the Public Purpose,* pp. 226, 228; Galbraith, *Anatomy of Power,* p. 139; John Kenneth Galbraith, "A New Treatise on Political Economy, Introduction," p. 3, John Kenneth Galbraith Collection, Box 96; Galbraith, *New Industrial State,* pp. 330–31.

40. Galbraith, *New Industrial State,* pp. 20, 62, 179, 234, 242, 307–8; Galbraith, *Economics and the Public Purpose,* p. 217. Cf. ibid., pp. 152, 171, 322.

41. Galbraith, *Anatomy of Power,* pp. 128, 142–45. Galbraith discounts the possibility of a real conjunction of interests.

42. Galbraith, *Economics, Peace and Laughter,* p. 76. Despite the Marxist allusion there is no Marxist conclusion.

43. Galbraith, *American Capitalism,* pp. 16, 94; Galbraith, *Economics and the Public Purpose.*

44. Galbraith, *American Capitalism,* pp. 13, 17, 167; Galbraith, *Anatomy of Power,* pp. 136–37.

45. This distinction fits Galbraith better than does a more orthodox concept of market failure. Cf. "Market failure arises in a number of different ways—in [1] public goods, [2] externalities, and [3] monopolies." Dieter Helm, "The Economic Borders of the State," in Dieter Helm, ed., *The Economic Borders of the State* (Oxford: Oxford University Press, 1989), p. 38. Galbraith's second type of market failure is

206   LIBERAL ECONOMICS AND DEMOCRACY

closest to (but broader than) public goods. Cf. "merit goods" in Wilfred Beckerman, "How Large a Public Sector?" in Helm, ed., *The Economic Borders of the State,* pp. 82–85.

46. Galbraith, *Culture of Contentment,* pp. 164–65, 179. Cf. Galbraith, *New Industrial State;* Galbraith, "The Way up from Reagan Economics," pp. 6–8, 12.

47. Galbraith, *Economics and the Public Purpose,* p. 13.

48. This is the theme of *The Affluent Society* and runs throughout his work. Keynesian policy is mentioned in *The Affluent Society* on pp. xvi, xix, xxii. The point about women is found in *Economics and the Public Purpose,* pp. 45–53, 251–58. Galbraith agrees that security requires high production.

49. Cf. Jacob Viner, *The Role of Providence in the Social Order: An Essay in Intellectual History* (Princeton, N.J.: Princeton University Press, 1972), pp. 86–113; Conrad P. Waligorski, *The Political Theory of Conservative Economists* (Lawrence: University Press of Kansas, 1990), pp. 85–93.

50. Galbraith, *Economics in Perspective,* pp. 6–7; John Kenneth Galbraith, "Nothing Succeeds Like Excess," *New York Times* (August 28, 1989), p. A17; John Kenneth Galbraith, "The Uses and Excuses for Affluence," *New York Times Magazine* (May 31, 1981), pp. 38–44 and following; Galbraith, *Affluent Society,* pp. 46, 50, 86; Galbraith, *Culture of Contentment,* pp. 18–20, 41, 96–97; Galbraith, *Economics, Peace and Laughter,* p. 74.

51. Galbraith, *Culture of Contentment,* p. 97; Galbraith, *Affluent Society,* pp. 87–99, 150–51.

52. John Kenneth Galbraith, "The Pros and Cons of Capitalism," *World Marxist Review* 32 (November 1989): 57–59; Galbraith, *American Capitalism,* pp. 104–5, 156; Galbraith, *Culture of Contentment,* pp. 171–72, 179–80; Galbraith, *Affluent Society,* pp. 46–57, 68–74, 86, 88–89.

53. Galbraith, *Economics and the Public Purpose,* pp. 10, 146–48, 216–20, 284, 287–89; Galbraith, *The Liberal Hour,* pp. 19–21. Cf. *Economics and the Public Purpose,* pp. 239–40, 268–69; Galbraith, *Culture of Contentment,* p. 179.

54. This is a constant theme in *American Capitalism* and *Economics and the Public Purpose.* A succinct summary appears in the latter on pp. 239–40, 268–70.

55. Galbraith, *Economics and the Public Purpose,* pp. 255–56, 278–80.

56. Galbraith discusses social justice, community, common interest, and social balance, but he systematically develops and justifies only social balance. A claim for less private consumption and more shared public goods could be more deeply defended with an argument that we are a community, a nation, that we have ties to one another, something in common; or that public spending is necessary to promote private welfare.

57. Galbraith, *Economics and the Public Purpose,* pp. 252–56, 323–24, 216, 278; Galbraith, *American Capitalism,* pp. 104–5. Cf. Galbraith, "Ideology and Economic

Reality," p. 7; John Kenneth Galbraith, "The Democrats: Profile of the Popular Party," pp. 11–12, John Kenneth Galbraith Collection, Box 98. On interpersonal utility comparisons, cf. Galbraith, *Life in Our Times,* p. 336.

58. Galbraith, *Culture of Contentment,* pp. 162, 44; John Kenneth Galbraith and Seymour E. Harris, "The Failure of Monetary Policy" [January 15, 1958], John Kenneth Galbraith Collection, Box 27; John Kenneth Galbraith, campaign speech, John Kenneth Galbraith Collection, Box 75, 1960 Presidential Campaign File; John Kenneth Galbraith, "The Conflict in the Labour Party: An Outside View," John Kenneth Galbraith Collection, Box 98. Cf. John Kenneth Galbraith, "Recession Without End," *Los Angeles Times* (November 3, 1991), pp. M1, 6; Galbraith, "Interest Groups by Any Other Name"; Galbraith, *Economics and the Public Purpose,* p. 328.

59. I owe this phrase to Denny Pilant. *Economics and the Public Purpose* indicates that economics is *public,* with public ramifications and collective needs, not just a private concern.

60. John Kenneth Galbraith, "Individualism, Collectivism and Economists" [n.d. (c. 1952?)], pp. 10–11, 23, John Kenneth Galbraith Collection, Box 100; Galbraith, *Affluent Society,* p. 126. Doing nothing allows the powerful to choose for all.

61. John Kenneth Galbraith, "Economics of Agriculture (Unpublished) Draft, chapter 1," p. 22 [c. 1949–1950?], John Kenneth Galbraith Collection, Box 96. See John Kenneth Galbraith, "The Economics of Great Events" [speech at Gettysburg College, November 18, 1957], pp. 6–7, John Kenneth Galbraith Collection, Box 105, for a discussion of public interest in "essentially private [economic] decisions." See also John Kenneth Galbraith, "Meet the Press" transcript [November 12, 1961], John Kenneth Galbraith Collection, Box 43. The existence of and legitimacy of meeting public needs is a major theme in *Affluent Society.* Cf. Galbraith, *Life in Our Times,* pp. 527, 528; Galbraith, *Economics in Perspective,* pp. 40, 234; Galbraith, *American Capitalism,* pp. 170–71.

62. Hession, *Galbraith and His Critics,* p. 84.

63. Galbraith, *The Good Society;* Galbraith, *Affluent Society,* pp. 126, 203, 234, 238; John Kenneth Galbraith, Notes for "Lecture at Cambridge YMCA" [11/24/58], p. 1, John Kenneth Galbraith Collection, Box 105. Compare Thomas Balogh, *The Irrelevance of Conventional Economics* (New York: Liveright Pub. Corp., 1982), pp. 89–92. Cf. Hession, *Galbraith and His Critics,* p. 106, for criticisms of the social imbalance argument.

64. Galbraith, *Affluent Society,* pp. xviii–xix, 116–28, 132, 149–54, 204, 219–22, 226–31; Galbraith, "Pros and Cons of Capitalism," p. 58; Galbraith, *American Capitalism,* pp. 63–67; Galbraith, *Economics in Perspective,* pp. 289–91; Galbraith, *Economics, Peace and Laughter,* pp. 17–18, 23–25; Galbraith, *Economics and the Public Purpose,* pp. 173, 309; Gambs, *John Kenneth Galbraith,* pp. 42–53, 59–60; Robert Lekachman, "Introduction," in Hession, *Galbraith and His Critics,* p. xv; Okroi, *Gal-*

braith, Harrington, Heilbroner, pp. 50–51.

65. Quality of life includes an individual's being "an end in himself." Galbraith, *Economics, Peace and Laughter,* pp. 24, 175–76; John Kenneth Galbraith, "A Free Society Against Depression," "draft" [no date or publication information], p. 1, John Kenneth Galbraith Collection, Box 99; John Kenneth Galbraith, address delivered to meeting of the National Policy Committee on Pockets of Poverty, December 13, 1963, pp. 6–7, John Kenneth Galbraith Collection, Box 19; Galbraith, *American Capitalism,* p. 146.

66. Charles Taylor, "What's Wrong with Negative Liberty," in Alan Ryan, ed., *The Idea of Freedom: Essays in Honour of Isaiah Berlin* (Oxford: Oxford University Press, 1979), p. 177. Taylor argues that negative theories can incorporate "some notion of self-realisation."

67. Author's Interview with Galbraith; Galbraith, *The Good Society,* p. 4; John Kenneth Galbraith, "Friendly Advice to a Shrinking Military," *New York Times* (November 22, 1989), p. A25; Galbraith, "Uses and Excuses for Affluence," pp. 38–44; Galbraith, *American Capitalism,* pp. 33–35; Galbraith, *New Industrial State,* pp. 412–13, 277–78; Galbraith, *Economics and the Public Purpose,* p. 241 (cf. pp. 241–50).

68. Galbraith, *American Capitalism,* pp. 33–35; Galbraith, "The Pros and Cons of Capitalism," p. 58.

69. Galbraith, "Interview: The Anatomy of Power," p. 31; Galbraith, *Anatomy of Power,* pp. 51, 186. See also Galbraith, *New Industrial State,* pp. 379–80, about expanding employee choices. See also John Kenneth Galbraith, "The Question of the Budget" [speech for John F. Kennedy], p. 5, John Kenneth Galbraith Collection, Box 74, 1960 Presidential Campaign File; John Kenneth Galbraith, "Economic Policy and the Art of Adaptation," 1952 *Farm Policy Forum,* April 1952, pp. 12–15, John Kenneth Galbraith Collection, Box 99. Cf. Galbraith, *Economics and the Public Purpose,* p. 244; Galbraith, "Friendly Advice to a Shrinking Military"; Galbraith, *The Liberal Hour,* pp. 63–64.

70. Galbraith, *Economics and the Public Purpose,* p. 91; John Kenneth Galbraith, "Economic Freedom" [speech at Wellesley College, October 13, 1954], John Kenneth Galbraith Collection, Box 104; John Kenneth Galbraith, speech to Adhesive Manufacturers Association [May 6, 1963], pp. 4, 7, John Kenneth Galbraith Collection, Box 104; John Kenneth Galbraith, "Individualism, Collectivism and Economists" [no date (c. 1952?)], pp. 23–24, John Kenneth Galbraith Collection, Box 100; John Kenneth Galbraith, "Farm Policy: The Problem and the Choices" [address before the National Farm Institute, February 14, 1958], pp. 11–12, John Kenneth Galbraith Collection, Box 27.

71. Galbraith, "Individualism, Collectivism and Economists"; Galbraith, *Affluent Society,* pp. 254, 223. On p. 223 he argues that the individuality, dignity, and personality of employees may be as important as production. See also Galbraith, *New Indus-*

trial State, pp. 379–80, 383, 333; Galbraith, *Economics, Peace and Laughter,* pp. 24, 27.

72. Lamson, *Speaking of Galbraith,* p. 46; Galbraith, "Ideology and Economic Reality," pp. 8–9; Galbraith, *Economics and the Public Purpose,* p. 156; Galbraith, *American Capitalism,* p. 200; Galbraith, *The Great Crash,* p. 27.

73. Galbraith, *New Industrial State,* p. 392; Galbraith, *Economics and the Public Purpose,* pp. 260, 235–36; Galbraith, *Culture of Contentment,* pp. 175–76, 22, 176–77; John Kenneth Galbraith, "The Democratic Approach to the Farm Problem," p. 10, John Kenneth Galbraith Collection, Box 23; John Kenneth Galbraith, "Economic Perceptions and the Farm Policy," John Kenneth Galbraith Collection, Box 99; Galbraith, *Affluent Society.*

74. The quote is from John Kenneth Galbraith, "Youth in the Social Context: The Basic Impact of Urbanization," p. 3, John Kenneth Galbraith Collection, Box 103. Cf. Galbraith as quoted in Charles A. Radin, "Reaffirming a Commitment to Liberalism," *Boston Globe* (October 27, 1988), p. 2: "Liberalism, certainly not conservatism, brought the worst of this suffering [the Great Depression] under control and performed the highly conservative function of saving the system." He also discussed what remains to be done. Keynes' economics ended "Marxism in the advanced countries." Galbraith, *Economics, Peace and Laughter,* p. 44.

75. John Kenneth Galbraith, "The Goldwater Phenomenon" [Presidential campaign speech, 1964], p. 13, John Kenneth Galbraith Collection, Box 51; Galbraith, notes for "Lecture at Cambridge YMCA," p. 3; Galbraith, *New Industrial State,* pp. 268–69; Galbraith, *Culture of Contentment,* pp. 175–77.

76. Galbraith, *Affluent Society,* p. 235.

77. John Kenneth Galbraith, "Basic Factors in Farm Price Policy" [memorandum for the Secretary of Agriculture, n.d.], John Kenneth Galbraith Collection, Box 97; John Kenneth Galbraith, "The American Economy: Substance and Myth," John Kenneth Galbraith Collection, Box 97; Galbraith, *Money,* p. 300; John Kenneth Galbraith, "Farm Policy: Some Proposals for Improvement" [lecture given before the graduate school of the U.S. Department of Agriculture, December 1, 1954], p. 5, John Kenneth Galbraith Collection, Box 97.

78. *Agriculture:* Galbraith's beginning as an agricultural economist has colored his orientation. *Price control:* Cf. Galbraith, *Economics and the Public Purpose,* pp. 84–85, 321–35. For why he no longer sees them as viable, see Galbraith, *New Industrial State,* p. xxxiv. *Inflation:* Cf. Galbraith, *The Liberal Hour,* pp. 62–69; Galbraith, *Economics and the Public Purpose,* pp. 203–11; Galbraith, *Affluent Society,* pp. 166–77. *Planning:* Cf. Galbraith, *Economics and the Public Purpose,* p. 337; Galbraith, *New Industrial State,* pp. 22–23, 268, 365–74. *Poverty:* See Galbraith, *Affluent Society;* Galbraith, *The Voice of the Poor. The Military:* While ambassador to India, Galbraith was sent to Vietnam by President Kennedy to make a personal assessment for Kennedy. Cf. Galbraith, *How to Control the Military;* Galbraith, *Culture of Contentment,* p. 181. *Development:* Cf. Galbraith, *The Voice of the Poor.*

Education: See Galbraith, *Affluent Society. Power:* See Galbraith, *Economics and the Public Purpose,* pp. 239–40, 268–69. *Urban reform:* See Galbraith, *New Industrial State,* pp. 367–72. *Welfare:* See Galbraith, *Affluent Society,* pp. 244–52; Galbraith, *Culture of Contentment,* p. 180. *Demand:* Cf. Galbraith, *New Industrial State,* pp. 230–36; Galbraith, *Culture of Contentment,* pp. 164, 177–78; Galbraith, *Economics and the Public Purpose,* pp. 321–22; Okroi, *Galbraith, Harrington, Heilbroner,* p. 40. *Taxes:* Cf. Galbraith, *Economics and the Public Purpose,* pp. 287–88, 323–24; Galbraith, *Culture of Contentment,* p. 179. *Regulation:* See Galbraith, *Culture of Contentment,* p. 179. Some of these views are summarized in *Culture of Contentment,* pp. 177–81, a less optimistic discussion of reform than his earlier work.

79. Despite his criticism of socialism, Galbraith was more inclined toward a liberal socialist alternative in the early 1970s than before or since. Cf. Galbraith, "The Pros and Cons of Capitalism"; John Kenneth Galbraith, *The Nature of Mass Poverty* (Harmondsworth, U.K.: Penguin Books, 1979), pp. 92–95; Galbraith, *Economics and the Public Purpose,* pp. 237–38, 292–303, 240; Galbraith, *New Industrial State,* pp. 104, 106–10, 406–7 ("new socialism"); John Kenneth Galbraith, "The Economic Problems of the Left," *New Statesman* 91 (February 20, 1976): 217–18. Cf. *New Industrial State,* p. 110: "The misfortune of democratic socialism has been the misfortune of the capitalist. When the latter could no longer control, democratic socialism was no longer an alternative." In *The Good Society,* Galbraith argues that both socialism and traditional capitalism are dead. Galbraith, *The Good Society,* pp. 17–20.

80. The quote is from Galbraith, "Wealth and Poverty." See also John Kenneth Galbraith, "Memorandum for the President," "*Tax Reduction, Tax Reform and the Problems in This Path,*" John Kenneth Galbraith Collection, Box 76; John Kenneth Galbraith, letter to John F. Kennedy [August 20, 1962], John Kenneth Galbraith Collection, Box 76; John Kenneth Galbraith, "MEMORANDUM FOR SENATOR JOHNSON" [September 1957], John Kenneth Galbraith Collection, Box 36; Galbraith, *Economics, Peace and Laughter,* pp. 26–27; Galbraith, "Time and the New Industrial State," p. 375; Galbraith, *Affluent Society,* pp. xx, 88, 236–38; Galbraith, *New Industrial State,* pp. 238–39, 350; Galbraith, *Voice of the Poor,* p. 78; Galbraith, "The Uses and Excuses for Affluence," pp. 50, 52; John Kenneth Galbraith, "What Tact the Press Showed," *New York Times* (December 22, 1987), p. A23.

81. Galbraith, *How to Control the Military,* p. 84; Galbraith, *Economics and the Public Purpose,* pp. 13, 312, 236, 241, 231; Galbraith, *New Industrial State,* pp. 399, 329; Galbraith, *The Good Society,* p. 2. Galbraith discusses bureaucracy more than he does government structure. For one of his few discussions of structure, see Galbraith, *Anatomy of Power,* pp. 145–47.

82. Galbraith, *Anatomy of Power,* pp. 142–46.

83. Galbraith, *New Industrial State,* pp. 8, 355–56, 393–94, 414; Galbraith, *Economics and the Public Purpose,* pp. 228–29, 236, 259–69, 241–46. See pp. 268–69 for measures to help emancipate the state, including more equality and enhancing the

power of the market system. See pp. 247–48 for a strong statement that liberalism is the only means for emancipation. Cf. Galbraith, *Culture of Contentment,* pp. 155–57; Okroi, *Galbraith, Harrington, Heilbroner,* p. 242; Hession, *Galbraith and His Critics,* p. 214. By 1985, Galbraith was less confident of the reforming potential of the "educational and scientific estate." See Galbraith, *New Industrial State,* p. xxxiv. See pp. xxix–xxxiv for system changes he had not foreseen. Nevertheless, as for most reform liberals, for Galbraith, education remains central to a good life. Galbraith, *The Good Society,* pp. 68–74. The emancipation argument answers people who see tendencies in Galbraith toward technological determinism. Size and organization are the inevitable result of technology; the nature of control is not. Technological determinism does not necessarily apply to relations or modes of governance. Society can choose how large organizations are governed and what they will do.

84. Perhaps a combination of recession, depression, "long-run economic desuetude," dangers of autonomous military power or military disaster, and urban unrest might shock people into demanding basic reform. Galbraith, *Culture of Contentment,* pp. 155–57, 172–73. That they have is integral to the contemporary conservative reaction.

85. Galbraith's most sustained discussion of democracy is in *Age of Uncertainty,* pp. 296, 324–39. See also Galbraith, *Culture of Contentment,* pp. 146–47; Galbraith, *The Good Society,* pp. 70–72, 138–43; Galbraith, *Anatomy of Power,* p. 128.

86. Author's interview with Galbraith; Galbraith, *Age of Uncertainty,* p. 327; Galbraith, "Economic Development: Engine of Democracy," p. 21; Galbraith, *Culture of Contentment,* p. 8; Galbraith, *The Good Society,* p. 72.

87. Galbraith, *Culture of Contentment,* pp. 174, 155, 125–26, 132–33, 138; Galbraith, *New Industrial State,* p. xxxiii; Galbraith, *The Good Society,* pp. 8, 142; Galbraith, "The Wealth of the Nation," p. 4; John Kenneth Galbraith, "The Limits of American Capacity" [1952], p. 11, John Kenneth Galbraith Collection, Box 106.

88. Galbraith, *Affluent Society,* p. 72; James Srodes, "Curmudgeon in Winter," *Financial World* 158 (November 28, 1989), pp. 82–83; Galbraith, *Anatomy of Power,* pp. 147–48; Galbraith, *Life in Our Times,* p. 528; Galbraith, *Economics, Peace and Laughter,* p. 60; Galbraith, *Economics and the Public Purpose,* pp. 68–70, 160, 228; Okroi, *Galbraith, Harrington, Heilbroner,* p. 244.

89. Galbraith, *Economics and the Public Purpose,* p. 236; John Kenneth Galbraith, review of *National Economic Planning* by Paul Baran [November 1951], John Kenneth Galbraith Collection, Box 98; John Kenneth Galbraith, review of *New Fabian Essays* edited by R. H. S. Crossman, John Kenneth Galbraith Collection, Box 98. Given the typical lack of shareholder control, ownership of shares is desirable on other grounds but is not democracy.

90. Cf. Robert L. Heilbroner, *Between Capitalism and Socialism: Essays in Political Economics* (New York: Vintage Books, 1970), pp. 53, 234–35.

91. Galbraith, *Economics and the Public Purpose*, pp. 247–48.

CHAPTER 5. LESTER THUROW

1. John Kenneth Galbraith, *Economics in Perspective: A Critical History* (Boston: Houghton Mifflin, 1987), pp. 288–89.

2. Lester Thurow, "An American Common Market" [book review], *Washington Post Book World* 23 (October 31, 1993): 10.

3. Lester C. Thurow, *Head to Head: The Coming Economic Battle Among Japan, Europe, and America* (New York: William Morrow, 1992); Lester C. Thurow, "GATT Is Dead," *Journal of Accountancy* 170 (September 1990): 36–39; Lester C. Thurow, "Money Wars: Why Europe Will 'Own' the 21st Century," *Washington Post* (April 19, 1992), pp. C1–2. "History is far from over. A new competitive phase is even now under way." Thurow, *Head to Head*, p. 14. Thurow develops all of these arguments in Lester C. Thurow, *The Future of Capitalism: How Today's Economic Forces Shape Tomorrow's World* (New York: William Morrow, 1996).

4. Thurow, *Head to Head*, pp. 15–16; Lester C. Thurow, *The Zero-Sum Solution: Building a World-Class American Economy* (New York: Simon & Schuster, 1985), pp. 137, 60.

5. Lester C. Thurow, *Dangerous Currents: The State of Economics* (New York: Vintage Books, 1983), pp. xiv–xv; Thurow, *Zero-Sum Solution*, p. 86; Lester C. Thurow, "An International Keynesian Yank," *Challenge* 26 (March–April 1983): 38.

6. Thurow, *Dangerous Currents*, pp. 226–28; Lester C. Thurow, *The Zero-Sum Society: Distribution and the Possibilities for Economic Change* (New York: Basic Books, 1980), pp. 6–16.

7. Thurow, *Dangerous Currents*, pp. 226–27, 193; Lester C. Thurow, "Companies Merge; Families Break Up," *New York Times* (September 3, 1995), p. E11; Thurow, *Future of Capitalism*, pp. 31–35; Thurow, *Zero-Sum Solution*, pp. 86, 60–68, 112; Lester C. Thurow, "Putting Capitalists Back into Capitalism," in Samuel Bowles, Richard C. Edwards, and William G. Shepherd, eds., *Unconventional Wisdom: Essays on Economics in Honor of John Kenneth Galbraith* (Boston: Houghton Mifflin, 1989), p. 195; Lester C. Thurow, "A Surge in Inequality," in Eleanor Brown, ed., *Readings, Issues and Questions in Public Finance* (Homewood, Ill.: Irwin, 1988), p. 43. Lester Thurow, "Fixing It," *Playboy* 41 (January 1994): 192; Lester C. Thurow, "We're Not Facing Up to Our Nation's Problems," *Washington Post* (February 11, 1990), pp. C1–2; Thurow, *Zero-Sum Society*, pp. 15, 65.

8. Thurow, *Head to Head*, pp. 113–14. Cf. Thurow, *Zero-Sum Solution*, p. 122.

9. Thurow, *Dangerous Currents*, pp. xviii–xix (cf. pp. 18–19).

10. Thurow, *Dangerous Currents*, pp. 227, 109, 173, 21–23, 3, 54–55, 87, 185–90, 16, 157–58, 12–13, 232, 184; Lester C. Thurow, "Why Do Economists Disagree?" *Dissent* 29 (Spring 1982): 181–82. Cf. Thurow, *Dangerous Currents*, pp. x–xi, 106,

117–21. Thurow's reference to Newton mixes separate historical events.

11. Thurow, *Dangerous Currents*, pp. 8, 216. Lester C. Thurow, *Generating Inequality: Mechanisms of Distribution in the U.S. Economy* (New York: Basic Books, 1975), pp. ix–x, 21–25.

12. Thurow, *Dangerous Currents*, pp. 24–27, 139; Thurow, "Why Do Economists Disagree?" pp. 176–77.

13. Thurow, *Future of Capitalism*, pp. 306, 16, 284–88, 295–97, 304; Thurow, *Zero-Sum Solution*, pp. 308, 60, 34, 156; Thurow, *Dangerous Currents*, pp. 226, 177, 157; Thurow, "Putting Capitalists Back into Capitalism," p. 190; Thurow, *Head to Head*, p. 118.

14. Thurow, *Zero-Sum Society*, pp. 20, 26, 9–12, 218–19 n. 1.

15. Thurow, *Head to Head*, pp. 118–19; Thurow, *Dangerous Currents*, pp. 219–20, 223–25, 216, 136, 115, 175; Lester C. Thurow, "The American Economy in the Year 2000," *American Economic Review* 62 (1972), p. 440; *Zero-Sum Solution*, p. 345. While the dominant theory ignores the political implications of actual want formation, Thurow at least acknowledges them.

16. Thurow, *Head to Head*, pp. 17–18, 105, 238; Thurow, *Zero-Sum Society*, p. 81; Lester C. Thurow, "Welfare State Keeps Capitalism Working," *Los Angeles Times* (December 20, 1987), sec. iv, p. 3.

17. Thurow, *Zero-Sum Society*, pp. 195–96.

18. Thurow, *Head to Head*, pp. 15, 32–39; Thurow, *Zero-Sum Society*, p. 174; Thurow, *Dangerous Currents*, p. 15.

19. Thurow, *Zero-Sum Society*, pp. 11–12, 17, 155; Thurow, *Dangerous Currents*, pp. 24–27; Thurow, "Why Do Economists Disagree?" p. 177; Thurow, *Zero-Sum Solution*, p. 11.

20. Thurow, *Zero-Sum Solution*, pp. 382, 117–18; Thurow, *Zero-Sum Society*, pp. 196, 154, 194–95, 17; Thurow, *Generating Inequality*, pp. ix–x, 21–23; Thurow, *Dangerous Currents*, pp. 224–25. Lester Thurow, "Toward a Definition of Economic Justice," *Public Interest* 31 (1973): 58, discusses attempts "to specify economic equity." In *Head to Head*, p. 97, Thurow notes that "Basic attitudes about fairness will have to change" in the transition from communism to capitalism.

21. Thurow, *Generating Inequality*, pp. ix–x, 24; Thurow, *Zero-Sum Solution*, pp. 120–21, 117; Lester C. Thurow, "Equity versus Efficiency in Law Enforcement," in Ryan C. Amacher, Robert D. Tollison, and Thomas D. Willett, eds., *The Economic Approach to Public Policy: Selected Readings* (Ithaca, N.Y.: Cornell University Press, 1976), p. 125; Lester C. Thurow, "Equity, Efficiency, Social Justice, and Redistribution," *Nebraska Journal of Economics and Business* 20 (Spring 1981): 5–24. See Thurow, *Zero-Sum Society*, pp. 200–201, for his proposed equity goals, and Thurow, "Toward a Definition of Economic Justice," pp. 75–79, for his definitions of equity and the common good.

22. Thurow, *Generating Inequality*, p. 22; Lester C. Thurow, "Response to

Buchanan," *Journal of Economic Issues* 16 (1982): 863; Thurow, "Equity, Efficiency, Social Justice," p. 7; Thurow, *Zero-Sum Society*, p. 194.

23. Thurow, *Head to Head*, p. 17; Thurow, "Welfare State Keeps Capitalism Working," p. 3.

24. Thurow, "Surge in Inequality," pp. 36–39, 42–43; Thurow, "Companies Merge; Families Break Up"; Thurow, *Zero-Sum Society*, pp. 159–62, 157; Thurow, "American Common Market," p. 10; Thurow, "Putting Capitalists Back into Capitalism," p. 189. Cf. Thurow, *Zero-Sum Solution*, pp. 65, 110–11, 117; Thurow, *Generating Inequality*, pp. 14–15, 61; Lester C. Thurow, "The Post-Industrial Era Is Over," *New York Times* (September 4, 1989), p. A27; Thurow, *Head to Head*, pp. 53, 138, 163–64.

25. Thurow, *Zero-Sum Solution*, pp. 114, 61–64; Thurow, "Surge in Inequality," pp. 39–41; Thurow, "Fixing It," p. 192.

26. Thurow, *Generating Inequality*, pp. 227, viii, xii, 44–45, 59–61, 133, 149–51, 154, 207–9; Thurow, *Future of Capitalism*, pp. 171–80; Thurow, *Dangerous Currents*, p. 153; Thurow, *Zero-Sum Society*, p. 175.

27. Conrad P. Waligorski, *The Political Theory of Conservative Economists* (Lawrence: University Press of Kansas, 1990), pp. 85–96. Cf. Martin Bronfenbrenner, "Equality and Equity," *Annals of the American Academy of Political and Social Science* 409 (September 1973): 9–23; Thurow, *Zero-Sum Society*, pp. 16–17.

28. Thurow, *Generating Inequality*, pp. 26–27; Thurow, *Zero-Sum Solution*, p. 320; Lester C. Thurow, "Of Grasshoppers and Ants" [review of Charles Murray, *Losing Ground: American Social Policy, 1950–1980*], *Harvard Business Review* 63 (July–August 1985): 44.

29. Thurow, "Why Do Economists Disagree?" pp. 179–80; Thurow, *Generating Inequality*, pp. 48–49; Thurow, "Equity, Efficiency, Social Justice," pp. 5, 7, 10; Thurow, *Zero-Sum Society*, pp. 7–8; Thurow, "Illusion of Economic Necessity," p. 252, 250, 256; Thurow, *Zero-Sum Solution*, pp. 216–18.

30. Thurow, *Zero-Sum Solution*, p. 127; Lester C. Thurow, "Trickle Skips Labor," *Boston Globe* (January 13, 1987), p. 28; Thurow, "Why Do Economists Disagree?" p. 180; Thurow, "Equity, Efficiency, Social Justice," pp. 8–9.

31. Thurow, *Future of Capitalism*, pp. 130, 165–67, 242–45, 270; Thurow, *Generating Inequality*, pp, 201–2, 208; Lester C. Thurow, "The Political Economy of Income Redistribution Policies," *Annals of the American Academy of Political and Social Science* 409 (September 1973): 147; Thurow, "Equity, Efficiency, Social Justice," pp. 7, 10–13; Thurow, *Head to Head*, pp. 64–65; Thurow, *Zero-Sum Solution*, p. 113; Thurow, *Zero-Sum Society*, pp. 203–6.

32. Thurow, *Zero-Sum Society*, pp. 195, 179–80, 189; Thurow, *Generating Inequality*, p. 27; Thurow, "Political Economy of Income Redistribution Policies," p. 155.

33. Thurow, *Generating Inequality*, pp. xii, 204–5; Thurow, *Zero-Sum Society*,

pp. 180–82.

34. Thurow, *Dangerous Currents*, p. 206; Thurow, *Generating Inequality*, p. xiii; Thurow, *Zero-Sum Society*, pp. 188–90; Lester Thurow, "Society's Economic Failure," *Boston Globe* (May 12, 1992), p. 42; Thurow, "Equity, Efficiency, Social Justice," pp. 22–23.

35. Thurow, "Equity, Efficiency, Social Justice," pp. 7, 10, 22–24; Thurow, "Of Grasshoppers and Ants"; Thurow, *Dangerous Currents*, p. 139; Thurow, *Zero-Sum Solution*, pp. 114–15; Thurow, *Head to Head*, pp. 64–65.

36. Thurow, "Welfare State Keeps Capitalism Working." Thurow adds that "demand for mass skills" and "mass compulsory education" are also essential to capitalism's evolution. Thurow, *Zero-Sum Solution*, pp. 18–21, 115, 173; Thurow, "Surge in Inequality," pp. 43–45.

37. Thurow, *Zero-Sum Solution*, p. 86; Thurow, *Zero-Sum Society*, pp. 6, 15–18, 24 and passim; Thurow, *Future of Capitalism*, pp. 159, 242. Pursuit of self-interest in a structure of agreed upon goals, rules, and purposes, something akin to a feeling of equity and community, would reduce zero-sum conflict. The danger of this conflict is present in his later work even if the arena of conflict shifts slightly.

38. Thurow, *The Future of Capitalism*, pp. 17–18, 242–55; Thurow, *Generating Inequality*, pp. 47–48; Thurow, *Head to Head*, p. 17; Thurow, *Zero-Sum Solution*, pp. 112, 117–18, 325–27, 382; Thurow, "We're Not Facing Up to Our Nation's Problems."

39. Thurow, *Zero-Sum Society*, p. 8.

40. Thurow, "We're Not Facing Up to Our Nation's Problems," p. 2; Thurow, *Head to Head*, pp. 266–67; Lester C. Thurow, "An Establishment or an Oligarchy?" *National Tax Journal* 42 (1989): 405–11; Thurow, "Fixing It," p. 248; Thurow, *Zero-Sum Society*, p. 16; Adam Smith, "Don't Bet on Us" [review of *Head to Head*], *New York Times* (April 26, 1992), sec. 7, p. 3. This is not Schumpeter-like elitism; Thurow argues that government must respond to popular demands. Cf. Joseph A. Schumpeter, *Capitalism, Socialism and Democracy* (New York: Harper and Row, 1976). Given inequality and private-sector power, the market cannot be the sphere of real democracy.

41. Thurow, *Zero-Sum Society*, pp. 12, 55, 154–57.

42. Thurow, *Dangerous Currents*, pp. 220–22; Thurow, *Head to Head*, pp. 117–18, 120–21. Cf. Thurow, *Generating Inequality*, p. 142.

43. Thurow, *Dangerous Currents*, pp. 220–22; Thurow, *Generating Inequality*, p. 48; Thurow, "American Common Market," p. 10.

44. Thurow, *Zero-Sum Society*, pp. 128–30, 212–14.

45. Thurow, *Zero-Sum Solution*, pp. 267, 345; Thurow, *Dangerous Currents*, pp. 169–70; Thurow, "An American Common Market," p. 10; Thurow, *Head to Head*, p. 238; Thurow, "Fixing It," pp. 192, 247–48; Thurow, *Future of Capitalism*, pp. 271–77.

46. Thurow, *Zero-Sum Society*, pp. 7–8, 139; Thurow, *Zero-Sum Solution*, pp. 295–96; Thurow, *Head to Head*, p. 37; Thurow, *Future of Capitalism*, p. 286; Thurow, "Welfare State Keeps Capitalism Going," p. 3; Thurow, *Dangerous Currents*, p. 28; Thurow, "Of Grasshoppers and Ants."

47. Thurow, *Zero-Sum Society*, p. 8.

48. Thurow, *Dangerous Currents*, pp. xvi, 51, 61, 137; Lester C. Thurow, "The Fed Goes Ghostbusting," *New York Times* (May 6, 1994), p. A29; Thurow, *Zero-Sum Society*, pp. 7, 66–67, 140, 146; Thurow, *Zero-Sum Solution*, pp. 21–22, 35, 203, 222, 242–47; Thurow, "We're Not Facing Up to Our Nation's Problems," p. 2.

49. Thurow, *Future of Capitalism*, pp. 271, 290, 295, 305; Lester C. Thurow, "History is Far from Over," *Boston Globe* (March 6, 1990), p. 28; Thurow, *Head to Head*, p. 290; Thurow, *Zero-Sum Society*, pp. 203–6, 208–9, 211.

50. Thurow, *Zero-Sum Solution*, p. 101.

51. Thurow, *Zero-Sum Solution*, pp. 266–98; 60; Thurow, *Head to Head*, pp. 15–16, 55–58, 144, 283, 259–99; Thurow, "Surge in Inequality," pp. 43–44; Thurow, *Zero-Sum Society*, p. 191; Lester C. Thurow, "America Needs a Strategy," *Boston Globe* (November 3, 1992), p. 42. Karen W. Arenson, "Debate Grows over Adoption of National Industrial Policy," *New York Times* (June 19, 1983) sec. 1, pp. 1, 38; Lester C. Thurow, *The Case for Industrial Policies* (Washington, D.C.: Center for National Policy, January 1984); Thurow, *Head to Head*, pp. 35–36; Thurow, *Future of Capitalism*, pp. 16, 252, 281, 284.

52. Thurow, *Dangerous Currents*, p. 120.

53. Thurow, "Of Grasshoppers and Ants," p. 44; Thurow, "American Economy in the Year 2000," p. 443; Thurow, *Head to Head*, pp. 118–20; Thurow, *Zero-Sum Solution*, pp. 142–44, 179; Thurow, *Dangerous Currents*, pp. 120–21; Thurow, *Zero-Sum Society*, p. 168. Cf. Judith N. Shklar, *American Citizenship: The Quest for Inclusion* (Cambridge, Mass.: Harvard University Press, 1991), pp. 63, 99–100.

54. Thurow, *Zero-Sum Solution*, pp. 143–44.

55. Thurow, *Zero-Sum Society*, pp. 203–4.

56. Thurow, *Head to Head*, pp. 122–23; Thurow, *Zero-Sum Solution*, pp. 143–44, 170–78; Thurow, *Generating Inequality*, pp. 17–18, 81–82, 112, 194–95; Thurow, *Dangerous Currents*, pp. 17–18, 173, 200–204, 209–13, 226. Cf. John Kenneth Galbraith, *The Affluent Society*, 2d ed. (New York: New American Library, 1969), p. 96, on the relation between economic security and production.

57. Thurow, *Zero-Sum Solution*, p. 129.

58. Thurow, *Zero-Sum Solution*, pp. 178–79; Thurow, *Zero-Sum Society*, p. 8.

59. Thurow, *Head to Head*, p. 58; Thurow, *Future of Capitalism*, pp. 214–17 and passim.

60. "The problems of slow productivity growth were magnified by the emergence of a world economy." Thurow, *Zero-Sum Solution*, p. 20.

61. Thurow, "Fixing It," p. 192; Thurow, "International Keynesian Yank," p. 38; Thurow, *Head to Head*, pp. 64–65; Thurow, *Future of Capitalism*, pp. 127–31, 216–17; Thurow, *Zero-Sum Solution*, pp. 107, 335; Thurow, "American Common Market," pp. 1, 10.

62. Thurow, *Head to Head*, pp. 200–201, 17, 24, 31, 55–66, 209, 238–39; Thurow, "GATT Is Dead," p. 39; Thurow, *Future of Capitalism*, pp. 120–27. Thurow, *Case for Industrial Policy*, p. 14; Thurow, *Zero-Sum Solution*, pp. 89, 156; Joe Cobb, "Bookshelf: Doing Economic Battle" [review of *Head to Head*], *Wall Street Journal* (May 28, 1992), p. A18.

63. Thurow, *Zero-Sum Solution*, pp. 123, 24, 315, 345, 348, 60, 122, 158; Thurow, *Dangerous Currents*, pp. 222–25, 202–4; Thurow, *Head to Head*, p. 32; Thurow, *Future of Capitalism*, p. 257. Individual versus common interest is a recurring theme in *Head to Head* and *Future of Capitalism*. Cf. Robert B. Reich, "America Pays the Price," *New York Times* (January 29, 1989), sec. 6, p. 32: "asset-arranging. . . . invites zero sum games. . . . Without trust, people won't engage in common goals."

64. Lester C. Thurow, "Visionless Liberalism," *Boston Globe* (December 24, 1991), p. 34.

65. Richard Parker, "Throwing Down the Economic Gauntlet" [review of *Head to Head*], *Washington Post* (June 8, 1992), p. C2.

66. Thurow, "Putting Capitalists Back into Capi*talism*," p. 190.

67. Thurow, *Zero-Sum Solution*, p. 60; Thurow, "Companies Merge; Families Break Up"; Thurow, "America Needs a Strategy," p. 42; Thurow, "Surge in Inequality," p. 44; Thurow, "American Common Market," p. 10.

CHAPTER 6. ROBERT REICH

1. Robert B. Reich, *Tales of a New America: The Anxious Liberal's Guide to the Future* (New York: Vintage Books, 1987), pp. xi, 227, 28–39, 44–45, 237, 114–15; Robert B. Reich, *The Next American Frontier* (New York: Times Books, 1983), pp. 17–19; Robert B. Reich, *The Resurgent Liberal (And Other Unfashionable Prophecies)* (New York: Vintage Books, 1991), pp. 278–82, 251; Robert B. Reich, *The Work of Nations: Preparing Ourselves for 21st-Century Capitalism* (New York: Vintage Books, 1992), p. 269. Cf. Robert B. Reich, "Toward a New Public Philosophy," *Atlantic Monthly* 255 (May 1985): 68–79. Most liberals view minority claims too narrowly, as summoning charity or obligation rather than as invoking a mutual responsibility.

2. Robert B. Reich, *Public Management in a Democratic Society* (Englewood Cliffs, N.J.: Prentice-Hall, 1990), p. 1.

3. Laura Tyson as quoted in Frank Swoboda, "The Return of Robert Reich," *Washington Post National Weekly Edition* (May 15–21, 1995), p. 19; Randy Cun-

ningham as quoted in Adam Clymer, "Republicans Push Stopgap Spending as Recess Nears," *New York Times* (September 29, 1995), pp. A1, 12; Catherine S. Manegold, "Labor Secretary Urges Cuts in 'Corporate Welfare' Too," *New York Times* (November 23, 1994), p. A11; Eric Alterman, "The Reich Stuff," *Mother Jones* (July/August 1995): 50–51.

4. Reich, *Tales of a New America*, pp. 236–37, 241; Reich, *Resurgent Liberal*, pp. 240–41, 246, 287–89, xii, 96. Community, participation, and common interest could address the adverse result of laissez-faire individualism—Thurow's zero-sum society.

5. Cf. Robert B. Reich, ed., *The Power of Public Ideas* (Cambridge, Mass.: Harvard University Press, 1988).

6. Reich, *Tales of a New America*, pp. xi–xii, 5–6.

7. Reich, *Tales of a New America*, pp. 5–6; Robert B. Reich, "Trade: With Whom? For What? A Citizen's Guide to the Trade Debate," *Journal of Policy Analysis and Management* 9 (Summer 1990): 391; Reich, *Power of Public Ideas*, p. 3; Reich, *Next American Frontier*, p. 232; Reich, *Work of Nations*, pp. 43, 154, 186, 262; Robert B. Reich, "Making Industrial Policy," *Foreign Affairs* 60(4) (Spring 1982): 878; Robert B. Reich, *An Industrial Policy for America: Is It Needed?* (Washington, D.C.: U.S. Government Printing Office, Subcommittee on Economic Stabilization of the Committee on Banking, Finance and Urban Affairs, House of Representatives, April 1983), p. 39. Cf. Reich, "Trade," p. 394.

8. The tales are "The Mob at the Gates," "The Triumphant Individual," "The Benevolent Community," and "The Rot at the Top," in Reich, *Tales of a New America*.

9. Reich, *Tales of a New America*, pp. 18–20, 8, 253; Reich, *Next American Frontier*, pp. 8, 32–33, 231, 278–80.

10. Cf. Walter Lippmann, *The Public Philosophy* (New York: Mentor Books, 1955).

11. Reich, *Tales of a New America*, pp. xi–xii; Reich, *Resurgent Liberal*, pp. xii, 96, 273, 289; Reich, *Next American Frontier*, pp. 280–81.

12. Reich, *Tales of a New America*, pp. 201, 48–49; Reich, *Resurgent Liberal*, pp. 201, 221; *Next American Frontier*, pp. 270, 273; Reich, *Industrial Policy for America*, p. 38; Reich, *Work of Nations*, p. 187. Cf. Reich, "Making Industrial Policy," pp. 871–74. Note the implied criticism of pluralism in this argument.

13. Reich, *Next American Frontier*, p. 5; Reich, "Making Industrial Policy," p. 878; Reich, *Resurgent Liberal*, p. 288; Robert B. Reich and John D. Donahue, *New Deals: The Chrysler Revival and the American System* (New York: Times Books, 1985), pp. 280, 54. Cf. Reich, *Next American Frontier*, p. 233, 251.

14. Reich, *Tales of a New America*, pp. 201–2; Reich, *Next American Frontier*, pp. 75–76.

15. Reich, *Next American Frontier*, p. 3; Reich, *Work of Nations*, p. 9.

16. Reich, *Next American Frontier*.

17. Reich, *Next American Frontier*, pp. 33, 49, 87–88, 93–96, 100–105; 267–68; Reich, *Resurgent Liberal*, p. 207; Reich, *Industrial Policy for America*, p. 11; cf. Robert

B. Reich, *Education and the Next Economy* (Washington, D.C., National Education Association, 1988), pp. 11–13; Reich, *Work of Nations*, pp. 46–52.

18. Reich, *Next American Frontier*, p. 231; Reich, *Industrial Policy for America*, pp. 3, 31–34; Reich, *Work of Nations*, pp. 70–77, 81, 136; 161–63; Ira C. Magaziner and Robert B. Reich, *Minding America's Business: The Decline and Rise of the American Economy* (New York: Harcourt Brace Jovanovich, 1982), p. 107.

19. Reich, *Tales of a New America*, pp. 41–42; Reich, *Work of Nations*, pp. 7–8, 24–28, 173–74, 177–90, 208–19, 268, 3; Reich, *Industrial Policy for America*, p. 29. Cf. Robert B. Reich, "Domestic Agenda: From the Left," *Christian Science Monitor* (February 11, 1991), p. 18. Reich claims that we failed to address these concerns in the 1980s. Cf. Robert Reich, "The Squandered Decade," *Village Voice* 35 (January 2, 1990): 40; Robert B. Reich, contribution to "The American 80's: Disaster or Triumph?: A Symposium," *Commentary* 90 (September 1990): 16–17; Manegold, "Labor Secretary Urges Cuts," p. A11.

20. Reich, *Industrial Policy for America*, p. 39; Reich, *Tales of a New America*; Reich, *Resurgent Liberal*, p. 287.

21. Reich, *Tales of a New America*, pp. 28–29; Reich, *Industrial Policy for America*, pp. 2–3; Magaziner and Reich, *Minding America's Business*, pp. 42–44, 62–63; Reich, *Education and the Next Economy*, p. 10; Reich, *Resurgent Liberal*, p. 57.

22. Reich, *Power of Public Ideas*, pp. 1–2; Reich, *Tales of a New America*, p. 198.

23. Reich, *Resurgent Liberal*, pp. 57, xiii, 7–19, 184; Reich, *Industrial Policy for America*, pp. 13–21, 25; Robert B. Reich, "Put a Brake on High-Tech Alliances," *Los Angeles Times* (March 20, 1989), sec. II, p. 5; Reich, *Next American Frontier*, pp. 236–37, 280; Robert B. Reich, "America Pays the Price," *New York Times* (January 29, 1989), sec. 6, p. 32; Reich, *Tales of a New America*, p. 222. Conservatives ignore "conservative planning [that]. . . . is done far more quietly [than liberal planning] and . . . tends to be run by large corporations and Wall Street. . . . [It] has an uncanny way of making the rich richer and the poor poorer." Reich, *Resurgent Liberal*, p. 254.

24. Reich, *Power of Public Ideas*, p. 4 (cf. p. 138). Reich, *Resurgent Liberal*, pp. 261, 269.

25. Reich, *Tales of a New America*, pp. 223–27, 48–49; Reich, *Next American Frontier*, p. 186; Reich, *Resurgent Liberal*, p. 218.

26. Magaziner and Reich, *Minding America's Business*, p. 331; Reich, *Industrial Policy for America*, p. 29; Reich and Donahue, *New Deals*, pp. 296, 54–55, 289–90; Reich, *Next American Frontier*, pp. 3, 234–35, 12; Reich, *Resurgent Liberal*, p. 97; Robert B. Reich, "Clinton: Spur Growth," *New York Times* (July 16, 1992), p. A25.

27. Reich, *Tales of a New America*, pp. 250, 47; Reich, *Resurgent Liberal*, pp. xi–xii, 241; Reich, *Next American Frontier*, pp. 278–80; 166; Robert B. Reich, "Forum: On the Brink of an Anti-Business Era," *New York Times* (April 12, 1987), sec. 3, p. 3.

28. Reich, *Tales of a New America*, pp. 130–45, 242; Reich, *Resurgent Liberal*,

```

pp. 37–47, 192, 194; Reich,"Forum," p. 3; Magaziner and Reich, *Minding America's Business*, pp. 149–50; Reich, *Next American Frontier*, p. 200. Cf. Reich, *Tales of a New America*, p. 177. Conservatives ignore how the spontaneous market creates "order" and insist that people accept whatever results from the market.

29. Reich, *Work of Nations*, pp. 173, 197–219, 273–74; Reich, *Next American Frontier*, pp. 117–20, 167; Reich, *Resurgent Liberal*, pp. 22, 62–63, 73, 79, 235; Magaziner and Reich, *Minding America's Business*, p. 150. Cf. Robert B. Reich, "As the World Turns," *New Republic* 200 (May 1, 1989): 23–28. In *Tales of a New America*, p. 272 n. 4, Reich notes that ownership of stocks, bonds, and tax-free securities is concentrated in the top 2 percent of households. Typically, he leaves it to readers to draw their own conclusions. Like Galbraith, Reich is puzzled that public reaction to growing inequality has been so muted. *Work of Nations*, p. 282.

30. Reich, *Tales of a New America*, pp. 106–7; Reich, *Work of Nations*, pp. 225–30, 291–92.

31. Reich, "As the World Turns," p. 23; Reich, *Tales of a New America*, pp. 105–16, 47; Reich, *Resurgent Liberal*, pp. 236–38.

32. Reich, *Resurgent Liberal*, pp. 96, 240–45; Reich, *Next American Frontier*, pp. 20–21, 229, 271; Frank Swoboda, "Helping the 'Anxious Class'," *Washington Post National Weekly Edition* (October 3–9, 1994): 19. The standard of living discussion is echoed in Reich, *Work of Nations*. Cf. Reich, *Power of Public Ideas*, p. 3.

33. Reich, *Work of Nations*, pp. 245–47.

34. Reich, *Tales of a New America*, pp. 182–83, 185, 194–95, 279; Reich, "As the World Turns," p. 28; Reich, *Work of Nations*, pp. 247–51. Cf. Reich, *Work of Nations*, pp. 283–95; Reich, *Next American Frontier*, pp. 202–12.

35. Reich, *Power of Public Ideas*, p. 123.

36. Reich, *Tales of a New America*, pp. 10–11, 16, 155–63, 168.

37. Reich, *Tales of a New America*, pp. 20, 237.

38. Reich, *Tales of a New America*, pp. 114–15, 172, 165; Reich, *Work of Nations*, pp. 250, 282; Reich, *Education and the Next Economy*, p. 25.

39. Reich, *Tales of a New America*, pp. 145, 242, 33; Reich, *Resurgent Liberal*, p. 219; Michael J. Sandel, "The Political Theory of the Procedural Republic," in Robert B. Reich, *The Power of Public Ideas*, p. 115. Cf. Reich, *Resurgent Liberal*, pp. 219–20.

40. Reich, *Next American Frontier*, pp. 274–75.

41. Cf. *Work of Nations*, pp. 9, 304.

42. Cf. Robert B. Reich, "Everyone Gives, Everyone Benefits," *New York Times* (April 1, 1990), sec. 6, p. 44: "A sense of national purpose—of historic, cultural, and principled connection to a common political endeavor—must transcend cosmopolitan economic ties if it is to elicit investment in the nation's future."

43. Reich, *Tales of a New America*, pp. 169–71; Reich, *Work of Nations*, pp. 252–58, 268, 276–79; Robert B. Reich, "Secession of the Successful," *New York Times Magazine* (January 20, 1991), sec. 6, pp. 16–17, 42ff.
```

44. Reich, *Work of Nations*, pp. 309–10, 259, 301; Reich, *Resurgent Liberal*, pp. 241, 80–83; Reich, *Tales of a New America*, pp. 105, 124–25, 150, 238, 252; Reich, *Industrial Policy for America*, p. 35; Reich and Donahue, *New Deals*, pp. 289, 296–97; Reich, *Next American Frontier*, p. 170.

45. Reich, *Tales of a New America*, pp. 37, 195–96; Reich, *Work of Nations*, p. 321; Reich, *Next American Frontier*, pp. 267–68, 200; Reich, *Resurgent Liberal*, pp. 81–83, 220, 242–46. Cf. Reich, "America Pays the Price," p. 40.

46. Reich, "Making Industrial Policy," p. 874; Reich, *Tales of a New America*, pp. 36–39; Reich, *Next American Frontier*, p. 3; Reich, *Resurgent Liberal*, pp. 280–81. Interest groups are, however, necessary to democracy. Reich, *Resurgent Liberal*, p. 218.

47. Reich, *Public Management in a Democratic Society*, pp. 2–4, 6; Reich, *Next American Frontier*, pp. 256, 268, 273.

48. Reich, *Next American Frontier*, pp. 75, 273; Reich, *Public Management in a Democratic Society*, pp. 5–6; Reich, *Work of Nations*, pp. 283–95; Reich, *Power of Public Ideas*, pp. 9–10; Reich, *Industrial Policy for America*, p. 29. Robert B. Reich, "Unacknowledged Legislators" [book review], *New Republic* 204 (January 21, 1991): 38–41; Robert B. Reich, "Policy Making in a Democracy," in Reich, *Power of Public Ideas*, pp. 123–38; Magaziner and Reich, *Minding America's Business*, p. 201. Cf. Reich and Donahue, *New Deals*, p. 268.

49. Reich, *Power of Public Ideas*, pp. 3, 10, 137–38, 143–44; Reich, *Tales of a New America*, p. 191; Reich, *Resurgent Liberal*, p. 262; Reich and Donahue, *New Deals*, p. 297; Reich, "Making Industrial Policy," p. 878; Reich, *Next American Frontier*, pp. 199–200.

50. Reich, *Resurgent Liberal*, pp. 217–21, 240–41; Reich, *Public Management in a Democratic Society*, pp. 7–8; Reich, "Policy Making in a Democracy," pp. 138–46.

51. Cf. Kenneth J. Arrow, *Social Choice and Individual Values* (New York: John Wiley & Sons, 1963).

52. For judgment, see Reich, *Public Management in a Democratic Society*, pp. 6–8; Reich, *Power of Public Ideas*, pp. 123, 144; Reich, *Resurgent Liberal*, pp. 220, 261–63.

53. Reich, *Power of Public Ideas*, pp. 3–4; Reich, *Resurgent Liberal*, pp. 261–63; Reich, "Policy Making in a Democracy," pp. 138, 144–46; Reich, *Public Management in a Democratic Society*, pp. 6–9; 123.

54. Reich, *Resurgent Liberal*, pp. 218–20.

55. Benjamin Barber, *Strong Democracy: Participatory Politics for a New Age* (Berkeley: University of California Press, 1984); Reich, *Power of Public Ideas*, pp. 229–30.

56. Reich, *Public Management in a Democratic Society*, pp. 8–9, 49, 63, 139–40, 173–75.

57. Reich, *Public Management in a Democratic Society*, pp. 161–75, 49, 63; Reich, *Power of Public Ideas*, p. 123.

222   LIBERAL ECONOMICS AND DEMOCRACY

58. Reich, *Resurgent Liberal*, p. 219; Reich, *Public Management in a Democratic Society*, p. 6.

59. Reich, *Power of Public Ideas*, pp. 229, 6, 9–10; Reich, *Resurgent Liberal*, p. 267.

60. Reich, *Industrial Policy for America*, pp. 32, 38; Reich, *Next American Frontier*, pp. 251, 248, 258–59; Reich, *Resurgent Liberal*, pp. 22, 74–75, 81–82, 221, 289; Reich, *Tales of a New America*, pp. 246–48.

61. Reich, *Work of Nations*, p. 304.

62. This also illustrates his acceptance of the market.

63. Conflict between the civic and the business culture does not address this issue. Cf. *Next American Frontier*, pp. 3–11.

64. Reich, *Public Management in a Democratic Society*, pp. 30, 173.

65. Theda Skocpol claims that Reich fails to propose sufficient political reforms. Skocpol, "The Legacies of New Deal Liberalism," in Douglas MacLean and Claudia Mills, eds., *Liberalism Reconsidered* (Totowa, N.J.: Rowman & Allanheld, 1983), p. 99. Reich discusses party reform in Robert B. Reich, "Yes: Blame Election Funds," *New York Times* (October 12, 1989), p. A29.

66. Community and public philosophy support his assertion that liberals must stand for something, and call into question claims that liberalism's first principle is neutrality between ultimate values. Reich accepts a milder notion of neutrality—fair or even-handed treatment—but one must have some basis for determining what is "fair."

67. Reich, *Public Management in a Democratic Society*, pp. 74, 6–7; Reich, *Tales of a New America*, pp. 228–30; Reich, "Unacknowledged Legislators," p. 40; Magaziner and Reich, *Minding America's Business*, p. 201. Cf. Reich, *Resurgent Liberal*, p. 218.

68. Reich, *Resurgent Liberal*, p. 218; Reich, *Next American Frontier*, pp. 272–73, 275, 269; Reich, "Policy Making in a Democracy," p. 138. Cf. Reich and Donahue, *New Deals*, pp. 54–55.

69. Reich, *Next American Frontier*, pp. 272–73; Reich and Donahue, *New Deals*, p. 297; Reich, "Policy Making in a Democracy," pp. 137–47.

70. Reich, *Next American Frontier*, pp. 5–6, 187–89, 232; Reich, *Tales of a New America*, pp. 223; Reich, *Work of Nations*, p. 186; Magaziner and Reich, *Minding America's Business*, pp. 331–42.

71. Reich, *Next American Frontier*, pp. 5–6, 87–89, 96–100; Reich, *Tales of a New America*, pp. 206–9; Magaziner and Reich, *Minding America's Business*, pp. 197–203, 224–32; Reich and Donahue, *New Deals*, pp. 71, 101; Reich, *Work of Nations*, pp. 39–41.

72. Reich, *Work of Nations*, pp. 41, 58–68, 159, 320; Reich, "Everyone Gives, Everyone Benefits," pp. 42, 45; Reich, *Tales of a New America*, pp. 231, 68–77; Reich, *Next American Frontier*, p. 189; Robert B. Reich, "Boost Productivity by Investing in People's Minds and Skills," *Los Angeles Times* (July 13, 1992), p. B5; Robert B.

Reich, "Behold! We Have an Industrial Policy," *New York Times* (May 22, 1988), sec. 4, p. 29; Reich, "Making Industrial Policy," p. 857; Reich, *Resurgent Liberal,* pp. 55–56; Reich and Donahue, *New Deals,* p. 293; Magaziner and Reich, *Minding America's Business,* pp. 201, 210, 255.

73. Magaziner and Reich, *Minding America's Business,* pp. 324, 370, 5, 241, 208; Reich and Donahue, *New Deals,* pp. 268, 282–88; Reich, "Making Industrial Policy," p. 860.

74. Reich, *Next American Frontier,* pp. 109, 177–81, 277–78, 234; Reich, *Industrial Policy for America,* p. 38; Reich, "The American 80's," p. 16; Reich, *Tales of a New America,* p. 251; Karen W. Arenson, "Debate Grows over Adoption of National Industrial Policy," *New York Times* (June 19, 1983), sec. 1, pp. 1, 38.

75. Magaziner and Reich, *Minding America's Business,* pp. 7, 332–35, 341; Reich, *Resurgent Liberal,* pp. 220–21; Reich, *Next American Frontier,* pp. 12, 20–21, 133.

76. Reich, *Work of Nations,* pp. 3, 34, 77, 154, 177–80, 303, 9. Cf. Reich, *Resurgent Liberal,* pp. 174–75; Reich, *Tales of a New America,* pp. 78–82; Robert B. Reich, "The Myth of 'Made in the U.S.A.'," *Wall Street Journal* (July 5, 1991), p. A6; John Dillin, "U.S. Could Lose Middle Class," *Christian Science Monitor* (June 18, 1991), p. 6. This argument contrasts with Keynes' determination to maintain national economic independence to ensure domestic social experimentation.

77. Cf. Richard B. McKenzie, "The First and Second Reich: The Taming of an Industrial Policy Advocate," *Cato Journal* 11(1) (Spring–Summer 1991): 47–64; Louis Uchitelle, "An Old Liberal, a New Sermon," *New York Times* (April 12, 1990), pp. D1, 5; John S. McClenahen, "Do We Need a National Industrial Policy?" *Industry Week* 240 (March 18, 1991): 56–62.

78. "Reich acknowledges a partial change of heart. 'My early musings about industrial policy in the 1970s . . . seem to me to be problematic.'" E. J. Dionne, Jr., "Changing the Gurus?" *Washington Post* (April 14, 1991), pp. H1, 6.

79. Reich, *Work of Nations,* pp. 5–6, 8, 264–65, 312–14, 153, 301–15; "Everyone Gives, Everyone Benefits," pp. 42–45.

80. Reich, *Work of Nations,* p. 168.

81. Reich, *Next American Frontier,* pp. 13, 201; Reich, *Work of Nations,* pp. 245–50, 255, 262–65; Dillin, "U.S. Could Lose Middle Class," p. 6; Robert B. Reich, "Who Champions the Working Class?" *New York Times* (May 26, 1991), sec. 4, p. 11; Reich, *Tales of a New America,* pp. 194–95; Reich, "America Pays the Price," p. 40.

82. Reich, *Next American Frontier,* p. 172; Reich, "Trade: With Whom?" p. 397–99; Magaziner and Reich, *Minding America's Business,* p. 3; Reich, "Everyone Gives, Everyone Benefits," p. 45; Reich, *Tales of a New America,* p. 67–68.

83. Reich, *Next American Frontier,* p. 233; Reich, *Work of Nations,* pp. 262–65; Reich, *Resurgent Liberal,* pp. 58–59; Dillin, "U.S. Could Lose Middle Class," p. 6; Reich, "Clinton: Spur Growth," p. 25.

84. Magaziner and Reich, *Minding America's Business,* p. 324.

85. Reich, *Next American Frontier,* p. 271.

86. Thomas L. Friedman, "World's Big Economies Turn to the Jobs Issue," *New York Times* (March 14, 1994), pp. C1, 4; Reich, *Next American Frontier,* pp. 255, 232; Reich, *Education and the Next Economy,* p. 7; Reich, *Resurgent Liberal,* p. 218; Reich, *Work of Nations,* p. 3; Reich, "The American 80's," pp. 16–17. The subtitle of *Work of Nations* is *Preparing Ourselves for 21st-Century Capitalism,* when capitalism will be different.

87. Randall Rothenberg, *The Neo-Liberals: Creating the New American Politics* (New York: Simon & Schuster, 1984); Herbert Mitgang, "Why Liberals and Their Beliefs Will Rise Again," *New York Times* (January 17, 1990), p. C19.

88. Mitgang, "Why Liberal and Their Beliefs Will Rise Again," p. 19. Peter Passell, "Clinton Economists Cast a Wide Net," *New York Times* (October 11, 1992), sec. 4, p. 3, calls many of Reich's policies "un-liberal." Reich believes his policy is in the spirit of New Deal liberalism.

89. Barber, *Strong Democracy.*

90. Cf. W. W. Rostow, "Where We've Been, Where We're Going" [review of *The Work of Nations*], *Wall Street Journal* (March 20, 1991), p. A20; Gavin Wright, "Beyond Economic Nationalism" [review of *The Work of Nations*], *Washington Post* (March 3, 1991), sec. WBK, p. 1; McKenzie, "First and Second Reich," pp. 63–64, celebrates "Transnational economic forces . . . imposing tight controls" on politics.

91. Reich, *Work of Nations,* pp. 317–23.

CHAPTER 7. ISSUES

1. H. J. Laski, *The Decline of Liberalism* (Oxford: Oxford University Press, 1940). See also Chapter 1 on contemporary usage of "liberal."

2. Dewey was a philosopher-activist, and Hobhouse can be understood in similar terms.

3. M. Francis, "A Case of Mistaken Paternity: The Relationship Between Nineteenth-Century Liberals and Twentieth-Century Liberal Democrats," *Australian Journal of Politics and History* 31 (1985): 282–99; D. A. Lloyd Thomas, "The Justification of Liberalism," *Canadian Journal of Philosophy* 2 (1972): 199–217.

4. Amy Gutmann, "How Liberal Is Democracy," in Douglas MacLean and Claudia Mills, eds., *Liberalism Reconsidered* (Totowa, N.J.: Rowman & Allanheld, 1983), p. 45: "The distinct language of democratic theory and liberal egalitarianism masks a good deal of commonality in the requirements of their ideal constitutions." See also Patrick M. Garry, *Liberalism and American Identity* (Kent, Ohio: Kent State University Press, 1992), pp. 35, 77–78; Michael Davis, "Liberalism and/or Democracy?" *Social Theory and Practice* 9 (Spring 1983): 51–72; Robert Eccleshall, "When Is a 'Liberal' Not a Liberal?" *Contemporary Review* 232 (April 1978): 187–93.

5. One might add civic republicanism, but it is outside the scope of this book.

6. Both concur that liberalism promotes elitism and bureaucracy.

7. See Conrad P. Waligorski, *The Political Theory of Conservative Economists* (Lawrence: University Press of Kansas, 1990), pp. 101–25. This argument is often called libertarian, but its criticism of equality, doubts about human reason, mistrust of popular rule, and search for objective order—albeit in market relations—resemble traditional conservatism. Ibid., pp. 5–9.

8. The quotes are from Dwight R. Lee, "Supply-Side Economics and the Political Order," *Modern Age* 28 (1984): 134–35; F. A. Hayek, "The Miscarriage of the Democratic Ideal," *Encounter* 50 (1978): 16; Milton Friedman, *Capitalism and Freedom* (Chicago: University of Chicago Press, 1962), p. 9; George Gilder, *Wealth and Poverty* (New York: Basic Books, 1981), p. 91; Friedrich A. Hayek, *The Road to Serfdom* (Chicago: University of Chicago Press, 1972), p. 69; James M. Buchanan, *Liberty, Market and State: Political Economy in the 1980s* (New York: New York University Press, 1986), p. 253; Friedrich A. Hayek, *Law, Legislation and Liberty: A New Statement of the Liberal Principles of Justice and Political Economy*, vol. 3, *The Political Order of a Free People* (Chicago: University of Chicago Press, 1979), p. 150. Occasional elections suffice to satisfy the terms of political democracy.

9. Cf. Michael Harrington, *Toward a Democratic Left: A Radical Program for a New Majority* (New York: Macmillan, 1968), pp. 17–18: "'Left' here . . . describe[s] a program" which appeals to "socialists and radicals" and "to the more traditional American aspirations for reform as well." It includes "extending democracy into significant areas of economic and social life" and "the possibilities of a rich society producing for popular need under popular control."

10. Don Lavoie, "Democracy, Markets, and the Legal Order: Notes on the Nature of Politics in a Radically Liberal Society," in Ellen Frankel Paul, Fred D. Miller, Jr., Jeffrey Paul, eds., *Liberalism and the Economic Order* (Cambridge: Cambridge University Press, 1993), p. 117.

11. Michael Harrington, "Liberalism According to Galbraith," *Commentary* 44(4) (October 1967): 80; Loren J. Okroi, *Galbraith, Harrington, Heilbroner: Economics and Dissent in an Age of Optimism* (Princeton, N.J.: Princeton University Press, 1988), pp. 139, 145–46, 152.

12. Benjamin Barber, *Strong Democracy: Participatory Politics for a New Age* (Berkeley: University of California Press, 1984), pp. 69, 101, 62, 253. Cf. Benjamin Barber, *The Conquest of Politics: Liberal Philosophy in Democratic Times* (Princeton, N.J.: Princeton University Press, 1988).

13. Cf. C. B. Macpherson, *Democratic Theory: Essays in Retrieval* (Oxford: Clarendon Press, 1973); C. B. Macpherson, "The Economic Penetration of Political Theory: Some Hypotheses," *Journal of the History of Ideas* 39 (1978): 101–18; C. B. Macpherson, *The Rise and Fall of Economic Justice, and Other Papers* (Oxford: Oxford University Press, 1985). The quotes are from C. B. Macpherson, *The Life*

and Times of Liberal Democracy (Oxford: Oxford University Press, 1977), pp. 92, 94, 100.

14. I am not discussing capitalism and democracy. Liberalism is related to but not coextensive with capitalism, of which there are many possible versions. Reform liberals, however, want "to make democracy and capitalism compatible." Garry, *Liberalism and American Identity*, p. 100.

15. Only Keynes did not address the division of authority between corporate and government officials, or address property as a source of power. Cf. Charles Lindblom, *Politics and Markets: The World's Political-Economic Systems* (New York: Basic Books, 1977); Charles Lindblom, "The Market as Prison," *Journal of Politics* 44 (1982): 324–36; Charles E. Lindblom, *Democracy and the Market System* (Oslo: Norwegian University Press, 1988).

16. Robert A. Dahl, *Democracy, Liberty and Equality* (Oslo: Norwegian University Press, 1986), p. 148; Robert A. Dahl, *After the Revolution? Authority in a Good Society* (New Haven, Conn.: Yale University Press, 1970), pp. 104–30; Robert A. Dahl, *A Preface to Economic Democracy* (Berkeley: University of California Press, 1985). Dahl argues that economic reform and equalization promote democratization.

17. Eccleshall, "When Is a 'Liberal' Not a Liberal?" pp. 188–89.

18. In addition to Thurow, cf. Brandeis, Keynes, Galbraith, and Reich.

19. Lester Thurow, "Toward a Definition of Economic Justice," *Public Interest* 31 (1973): 75; Philippa Strum, *Brandeis: Beyond Progressivism* (Lawrence: University Press of Kansas, 1993), pp. 22, 47–48, 96; John Dewey, *Freedom and Culture* (Buffalo, N.Y.: Prometheus Books, 1989), p. 53.

20. Robert B. Reich, *The Next American Frontier* (New York: Times Books, 1983), pp. 75–76; John Kenneth Galbraith, *Economics and the Public Purpose* (Harmondsworth, U.K.: Penguin Books, 1975), pp. 9, 173–79.

21. Compare Garry, *Liberalism and American Identity*, p. 134; Wilfred Beckerman, "How Large a Public Sector?" in Dieter Helm, ed., *The Economic Borders of the State* (Oxford: Oxford University Press, 1989), pp. 67–68.

22. Herbert J. Gans, *Middle American Individualism: The Future of Liberal Democracy* (New York: Oxford University Press, 1991), p. 123, argues that middle American individualism and "habits of political avoidance" frustrate hope for participatory democracy.

23. See the Macpherson titles cited in note 13. See also William M. Sullivan, *Reconstructing Public Philosophy* (Berkeley: University of California Press, 1986), p. 178; Barber, *Strong Democracy*, pp. 106–7, 215–17, 252. Because of their books' clear writing, wide availability, and broad acceptance in the academic community, Barber and Sullivan are important. They believe that political participation will address economic problems. Charles Anderson, *Pragmatic Liberalism* (Chicago: University of Chicago Press, 1990), p. 104, argues "Full employment is, in effect, a proxy for the liberal commitment to equality and social justice." Cf. Anderson, *Pragmatic*

Liberalism, p. 105.

24. John Maynard Keynes, *The Collected Writings of John Maynard Keynes,* edited by Donald Moggridge, vol. 9, *Essays in Persuasion* (London: Macmillan, 1972), p. 211.

25. Reform liberals accept Keynes' argument that functioning markets can protect diversity, individualism, efficiency, self-interest, freedom, choice, and "the variety of life." John Maynard Keynes, *The Collected Writings of John Maynard Keynes,* edited by Donald Moggridge, vol. 7, *The General Theory of Employment Interest and Money* (London: Macmillan, 1973), p. 380. For them, markets satisfy many legitimate wants and coordinate behavior, although not as extensively as in laissez-faire theory.

26. Although specifically addressed to workfare, Reich's argument also applies to welfare: the program's purpose is to "increase people's capacity to take active responsibility for their fate." Robert B. Reich, *Tales of a New America: The Anxious Liberal's Guide to the Future* (New York: Vintage Books, 1987), p. 183. Cf. Lester C. Thurow, "Welfare State Keeps Capitalism Working," *Los Angeles Times* (December 20, 1987), sec. 4, p. 3.

27. John Kenneth Galbraith, *Economics in Perspective: A Critical History* (Boston: Houghton Mifflin, 1987), p. 298: "economics does not usefully exist apart from politics, and so it will not in the future." Separation masks power. Ibid., p. 299.

28. John Kenneth Galbraith, *The Affluent Society,* 2d ed. (New York: New American Library, 1969), p. xxii: "The thrust of this book is that increased production is not the final test of social achievement, the solvent of all social ills. Thus it challenges the very foundation of Keynesian policy with its nearly total emphasis on the expansion of economic output and income."

29. Cf. Strum, *Brandeis,* p. 138; John Dewey, *Liberalism and Social Action* (New York: Capricorn Books, 1963), pp. 7-8, 48; Michael Kammen, *Spheres of Liberty: Changing Perceptions of Liberty in American Culture* (Madison: University of Wisconsin Press, 1986), pp. 5, 8, 17, 129, 131-32, 148-50; David Spitz, *The Real World of Liberalism* (Chicago: University of Chicago Press, 1982), pp. 92-93; Anthony Downs, "The Evolution of Democracy: How Its Axioms and Institutional Forms Have Been Adapted to Changing Social Forces," *Daedalus* 116 (Summer 1987): 124. Michael Freeden, *Rights* (Minneapolis: University of Minnesota Press, 1991), p. 41, argues "Many rights are . . . still being discovered or invented." Mill's "tyranny of the majority" recognizes that obstacles other than force or government exist and that society may be oppressive. John Stuart Mill, *The Philosophy of John Stuart Mill: Ethical, Political and Religious* (New York: Modern Library, 1961), pp. 97, 191-92, 221, 255, 265.

30. The necessary conditions for freedom and freedom itself are not the same, but "If we want individuals to be free we must see to it that suitable conditions exist." Dewey, *Freedom and Culture,* p. 33.

31. Contentious policy debates over issues such as health care, welfare changes,

affirmative action, abortion, and tax policy are partly debates over the role of government in guaranteeing freedom and over the fundamental meaning of freedom.

32. Dieter Helm, "The Economic Borders of the State," in Helm, *Economic Borders of the State*, pp. 40–41; H. J. McCloskey, "The Problem of Liberalism," *Review of Metaphysics* 19 (1965): 260–61.

33. Carl Cohen, *Democracy* (New York: Free Press, 1971), p. 121; Isaiah Berlin, *Four Essays on Liberty* (London: Oxford University Press, 1969), p. xlviii.

34. Charles Taylor, "What's Wrong with Negative Liberty," in Alan Ryan, ed., *The Idea of Freedom: Essays in Honour of Isaiah Berlin* (Oxford: Oxford University Press, 1979), p. 177, says self-realization can be part of negative freedom. Given a desire to reduce restraints and a broad view of what issues can be addressed, this interpretation places reform liberals among the proponents of negative freedom.

35. Reich, *Tales of a New America*, p. 185.

36. "With affluence, consumers and workers have alternatives; it is less necessary, accordingly, that they submit to any given exercise of authority." John Kenneth Galbraith, *The Anatomy of Power* (Boston: Houghton Mifflin, 1983), p. 186. Galbraith adds "unemployment compensation" and "welfare payments." John Maynard Keynes, *The Collected Writings of John Maynard Keynes*, edited by Donald Moggridge, vol. 27, *Activities 1940–1946: Shaping the Post-War World: Employment and Commodities* (London: Macmillan, 1980), p. 445; Karl de Schweinitz, Jr., "The Question of Freedom in Economics and Economic Organization," *Ethics* 89 (1979): 352; O. H. Taylor, *Economics and Liberalism: Collected Papers* (Cambridge, Mass.: Harvard University Press, 1955), p. 176.

37. Waligorski, *Political Theory of Conservative Economists*, pp. 147–48. The desire for community is seen as a primitive emotion.

38. Russell Kirk, *A Program for Conservatives* (Chicago: Henry Regnery, 1962), pp. 140–50, 209–10. See also National Conference of Catholic Bishops, *Economic Justice for All: Pastoral Letter on Catholic Social Teaching and the U.S. Economy* (Washington, D.C.: United States Catholic Conference, 1986).

39. Barber, *Strong Democracy*, pp. 68–72, 101.

40. Sullivan, *Reconstructing Public Philosophy*, pp. 98–99, 105–6, 182–83, 21.

41. Michael Walzer, "The Communitarian Critique of Liberalism," *Political Theory* 18 (February 1990), p. 9. Cf. Gans, *Middle American Individualism*, pp. 98–104.

42. Michael Williams, "Liberalism and Two Conceptions of the State," in MacLean and Mills, eds., *Liberalism Reconsidered*, p. 125.

43. "We must worry about the cohesion of our society." Robert B. Reich, "The Unprepared American," *Christian Science Monitor* (April 11, 1991), p. 19.

44. Barber, *Strong Democracy*, pp. 106–10. Cf. Sullivan, *Reconstructing Public Philosophy*, pp. xii, 32.

45. Thus private economy refers to ownership—not use of common resources or impact on others.

46. Robert Skidelsky, *John Maynard Keynes,* vol. 2, *The Economist as Saviour* (New York: Penguin Books, 1994), p. 270.

47. Galbraith, *Economics and the Public Purpose,* p. 173.

48. Wallace C. Peterson, "Market Power: The Missing Element in Keynesian Economics," *Journal of Economic Issues* 23 (June 1989): 385, 388.

49. This need not be personal, physical, or manifestly arbitrary.

50. Cf. Lindblom, *Politics and Markets,* pp. 47–48.

51. Cf. Ronald Dworkin, "Neutrality, Equality, and Liberalism," in MacLean and Mills, eds., *Liberalism Reconsidered,* pp. 1–11; Will Kymlicka, "Liberal Individualism and Liberal Neutrality," *Ethics* 99 (1989): 883–905; Patrick Neal, "Liberalism and Neutrality," *Polity* 17 (1985): 664–84; Richard C. Sinopoli, "Liberalism and Contested Conceptions of the Good," *Journal of Politics* 55 (August 1993): 644–63; William Galston, *Liberal Purposes: Goods, Virtues, and Diversity in the Liberal State* (Cambridge: Cambridge University Press, 1991); Robert E. Goodin and Andrew Reeve, eds., *Liberal Neutrality* (London: Routledge, 1989).

52. Cf. Brandeis: "Neutrality is at times a graver sin than belligerence." As quoted in Strum, *Brandeis,* p. 158.

53. Joan Robinson, *Economic Philosophy* (Harmondsworth, U.K.: Penguin Books, 1962), p. 72.

54. Cf. Douglas Rae, *Equalities* (Cambridge, Mass.: Harvard University Press, 1981), pp. 70–71; Eccleshall, "When Is a 'Liberal' Not a Liberal?" pp. 191–92.

55. Successful markets and government failure produce a double defense for leaving things alone.

56. Herbert Stein, "Shrinking Government May Not Be the Answer," *Washington Post National Weekly Edition* (March 6–12, 1995).

57. Dewey, *Liberalism and Social Action,* p. 60. Psychological damage from insecurity pervades the lives of millions, undermining "robust individuality." John Dewey, *Individualism Old and New* (New York: Minton, Balch, 1930), p. 55.

58. Waligorski, *Political Theory of Conservative Economists,* especially pp. 153–59, 166–70. Cf. Steven E. Rhoads, *The Economist's View of the World: Government, Markets, and Public Policy* (Cambridge: Cambridge University Press, 1985), pp. 67–75.

59. Cf. John E. Schwarz, *America's Hidden Success: A Reassessment of Public Policy from Kennedy to Reagan* (New York: W. W. Norton, 1988).

60. Francis, "Case of Mistaken Paternity," p. 295; Roger King, *The State in Modern Society: New Directions in Political Sociology* (Chatham, N.J.: Chatham House, 1986), pp. 2, 14; Michael Freeden, *The New Liberalism: An Ideology of Social Reform* (Oxford: Clarendon Press, 1978), p. 60; James Ronald Stanfield, "The Dichotomized State," *Journal of Economic Issues* 25(3) (September 1991): 765.

61. John Maynard Keynes, *The Collected Writings of John Maynard Keynes,* edited by Donald Moggridge, vol. 21, *Activities 1931–1939, World Crisis and Policies in Britain and America* (London: Macmillan, 1982), p. 84.

62. Theda Skocpol, "The Legacies of New Deal Liberalism," in MacLean and Mills, eds., *Liberalism Reconsidered*, p. 99.

63. Galbraith and Reich especially; Brandeis, Dewey, Keynes, and Thurow to a lesser extent.

64. Nothing in Keynes' theory required that postwar Keynesianism exclude popular participation.

65. Cf. "Keynesian economics was . . . extraordinarily conservative. Would that all revolutions were so restrained." John Kenneth Galbraith, *The New Industrial State*, 4th ed. (Boston: Houghton Mifflin, 1985), p. xvii.

66. John Kenneth Galbraith, *A Journey Through Economic Time: A Firsthand View* (Boston: Houghton Mifflin, 1994), p. 157.

67. John Kenneth Galbraith, "The Wealth of the Nation" [review of Samuel Bowles, David Gordon, and Thomas E. Weisskopf, *Beyond the Waste Land: A Democratic Alternative to Economic Decline*], *New York Review of Books* 30 (June 2, 1983): 3–6.

68. Lindblom distinguishes synoptic planning—a total planning effort based on a comprehensive theory—from strategic planning, which emphasizes process, procedure, feedback, incremental changes, and trial and error. *Politics and Markets*, pp. 314–19. For Keynes, Galbraith, and Reich, "planning" means strategic planning.

69. I owe this point to Kenneth Dolbeare.

70. Judith N. Shklar, "The Liberalism of Fear," in Nancy L. Rosenblum, ed., *Liberalism and the Moral Life* (Cambridge, Mass.: Harvard University Press, 1989), p. 26.

Bibliography

INTERVIEWS

John Kenneth Galbraith, October 26, 1992.
Lord Kahn, October 16, 1980.

ARCHIVES

John Kenneth Galbraith Collection at the John F. Kennedy Presidential Library,
  Boston, Massachusetts.
Keynes Papers, Kings College Library, Cambridge University, Cambridge, United
  Kingdom.
Public Record Office, London, Treasury File T.247, John Maynard Keynes' file
  while working in the Treasury during World War II.

PRINTED SOURCES

Abrams, Elliott. 1976. "What Is a Liberal—Who Is a Conservative: A Symposium."
  Commentary 62 (September): 34–35.
Adelstein, Richard P. 1991. "'The Nation as an Economic Unit': Keynes, Roosevelt
  and the Managerial Ideal." *Journal of American History* 78: 160–87.
Alterman, Eric. 1995. "The Reich Stuff." *Mother Jones* (July/August 1995): 50–51.
Anderson, Carol Leutner. 1982. "Economics and Metaphysics: Framework for the
  Future." *Review of Social Economy* 40 (1982): 199–226.
Anderson, Charles. 1990. *Pragmatic Liberalism.* Chicago: University of Chicago
  Press.
Arenson, Karen W. 1983. "Debate Grows over Adoption of National Industrial Pol-
  icy." *New York Times* (June 19), sec. 1, pp. 1, 38.
Arrow, Kenneth J. 1963. *Social Choice and Individual Values.* New York: John Wiley
  & Sons.
Balogh, Thomas. 1982. *The Irrelevance of Conventional Economics.* New York: Live-
  right.
Barash, David P. 1992. *The L Word: An Unapologetic, Thoroughly Biased, Long-Over-
  due Explication and Celebration of Liberalism.* New York: William Morrow.

Barber, Benjamin. 1988. *The Conquest of Politics: Liberal Philosophy in Democratic Times*. Princeton, N.J.: Princeton University Press.

———. 1984. *Strong Democracy: Participatory Politics for a New Age*. Berkeley: University of California Press.

Barker, Rodney. 1978. *Political Ideas in Modern Britain*. London: Methuen.

Barraclough, John. 1977. "The Keynesian Era in Perspective." In Robert Skidelsky, ed., *End of the Keynesian Era* (New York: Holmes & Meier), pp. 104–11.

Bartlett, Bruce. 1984. "Keynes as a Conservative." *Modern Age* 28: 128–33.

Beckerman, Wilfred. 1989. "How Large a Public Sector?" In Dieter Helm, ed., *The Economic Borders of the State* (Oxford: Oxford University Press), pp. 66–91.

Berlin, Isaiah. 1969. *Four Essays on Liberty*. London: Oxford University Press.

Birnbaum, Jeffrey H. 1988. "Brave New Liberalism." *Business Month* 132 (October): 48–53.

Blumenthal, Sidney. 1986. *The Rise of the Counter-Establishment: From Conservative Ideology to Political Power*. New York: Times Books.

Brandeis, Louis D. (Osmond K. Fraenkel, ed.) 1935. *The Curse of Bigness: Miscellaneous Papers*. New York: Viking Press.

———. [1915] 1969. "Industrial Democracy" [testimony before the United States Commission on Industrial Relations, 1915]. Excerpts in Walter E. Volkomer, ed., *The Liberal Tradition in American Thought* (New York: Capricorn Books), pp. 288–96.

Bronfenbrenner, Martin. 1973. "Equality and Equity." *Annals of the American Academy of Political and Social Science* 409 (September): 9–23.

Buchanan, James M. 1986. *Liberty, Market and State: Political Economy in the 1980s*. New York: New York University Press.

Bullock, Alan, and Shock, Maurice, eds. 1966. *The Liberal Tradition: From Fox to Keynes*. London: Adam & Charles Black.

Burke, James. 1985. *The Day the Universe Changed*. Boston: Little, Brown.

Caporaso, James A., and Levine, David P. 1992. *Theories of Political Economy*. Cambridge: Cambridge University Press.

Cate, Tom. 1983. "Keynes and Thurow: The Socialization of Investment." *Eastern Economic Journal* 9 (May–September): 205–12.

Chernomas, Robert. 1984. "Keynes on Post-Scarcity Society." *Journal of Economic Issues* 18 (December): 1007–26.

Ciscel, David H. 1984. "Galbraith's Planning System as a Substitute for Market Theory." *Journal of Economic Issues* 18: 411–18.

Clarke, Peter. 1994. "Keynes in History." *History of Political Economy* 26: 117–35.

———. 1978. *Liberals and Social Democrats*. Cambridge: Cambridge University Press.

Clymer, Adam. 1995. "Republicans Push Stopgap Spending as Recess Nears." *New York Times* (September 29), pp. A1, 12.

Cobb, Joe. 1992. "Bookshelf: Doing Economic Battle" [review of Lester Thurow, *Head to Head: The Coming Economic Battle Among Japan, Europe, and America*]. *Wall Street Journal* (May 28), p. A18.

Cohen, Carl. 1971. *Democracy*. New York: Free Press.

Cook, Terrence E. 1991. *The Great Alternatives of Social Thought: Aristocrat, Saint, Capitalist, Socialist*. Savage, Md.: Rowman & Littlefield.

Cranston, Maurice. 1978. "Keynes: His Political Ideas and Their Influence." In A. P. Thirlwall, ed., *Keynes and Laissez-Faire: The Third Keynes Seminar at Canterbury 1976* (London: Macmillan), pp. 100–115.

Crotty, James R. 1990. "Keynes on the Stages of Development of the Capitalist Economy: The Institutional Foundation of Keynes' Methodology." *Journal of Economic Issues* 24 (September): 761–80.

Dahl, Robert A. 1970. *After the Revolution? Authority in a Good Society*. New Haven, Conn.: Yale University Press.

———. 1986. *Democracy, Liberty and Equality*. Oslo: Norwegian University Press.

———. 1985. *A Preface to Economic Democracy*. Berkeley: University of California Press.

Damico, Alfonso J. 1978. *Individuality and Community: The Social and Political Thought of John Dewey*. Gainesville: University Presses of Florida.

Davidson, Paul. 1989. "Achieving a Civilized Society." *Challenge* 32 (September–October): 40–46.

Davis, Michael. 1983. "Liberalism and/or Democracy?" *Social Theory and Practice* 9 (Spring): 51–72.

Dawson, Nelson L. 1984. "Louis D. Brandeis, George Gilder, and the Nature of Capitalism." *The Historian* 47 (November): 72–85.

Dewey, John. [1939] 1989. *Freedom and Culture*. Buffalo, N.Y.: Prometheus Books.

———. 1939. "The Future of Liberalism or the Democratic Way of Change." In John Dewey, Boyd H. Bode, and T. V. Smith, *What Is Democracy? Its Conflicts, Ends and Means* (Norman, Okla.: Cooperative Books), pp. 3–10.

———. 1930. *Individualism Old and New*. New York: Minton, Balch.

———. [1935] 1963. *Liberalism and Social Action*. New York: Capricorn Books.

———. (Debra Morris and Ian Shapiro, eds.) 1993. *The Political Writings*. Indianapolis: Hackett.

Dillard, Dudley. 1948. *The Economics of John Maynard Keynes: The Theory of a Monetary Economy*. New York: Prentice-Hall.

Dillin, John. 1991. "U.S. Could Lose Middle Class." *Christian Science Monitor* (June 18), p. 6.

Dionne, Jr., E. J. 1991. "Changing the Gurus?" *Washington Post* (April 14), pp. H1, 6.

Dolbeare, Kenneth M., and Dolbeare, Patricia. 1973. *American Ideologies*. Chicago: Markham.

Downs, Anthony. 1987. "The Evolution of Democracy: How Its Axioms and Institutional Forms Have Been Adapted to Changing Social Forces." *Daedalus* 116 (Summer): 119–48.

Drucker, Peter F. 1971. *Men, Ideas and Politics.* New York: Harper & Row.

Dworkin, Ronald. 1983. "Neutrality, Equality, and Liberalism." In Douglas MacLean and Claudia Mills, eds., *Liberalism Reconsidered* (Totowa, N.J.: Rowman & Allanheld), pp. 1–11.

Eccleshall, Robert. 1978. "When Is a 'Liberal' Not a Liberal?" *Contemporary Review* 232 (April): 187–93.

Fine, Sidney. 1956 [1964]. *Laissez-Faire and the General Welfare State: A Study of Conflict in American Thought 1865–1901.* Ann Arbor: University of Michigan Press.

Fitzgibbons, Athol. 1988. *Keynes's Vision: A New Political Economy.* Oxford: Clarendon Press.

Francis, M. 1985. "A Case of Mistaken Paternity: The Relationship Between Nineteenth-Century Liberals and Twentieth-Century Liberal Democrats." *Australian Journal of Politics and History* 31: 282–99.

Frankfurter, Felix, ed. 1932. *Mr. Justice Brandeis.* New Haven, Conn.: Yale University Press.

_____ . 1932. "Mr. Justice Brandeis and the Constitution." In Felix Frankfurter, ed., *Mr. Justice Brandeis* (New Haven, Conn.: Yale University Press), pp. 47–125.

Freeden, Michael. 1978. *The New Liberalism: An Ideology of Social Reform.* Oxford: Clarendon Press.

_____ . 1993. "A Non-Hypothetical Liberalism: The Communitarianism of J. A. Hobson." Paper presented at the American Political Science Association, September 3.

_____ . 1991. *Rights.* Minneapolis: University of Minnesota Press.

Friedman, Milton. 1962. *Capitalism and Freedom.* Chicago: University of Chicago Press.

Friedman, Thomas L. 1994. "World's Big Economies Turn to the Jobs Issue." *New York Times* (March 14), pp. C1, 4.

Fukuyama, Francis. 1989. "The End of History?" *National Interest* 16 (Summer): 3–18.

_____ . 1989–1990. "A Reply to My Critics." *National Interest* 18 (Winter): 21–28.

G., A. G. 1923. "The Spirit of Liberalism." *The Nation and the Athenaeum* 34 (July 21): 512–13.

Galbraith, John Kenneth. [1958] 1965. *The Affluent Society.* Toronto: Mentor Books.

_____ . 1969. *The Affluent Society,* 2d ed. New York: New American Library.

_____ . 1977. *The Age of Uncertainty.* Boston: Houghton Mifflin.

_____ . 1956. *American Capitalism: The Concept of Countervailing Power,* rev. ed. Boston: Houghton Mifflin.

_____ . 1983. *The Anatomy of Power.* Boston: Houghton Mifflin.

_____ . 1979. *Annals of an Abiding Liberal.* Boston: Houghton Mifflin.

_____ . 1988. "Baseball: Socialist as Apple Pie." *New York Times* (August 7), sec. 4, p. 23.

_____ . 1988. "Coolidge, Carter, Bush, Reagan . . . ." *New York Times* (December 12), p. A19.

_____ . 1992. *The Culture of Contentment.* Boston: Houghton Mifflin.

_____ . 1989. "The Death of Liberalism." *Observer* (March 26): 33–34.

_____ . 1987. "Economic Development: Engine of Democracy." *New York Times* (August 25), p. A21.

_____ . 1976. "The Economic Problems of the Left." *New Statesman* 91 (February 20): 217–18.

_____ . 1975. *Economics and the Public Purpose.* Harmondsworth, U.K.: Penguin Books.

_____ . 1987. *Economics in Perspective: A Critical History.* Boston: Houghton Mifflin.

_____ . 1971. *Economics, Peace and Laughter.* New York: Signet.

_____ . 1989. "Friendly Advice to a Shrinking Military." *New York Times* (November 22), p. A25.

_____ . 1996. *The Good Society: The Humane Agenda.* Boston: Houghton Mifflin.

_____ . 1975. *The Great Crash, 1929.* Harmondsworth, U.K.: Penguin Books.

_____ . 1969. *How to Control the Military.* New York: Signet.

_____ . 1989. "Ideology and Economic Reality." *Challenge* 32 (November–December): 4–9.

_____ . 1988. "Interest Groups by Any Other Name." *New York Times* (May 29), sec. 4, p. 17.

_____ . 1983. "Interview: The Anatomy of Power" [conducted by Richard D. Bartel]. *Challenge* 26 (July–August): 26–33.

_____ . 1994. *A Journey Through Economic Time: A Firsthand View.* Boston: Houghton Mifflin.

_____ . 1960. *The Liberal Hour.* New York: New American Library.

_____ . 1981. *A Life in Our Times: Memoirs.* New York: Ballantine Books.

_____ . 1975. *Money: Whence It Came, Where It Went.* Boston: Houghton Mifflin.

_____ . 1979. *The Nature of Mass Poverty.* Harmondsworth, U.K.: Penguin Books.

_____ . 1985. *The New Industrial State,* 4th ed. Boston: Houghton Mifflin.

_____ . 1989. "Nothing Succeeds Like Excess." *New York Times* (August 28), p. A17.

_____ . 1991. "Paying the Price for the Reagan Years" [review of Haynes Johnson, *Sleepwalking Through History*]. *Washington Post Book World* (February 24): 1–2.

_____ . 1989. "The Pros and Cons of Capitalism." *World Marxist Review* 32 (November): 57–59.

_____. 1991. "Recession Without End." *Los Angeles Times* (November 3), pp. M1, 6.

_____. 1990. *A Tenured Professor: A Novel.* Boston: Houghton Mifflin.

_____. 1988. "Time and the New Industrial State." *American Economic Review: Papers and Proceedings* 78 (May): 373–82.

_____. 1981. "The Uses and Excuses for Affluence." *New York Times Magazine* (May 31), sec. 6, pp. 38–44.

_____. 1983. *The Voice of the Poor: Essays in Economic and Political Persuasion.* Cambridge, Mass.: Harvard University Press.

_____. 1982. "The Way Up from Reagan Economics." *Harvard Business Review* 60 (July–August): 6–8, 12.

_____. 1983. "The Wealth of the Nation" [review of Samuel Bowles, David Gordon, and Thomas E. Weisskopf, *Beyond the Waste Land: A Democratic Alternative to Economic Decline*]. *New York Review of Books* 30 (June 2): 3–6.

_____. 1987. "What Tact the Press Showed." *New York Times* (December 22), p. A23.

Galston, William. 1991. *Liberal Purposes: Goods, Virtues, and Diversity in the Liberal State.* Cambridge: Cambridge University Press.

Gambs, John S. 1975. *John Kenneth Galbraith.* Boston: Twayne.

Gans, Herbert J. 1991. *Middle American Individualism: The Future of Liberal Democracy.* New York: Oxford University Press.

Garry, Patrick M. 1992. *Liberalism and American Identity.* Kent, Ohio: Kent State University Press.

Gilder, George. 1981. *Wealth and Poverty.* New York: Basic Books.

Goodin, Robert E., and Reeve, Andrew, eds. 1989. *Liberal Neutrality.* London: Routledge.

Green, Philip. 1992. "In the American Tradition: A Few Kind Words for Liberalism." *Nation* 255 (September 28): 309ff.

Gutmann, Amy. 1983. "How Liberal Is Democracy." In Douglas MacLean and Claudia Mills, eds., *Liberalism Reconsidered* (Totowa, N.J.: Rowman & Allanheld), pp. 25–50.

Hall, John A. 1987. "Classical Liberalism and the Modern State." *Daedalus* 116 (Summer): 95–118.

_____. 1987. *Liberalism: Politics, Ideology and the Market.* Chapel Hill: University of North Carolina Press.

Hall, Peter A. 1994. "Keynes in Political Science." *History of Political Economy* 26 (1994): 137–53.

Hardin, Russell. 1993. "Liberalism: Political and Economic." In Ellen Frankel Paul, Fred D. Miller, Jr., and Jeffrey Paul, eds., *Liberalism and the Economic Order* (Cambridge: Cambridge University Press), pp. 121–44.

Harrington, Michael. 1967. "Liberalism According to Galbraith." *Commentary* 44 (October): 77–83.

———. 1968. *Toward a Democratic Left: A Radical Program for a New Majority.* New York: Macmillan.

Harris, Seymour E. 1947. *The New Economics: Keynes' Influence on Theory and Public Policy.* New York: Alfred A. Knopf.

Harrod, R. F. [1951] 1972. *The Life and Times of John Maynard Keynes.* Harmondsworth, U.K.: Penguin Books.

Hayek, Friedrich A. 1979. *Law, Legislation and Liberty: A New Statement of the Liberal Principles of Justice and Political Economy,* vol. 3, *The Political Order of a Free People.* Chicago: University of Chicago Press.

———. 1978. "The Miscarriage of the Democratic Ideal." *Encounter* 50: 14–17.

———. [1944] 1972. *The Road to Serfdom.* Chicago: University of Chicago Press (with a new Preface by the author, 1976).

Heilbroner, Robert L. 1970. *Between Capitalism and Socialism: Essays in Political Economics.* New York: Vintage Books.

———. 1988. *Beyond the Veil of Economics: Essays in the Worldly Philosophy.* New York: W. W. Norton.

———. 1984. "Economics and Political Economy: Marx, Keynes, and Schumpeter." *Journal of Economic Issues* 18 (September): 681–95.

———. 1985. *The Nature and Logic of Capitalism.* New York: W. W. Norton.

———. 1989. "The Triumph of Capitalism." *New Yorker* 64 (January 23): 98–109.

———. 1993. *21st Century Capitalism.* New York: W. W. Norton.

———. 1980. *The Worldly Philosophers.* New York: Simon & Schuster.

Helm, Dieter. 1989. "The Economic Borders of the State." In Dieter Helm, ed., *The Economic Borders of the State* (Oxford: Oxford University Press), pp. 9–45.

Herzog, Don. 1989. "Up Toward Liberalism." *Dissent* 36: 355–59.

Hession, Charles H. 1972. *John Kenneth Galbraith and His Critics.* New York: New American Library.

Hirschman, Albert O. 1977. *The Passions and the Interests: Political Arguments for Capitalism Before Its Triumph.* Princeton, N.J.: Princeton University Press.

Hobhouse, L. T. [1904] 1972. *Democracy and Reaction.* Brighton, U.K.: Harvester Press.

———. 1922. *The Elements of Social Justice.* New York: Henry Holt.

———. [1911] 1964. *Liberalism.* London: Oxford University Press.

———. 1911. *Social Evolution and Political Theory.* New York: Columbia University Press.

Hoover, Kenneth R. 1994. *Ideology and Political life.* Belmont, Calif.: Wadsworth.

Jeffries, John W. 1990. "The 'New' New Deal: FDR and American Liberalism, 1937–1945." *Political Science Quarterly* 105: 397–418.

Johnson, Elizabeth. 1974. "John Maynard Keynes: Scientist or Politician?" *Journal of Political Economy* 82: 99–111.

Johnson, Elizabeth S., and Johnson, Harry G. 1978. *The Shadow of Keynes: Understanding Keynes, Cambridge and Keynesian Economics.* Chicago: University of Chicago Press.

Kammen, Michael. 1986. *Spheres of Liberty: Changing Perceptions of Liberty in American Culture.* Madison: University of Wisconsin Press.

Katouzian, Homa. 1980. *Ideology and Method in Economics.* New York: New York University Press.

Kelman, Steven. 1988. "Why Public Ideas Matter." In Robert B. Reich, ed., *The Power of Public Ideas* (Cambridge, Mass.: Harvard University Press), pp. 31–53.

Keynes, John Maynard. (Donald Moggridge, ed.) 1971. *The Collected Writings of John Maynard Keynes,* vol. 1, *Indian Currency and Finance.* London: Macmillan.

———. (Donald Moggridge, ed.) 1971. *The Collected Writings of John Maynard Keynes,* vol. 2, *Economic Consequences of the Peace.* London: Macmillan.

———. (Donald Moggridge, ed.) 1971. *The Collected Writings of John Maynard Keynes,* vol. 4, *A Tract on Monetary Reform.* London: Macmillan.

———. (Donald Moggridge, ed.) 1971. *The Collected Writings of John Maynard Keynes,* vol. 5, *A Treatise on Money,* vol. 1, *The Pure Theory of Money.* London: Macmillan.

———. (Donald Moggridge, ed.) 1971. *The Collected Writings of John Maynard Keynes,* vol. 6, *A Treatise on Money,* vol. 2, *The Applied Theory of Money.* London: Macmillan.

———. (Donald Moggridge, ed.) 1973. *The Collected Writings of John Maynard Keynes,* vol. 7, *The General Theory of Employment Interest and Money.* London: Macmillan.

———. (Donald Moggridge, ed.) 1973. *The Collected Writings of John Maynard Keynes,* vol. 8, *A Treatise on Probability.* London: Macmillan.

———. (Donald Moggridge, ed.) 1972. *The Collected Writings of John Maynard Keynes,* vol. 9, *Essays in Persuasion.* London: Macmillan.

———. (Donald Moggridge, ed.) 1972. *The Collected Writings of John Maynard Keynes,* vol. 10, *Essays in Biography.* London: Macmillan.

———. (Donald Moggridge, ed.) 1973. *The Collected Writings of John Maynard Keynes,* vol. 13, *The General Theory and After, Part 1, Preparation.* London: Macmillan.

———. (Donald Moggridge, ed.) 1973. *The Collected Writings of John Maynard Keynes,* vol. 14, *The General Theory and After.* London: Macmillan.

———. (Elizabeth Johnson, ed.) 1971. *The Collected Writings of John Maynard Keynes,* vol. 15, *Activities 1906–1914: India and Cambridge.* London: Macmillan.

———. (Donald Moggridge, ed.) 1977. *The Collected Writings of John Maynard*

Keynes, vol. 17, *Activities: 1920–1922: Treaty Revision and Reconstruction*. London: Macmillan.

———. (Donald Moggridge, ed.) 1978. *The Collected Writings of John Maynard Keynes*, vol. 18, *Activities 1922–1932, The End of Reparations*. London: Macmillan.

———. (Donald Moggridge, ed.) 1981. *The Collected Writings of John Maynard Keynes*, vol. 19, part 1, *Activities 1922–1929: The Return to Gold and Industrial Policy*. London: Macmillan.

———. (Donald Moggridge, ed.) 1981. *The Collected Writings of John Maynard Keynes*, vol. 19, part 2, *Activities 1922–1929: The Return to Gold and Industrial Policy*. London: Macmillan.

———. (Donald Moggridge, ed.) 1981. *The Collected Writings of John Maynard Keynes*, vol. 20, *Activities 1929–1931: Rethinking Employment and Employment Policy*. London: Macmillan.

———. (Donald Moggridge, ed.) 1982. *The Collected Writings of John Maynard Keynes*, vol. 21, *Activities 1931–1939, World Crisis and Policies in Britain and America*. London: Macmillan.

———. (Donald Moggridge, ed.) 1978. *The Collected Writings of John Maynard Keynes*, vol. 22, *Activities: 1939–1945, Internal War Finance*. London: Macmillan.

———. (Donald Moggridge, ed.) 1979. *The Collected Writings of John Maynard Keynes*, vol. 24, *Activities: 1944–1946, The Transition to Peace*. London: Macmillan.

———. (Donald Moggridge, ed.) 1980. *The Collected Writings of John Maynard Keynes*, vol. 25, *Activities 1940–44, Shaping the Post-War World: The Clearing Union*. London: Macmillan.

———. (Donald Moggridge, ed.) 1980. *The Collected Writings of John Maynard Keynes*, vol. 26, *Activities 1941–1946, Shaping the Post-War World: Bretton Woods and Reparations*. London: Macmillan.

———. (Donald Moggridge, ed.) 1980. *The Collected Writings of John Maynard Keynes*, vol. 27, *Activities 1940–1946: Shaping the Post-War World: Employment and Commodities*. London: Macmillan.

———. (Donald Moggridge, ed.) 1982. *The Collected Writings of John Maynard Keynes*, vol. 28, *Social, Political and Economic Writings*. London: Macmillan.

———. (Donald Moggridge, ed.) 1979. *The Collected Writings of John Maynard Keynes*, vol. 29, *The General Theory and After: A Supplement*. London: Macmillan.

———. 1939. "Democracy and Efficiency." *New Statesman and Nation* (January 28): 121–23.

———. 1924. "Does Unemployment Need a Drastic Remedy?" *Nation and Athenaeum* (May 24): 235–36.

———. 1933. "National Self-Sufficiency." *Yale Review* 22: 755–69.

Keynes, Milo, ed. 1974. *Essays on John Maynard Keynes*. Cambridge: Cambridge University Press.

King, Roger. 1986. *The State in Modern Society: New Directions in Political Sociology* [chapter 8 by Graham Gibbs]. Chatham, N.J.: Chatham House.

Kirk, Russell. [1954] 1962. *A Program for Conservatives.* Chicago: Henry Regnery.

Kristol, Irving. 1967. "Professor Galbraith's 'New Industrial State'." *Fortune* 76 (July): 90–91ff.

Kymlicka, Will. 1989. "Liberal Individualism and Liberal Neutrality." *Ethics* 99: 883–905.

Lamson, Peggy. 1991. *Speaking of Galbraith: A Personal Portrait.* New York: Ticknor & Fields.

Lane, Robert E. 1986. "Market Justice, Political Justice." *American Political Science Review* 80: 383–402.

Laski, H. J. 1940. *The Decline of Liberalism.* Oxford: Oxford University Press.

Lavoie, Don. 1993. "Democracy, Markets, and the Legal Order: Notes on the Nature of Politics in a Radically Liberal Society." In Ellen Frankel Paul, Fred D. Miller, Jr., and Jeffrey Paul, eds., *Liberalism and the Economic Order* (Cambridge: Cambridge University Press), pp. 103–20.

Lawson, R. Alan. 1971. *The Failure of Independent Liberalism (1930–1941).* New York: Capricorn Books.

Lee, Dwight R. 1984. "Supply-Side Economics and the Political Order." *Modern Age* 28: 134–42.

Lekachman, Robert. 1966. *The Age of Keynes.* New York: Random House.

_____ . 1964. *Keynes' General Theory: Reports of Three Decades.* New York: St. Martin's Press.

_____ . 1977. "The Radical Keynes." In Robert Skidelsky, ed., *The End of the Keynesian Era: Essays on the Disintegration of the Keynesian Political Economy* (New York: Holmes & Meier), pp. 59–66.

Lerner, Max. 1932. "The Social Thought of Mr. Justice Brandeis." In Felix Frankfurter, ed., *Mr. Justice Brandeis* (New Haven, Conn.: Yale University Press), pp. 7–45.

Lichtenstein, Peter M. 1984. "Some Theoretical Coordinates of Radical Liberalism." *American Journal of Economics and Sociology* 43: 333–39.

Lief, Alfred. 1941. *The Brandeis Guide to the Modern World.* Boston: Little, Brown.

Lindblom, Charles E. 1988. *Democracy and the Market System.* Oslo: Norwegian University Press.

_____ . 1982. "The Market as Prison." *Journal of Politics* 44: 324–36.

_____ . 1977. *Politics and Markets: The World's Political-Economic Systems.* New York: Basic Books.

Lippmann, Walter. 1955. *Essays in the Public Philosophy.* New York: Mentor Books.

Lloyd Thomas, D. A. 1972. "The Justification of Liberalism." *Canadian Journal of Philosophy* 2: 199–217.

Locke, John. (Peter Laslett, ed.) [1690] 1965. *The Second Treatise of Government.* In John Locke, *Two Treatises of Government.* New York: Mentor Books.

Macpherson, C. B. 1973. *Democratic Theory: Essays in Retrieval.* Oxford: Clarendon Press.

_____ . 1978. "The Economic Penetration of Political Theory: Some Hypotheses." *Journal of the History of Ideas* 39: 101–18.

_____ . 1977. *The Life and Times of Liberal Democracy.* Oxford: Oxford University Press.

_____ . 1962. *The Political Theory of Possessive Individualism: Hobbes to Locke.* Oxford: Clarendon Press.

_____ . 1985. *The Rise and Fall of Economic Justice and Other Papers.* Oxford: Oxford University Press.

Magaziner, Ira C., and Reich, Robert B. 1982. *Minding America's Business: The Decline and Rise of the American Economy.* New York: Harcourt Brace Jovanovich.

Malthus, Thomas Robert. [1872] 1986. *An Essay on the Principle of Population,* 7th ed. London: Reeves & Turner [reprinted by Augustus M. Kelley, Fairfield, N.J.].

Manegold, Catherine S. 1994. "Labor Secretary Urges Cuts in 'Corporate Welfare' Too." *New York Times* (November 23), p. A11.

Manning, D. J. 1976. *Liberalism.* New York: St. Martin's Press.

Mason, Alpheus Thomas. 1955. *Security Through Freedom: American Political Thought and Practice.* Ithaca, N.Y.: Cornell University Press.

McClenahen, John S. 1991. "Do We Need a National Industrial Policy?" *Industry Week* 240 (March 18): 56–62.

McCloskey, H. J. 1965. "The Problem of Liberalism." *Review of Metaphysics* 19: 248–75.

McKenzie, Richard B. 1991. "The First and Second Reich: The Taming of an Industrial Policy Advocate." *Cato Journal* 11(1) (Spring–Summer): 47–64.

Merquior, J. G. 1991. *Liberalism: Old and New.* Boston: Twayne.

Mill, John Stuart. [1861] *Considerations on Representative Government.*

_____ . (Marshall Cohen, ed.) 1961. *The Philosophy of John Stuart Mill: Ethical, Political and Religious.* New York: Modern Library.

_____ . 1970. *Principles of Political Economy.* Harmondsworth, U.K.: Penguin Books.

Minsky, Hyman P. 1975. *John Maynard Keynes.* New York: Columbia University Press.

Mitgang, Herbert. 1990. "Why Liberals and Their Beliefs Will Rise Again." *New York Times* (January 17), p. C19.

Moggridge, D. E. 1974. "The Influence of Keynes on the Economics of his Time." In Milo Keynes, ed., *Essays on John Maynard Keynes* (Cambridge: Cambridge University Press), pp. 73–81.

_____ . 1976. *Keynes.* Glasgow: Fontana/Collins.

Morris, Charles R. 1986. *A Time of Passion: America, 1960–1980.* New York: Penguin Books.

National Conference of Catholic Bishops. 1986. *Economic Justice for All: Pastoral Letter on Catholic Social Teaching and the U.S. Economy.* Washington, D.C.: United States Catholic Conference.

Neal, Patrick. 1985. "Liberalism and Neutrality." *Polity* 17: 664–84.

New York Times staff. 1992. "A Who's Who of Men Advising Clinton." *New York Times* (September 13), sec. 1, p. 36.

Okroi, Loren J. 1988. *Galbraith, Harrington, Heilbroner: Economics and Dissent in an Age of Optimism.* Princeton, N.J.: Princeton University Press.

Paine, Thomas. 1978. *Political Writings.* Franklin Center, Pa.: Franklin Library.

Parker, Richard. 1992. "Throwing Down the Economic Gauntlet" [review of Lester Thurow, *Head to Head: The Coming Economic Battle Among Japan, Europe, and America*]. *Washington Post* (June 8), sec. C, p. 2.

Parsons, Wayne. 1983. "Keynes and the Politics of Ideas." *History of Political Thought* 4 (Summer 1983): 367–92.

Passell, Peter. 1992. "Clinton Economists Cast a Wide Net." *New York Times* (October 11), sec. 4, p. 3.

Peterson, Wallace C. 1989. "Market Power: The Missing Element in Keynesian Economics." *Journal of Economic Issues* 23 (June): 371–91.

Peterson, William H. 1992. Review of Lester C. Thurow, *Head to Head: The Coming Economic Battle Among Japan, Europe, and America. The Freeman* 42 (October): 401–3.

Rabinovitz, Jonathan. 1994. "Liberal Coalition Has Biggest Victory." *New York Times* (September 20), p. A15.

Radin, Charles A. 1988. "Reaffirming a Commitment to Liberalism." *Boston Globe* (October 27), p. 2.

Rae, Douglas. 1981. *Equalities.* Cambridge, Mass.: Harvard University Press.

Reich, Robert B. 1989. "America Pays the Price." *New York Times* (January 29), sec. 6, p. 32.

_____ . 1989. "As the World Turns." *The New Republic* 200(18) (May 1): 23–28.

_____ . 1988. "Behold! We Have an Industrial Policy." *New York Times* (May 22), sec. 4, p. 29.

_____ . 1983. "Beyond Free Trade." *Foreign Affairs* 61: 773–804.

_____ . 1992. "Boost Productivity by Investing in People's Minds and Skills." *Los Angeles Times* (July 13), p. B5.

_____ . 1992. "Clinton: Spur Growth." *New York Times* (July 16), sec. A, p. 25.

_____ . 1990. Contribution to "The American 80's: Disaster or Triumph?: A Symposium." *Commentary* 90 (September): 16–17.

_____ . 1991. "Domestic Agenda: From the Left." *Christian Science Monitor* (February 11), p. 18.

_____ . 1988. "The Economics of Illusion and the Illusion of Economics." *Foreign Affairs* 66: 512–28.

_____ . 1988. *Education and the Next Economy.* Washington, D.C., National Education Association.

_____ . 1990. "Everyone Gives, Everyone Benefits." *New York Times* (April 1), sec. 6, pp. 42–45.

_____ . 1987. "Forum: On the Brink of an Anti-Business Era." *New York Times* (April 12), sec. 3, p. 3.

_____ . 1991. "Here's an Economic Policy." *New York Times* (November 3), sec. 4, p. 15.

_____ . 1983. *An Industrial Policy for America: Is It Needed?* Washington, D.C.: U.S. Government Printing Office, Subcommittee on Economic Stabilization of the Committee on Banking, Finance and Urban Affairs, House of Representatives, April 1983.

_____ . 1982. "Making Industrial Policy." *Foreign Affairs* 60: 852–81.

_____ . 1991. "The Myth of 'Made in the U.S.A.'" *Wall Street Journal* (July 5), p. A6.

_____ . 1983. *The Next American Frontier.* New York: Times Books.

_____ . 1988. "Policy Making in a Democracy." In Robert B. Reich, ed., *The Power of Public Ideas* (Cambridge, Mass.: Harvard University Press), pp. 123–56.

_____ , ed. 1988. *The Power of Public Ideas.* Cambridge, Mass.: Harvard University Press.

_____ . 1990. *Public Management in a Democratic Society.* Englewood Cliffs, N.J.: Prentice-Hall.

_____ . 1989. "Put a Brake on High-Tech Alliances." *Los Angeles Times* (March 20), sec. II, p. 5.

_____ . [1989] 1991. *The Resurgent Liberal (And Other Unfashionable Prophecies).* New York: Vintage Books.

_____ . 1991. "Secession of the Successful." *New York Times Magazine* (January 20), sec. 6, pp. 16–17, 42ff.

_____ . 1990. "The Squandered Decade." *Village Voice* 35 (January 2): 40.

_____ . 1987. *Tales of a New America: The Anxious Liberal's Guide to the Future.* New York: Vintage Books.

_____ . 1985. "Toward a New Public Philosophy." *Atlantic Monthly* 255 (May): 68–79.

_____ . 1990. "Trade: With Whom? For What? A Citizen's Guide to the Trade Debate." *Journal of Policy Analysis and Management* 9 (Summer): 391–99.

_____ . 1991. "Unacknowledged Legislators" [book review]. *New Republic* 204 (January 21): 38–41.

———— . 1991. "The Unprepared American." *Christian Science Monitor* (April 11), p. 19.

———— . 1991. "Who Champions the Working Class?" *New York Times* (May 26), sec. 4, p. 11.

———— . 1992. *The Work of Nations: Preparing Ourselves for 21st-Century Capitalism.* New York: Vintage Books.

———— . 1989. "Yes: Blame Election Funds." *New York Times* (October 12), p. A29.

Reich, Robert B., and Donahue, John D. 1985. *New Deals: The Chrysler Revival and the American System.* New York: Times Books.

Rhoads, Steven E. 1985. *The Economist's View of the World: Government, Markets, and Public Policy.* Cambridge: Cambridge University Press.

Richberg, Donald R. 1932. "The Industrial Liberalism of Mr. Justice Brandeis." In Felix Frankfurter, ed., *Mr. Justice Brandeis.* New Haven, Conn.: Yale University Press, pp. 127–39.

Risen, James. 1994. "Reich Feels Clinton Not Getting Credit for Economic Recovery." *Morning News of Northwest Arkansas* (September 6), p. 5A.

Robinson, Joan. 1962. *Economic Philosophy.* Harmondsworth, U.K.: Penguin Books.

———— . 1974. "What Has Become of the Keynesian Revolution?" In Milo Keynes, ed., *Essays on John Maynard Keynes* (Cambridge: Cambridge University Press), pp. 123–32.

Rostow, W. W. 1991. "Where We've Been, Where We're Going" [review of Robert Reich, *The Work of Nations: Preparing Ourselves for 21st-Century Capitalism*]. *Wall Street Journal* (March 20), sec. A, p. 20.

Rothenberg, Randall. 1984. *The Neo-Liberals: Creating the New American Politics.* New York: Simon & Schuster.

Rotunda, Ronald D. 1968. "The 'Liberal' Label: Roosevelt's Capture of a Symbol." *Public Policy* 17: 377–408.

———— . 1986. *The Politics of Language: Liberalism as Word and Symbol.* Iowa City: University of Iowa Press.

Ryan, Alan. 1989. "Communitarianism: The Good, The Bad, & the Muddly." *Dissent* 36: 350–54.

Salvadori, Massimo. 1977. *The Liberal Heresy: Origins and Historical Development.* London: Macmillan.

Sandel, Michael J. 1988. "The Political Theory of the Procedural Republic." In Robert B. Reich, ed., *The Power of Public Ideas* (Cambridge, Mass.: Harvard University Press), pp. 109–21.

Schapiro, Salwyn. 1958. *Liberalism: Its Meaning and History.* Princeton, N.J.: D. Van Nostrand.

Schlesinger, Arthur, Jr. 1956. "The Challenge of Abundance." *Reporter* 14 (May 3): 8–11.

Schoettli, Urs. 1986. "The State of Liberalism—Challenges from Left and Right." *Contemporary Review* 248: 79–85.

Schumpeter, Joseph A. 1976. *Capitalism, Socialism and Democracy.* New York: Harper & Row.

_____ . 1951. *The Great Economists: From Marx to Keynes.* New York: Oxford University Press.

Schwarz, John E. 1988. *America's Hidden Success: A Reassessment of Public Policy from Kennedy to Reagan.* New York: W. W. Norton.

Schweinitz, Karl de, Jr. 1979. "The Question of Freedom in Economics and Economic Organization." *Ethics* 89 (July): 336–53.

Shapiro, Walter. 1988. "The Party's New Soul." *Time* 132 (July 25): 17–19.

Shklar, Judith N. 1991. *American Citizenship: The Quest for Inclusion.* Cambridge, Mass.: Harvard University Press.

_____ . 1989. "The Liberalism of Fear." In Nancy L. Rosenblum, ed., *Liberalism and the Moral Life* (Cambridge, Mass.: Harvard University Press), pp. 21–39.

Siedentop, Larry. 1979. "Two Liberal Traditions." In Alan Ryan, ed., *The Idea of Freedom: Essays in Honour of Isaiah Berlin.* (Oxford: Oxford University Press), pp. 153–74.

Silk, Leonard. 1976. *The Economists.* New York: Avon Books.

Sinopoli, Richard C. 1993. "Liberalism and Contested Conceptions of the Good." *Journal of Politics* 55 (August): 644–63.

Skidelsky, Robert, ed. 1977. *The End of the Keynesian Era: Essays on the Disintegration of the Keynesian Political Economy.* New York: Holmes & Meier.

_____ . [1983] 1986. *John Maynard Keynes,* vol. 1, *Hopes Betrayed 1883–1920.* New York: Viking.

_____ . [1992] 1994. *John Maynard Keynes,* vol. 2, *The Economist as Saviour.* New York: Penguin Books.

_____ . 1993. "Keynes and the Left." *New Statesman and Society* 6 (April 16): 16–17.

_____ . 1979. "Keynes and the Reconstruction of Liberalism." *Encounter* 52 (April): 29–39.

Skocpol, Theda. 1983. "The Legacies of New Deal Liberalism." In Douglas MacLean and Claudia Mills, eds., *Liberalism Reconsidered* (Totowa, N.J.: Rowman & Allanheld), pp. 87–104.

Smith, Adam. 1992. "Don't Bet on Us" [review of Lester Thurow, *Head to Head: The Coming Economic Battle Among Japan, Europe, and America*]. *New York Times* (April 26), sec. 7, p. 3.

Smith, Adam. [1776] 1965. *An Inquiry into the Nature and Causes of the Wealth of Nations.* New York: Modern Library.

Sowell, Thomas. 1987. *A Conflict of Visions: Ideological Origins of Political Struggles.* New York: Quill.

Spitz, David. 1982. *The Real World of Liberalism.* Chicago: University of Chicago Press.

Srodes, James. 1989. "Curmudgeon in Winter." *Financial World* 158 (November 28): 82–83.

Stanfield, James Ronald. 1991. "The Dichotomized State." *Journal of Economic Issues* 25 (September): 765–80.

Stein, Herbert. 1995. "Shrinking Government May Not Be the Answer." *Washington Post National Weekly Edition* (March 6–12).

Stelzer, Irwin M. 1992. "Old Wine" [review of Lester Thurow, *Head to Head: The Coming Economic Battle Among Japan, Europe, and America*]. *Commentary* 94 (October): 51–54.

Stigler, George. 1965. "The Intellectual and the Marketplace." In Adrian Klaasen, ed., *The Invisible Hand* (Chicago: Gateway Editions), pp. 31–42.

Strum, Philippa. 1993. *Brandeis: Beyond Progressivism.* Lawrence: University Press of Kansas.

_____ , ed. 1995. *Brandeis on Democracy.* Lawrence: University Press of Kansas.

Sullivan, William M. 1986. *Reconstructing Public Philosophy.* Berkeley: University of California Press.

Sweezy, Paul L. 1981. "Keynes as a Critic of Capitalism." *Monthly Review* 32 (April): 33–36.

Swoboda, Frank. 1994. "Helping the 'Anxious Class'." *Washington Post National Weekly Edition* (October 3–9): 19.

_____ . 1995. "The Return of Robert Reich." *Washington Post National Weekly Edition* (May 15–21): 19.

Taylor, Charles. 1979. "What's Wrong with Negative Liberty." In Alan Ryan, ed., *The Idea of Freedom: Essays in Honour of Isaiah Berlin* (Oxford: Oxford University Press), pp. 175–93.

Taylor, O. H. 1955. *Economics and Liberalism: Collected Papers.* Cambridge, Mass.: Harvard University Press.

Thurow, Lester C. 1992. "America Needs a Strategy." *Boston Globe* (November 3), p. 42.

_____ . 1993. "An American Common Market" [book review]. *Washington Post Book World* 23 (October 31): 1, 10.

_____ . 1972. "The American Economy in the Year 2000." *American Economic Review* 62: 439–43.

_____ . 1981. "Beware of Reagan's Military Spending." *New York Times* (May 31), sec. 3, p. 3.

_____ . 1984. *The Case for Industrial Policies.* Washington, D.C.: Center for National Policy.

_____ . 1991. "Centennial Essay." *American School Board Journal* 178 (September): 40–43.

_____ . 1995. "Companies Merge; Families Break Up." *New York Times* (September 3), p. E11.

_____ . 1983. *Dangerous Currents: The State of Economics.* New York: Vintage Books.

_____ . 1981. "Equity, Efficiency, Social Justice, and Redistribution." *Nebraska Journal of Economics and Business* 20 (Spring): 5–24.

_____ . 1976. "Equity versus Efficiency in Law Enforcement." In Ryan C. Amacher, Robert D. Tollison, and Thomas D. Willett, eds., *The Economic Approach to Public Policy: Selected Readings* (Ithaca, N.Y.: Cornell University Press), 124–32.

_____ . 1989. "An Establishment or an Oligarchy?" *National Tax Journal* 42: 405–11.

_____ . 1994. "The Fed Goes Ghostbusting." *New York Times* (May 6), p. A29.

_____ . 1994. "Fixing It." *Playboy* 41 (January): 190–92, 247–48.

_____ . 1996. *The Future of Capitalism: How Today's Economic Forces Shape Tomorrow's World.* New York: William Morrow.

_____ . 1987. "Galbraith, John Kenneth." In John Eatwell, Murray Milgate, and Peter Newman, eds., *The New Palgrave: A Dictionary of Economics* (London: Macmillan), vol. 2, pp. 455–56.

_____ . 1990. "GATT Is Dead." *Journal of Accountancy* 170 (September): 36–39.

_____ . 1975. *Generating Inequality: Mechanisms of Distribution in the U.S. Economy.* New York: Basic Books.

_____ . 1992. *Head to Head: The Coming Economic Battle Among Japan, Europe, and America.* New York: William Morrow.

_____ . 1990. "History Is Far from Over." *Boston Globe* (March 6), p. 28.

_____ . 1981. "The Illusion of Economic Necessity." In Robert A. Solo and Charles W. Anderson, eds., *Value Judgment and Income Distribution* (New York: Praeger), pp. 250–75.

_____ . 1983. "An International Keynesian Yank." *Challenge* 26 (March–April): 36–39.

_____ . 1991. "Let's Learn from the Japanese." *Fortune* 124 (November 18): 183–87.

_____ . 1988. "Let's Put Capitalists Back into Capitalism." *Sloan Management Review* 30 (Fall): 67–71.

_____ . 1982. "The Missing Mosaic." *Social Science Quarterly* 63: 376–80.

_____ . 1992. "Money Wars: Why Europe Will 'Own' the 21st Century." *Washington Post* (April 19), p. C1.

_____ . 1985. "Of Grasshoppers and Ants" [review of Charles Murray, *Losing Ground: American Social Policy, 1950–1980*]. *Harvard Business Review* 63 (July–August): 44–45, 48.

_____ . 1973. "The Political Economy of Income Redistribution Policies." *Annals of the American Academy of Political and Social Science* 409 (September): 146–55.

_____ . 1989. "The Post-Industrial Era Is Over." *New York Times* (September 4), p. A27.

_____ . 1989. "Putting Capitalists Back into Capitalism." In Samuel Bowles, Richard C. Edwards, and William G. Shepherd, eds., *Unconventional Wisdom: Essays on Economics in Honor of John Kenneth Galbraith* (Boston: Houghton Mifflin), pp. 189–204.

_____ . 1982. "Response to Buchanan." *Journal of Economic Issues* 16: 863–64.

_____ . 1992. "Society's Economic Failure." *Boston Globe* (May 12), p. 42.

_____ . 1988. "A Surge in Inequality." In Eleanor Brown, ed., *Readings, Issues and Questions in Public Finance* (Homewood, Ill.: Irwin, 1988), pp. 36–46.

_____ . 1973. "Toward a Definition of Economic Justice." *Public Interest* 31: 56–80.

_____ . 1991. "Visionless Liberalism." *Boston Globe* (December 24), p. 34.

_____ . 1987. "Welfare State Keeps Capitalism Working." *Los Angeles Times* (December 20), sec. iv, p. 3.

_____ . 1990. "We're Not Facing Up to Our Nation's Problems." *Washington Post* (February 11), pp. C1–2.

_____ . 1982. "Why Do Economists Disagree?" *Dissent* 29 (Spring): 176–82.

_____ . 1980. *The Zero-Sum Society: Distribution and the Possibilities for Economic Change* (New York: Basic Books).

_____ . 1985. *The Zero-Sum Solution: Building a World-Class American Economy.* New York: Simon & Schuster.

Uchitelle, Louis. 1990. "An Old Liberal, a New Sermon." *New York Times* (April 12), pp. D1, 5.

Ulmer, Melville J. 1983. "The War of the Liberal Economists." *Commentary* 76 (October): 53–56.

Viner, Jacob. 1972. *The Role of Providence in the Social Order: An Essay in Intellectual History.* Princeton, N.J.: Princeton University Press.

Waligorski, Conrad P. 1994. "Keynes and Democracy." *Social Science Journal* 31: 79–91.

_____ . 1990. *The Political Theory of Conservative Economists.* Lawrence: University Press of Kansas.

Waligorski, Conrad, and Hone, Thomas. 1981. *Anglo-American Liberalism: Readings in Normative Political Economy.* Chicago: Nelson Hall.

Walzer, Michael. 1990. "The Communitarian Critique of Liberalism." *Political Theory* 18: 6–23.

_____ . 1984. "Liberalism and the Art of Separation." *Political Theory* 12: 315–30.

Weisskopf, Walter A. 1977. "Normative and Ideological Elements in Social and Economic Thought." *Journal of Economic Issues* 11: 103–17.

Westbrook, Robert B. 1991. *John Dewey and American Democracy.* Ithaca, N.Y.: Cornell University Press.

Will, George. 1995. "Fringe Is Marginal No More." *Morning News of Northwest Arkansas* (January 1), p. 9D.

Williams, Michael. 1983. "Liberalism and Two Conceptions of the State." In Douglas MacLean and Claudia Mills, eds., *Liberalism Reconsidered* (Totowa, N.J.: Rowman & Allanheld), pp. 117–29.

Wilson, Woodrow. 1913. *The New Freedom: A Call for the Emancipation of the Generous Energies of a People.* New York: Doubleday, Page.

Winch, Donald. 1978. *Adam Smith's Politics: An Essay in Historiographic Revision.* Cambridge: Cambridge University Press.

———. 1969. *Economics and Policy: A Historical Study.* London: Hodder & Stoughton.

Wines, Michael. 1992. "White House Links Riots to Welfare." *New York Times* (May 5), pp. A1, 12.

Wogaman, J. Philip. 1977. *The Great Economic Debate: An Ethical Analysis.* Philadelphia: Westminster Press.

Wolfe, Alan. 1995. "Dispassionate Romantic" [review of Alan Ryan, *John Dewey and the High Tide of American Liberalism*]. *Civilization* 2 (July–August): 82–83.

Wright, Gavin. 1991. "Beyond Economic Nationalism" [review of Robert B. Reich, *The Work of Nations: Preparing Ourselves for 21st-Century Capitalism*]. *Washington Post* (March 3), sec. WBK, p. 1.

Index

CPSIA information can be obtained at www.ICGtesting.com
Printed in the USA
BVOW02*2009060913

330300BV00003B/116/P